Monterey Bay Area:
Natural History and Cultural Imprints

Burton L. Gordon

THIRD EDITION

SINCE 1952

Pacific Grove, California, USA

Distributed by:

The Boxwood Press
183 Ocean View Blvd.
Pacific Grove, CA 93950 USA
Phone: 408-375-9110
Fax: 408-375-0430
e-mail: boxwood@cruzio.com

Gordon, B. Le Roy (Burton Le Roy), 1920-
    Monterey Bay area: natural history and cultural imprints/Burton L.
Gordon—3rd ed.
        p.   cm.
    Includes bibliographical references (p.) and index.
    ISBN 0-940168-38-3 (alk. paper)
    1. Natural history—California—Monterey Bay. 2. Human ecology-
-California-Monterey Bay. 3. Monterey Bay (Calif.)-Environmental
conditions. I. Title.
QH105.C2G67 1996
508.794'7—dc20   95-25409
                                                      CIP

Printed in the USA

Preface to the Third Edition

IN THE TWENTY YEARS since the first edition of this book appeared, there have been changes in the way Americans speak of themselves and other cultural groups. In keeping with the historical emphasis of the text, some currently less-favored geopolitical and cultural designations, such as "Indians," have been retained as being consistent with the historical documents quoted herein. (In the case of Monterey Bay area's aboriginal peoples, who originated not here but across the Bering Straits, and whose culture here was largely extinguished before the area became American territory, the now-preferred "Native Americans" is doubly inappropriate.) We realize that not everyone will agree with such usage and want it known that these are "errors" of commission, not omission.

I AM DEEPLY indebted to Susan Hawthorne, Associate Editor of The Boxwood Press: Without her advice and help this third edition would not have been completed.

This edition, like the first, owes much to the encouragement given by friends and former students at Moss Landing Marine Laboratories—especially John Oliver, Peter Slattery, Bruce Stewart, and Rick Kvitek.

Thanks are also due the following people for information they generously provided: John Pearse, University of California, Santa Cruz; Michael Tripp, University of Victoria; Margaret Bradbury, San Francisco State University; Derrin Banks, Santa Ana Botanic Garden; David Dixon and David Rodriguez, Marina State Beach; Jack Levitz, Jacks Peak County Park; David Lindberg, Museum of Paleontology, University of California, Berkeley; Laura Lee Lienk, Watershed Ecology Outreach Program; William Desmond, Map Librarian, University of California, Santa Cruz; and Bruce Delgado, Bureau of Land Management.

Burton L. Gordon

Santa Cruz, California
August, 1995

Preface

This study, which has grown from notes prepared for a field course, "Human Ecology of the Monterey Bay Area," benefitted greatly from my association with graduate students at Moss Landing Marine Laboratories—particularly Shane Anderson, Richard Avey, John Hansen, Robert Morey, and Larry Talent. (Specific factual contributions from class members and others are acknowledged in the text.) I am also much indebted to my colleagues at Moss Landing Marine Laboratories for encouragement—especially Dr. Victor Morejohn and Mary Jean Bilek for editorial improvements in the manuscript and Dr. Robert Hurley, Director, for implementing its publication.

Dr. Ralph Buchsbaum, formerly of the University of Pittsburgh, and Dr. James Griffin of Hastings Natural History Reservation generously contributed time to read the manuscript and make valuable suggestions. Jack Stirton, U.S. Army Corps of Engineers, made helpful comments on the section dealing with wave erosion and littoral drift. Allyn Smith and Barry Roth of the California Academy of Sciences kindly identified many of the mollusks discussed in the text. Professor Georg Treichel, Dr. John Westfall, Sharon Johnson, and Byron Wood of San Francisco State University gave liberal advice on bibliographic and map resources.

I wish to thank Stanley Clayton, Monterey County Agricultural Commissioner's Office; Howard Greenfield, Salinas Valley Mosquito Abatement Board; Tom Gould, Mount Madonna County Park Ranger; and Dave Steaffens, Toro Regional Park Ranger for freely sharing their knowledge of the natural history of the Monterey Bay area.

I am especially grateful to Nat Bracco, Ronnie Chinn, Jack Dolan, George Flath, John Giannini, Bob Rubis, Hans Struve, and Harry Xanthus, long-time residents of the area, for their warm hospitality and for historical and other information heretofore not available in print.

And finally, my thanks to my wife, Myra, for contributing many careful observations of her own on plant and animal life, and for her patience and industry in typing several versions of the manuscript.

An alphabetical list of the common names of animals and plants discussed appears at the end of the book, along with their scientific names. The bracketed comments in quoted passages are mine.

Burton L. Gordon

Santa Cruz, California
August, 1974

Contents

ON THE COVER
Then and Now (clockwise from left): ▫ Map of Monterey Bay is the oldest detailed physiographic rendering of the area, published in 1871 by the State Geological Survey of California. ▫ Tanbark oak acorns were a staple food of the Costanoan Indians; later the bark was harvested exhaustively for use in the tanning of hides. A resilient species, the tanbark oak is today reclaiming much territory hereabouts. ▫ Urban land use planning can do much to restore and enhance the balance of plant, animal, and human habitats in the Monterey Bay area now, and in the future.

1

Introduction

THE MONTEREY BAY AREA is being rapidly transformed into yet another major California urban center: The attendant problems range, characteristically, from congested traffic to inadequate supplies of fresh water. Suburbs have spread to the rural landscape, and the last remaining tracts of undisturbed vegetation are being cleared for residential development. It has become increasingly clear to residents and visitors alike that the area's dwindling biotic and scenic resources must be preserved (on economic grounds alone, if not for more cogent reasons). The great challenge ahead lies in developing a comprehensive program for renewing such resources in an appropriate semblance of their natural condition, and for managing them on a sustainable basis. The main purposes of this book are (1) to describe the character and extent of ecological change produced by human action in the Monterey Bay area and (2) to suggest applications of such information to land-use planning. For example, the book may be helpful to those engaged in planning an ecologically suitable hinterland for the Monterey Bay National Marine Sanctuary, established in 1992.

The clearing and changing of the natural plant cover, and other alterations of the terrain, are emphasized because these are among the activities of humans which have had the greatest ecological

1

consequences. Locally, species have been exterminated and habitats destroyed. Numerous domesticated and game species and species commensal with humans (such as insect and rodent pests) have been introduced. An even larger number of native species have been exposed to unplanned disruptive and selective action. Changes in animal habits and food sources have taken place. As a result of agricultural and industrial developments, natural hydrological patterns have been changed, and the chemical content of the air, soil, and water altered. Thus, new habitats for plants and animals, and for people themselves, are being created. The theme is an old one, first dealt with in detail in 1863 by George P. Marsh in *The Earth as Modified by Human Action.*

The strongly historical emphasis of the text allows the reader who knows the bay area as it is to review what it has been and to see what it is *becoming*. Many contemporary problems are involved. In "preserving nature" what, in fact, are the conditions we are trying to preserve—a landscape already molded by centuries of human occupancy? A beach is eroded by wave action. Was its disappearance a result of natural littoral processes only, or partially the consequence of a jetty's having been built upcoast? A species becomes locally extinct. Was this a result of natural evolutionary processes, of fluctuations in climate, or of human modification of its habitat? Effluent materials are suspected of damaging aquatic life near a pipe outfall. But how can the fact be established with certainty when knowledge of the biological conditions existing when the pipe was laid is lacking? Many exotic plants and animals now inhabit the area. Has the introduction of certain of these species been detrimental? Clearly this question is important for regional planning purposes, but a useful answer can be given only if we know which species were, in fact, introduced and the history of their effects.

Many questions remain unanswered for lack of adequate chronological detail. Without historical data it is almost impossible to distinguish biotic and environmental changes which are the result of natural processes from those actually produced by human industry— a circumstance which may be exploited by those seeking to avoid responsibility. An attempt is made on the following pages to sketch a number of what might be called *fiducial ecosystems* and to establish a chronological series of ecological reference points useful in interpreting future environmental change in the area.

Although this study is largely descriptive and is meant to be without philosophical pretensions, it is written with certain assumptions in mind. Most of these are readily apparent. Such assumptions do not affect the accuracy of facts stated in the text. However, some may be subject to question. The author has assumed, for example, that achievement of maximum ecological diversity should be something of an ideal in land-use planning; that a varied, species-rich biota, based upon multiple food chains, is desirable; that an underlying biotic potential manifests itself in such features as the natural plant associations; that even where these associations have been altered or removed, regenerative forces continue to operate because, for example, climatic and edaphic patterns persist; that the idea of a potential natural vegetation is a useful planning concept and that a knowledge of plant succession is essential to attaining optimum land use; that diversity will be partially ensured by maintaining and, where necessary, restoring tracts of the original plant associations—and further increased by keeping all successional phases of plant cover in existence somewhere within the area at all times; that only by control of vegetation can terrestrial animal numbers, in certain species, be maintained above critically low values (though admittedly such values have not as yet been adequately determined); that further extinction of species in the Monterey Bay area, as elsewhere, should be prevented at all costs; and that biotic enrichment can also be attained through judicious introduction and exclusion of exotic species.

1. Definition of Terms

The Monterey Bay area, as defined for this study, extends along the California coast from the Monterey Peninsula (including Carmel) northward to Año Nuevo Island. The definition accords with old usage.

The northern extent of the embayment is not as sharply defined as the southern, and in early accounts Año Nuevo, then referred to as "Point Año Nuevo," was taken as the bay's north limit. For example, Father Pedro Font, in his diary written in 1776, said ". . . the bay formed by Cabo de Pinos [Cape of Pines—i.e., Point Pinos] and Punto de Año Nuevo is very large" (Bolton, 1933, p. 308). Later, in 1792, Captain George Vancouver described the limit of the Monterey Bay: "This famous bay is situated between Point Pinos and Point Año Nuevo . . . . This spacious but very open bay is formed by the coast falling back from the line of the two points, nearly four leagues" (Vancouver, 1933, p. 77; Beechey, 1831, p. 84). On its seaward side, the area includes the littoral zone. Inland, it includes the watersheds of the rivers and streams draining into Monterey Bay, excepting the upper Salinas River, which has its headwaters far to the south. Biogeographically the upper Salinas Valley is as strongly associated with southern California as it is with the shores of Monterey Bay. Hence, the southern limit of the area discussed here is placed arbitrarily across the Salinas Valley from Palo Escrito Peak at the southern end of the Sierra de Salinas to Pinnacles National Monument in the Gabilan Mountains—that is, roughly at the old boundary between the Costanoan and Salinan Indians.

Much use of the terms *natural landscape* and *cultural landscape* has been made (see Krebs, 1923). The most obvious example of a natural landscape, as the term is used here, is an area neither occupied by nor affected by people. Virtually no such environment remains on earth; but even in long-settled areas the concept of a natural versus a cultural landscape preserves an important and useful distinction. In defining the natural landscape, we picture the countryside as it would be if people and their works were removed leaving behind those environmental features which may exist independently of humankind—for example, mountains, unpolluted streams, and indigenous plant formations.

The term *cultural landscape* is applied to all features of the physical environment which are attributable to human presence—such as roads, cities, orchards, deforested tracts, introduced species, and smog. In addition to a panorama of crops, pastures, towns, and the like, the effects of people on life and environment can be seen in a thousand details: Birds aligned on telephone wires; gulls following a plough; swallow's nests under the eaves of a building; tree rings around sawn stumps in a redwood forest; dust plumes rising from a cement plant (Davenport); a change in plant cover at the boundaries of an old Spanish land grant; the multicolored waters of salt ponds (Moss Landing); barnacles colonizing newly laid jetty rocks; clumps of mussels clinging to old pilings; a herd of sea lions hauled out on a breakwater (Monterey); mine scars on a mountain slope (Natividad); the contour-terrace paths made by cattle grazing a hillside; a skyline formed by groves of an Australian tree (*Eucalyptus*); jet trails overhead; and so on. Thus the cultural landscape is an environmental catalog of human accomplishment in the area—for better or for worse. (A note of justification for this use of terms and for what may seem an arbitrary division: It is sometimes said, "everything is natural, humanity included." This usage is rejected here: Unless contrasted with something "unnatural" or artificial, such as the products of human culture, "things natural" can mean little more than "things in general".)

In describing the development of the cultural landscape in the Monterey Bay area the implied reference date is the time, probably at the close of the Pleistocene period (late, by Old World standards), when people first appeared in this part of the western hemisphere. The reference condition, logical but necessarily hypothetical, is a scene lacking all human influence—the natural landscape, or fundament, upon which people have acted. Because this fundament has itself been subject to change by, among other forces, seasonal and longer-term climatic variations, the natural landscape is constantly being reposed with slight variations for cultural modification.

Related to the concept of natural landscape is that of a *potential natural vegetation*, this being the vegetation that would come into existence if people were suddenly removed from the scene and all the ensuing stages of plant succession were concentrated into a single moment (Tüxen, 1956, p. 5).

An archaic term, *anthropurgic* (from the Greek for man + work), is revived here because it expresses this idea of the human species as a unique agent of change. Anthropurgic is defined as "influenced by the exercise of human power; operated upon by humans," as distinguished from *physiurgic*, i.e., produced "in the course of nature, without the intervention of humans." Hence, a subtitle of this study could well be "An Anthropurgic Ecology of the Monterey Bay Area."

2. Controls for the Study of Ecological Change

When the Monterey Bay area was discovered by Europeans, the biota was not in an unaltered condition. Even then, the areas of natural plant cover—natural in the sense of being uninfluenced by people—had been reduced. Today such vegetation probably no longer exists.

In very many parts of the world, Old and New, man has been on hand for so long and in such numbers that great deformation of the vegetation has resulted. We can then hardly speak of a natural balance without him, since man has been exerting sustained and selective pressures. Except at the climatic extremes, there may be no such thing as undisturbed or natural vegetation. (Sauer, 1952, p. 18)

However, the circumstances in coastal central California were unusual. This land had not been subjected to those profound ecological changes associated with the development of agriculture, cities, and technology in many parts of the Americas and in the Old World. A lithic culture survived here into the nineteenth century. The aboriginal inhabitants of the Monterey Bay area were without agriculture and domesticated animals, other than dogs. Despite changes in plant cover and animal life made by the Indians, the biotic conditions observed here by the first Spaniards were probably closer to natural than those existing elsewhere in these latitudes, excepting in Australia.

Several general sources of information are available concerning the environmental conditions upon which human-made changes have been imposed. A number of prehistoric human-environment relationships can be glimpsed by inspecting the content and environs of kitchen middens marking the sites of old Indian settlements.

Dated descriptions and collections by explorers and naturalists present views of environmental conditions in the Monterey Bay area at the time of its discovery and settlement by Europeans, before the most sweeping changes in the natural landscape had been made. Accounts by the explorers Lieutenant Pedro Fages and Father Juan Crespi are indispensable. Coulter, Douglas, Eschscholz, Haenke, Hartweg, Menzies, Nuttall, and von Chamisso are among the illustrious early naturalists who collected in the area.

Insight into early, more nearly natural conditions can also be obtained from contemporary field studies in those parts of the landscape farthest removed from archaeological remains and human presence (and hence presumably vestiges of the natural environment) and by observing the successional and regenerative trend of biotic events in abandoned areas previously utilized by people in some way and not presently subject to human activities.

In the absence of historical evidence it is often difficult to disentangle the cultural and the natural. Even thoroughgoing biotic alterations and the presence of a well-developed cultural landscape may go quite unnoticed: ". . . man dominated landscapes do not betray their origin to the casual observer. Take the grasslands of California, the rolling hills back from the coast . . . . Here are stretches of what looks like indigenous vegetation. Much of this mantle is not obviously tended by man; it has the look of something that has been in California as long as the oaks it grows among, yet the bulk of it came, all uninvited . . . . Most of it had a long history of association with man when it made the trip . . . . Native plants are there, even some native grasses, but it takes a well-informed botanist going over the vegetation item by item to show how small a percentage is made up of indigenous California plants" (Anderson, 1956, p. 763).

2

The Natural Landscape

A FEW PRINCIPAL CHARACTERISTICS of the physical environment—land, sea, air, and their seasonal interaction—are reviewed below so that the effects of human occupancy can be seen within a framework of inanimate nature.

1. Physiographic Features and Surface-Forming Materials

Throughout its geomorphic history a hidden yet dominant and controlling influence on the Monterey Bay area has been the great submarine canyon which heads at Moss Landing and extends out of the bay into the Pacific. The courses of the principal rivers—the San Lorenzo, Pajaro, and Salinas—are directed toward the canyon. Offshore contours show that this converging pattern continues beneath the sea—a vestige of an older and similar drainage pattern that existed when the Pleistocene Pacific was several hundred feet below its present level. Despite the considerable depths in the canyon itself (it is more than half a mile [1 km] deep 6 miles [10 km] west of Moss Landing), the larger part of the bay, lying on the continental shelf, is less than 98 feet (30 m) deep. Other major factors controlling geomorphic development in the area include the long-term rise and fall of sea level and the frequent tectonic activity along the San Andreas fault (of which the Loma Prieta temblor in 1989 was an emphatic reminder).

A notable feature of the Monterey Bay is its symmetrical outline, with the canyon midway between Santa Cruz and Point Pinos. As one approaches the bay from the open sea and looks eastward, the skyline is formed by the crests of the Santa Cruz Mountains toward the left and center of the horizon, and by the Gabilan and Santa Lucia mountains to the right—the latter two ranges being separated by the Salinas Valley. Loma Prieta in the Santa Cruz Mountains and Fremont Peak in the Gabilans stand out as landmarks.

Between the coast and the mountain crests in the northern half of the bay area lies an expanse of low hills, while in the southern half alluvial plains are extensive. Thus the San Lorenzo River is almost without an alluvial plain; the plain of the Pajaro is much broader; and the Salinas River has produced by far the greatest expanse of alluvium in the area.

Igneous and metamorphic rocks are exposed along parts of the mountain crests in both the Santa Cruz and the Santa Lucia mountains, but sedimentary rocks are predominant.

Differences in surface-forming materials account for several contrasts between the southern and northern ends of the bay. The rough boulder-strewn headlands of Point Pinos are made up of granitic rock. Sedimentary rocks, especially shales, form both the slopes of the Salinas Valley and the flat coastal shelf at the north end of the bay between Santa Cruz and Davenport. Around Point Pinos, quartz and feldspar derived from the weathering of granite have supplied the sands in the white dunes and beaches of Pacific Grove and Carmel. The clear offshore water there, with its good subsurface visibility, is appreciated by scuba divers. Within the bay and northward finer deposits, coming from the Salinas River or eroded from shoreline cliffs, yield gray and tan beach silts and sands, and make for turbid offshore waters.

As the last continental glaciers of the Pleistocene Epoch melted, world sea level rose. A large expanse of coastal land was submerged, markedly changing the shape of Monterey Bay.

High-altitude view eastward over Monterey Bay and central California, to the Sierra Nevada. The San Andreas fault is shown extending from north to south across the photograph. The land on the seaward side of the fault line has sporadically experienced lateral displacement northward, relative to the more easterly parts of California. The head of Monterey Bay Submarine Canyon is shown at Moss Landing. Not all of the events that contributed to the formation of the canyon are known; but that it is, in fact, of "polygenetic origin" (Starke and Howard, 1968) is generally acknowledged. An approximate outline of Pleistocene Lake San Benito (Jenkins, 1973) is shown east of Elkhorn Slough; the area is now drained by the Pajaro River through Pajaro Gap. The lake was some 122 m above present sea level. The 125 m submarine contour for Monterey Bay is also shown, this being roughly the shoreline of the bay during maximum late Pleistocene

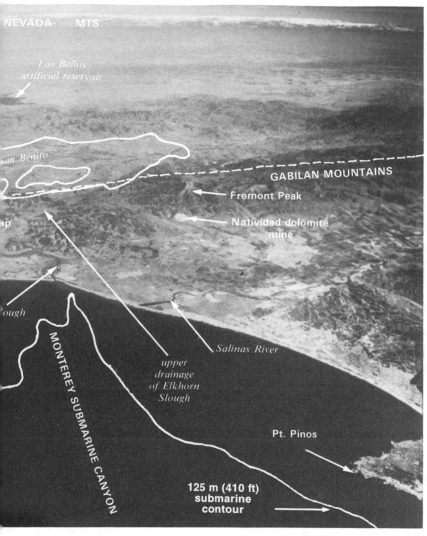

NEVADA MTS.

Los Baños artificial reservoir

an Benito

GABILAN MOUNTAINS

Fremont Peak

Natividad dolomite mine

p

ough

MONTEREY SUBMARINE CANYON

upper drainage of Elkhorn Slough

Salinas River

Pt. Pinos

125 m (410 ft) submarine contour

lowering of sea level (Lajoie, 1972, p. 32). Thus the water in Lake San Benito may at times have stood 247 m or more above the Pleistocene shoreline, located less than 20 km distant at the head of the submarine canyon near Moss Landing. Topographic evidence indicates that Lake San Benito found a temporary outlet across the fault into Elkhorn Slough (Jenkins, 1973, p. 159). It is not unreasonable to conjecture (considering the abrupt changes in drainage known to have occurred elsewhere along the San Andreas fault) that the lake found such an outlet suddenly and, given so steep a gradient, drained torrentially into the submarine canyon, cutting terraces along the slough, producing turbidity currents that scoured the upper parts of the canyon, and depositing masses of large-grained sediment well offshore. (On turbidity currents in the canyon, see Garfield et al., 1994). (Photo by U. S. Army Corps of Engineers)

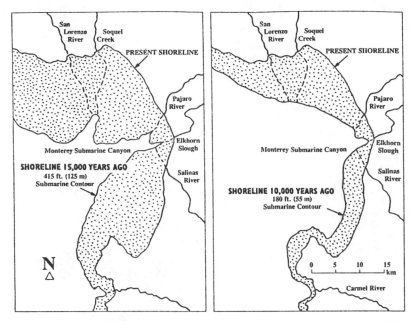

Changing shape of the Monterey Bay area during the estimated period of human occupancy. *Left*, approximate outline of Monterey Bay about 15,000 years ago, during the last major continental glaciation, when the sea was some 125 m lower than now. *Right*, approximate outline of the Bay about 10,000 years ago (near the beginning of the Holocene period), when sea level was still about 55 m lower than at present. Stippled areas represent former coastland now covered by seawater.

Because archaeological evidence within this area has been lost to a rising sea, the date of the earliest human coastal settlement (and thus the contemporary outline of the bay itself) is problematical. Most archaeologists believe that people arrived in California some eleven thousand years ago. Others defend dates several thousand years earlier (Orr, 1969). But "even the most conservative scholar believes much of the Pacific coast to have been settled and inhabited by at least 8,000 to 10,000 years ago" (Meighan, 1965, p. 709). Whichever of these estimates we accept, the bay's shape has changed greatly since it was first seen by humans.

When sea level was at its lowest, subaerial land extended westward to or slightly beyond the edge of the continental shelf, now at a depth of roughly 350-400 feet (105-120 m). No doubt the landscape supported plant and animal communities similar to those that exist in the Monterey Bay area today. But it is now almost impossible to reconstruct in detail the topography—much less the biogeography—because the whole continental shelf is covered by a blanket of sand or mud, in places over 3 feet (1 m) thick (Yancey, 1968, pp. 82-83). Any hills that may have existed were leveled by wave action, reduced to sand, and scattered over the seabed by longshore drift. The former lower valleys of the Salinas, Pajaro, and San Lorenzo rivers (between present shoreline and the submarine canyon) are almost filled with sediment. The hill-lands which stood off Point Sur are now submerged. Only the highest elevations of this once-extensive California lowland still stand above the sea—for example, the Channel Islands to the south of the Monterey Bay area, and the Farallons to the north.

Despite all this, a few of the original physiographic features in this drowned landscape survive; for instance, at least one submerged shoreline is still discernible at a depth of about 100 feet (30 m) (Yancey, 1968, p. 83). Thus pockets of relict subaerial deposits containing fossil (or even archaeological) evidence may someday be found: Buried objects covered by only a shallow layer of buffering material sometimes escape destruction during changes in sea level. For example, during a late-Pleistocene lowering of the sea, patches of mollusk beds near Lighthouse Point in Santa Cruz were left virtually undisturbed by the retreating surf: Littleneck clam shells in these beds remain unabraded, and "so tightly closed that the interior is devoid of sediment" (Addicott, 1966, p. C6).

Not all recent changes hereabouts have been initiated by people. Coastal physiography is characterized by especially rapid natural change. Año Nuevo Island is itself an example: All early accounts refer to *Point* Año Nuevo, not to Año Nuevo *Island*. Captain Vancouver evidently approached the point and inspected it closely: "Near *Point* Año Nuevo are some small rocks detached from the coast a very little distance" (Vancouver, 1798. p. 78). Seen from the sea the island might simply have been indistinguishable from the headland, but Father Crespi's party approached Año Nuevo by land and camped nearby in 1770. His account, too, refers to "the *point* of Año Nuevo, which is low with rocky reefs" (Bolton,   1927, p. 251). And a

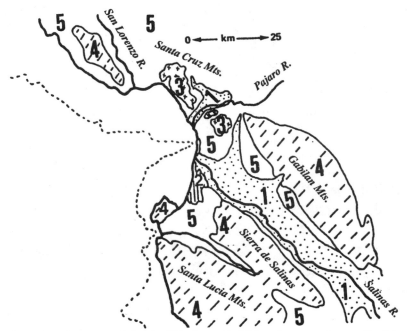

Surface-forming materials. **1**. Alluvium. **2**. Old and recent dunes **3**. Aromas red sands. **4**. Igneous rocks. **5**. Undifferentiated sedimentary rocks.

description from the diary of Palou, upon his reaching the beach near Waddell Creek in 1776 after traveling overland, reads:

> The Punta de Año Nuevo, which we have so close at hand, is a tongue of low land, rocks, and reefs of very low elevation but it extends a long way into the sea, and to sailors doubtless it would look very high because of the range of hills and sierras which it has very near by. (Bolton, 1930, p. 443)

Studies of cliff erosion along this coast indicate that, in places, wave action is displacing the shoreline inland at an average of over 6 inches (15 cm) per year. Año Nuevo Point, subjected to strongly refracted and focused waves approaching from both sides, was breached leaving an island of resistant materials offshore. The idea that in early historical times Año Nuevo was a peninsula rather than an island is discounted in one study (Orr and Poulter, 1962, p. 14). However, a permanently separate island has existed for only a short time. As early as 1798, the promontory probably appeared as either an island or a peninsula, depending on whether it was viewed at low or high tide, in winter or summer. But as late as 1857, one official and detailed map shows no Año Nuevo Island, only Año Nuevo Point; the seaward tract of higher land that now forms the island was then connected to the mainland by a sandbar (Plat of the Rancho Punta Año Nuevo, surveyed by J. Kellenberger, under orders of the U.S. Surveyor General, June 1857). One measure of how recently water depths have changed: Old residents in the neighborhood, questioned in the 1970s, said that building materials for the Coast Guard houses (now abandoned), were hauled to the island by wagon at low tide.

2. Climate and Season

Superficially, seasons are weakly developed in the Monterey Bay area. Immigrants coming from the eastern United States and northern Europe sometimes say they miss the thunderous summers, the colorful autumns, and (strangely) the icy winters. (A few even claim that, lacking such cyclical promptings, they feel "suspended in time"—that their years slip away hardly noticed.) But this contrast is easily exaggerated: Seasonal rhythms are characteristic of life everywhere except in the most artificial human environments. Though no doubt less conspicuous than in some places, such rhythms are well developed in the Monterey Bay area, too. The human species has, unlike other mammals, found a home in all of the world's climates—and, through its cultural innovations (artificial heating, lighting, etc.), not only modified the natural cycles but created new ones of its own.

The important subject of phenology remains poorly covered for the Monterey Bay area. Phenology deals with the time of appearance of characteristic periodic events in the life cycles of plants and animals, especially those events influenced by seasonal changes in temperature, photoperiod, and rainfall—but including other cyclic influences in the physical environment as well. Although the seasonal development of many local species has been described there has, as yet, been no attempt to assemble and interrelate the abundant (though patchy) phenological data available for the area as a whole—and this despite the fact that seasonal interactions govern and trigger the enactment of most ecological processes. Although seasonal progressions on land are quite different from those at sea, little seems to have been written contrasting the two, or showing how they interact near shoreline. A brief introduction to the subject follows.

2.1. Seasonal Cycles on Land

The most conspicuous seasonal influences on landscape arise from variations in rainfall. Grass-covered hills, green under winter rains, are parched to yellows and tans in summer. January and February are usually the wettest months, while July and August are virtually without rainfall. Rainfall increases from south to north along the coast. At Monterey the average is about 15 inches (38 cm) a year; at Santa Cruz the average is 27 inches (69 cm) per year. Rainfall also generally increases with elevation. For example, at Boulder Creek, which is some 600 feet (183 m) higher than Santa Cruz, the average rainfall is about 54 inches (137 cm) per year.

During the winter season, when rain-bearing air masses arrive from a westerly direction, there is a marked rainshadow in the Salinas Valley and on the western slopes of the Gabilans, these being on the lee side of the Santa Lucia Range. Thus, annual rainfall values in the Salinas Valley are less than those of coastal sites such as Monterey and Santa Cruz. Soledad, in the valley, receives only a little over 9 inches (23 cm) yearly. Stations along the crest of the Santa Lucia Range average as much as 60 inches (152 cm) per year, whereas those at about the same elevation along the crest of the Gabilans average only around 20 inches (50 cm) per year.

In accordance with the season of rainfall, river and creek flow is mainly in the winter; in summer, most stream courses are dry.

The averaging of annual rainfall values obscures a climatic factor of great importance to the biota, namely the considerable variation in rainfall from year to year. For example, at King City near the southern edge of the area, the average rainfall from 1888 to 1954 was 10.5 inches (26.4 cm), the maximum 25 inches (64 cm) and the minimum only 4 inches (10 cm). At irregular intervals, severe drought may force

View northeastward from the northern Sierra de las Salinas. A tongue of fog extends from left to right, up the Salinas Valley. The Gabilan Mountains appear in the background with Fremont Peak rising to the left of center. (Photo Nancy Burnett)

vegetation and animal life to adjust to arid conditions, sometimes for prolonged periods. One of the worst of these droughts culminated in 1864; others occurred between 1928 and 1934, and between 1987 and 1992. In the same way, significant temperature ranges are often hidden by averaging: No plant is killed by a monthly average, but the record low temperatures in December of 1990 carried off shrubs and trees all around the Monterey Bay—particularly imported species.

Winter weather is likely to alternate between cloudy, rainy, and fair. In the summer, more stable air and recurrent summer fog are characteristic. Under these stable summer conditions, strong convection and associated thunder and lightning is rare. Lightning flashes are seen mainly in the rainy season, when the danger of natural forest fires is minimal.

Except at higher elevations, snow cover is rarely a part of the area's scenery. From Santa Cruz, patches of snow can be seen atop El Toro Peak for a week or two in most winters. And from Monterey, snow can be seen occasionally on Fremont Peak in the Gabilan Mountains, across the Salinas Valley to the east.

Along the coast summer winds are generally northwesterly—and winter winds variable, often westerly or southwesterly. Over much of the area the strongest winds are felt in winter. However, this is not so in the Salinas Valley:

In the Salinas Valley summer winds are stronger than winter winds. Entering the Salinas Valley from Monterey Bay, they sweep up the valley with increasing regularity and force as the valley narrows and the heated interior is approached. The movement generally begins in the forenoon, reaches a maximum in the early afternoon, and gradually subsides as evening approaches. Heated as they move inland, they increase transpiration and evaporation. (Carpenter and Cosby, 1929, p. 5)

Granted, autumn is not a colorful season by eastern standards. Yet the leaves of poison oak supply a little red, sycamore trees growing along the upper river courses turn yellow, and in the salt marshes around Elkhorn Slough pickleweed marks out broad patches of pink and salmon.

Photoperiod, the interval in a 24-hour period during which an organism is exposed to daylight, is a major seasonal influence. In many terrestrial plants this day-length cycle initiates leafing, flowering, and fruiting, and for many animals it determines times of reproduction and migration—in the dark-eyed junco, for instance. Because the daylight period varies in length (depending on the geographical latitude) with a clock-like regularity during the year, photoperiod is one of the most regular of cycles. In the seasonal behavior of many species, changes in day length are more important than changes in temperature.

2.2. Seasonal Cycles at Sea

In the open sea, the seasons are distributed differently over the year from those on land, and seasonal extremes are less severe.

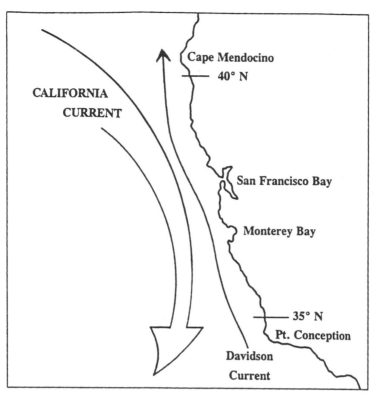

Oceanic circulation along the California coastline.

On land, the year is customarily divided into four seasons (though in the Monterey Bay area, the year is basically two-seasonal, with a cooler, wetter winter season and a warmer, drier summer season). In the open sea, on the other hand, the year is described as having three seasons: (1) An upwelling period, from March to August; (2) an oceanic period of increased surface temperatures from September to November; and (3) a Davidson-Current period, from December to February, in which a narrow current flows northward near the coast (Bolin and Abbott, 1963).

Seasons are less pronounced in the sea. The reason for these more uniform conditions is mostly explained by the remarkable thermal properties of water. Water has a specific heat (thermal capacity) of 1, whereas granite, a common surface-forming rock on land, has a specific heat of only 0.25. Thus, it takes four times as many calories to raise the temperature of water 1 degree centigrade as it does granite. Maintaining relatively constant temperatures, ocean waters have a regulatory, or thermostatic, effect on the atmosphere above—and thus on the neighboring coasts.

Temperature extremes are lessened not only by the special properties of water but also by the movements of ocean currents, with the California Current bringing colder water from the north—and the Davidson Current, warmer water from the south.

During summers, the winds move surface water southward and, under the deflective force of the earth's rotation, slightly away from the coast. This displacement brings cold water from the depths to the surface where it chills the air above it. Condensation of water vapor in the air occurs, and fog is formed. Instead of the normal decrease with altitude, air temperatures actually increase upward. Thus, the upwelling of ocean water and the cold California current are responsible for two distinctive features of the coastal climate—fogs and temperature inversions—conditions that often extend well inland to the coastal mountains.

As marine organisms die, they sink toward the bottom of the sea, carrying their stored mineral nutrients with them. Upwelling lifts these nutrients to the sunlit surface where they can be used by phytoplankton, the basic food suppliers for marine animal life. Thus primary biomass production is at a maximum during the upwelling period.

On land, where nutrients are released for plant use gradually by the leaching of surface-forming rocks, nothing comparable to this great seasonal resupply occurs. On land, it is winter rains that bring forth a whole new generation of plant and animal life—while on the neighboring sea, rainfall gives rise to no such spectacular renewal. (These natural contrasts are, of course, much diminished by human artifice—for example, where agriculturalists apply mineral fertilizers to, or irrigate, the soil.) The droughts which are so important to land life have little influence in the sea; for marine organisms, desiccation is a limiting factor only along shoreline at the higher tidal levels.

On land, summer fog is especially heavy in the mornings and near the coast, usually clearing with rising surface temperatures in the afternoons. The fog forms a thin blanket, usually no more than a few hundred meters thick.

Those who have driven along Highway 17 from Los Gatos to Santa Cruz may recognize this description of an August view from the crest of the Santa Cruz Mountains, written by a traveling botanist in 1861:

> To the south lie the whole Bay of Monterey and a vast expanse of ocean . . . . Monterey is obscured by fog, but the mountains rise above it in the clear air. Fog forms at the head of the bay and rolls up the Salinas Valley . . . [which] seems like a great arm of the sea. (Brewer, 1949, p. 155)

The same traveler noted the inversion of temperatures in this area: "There is a very curious meteorological fact connected with these hills. It is cooler in the large valleys and hotter on the hills" (Brewer, 1949, p. 124). Nowadays, residents in the upper Santa Cruz mountains sometimes seek relief from August heat by driving down to Santa Cruz.

One of the bigger contrasts between marine and terrestrial life involves their very different biotas: Insects and flowering plants— major life forms on land—are rare in the sea. Thus, a good illustration of the importance of seasonal precipitation to land life is given by a flowering plant and its insect associates: Coyote brush, a common and ecologically important coastal shrub in the Monterey Bay area, is the principal support for a community of some 144 insect species:

> Briefly, the plant's growth is dependent on the seasonal wet-dry cycle, and the insects are correspondingly adjusted . . . . Developmental stages of the insects reach a peak during the spring period of greatest growth . . . . Insects of all sorts are less common on the plant during the summer dormancy. (Tilden, 1951, p. 153)

At sea there is, of course, no corresponding wet-dry cycle, and no summer dormancy of invertebrate herbivores.

Among the more fundamental seasonal distinctions are those based on changes in biomass production—and in this regard, the terrestrial environment differs significantly from the marine. On land, chlorophyll production is at a maximum in winter and slackens in late spring (hills turn green in November, and yellow in May). But in the bay, phytoplankton growth is at a minimum in winter, and greatest during the summer months June through August. The marked difference in productivity seasons is well illustrated by the example of coyote brush given above.

The oceanic period, September to November, brings pelagic (open sea) birds in the greatest numbers and variety to the bay (Stallcup, 1976, p. 114). Yet, this is the very time that bird activity is weakest on land: In the upper Carmel Valley, "the first half of September is the quietest part of the bird year at Hastings Reservation" (Davis and Baldridge, 1980, p. 80).

A number of marine organisms have a 24-hour (diel) cycle in which they migrate toward the surface of the sea at night to feed on phytoplankton, and sink during the day: for example, various krill species (Youngbluth, 1976) and such fish as the northern anchovy (Frey, 1971, p. 49). Nothing similar occurs on land.

At sea, there are lunar seasons—insignificant on land. Tides are produced by the gravitational attraction of the sun and moon. Since the moon exerts much the stronger pull, the tides are principally a lunar effect. Along this coast, there are two high tides and two low tides each day. The highest tides occur near the time of the full moon—the lowest, near the time of new moon. The greatest range between high and low tides occurs every two weeks when the sun, moon, and earth are approximately in a straight line: these are known as "spring" tides; during spring tides, beaches are covered and uncovered throughout their full extent. The smallest tidal ranges occur one week after spring tides; these are called "neap" tides. Near shoreline, this complex but regular tidal periodicity establishes some "six or seven zones in the intertidal vegetational cover" (Doty, 1946, p. 315). The breeding cycle of the grunion provides one of the more remarkable examples of the lunar-tidal influence (see p. 219). An upper intertidal alga, *Pelvetia,* is also said to reproduce according to a lunar cycle.

2.3. Reciprocal Influences of Land and Sea on Season

In summer, land and sea breezes (blowing offshore in the mornings and onshore in the afternoons, respectively) often give parts of Monterey Bay area a change of air every 24 hours—and help disperse the smog that is becoming increasingly common.

In terms of world climate, the influences of land and sea are mutual and inseparable, but from place, to place, one influence or the other may be stronger: In the Monterey Bay area, the maritime influence predominates.

As noted above, summer fog is a major marine influence on the inland climate. During the dry season, fog dripping from trees may amount to the equivalent of several inches of rainfall. When trees are felled, this precipitation is lost, because brush and grass collect fewer fog droplets. The growth of several native plants, including the stream orchid and phantom orchid, is said to be favored by this fog drip (Oberlander, 1956, p. 851). Many other native plants are associated with the summer fog: The lace lichen, said to be the largest of American lichens (Herre, 1910, p. 219) grows best in trees exposed to heavy fog; the closed-cone conifer forests of Monterey Peninsula and Año Nuevo, and the maritime chaparral that extends along the coast between them, are typical fog-belt vegetation; and the inland extent of the coast redwood is closely associated with the number of foggy days in summer.

Airborne salt from the surf zone limits the approach of various land plants to shoreline—the redwood, for instance.

The head of the submarine canyon—with its deep, cold, upwelling waters—brings many deepwater species closer to shoreline, and extends the marine influence strongly into Elkhorn Slough.

Twice each tidal day, the sea rises some 2.5 feet above its mean level, and seawater flows into small coastal lagoons and Elkhorn Slough, sustaining the salt marshes there. In Elkhorn Slough, tidal ebb and flow also produce extensive mudflats—grayish, almost bare, surfaces of mud and sand that are alternately seabed and mainland.

Land influences on the sea are less evident: Winter flooding of coastal streams has a pronounced effect on both the turbidity and salinity of coastal waters. Though temporary and localized, these floods produce considerable changes in marine life: for instance, some marine mollusks, such as oysters, are killed by fresh water. Water salinity off the mouths of flooding rivers and streams may be lowered to nearly zero. (In southern California, the salinity of surface waters may be lowered by flooding rivers from 33.5—roughly the average along this coast—to 28 parts per thousand as much as 10 miles offshore [Zierer, 1956, p. 86].)

2.4. The Seasons in Sand at the Interface

The importance of sand as a habitat is reflected in the names of numerous plants and animals: sanderling, sand piper, sand verbena, sand gilia, sand dollar, etc. Beaches and dunes are the principal physiographic features made of sand, and winds and waves are the principal agents in their formation and their seasons. Following is a rough outline of major seasonal beach changes.

Along the California coast wind, current, and ocean-wave directions are mainly controlled by seasonal changes in the general pattern of atmospheric circulation over the eastern Pacific Ocean.

Most ocean waves are wind generated: The velocity, fetch, and duration of winds over the open sea determine the characteristics of the waves they generate—especially wave length, height, and period. These characteristics, in turn, determine the behavior of waves as they approach the coastal shallows and shoreline. Wind-generated waves travel in groups, or trains, of similar period and height. Most trains reach the beach with periods that may be as long as 16 seconds, and as short as 6 seconds (Bascom, 1964, p. 62). Thus each wave-train period sets a schedule for the feeding sanderlings that race back and forth at the water's edge.

Littoral drift is the transport of sand parallel to the shoreline by waves and wave-generated currents. Because prevailing winds along the California coast are from the northwest, most ocean waves arrive from that direction. Accordingly, the net movement of sand is southward, or downcoast. In the winter season, however, there are periods during which this downcoast movement is interrupted by winds and waves that arrive from the west or southwest, resulting in an upcoast transport of sand at those times.

Nearshore life is adapted to a changeable, often violent, environment—but in winter, wave action is especially disruptive. The heights of ocean waves vary seasonally, with winter waves the highest. These high waves transport sand to the offshore zone, removing the beaches completely or leaving them narrow and steep. Unprotected by beaches, cliffs are attacked, and eroded. Flooding streams and the heavy wave action result in turbid winter waters in the nearshore zone. There, sand is winnowed by the waves and transported to the outer edge of the surf zone (though rarely to depths much greater than 30 feet (10 m); sand dollars and olivellas are among the better-known inhabitants of these subtidal sands. The suspended mud is carried into deeper water, and deposited as a thin blanket on the sea bottom (Wolf, 1970, p. 334).

Summer waves move the sand back again, forming broad, gently-sloping beaches. Mosslike green algae, *Enteromorpha,* which cover rocks and ledges well within the splash zone in winter, wither and disappear when the summer beaches reform.

Beaches appear barren, but much of their life is beneath the surface. Although there are fewer species than in most other coastal habitats, populations are often large. Burrowing animals are characteristic, and life is distributed roughly in zones: Pill bugs are found above the tides. In the intertidal zone, beach hoppers burrow in wet sand, just beyond reach of the waves (Ricketts and Calvin, 1968, p. 214). Sand crabs favor the lower beach, where their uplifted feeding organs make echelon-shaped ripples in backwash.

The breadth of these zones varies with the tidal range as determined by the lunar cycle.

Birds also have their favorite feeding zones: Snowy plovers feed above the tides; sanderlings, on the wetted sand; and lower still, willets feed while wading in shallow water. For beach birds, the tidal cycle, by controlling the available feeding space, determines which species are present and their numbers (Recher, 1969, p. 393 and p. 403).

Both beach profile and sand-particle size change seasonally: winter beaches, coarser sand; summer beaches, finer sand. The size of sand particles affects the kinds of beach life present. For example, in coarse sand such tiny animals as the thread worms (nematodes), instead of burrowing, slide through the thin films of water that separate sand grains.

As with the phytoplankton of the open sea, benthic marine algae (feather boa kelp, giant kelp, bullwhip kelp, etc.) have their peak growth season in late summer or early fall (that is, at the very time that growth of land plants is at its minimum). All of this influences the seasonal development of invertebrate life on the beaches: Mixed in tangled masses, rafts of kelp drift ashore in greatest quantities in the fall, when wave heights increase. As they decay on the beach, the kelp piles support swarms of beach hoppers, kelp flies, beetles, and other invertebrates. Animal life in the decaying kelp provides food for a number of shorebirds, and especially for black turnstones.

In summer, the effluents of many streams are blocked by beach sand, and small lagoons of brackish water are formed—a condition that gives Laguna Creek, north of Santa Cruz, its name. (Anadromous fish are able to enter small coastal streams only in the rainy season; for instance, the coho salmon spawns in Waddell Creek between November and January.)

Because beaches are located at the interface of land and sea, their seasons are an intermixture, and an amplification, of influences from those two, very different, environments. Thus cyclical physiographic changes on beaches are of much greater magnitude than those farther inland; and tidal cycles, though characteristic of the marine environment, are accentuated here at the ocean's edge.

Seasonal changes in animal life may reflect climatic extremes experienced elsewhere rather than within the Monterey Bay area itself. The appearance of migratory birds is an example. In late summer (mid-July through August) sooty shearwaters appear in huge flocks offshore. Inland, snow geese visit Elkhorn Slough in winter, and cedar waxwings arrive to feed on pyracantha berries in city gardens.

The explanation of seasonal progressions is greatly complicated by the fact that many species have inherent (endogenous) rhythms, or "inner clocks"—established in their progenitors either by ancient or different environments. Thus, instead of falling into phase with our seasonal cycle, some plants introduced here from Australia and southern Africa continue to follow a southern-hemisphere schedule. These include Hottentot ivy, some red-flowered eucalypts, several acacias, and cape oxalis: The Hottentot ivy, for example, flowers heavily in mid-December and sets seed in February—and inland, eucalyptus trees are sometimes nipped by frost in their flowering season, as is the Brazilian Christmas cactus, if unprotected.

It should be noted here that other events which are recurrent but not necessarily periodic, are also of great ecological importance in the Monterey Bay area—for instance, the prolonged droughts on land, and at sea the occasional northward extensions of El Niño.

3. Natural Plant Associations

The Monterey Bay area is uncommonly rich in endemic plant species (Stebbins and Major, 1965, p. 23) and is also known for the large number of species that find here either their northern or southern limits (Thomas, 1961, p. 30). Such diversity makes conservational problems here more complicated than in most areas of similar size. At least a dozen major plant associations can be distinguished, each having a more or less distinctive native fauna. (See table of natural plant associations, pp. 28-29.)

NATURAL PLANT ASSOCIATIONS

(Adapted from Munz, 1959; Jensen, 1947; and Smith, 1959.)

Natural Plant Formations or Groupings	Dominant or Conspicuous Species	Location of Examples
(1) Offshore kelp forests	Proceeding from deepwater shoreward, a succession of beds: bull whip kelp, giant kelp, feather kelp, and woody chain bladder	The beds are found in the shallow offshore zone, mainly at depths of less than 18 m, particularly around the Monterey Peninsula, at Soquel Point and Soquel Cove, West Cliff Drive, and elsewhere within the bay. Their distribution is controlled mainly by the availability of hard bottom for kelp holdfasts, by the depth of the water, and by the wave refraction pattern within the bay. Giant kelp is widely distributed and forms most of the kelp beds in the area; there is a large seasonal stand of woody chain bladder off Cannery Row
(2) Intertidal and splash zone vegetation	Surf grass (or narrow-leaved eel grass), and such algae as feather boa kelp and *Enteromorpha intestinalis*	In this narrow strip numerous marine algae grow in a marked vertical zonation, the zonal limits being determined by lighting, wave exposure, and tidal action; particularly abundant where rocky ledges, boulders, and cobble form the shoreline, e.g., between Natural Bridges Beach and Point Santa Cruz, at Opal Cliffs, and around Point Pinos. Surf grass is found in the surf zone of rocky shorelines where there is a certain amount of sand; it is common at Año Nuevo, Natural Bridges Beach State Park, along West Cliff Drive, and on the Monterey Peninsula. Eel grass is estuarine; it is found only near the mouth of Elkhorn Slough, where there are several stands, e.g., a little south of the small-craft harbor. *E. intestinalis* is a bright yellowish-green alga which grows between plus 1 m and mean low tide; it is particularly common on the mudflats of Elkhorn Slough—as is another alga, the dull reddish *Gracilaria lemaneiformis*
(3) Strand vegetation: herbs and shrubs	(a) Dune and beach vegetation: beach-bur, coastal sagewort, common and yellow sand verbena, sea rocket	Young dunes and inner beach margins, especially between Sunset Beach and the mouth of the Salinas and River, and at Point Año Nuevo
	(b) Coastal scrub: mock heather, coast buckwheat, California sage, blue beach lupine, bluff lettuce	Old dunes, coastal cliffs, and hills, esp. between Moss Landing and Mulligan Hill and between Año Nuevo and Santa Cruz, and near Marina

(4) Coastal salt-marsh vegetation	Pickleweed, saltgrass, salt rush	Elkhorn Slough, Moro Cojo Slough, near the Pajaro River mouth and the mouth of Baldwin Creek, north of Santa Cruz
(5) Riparian vegetation	(a) Freshwater marsh: California tule, cat-tails, sedges	Areas of sluggish drainage along the lower courses of the major streams —e.g., the lower Pajaro River and Salinas River floodplains, and around lakes and (now) irrigation ponds
	(b) Riparian woodland: willows, cottonwoods, box elder, sycamore	Recent alluvium on floodplains of the larger streams, the Salinas River, Pajaro River, Branciforte Creek, Aptos Creek, etc.
(6) Closed-cone conifer forest	Monterey pine, knobcone pine, Monterey cypress, Gowen cypress, Santa Cruz cypress	Año Nuevo: Monterey pine and knobcone pine; on the Monterey Peninsula: Monterey pine, Gowen cypress and Monterey cypress; Bonny Doon: Santa Cruz cypress
(7) Redwood and mixed redwood Douglas fir forest	Coast redwood, Douglas fir, sword fern, redwood sorrel	Middle elevations on slopes of Santa Cruz Mountains; at its margins, redwood forest is intermixed with Douglas fir. Although not found at shoreline, redwoods extend downslope to within a few hundred meters of the sea on some leeward slopes—e.g., along Aptos Creek
(8) Broadleaf evergreen forest	Madrone, tanbark oak, coast and interior live oak, California laurel, blue blossom	On higher hills and slopes of the Santa Cruz Mountains, intermixed with tracts of redwood and Douglas fir forest; e.g., Nisene Marks State Park and Mount Madonna County Park
(9) Coast live-oak woodland	Coast live oak intermixed with poison oak, coffee berry, Ceanothus, etc.	The Aromas Red Sands area, including the Prunedale district and Royal Oaks County Park. A large uninterrupted stand lies between Aptos and Watsonville along Highway 1. In the Fort Ord area, where the dunes have weathered to a normal soil profile
(10) Foothill woodland	Blue oak, maul oak, black oak, diggerpine, Coulter pine	On the slopes of the Gabilan Mountains and the Sierra de Salinas. In the Monterey Bay area as defined here, Coulter pine grows only in the northern Gabilans—on Fremont Peak and southward to Gloria Pass
(11) Chaparral	Chamise, manzanita, and Ceanothus	Slopes and ridges of the Santa Cruz and Gabilan mountains and the Sierra de Salinas
(12) Grassland	Perennial bunchgrasses—e.g., needlegrass	No sizeable tracts of this plant cover remain. The largest area was probably located in the lower Salinas Valley; it was largely converted to annual grassland soon after European settlement and then, in part, to cropland

3

The Cultural Landscape and Its Development

THE HUMAN SPECIES is the product of long evolution in the Old World. There the species remained until late in its history, gradually occupying higher latitudes. Advancing across the Bering Straits, the earliest human immigrants (the real discoverers of America and first in a long line of colonists) found a hemisphere as completely without human influence as some distant planet—truly, a "New World." (Nevertheless, by the time Europeans arrived and actually applied that name, much of this newly-found hemisphere bore its own heavy human imprint.)

Historically, the Monterey Bay area has been occupied successively by three major cultural groups: American Indians of the Costanoan group; Spanish-Mexicans; and Americans. The last named is plainly a very general grouping; it includes diverse elements, each of which has made contributions to the area's development: Americans from the eastern seaboard, Chinese, Italians, Japanese, Portuguese, Yugoslavians, and others. The existing cultural landscape is the cumulative effect of occupancy of the area by these several groups.

1. Indian Occupancy

The Monterey Bay area is within the former territory of the Costanoan (Ohlone) Indians. Although Costanoan territory included all the land draining into Monterey Bay except the upper Salinas Valley, and extended inland into the Santa Clara Valley, the typical Costanoan habitat was coastal. Indeed, the name Costanoan itself is derived from the Spanish word meaning "coast people."

1.1. Costanoan Village Sites and Population Centers

Archeological evidence, including radiocarbon dating, suggests that the earliest human occupancy of coastal California began at least 10,000 years ago with immigrants who were primarily hunters, and that a strong dependence on shoreline resources and seed gathering developed some time later, about 7500 years ago (Meighan, 1965, p. 712). The Costanoan economy was a continuation of this tradition.

As noted above, the Costanoans practiced no agriculture and raised no domesticated plants or animals, except the dog. Their subsistence was based on gathering and hunting, and their economy was predominantly biotechnic. The littoral zone appears to have supplied much of the gathered part of their diet. Old habitation sites can be located today by kitchen midden deposits, now commonly called shellmounds because they consist largely of mollusk shells.

Along the shore, Indian food sources were concentrated in the intertidal zone. Shellfish and associated organisms are abundant near rocky ledges, reefs, and tide pools, especially on the Monterey Peninsula and at Año Nuevo. Rocky shoreline is not extensive between Santa Cruz and the Monterey Peninsula, but shellmounds are common too in the mid-coastal part of the bay around Elkhorn Slough and the mouth of the Pajaro River, an area rich in bivalves.

On the coast itself several of the larger kitchen-midden sites are on dunes. For example, the midden at Sand Hill bluff, near the mouth of Laguna Creek, is on the only large patch of dune in this stretch. The largest accumulation of midden north of the Monterey Peninsula is on the dunes of Año Nuevo Point. (This midden area extends on northward to Gazos Creek, as far as the dunes themselves.) No obvious reasons come to mind for this shoreline congregation of the Indians on dunes. Perhaps good drainage made their surface more attractive in winter than most of the flat coastal terrace, because the dunes were less muddy.

Since this part of California has little rain for about six months of the year, proximity to a permanent water supply was an important factor in the selection of habitation sites. The Indians seldom lived far from streams or springs. Some of the larger villages, such as those on Año Nuevo and Laguna creeks, were back a little way from the shoreline, in spots protected from coastal winds by the surrounding terrain.

Although the Spanish remark on fighting among coastal tribes, well-organized intertribal warfare was uncommon, and considerations of defense were probably of slight importance in the selection of village sites.

1.2. Costanoan Middens, Subsistence, and Environmental Effects

The content of Costanoan middens is the principal source of information on relationships between these aboriginal people and their environment.

Costanoans made no pottery. They cooked in large, watertight baskets by an extremely laborious, fuel-consuming process called stone boiling. Stones were heated, dropped into baskets filled with water, and, when cooled, replaced with freshly heated ones. Little by little the water was brought to the boiling point. Food materials were added and the heating process continued. Gathering large quantities of broken limbs and twigs for fuel must have been a major chore, as the Costanoans lacked cutting tools before the arrival of Europeans.

The shore was an important source of food for Indians well back from the coast. Kitchen middens rich in shells are to be found miles from the shoreline (e.g., at Bonny Doon and on the University of California campus at Santa Cruz). For the area as a whole, the California mussel is the most abundant shell in the mounds, although locally other shells predominate.

Laguna Creek and Sand Hill Bluff (*above*) south of Davenport, showing two Indian habitation sites: sand dunes at shoreline and lee positions at streamsides. Laguna Creek, left foreground. The dunes on Sand Hill Bluff, background, are covered by a thick midden deposit. Marine erosion has changed topography greatly since midden accumulation began. Taking the settlement date as 5600 years ago (radio-carbon dating, Morejohn, p. 208), and the rate of cliff recession as 15 cm per year, the shoreline was then located about 0.8 km seaward of its present position. Rock ledges at bases of bluffs, exposed at low tide, and nearby kelp beds were rich in marine foods. Laguna Creek supplied fresh water. Oak groves and buckeyes grow a short distance inland. *Below*, **Dunes on Sand Hill Bluff**. The slope is covered with shell fallen from the thick midden deposit (dark layer, arrow, at top of mound). Archaeological remains are abundant in the upper drainage basin of Laguna Creek, near Bonny Doon. (Photos B. Gordon)

Shells in midden at Sandhill Bluff. a. limpet; b. littleneck clam; c. red abalone; d. gumboot chiton; e. dogwinkle; f. California mussel; g. barnacle. (Photo R. Buchsbaum)

More than a dozen shellmounds are located on the dunes at Año Nuevo (Barnes, et al., 1925). As wind winnows the sand, shells and artifacts are exposed from time to time. We found the following remains of animals on the surface at one site: shells of California mussel (which predominate), black turban, shell limpet, littleneck clam, purple-hinged scallop, olivella, red abalone, barnacle, and some large sea snails, e.g., red turban; gumboot chiton plates; purple sea urchin tests; crab claws; and fish, mammal, and bird bones. Intermixed with the animal remains are great quantities of chipped chert and flint, many flat, rounded stones, a little larger than the fist (used in stone boiling), and a few pieces of obsidian.

At a site on a tributary of Scott Creek, about 1.6 km north of Swanton and a little over 1.6 km from the shoreline, the California mussel is again the most abundant mollusk, and the list of shells collected is much the same as that for Point Año Nuevo: Besides the mussel, we found mossy chiton, gumboot chiton, barnacles, red abalone, black abalone, littleneck clam, black turban, slipper shell, shield limpet, purple sea urchin tests, and blue top shell. The following passage, written in 1914 of mounds, a few kilometers northwest of Santa Cruz, is one of the first published accounts of an excavation in the area: "The shells composing the mounds are mostly mussel, though there are many other kinds, and quite a few bones of birds, crabs, and seals; that are in a very good state of preservation." (Dodge, 1914, p. 120)

The Costanoans fed omnivorously on shorelife. White, butterfly-shaped plates of cryptochitons are numerous in the mounds. The Pomo still eat these chitons, although some of the least finicky and convention-bound modern inhabitants have found cryptochitons unsuitable fare: "After one experiment we decided to reserve the animals for times of famine" (Ricketts and Calvin, 1968, p. 91).

The Indians gathered all shellfish regardless of size. Shells of many limpets, turbans, and other sea snails found in the mounds are so small that they seem hardly worth collecting. Some may have been carried in with clumps of mussels, but they are too numerous for all of them to have been brought in accidentally. Since these shells are usually unbroken, they may have been boiled, whole, for soups.

Gathering mollusks seems to have been women's work: A Scot naturalist visiting the missionized Indians at Carmel in 1792 noted, "Their food at this time was chiefly shellfish which the women collected along the shore, while the men lounged about the country with their bows and arrows, killing rabbits and quails" (Menzies, 1924, pp. 293-294).

The middens suggest very closely clustered people. Perhaps cooking was communal, as there is hardly space for both dwellings and individual family fires around the mound surfaces.

The Costanoans did not make canoes (Fages, 1937, p. 65), but instead used reed rafts, or balsas, as the Spanish called them (Costansó, 1910, pp. 65-67). Accounts by the explorer Pedro Fages, written in 1769-1770, are among the most valuable of the historical materials on Costanoan life. The Spaniard describes the Indians at Año Nuevo as being:

very clever at *going out to fish embarked on rafts of reeds*, and they succeed, during good weather, in getting their provisions from the sea . . . the land also provides them with an abundance of seeds and fruits. (Fages, 1937, pp. 65 and 70)

The reefs and rocky shoreline favored by mussels and abalones are absent from the mudflats of Elkhorn Slough, and their shells rarely appear in middens thereabouts. At least two sites are located on the slopes of the low hills that stand above the lower end of the slough on its north side.

The first site, farthest up the slough, is located on the big bend where it turns from a southerly course westward into the bay. The most plentiful shells there are those of the Washington clam (moneyshell clam); fragments of the native Olympia oyster also are present. On the second site, not far from the salt ponds at the lower end of the slough, are shells of the basket cockle and the white sand clam.

Abalones and mussels are the most common shells in the middens on the Monterey Peninsula. Two species of the former, the red abalone and the black abalone, were especially important to the Indians as food; "they are found by the thousands in all stages of decomposition" (Keen, 1896).

Marine invertebrate remains in great variety are present in the middens on the Monterey Peninsula, as at Año Nuevo. The species present are for the most part the same in the two areas. A surface collection of invertebrates made at Fan Shell Beach included sea urchin tests, snails, crabs, and barnacles, and "chiton plates are indeed numerous" (Fisher, 1935). Another site yielded abalones, mussels, snails, limpets, and barnacles. A midden excavated at the Monterey Custom House Flagpole contained shells of abalones, mussels, clams, limpets, oysters, and land snails (Beardsley, 1896, p. 22).

Water fowl, including migrant species, were hunted. In November 1770, traveling from Monterey toward the Santa Clara Valley, Fages described the country near the head of Elkhorn Slough. He mentioned passing through

many reed patches crossed by *numerous bear trails*. At one place where they end there was a very large pond, and at the head of this a village of heathen, in which we saw about fifty souls. Two of these heathen went about with two *little rafts hunting ducks on the pool* . . . two of them hastened off across the plain to inform two very large villages of our passing; these villages were in sight, midway of our march . . . . They were very much surprised to see a soldier *kill in passing nine geese at three shots*. (Fages, 1911, p. 140)

Another characteristic of Costanoan subsistence—namely, the importance of hunting and gathering activities on land—is suggested by the fact that arrow points and baskets were among their principal artifacts. Año Nuevo Point was the chief Costanoan quarry and stone-working center. At the seaward end of the point there is an outcrop of banded gray, white, and brown chert. Great quantities of chert fragments, purposely chipped, are present in shellmounds scattered through the neighboring dunes; in fact, in terms of amounts of worked stone, Año Nuevo Point is probably one of the largest Stone Age quarries known. Complete arrow points are, however, very scarce. The probable explanation for the absence of completed points is that only "blanks," i.e., preliminary flakes, were prepared here, and these were then carried away for completion elsewhere (Heizer and Treganza, 1944, p. 314). Another large arrowsmith site was located in the dunes near the mouth of Laguna Creek. Banded chert, probably from Año Nuevo or Laguna Creek, is also found in shellmounds northward at Half Moon Bay and southward around Elkhorn Slough.

The Costanoans were more mobile than their large accumulations of shell midden alone would suggest. Actually, they spent much time hunting and frequently changed residence (La Pérouse, 1799, p. 447); their dwellings were designed accordingly, each consisting of little more than a lean-to of stakes covered with bundles of straw:

The Indians say that they love the open air, that it is convenient to set fire to their house when the fleas become troublesome, and that they can build another in less than two hours. (La Pérouse, 1799, p. 447)

Early European observers writing on Costanoan custom commonly indulged themselves in short essays on the relative merits of cultures–such essays being, for the most part, highly self-congratulatory in tone. On the other hand, Indian knowledge of the local natural history did stimulate favorable comment from outsiders; for example, several accounts admiringly describe skilled and subtle imitations of animal behavior used by the Indians in hunting operations (Petit-Thouars, 1956, pp. 81-82; Vancouver, 1798, p. 36).

Large land mammals such as deer, elk, and antelopes were important sources of food. In crossing the lower Salinas Valley in 1769, near the present site of Chualar, Spanish explorers noted:

Many antelope were seen going by, and the place was named Real de los Cazadores [Place of the Hunters], for there were then round about it some Indians who were so absorbed and occupied in hunting game that they did not notice us. . . . (Fages, 1911, p. 61)

A surprising fact not recorded in the historical sources but made clear from archaeological finds is that sea mammals were another major source of Indian food. In a collection of bones from the surfaces of two sites on the Monterey Peninsula, the following were counted (see manuscript by Edna Fisher):

Seal and sea lion	116	bones
Fish	190	"
Sea otter	250	"
Deer and elk	157	"
Birds	352	"
Coyotes	8	"
Rodents (gophers. mice, and rabbits)	23	"
Unidentified carnivores	6	"

Although such counts are difficult to interpret, they do provide an idea of the relative importance of various food items for purposes of reconstructing a typical Indian diet. The list shows that the Indians had the same unprejudiced taste for vertebrates as for invertebrates—all kinds were eaten, including carnivores. Among the large carnivores, pinnipeds were especially important. More sea otter bones were found than deer and elk bones, probably because the site is near the shoreline. The abundance of sea otter bones suggests that the otters may have been captured on land as well as in the kelp beds, and this conclusion is confirmed by an early historical account. The French explorer La Pérouse, who arrived in Monterey Bay September 15, 1786, commented on the Indian methods of otter hunting:

> The Indians . . . whose boats at Monterey are only made of reeds, catch them either on shore with snares, or kill them with large sticks, when they find them at a distance from the sea. For this purpose they conceal themselves behind the rocks, this animal being frightened at the least noise and plunging immediately into the water. (La Pérouse, 1799, p. 457)

The southern sea otter, now reduced to a small population, has changed its habits. Nowadays, it rarely comes on shore.

The bones of coastal birds, never taken for food today, also appear in the middens on the Monterey Peninsula; most common are bones of cormorant species, but those of the brown pelican, common loon, and common murre are present too (Fisher, 1934, p. 353); they provide further evidence that the Costanoans not only fished offshore but also hunted there, around stacks and rocks.

Local differences in predominant species in the middens can usually be explained by variations in neighboring marine habitats. However, there are few abalone shells in the midden at Año Nuevo Point, despite the fact that the point is now known as an excellent abalone fishing ground. Abalone (and *Olivella*) shells are known to have been traded out of the Monterey Bay area in aboriginal times, but it seems unlikely that this can account for their scarcity in the Año Nuevo mounds. The sea otter, for which the abalone is an important food, existed at Año Nuevo in Costanoan times, but it is not present there in any numbers now. A former abundance of otters might explain the scarcity of abalones in the Indian middens. On the other hand, Año Nuevo may be a much more favorable habitat for abalone now than it was two centuries ago. After the early-historic peninsula was breached to form the existing island, beaches in the vicinity were probably eroded and offshore sands displaced downcoast by littoral drift; thus broad expanses of rocky platform and reef suitable for the support of marine algae, and thus of abalone populations, were uncovered.

Like other coastal tribes, the Costanoans probably dried the meat of mollusks both for their own use and for trade: "throughout prehistoric time the coast natives exported large amounts of shellfish to the interior . . . both shells and dried meat" (Cook, 1946, p. 51). In the absence of any ethnographic description of these drying operations, an old account of middens west of Santa Cruz, written in 1914, contains an interesting note on the caves in the shale and limestone hills nearby:

> That the Indians carried mussels back to the hills is proved by the abundance of shells in the ground, and *every little cave has its complement, as if they used them for ovens. Shell fragments in the caves seem to have been burned, and the cave walls are discolored by fires.* (Dodge, 1914, p. 120)

The kitchen middens are the best sources of information on animals used by the Costanoans. For information on the plants they used, historical and ethnographic accounts are the principal sources.

Quantities of acorns and buckeyes were collected for food. Both contain a bitter material which was removed by crushing and leaching the fruit. The leaching was done either in specially made baskets or in sand pits dug for the purpose. After leaching, the meal was dried and stored.

Acorns were the main staple of the north and central California Indians as a whole (Baumhoff, 1963, p. 176), and even coastal Indians depended heavily on them. The protein content of shellfish is high, but acorns added a needed supply of carbohydrates and fats (Cook, 1946, p. 51). In an old history of Monterey County, it is noted that "large quantities of acorns were stored in baskets made of willow, and placed in trees fifteen to twenty feet from the ground, and secured

Branchlet and acorns of the tanbark oak, a medium-sized native evergreen tree. The acorns were a major Indian food. Later, large quantities of the tree's bark were used by Americans in the tanning industry. The acorns are an important wildlife food. (Photo B. Gordon)

from rain, and kept for winter use" (Elliott and Moss, 1881, p. 96; whether this account refers to Costanoans or Salinans is uncertain). California Indian population densities were generally at their highest in oak-covered areas.

The large acorns of the tanbark oak grow in clusters and, in October, are easily plucked. Those that cannot be reached can be collected from the ground a month or so later. Regular seasonal visits to tanbark groves were customary for the coastal Indians. In the Monterey Bay area, tanbark oak is concentrated mainly on the western slopes of the Santa Cruz Mountains. It was by far the most important acorn source. Its acorns were preferred over others, and no other California oak produces such a heavy crop. (Strictly speaking, the tanbark is not a true oak, belonging as it does in the genus *Lithocarpus*, rather than *Quercus*.)

Of the common oak species, the acorns of the coast live oak, the most abundant oak in coastal parts of the Monterey Bay area, were the least important as food for the Indians (Baumhoff, 1963, p. 165). The yield is small, variable, and of inferior quality.

In addition to the rich acorn source in tanbark groves of the Santa Cruz Mountains, there must have been something of a concentration of the area's diversified acorn resource in the Sierra de Salinas and northern Santa Lucia Mountains, where blue oak, valley oak, interior live oak, and black oak—major acorn producers—are found, along with some tanbark oak. Sources of acorns in both these areas were denied to the newly converted Indians on the Monterey Peninsula, according to one of the earliest accounts of mission days:

> The hill Indians also of the Sierra de Santa Lucia who live between this mission [Carmel] and that of San Antonio de las Robles [Paso Robles], persecute indiscriminately the New Christians of this region [that is, the Indian converts of Monterey Peninsula] whenever they enter the range to search for acorns, which the hill Indians guard and desire to keep for their own. These unhappy people encounter the same resistance when they go along the beach above Monterey [that is, northward to the tanbark groves of the Santa Cruz Mountains] on the same quest . . . . (Fages, 1937, p. 64)

Acorns were scarce in the mainly coast live oak-Monterey pine country around Carmel and elsewhere on the Monterey Peninsula. Use of what is clearly the buckeye was noted there by the Spanish sources:

> Those who are in this mission and nearby obtain few acorns, the lack of which they supply in part with blackberries and strawberries, which abound around the point of the Monte de Pinos: there are many *boletes* or mushrooms, and *another wild fruit about the size of an ordinary pear which is eaten roasted and boiled though it is somewhat bitter. The tree which bears it is rather whitish, like a fig tree, but not very tall. When it bears fruit it sheds its leaves entirely.* (Fages, 1937, p. 68)

Early accounts of burning are especially numerous from Santa Cruz northward to Año Nuevo and beyond. Grass seed, which may have been of some importance as food there, was gathered elsewhere also. Between the Pajaro and Salinas rivers, and about 4.2 km from the latter, Spanish explorers noted, "We saw near a lake some women who were gathering grass seeds" (Bolton, 1930, p. 452). This must have been in the vicinity of Lake Espinosa; an archaeological site exists on one of the nearby Vierra Lakes.

A variety of fiber plants were used. The following account is of Indians south of Monterey.

> There are two plants from which the natives obtain thread sufficiently strong for their needs. One of them grows on a moist soil and is very like true hemp, at least I take it to be so, and the other grows on dry ground and has leaves like a walnut, ashy colored and downy, with a white flower . . . . Neither of these plants grows to a height of more than three of four spans. (Fages, 1937, p. 80)

These are good descriptions of two widely used aboriginal fiber plants, Indian hemp and milkweed.

The crafts of nearby tribes have been thoroughly studied. The beautiful basketry of the Pomo to the north and the Salinan to the south is well known, but few specimens of Costanoan basketry are in existence. Probably Costanoan baskets were similar to those made by their neighbors. Good-quality basketry is essential to the practice of stone boiling.

The Costanoans must have used a large part of their energy in canvassing the country to gather food. Although the annual range in temperature in the area is not great, the inland supply of wild foods varies greatly because of seasonal rainfall. This was probably an important reason for the concentration of Indian populations along the coast. Being seasonally less variable, the intertidal zone offers gatherers a more dependable food source than does the inland zone. Although shoreline foods were the mainstay, Costanoan life was probably at its best in the fall, when inland acorns, buckeyes, islay prune, and blackberries ripened, grass seeds matured, and migrant flocks of ducks and geese arrived.

1.3. Disappearance of the Costanoans

The Indians, first concentrated in the missions by the Spanish, were dispersed during the Mexican period, when the missions were secularized.

The naturalist Menzies, visiting Mission Carmel in 1792 during the Spanish administration, wrote, "Close by, we saw a large village of huts containing about seven hundred Indians converted to the Christian religion" (Menzies, 1924, p. 284).

An American who visited San Juan Bautista in 1833, immediately before secularization, found it "containing from six to seven hundred inhabitants–all of whom are Indians, with the exception of the priests and fifteen or twenty people who are occupied in teaching and instructing these heathens" (Leonard, 1934, p. 161).

Richard Dana, author of *Two Years Before The Mast*, visited Monterey in 1836-1837 while it was still Mexican territory and commented on

the pure Indian, who runs about with nothing upon him but a small piece of cloth, kept up by a wide leather strap drawn around his waist . . . . The Indians, as I have said before, do all the hard work, two or three being attached to each [Spanish] house; and the poorest persons are able to keep one, at least, for they have only to feed them. (Dana, 1911, pp. 82, 86)

Since Dana (p. 74) also states that there were about a hundred houses in Monterey, several hundred Indians must have been working there as servants at the time.

The Costanoan way of life was greatly altered during the Spanish-Mexican period. Within a short time they learned something of agriculture (Petit-Thouars, 1956, p. 80). An American traveler in 1833 who described his position as being about 64 km (40 miles) south of San Francisco and 97 or 113 km (60 or 70 miles) north of Monterey (i.e., somewhere near Point Año Nuevo), remarked, "In some parts the natives raise a small quantity of corn, pumpkins, melons, etc." (Leonard, 1934, p. 91). At a point farther south, closer to Monterey, he observed, "Some of the natives live well, as they cultivate pumpkins, beans, and some of them Indian corn" (Leonard, 1934, p. 95). Although domesticated in the Americas, these agricultural plants were introduced here by the Spanish. Tillage and the growing of vegetable products had little appeal to the Spanish cattlemen, who willingly relegated those tasks to the Indian. Accounts written around the middle of the nineteenth century show that the Costanoans were finding a role as tillers in an otherwise pastoral economy—but this development was quickly cut short by American settlement.

During the early Spanish period the Indians had been mainly transferred to the missions at San Juan Bautista, Soledad, and Carmel from the Pajaro Valley. After secularization some drifted back to the valley as laborers. An American settler in the valley recorded that, in 1852, "We had a great many Indians in the valley. They made good hands to dig potatoes and bind grain. The squaws gathered wheat after the crops were harvested" (Kitchen, 1952, unpaginated). Kitchen probably means "a great many" relative to the total population, which was very small at the time. Costanoan culture did not last long in the American period of occupancy. The note above is one of the last published references to Indians living in the Pajaro Valley. As late as 1869, however, a few occasionally returned to one of their old village sites on a tributary of the Pajaro River a few kilometers south of Watsonville to "fish, hunt, and gather seed" (Reid, 1963).

A few Indians may have survived in the hills northwest of Santa Cruz until around the middle of the nineteenth century practicing, to some extent, their traditional livelihood. The following note, written in 1914, refers to a large shellmound about five miles upcoast from Santa Cruz: "Old timers tell me that the Indians used to come from the hills to this place, gather and cook shell fish, and throw the shells on the heap" (Dodge, 1914, p. 120). Until the beginnings of American settlement, Costanoans still occupied a considerable part of the Monterey Bay area. For example, in 1843, "there were but a few people except Indians in Carmel Valley" (Swan, 1874); and in 1851 the Salinas Valley was still "dotted with Indian huts" (Garnier, 1967, p. 33).

Introduced European diseases, particularly whooping cough and measles, are known to have decimated other California Indian groups, and a few records exist of their effects on the Costanoans. For example, in 1843, "The Indians were then numerous about Monterey and Carmelo, *for the small-pox was not brought to Monterey till next spring, which thinned them off*" (Swan, 1874).

The first destructive effects of European settlement, both Spanish and American, on Costanoan culture bore most heavily upon the Indians' food sources: they were taken or driven away from their food supply, or the food resource itself was destroyed in place (Cook, 1943, p. 26). This exclusion of the Indians from their food supply is well described in the following account (probably written in the late 1870s) which also indicates the interruption of trade relations between Costanoans and their inland neighbors, the Yokuts.

A large band of Indians from the Tulare Lake section passed through Salinas yesterday on their way to Monterey Bay to catch fish and dry abalone . . . . [According to] Chief Joaquin, who was a Mission Indian and speaks good Spanish, . . . formerly they had hundreds on this annual gathering at the sea, while now they have less than a hundred. He spoke of the disappearance of the game, and said that formerly he never saw a fence, while now they are found everywhere. Also they formerly had regular campgrounds, where mortars and pestles were left to grind the acorns, but since the advent of the white man, these caches had been disturbed. (*Salinas Daily Journal*, July 29, 1924, quoting a passage from old files of the *Daily Journal*)

The total Costanoan population has been estimated at 11,000 at the time the first Europeans arrived. Probably at least a third of them lived in the Monterey Bay area. In 1920, there were 56 survivors (Cook, 1943, p. 40). They are now virtually extinct. Today a few people of partly Costanoan descent reside in the area, mainly near San Jose and around the old mission San Juan Bautista. But their mission-Costanoan forebears abandoned most tribal customs more than a century ago.

The content of Costanoan shellmounds shows that the central California littoral had been subjected to a thoroughgoing human influence long before the coming of Europeans.

The total volume of shell in California middens was so great that the shell was sometimes mined. Foreigners visiting Spanish pueblos commented on their burning shells to make lime for their buildings–apparently a sizable industry (Egenhoff, 1952): lime was made "by burning seashells, of which there was a never-failing supply" (Duflot de Mofras, 1937; written in 1842) and "The lime they use is made of seashells, principally from the *ear shell* [i. e. , the abalone, *Haliotis*; its generic name means, literally, "sea ear"], which is of a large size and *in great numbers on the shores*" (Vancouver, 1798, p. 35). On the San Francisco Peninsula, Americans used midden as a road-surfacing material. Midden from a site described as being about five miles upcoast from Santa Cruz (near Laguna Creek?) was also used as a chicken food adjunct, for hardening egg shells:

On the coast is a large shell mound about 270 feet [82 m] long and 90 feet [27 m] wide. How high it formerly was cannot be told, *as most of it has been removed by poultry men who used to haul it away by the wagon loads*; at this time the mound was about 20 feet [6 m] high. (Dodge, 1914, p. 120)

The larger shell middens are at shoreline itself. Keeping in mind the rising sea, the rate of wave erosion along this coast, and the some 7000 years of occupancy by aboriginal shell collectors, it is clear that even the quantities of shell described above are but a small measure of the total biomass diverted here from marine ecosystems to human use. Within this period of time, shoreline has been displaced inland, probably in places by as much as a kilometer; many shell middens have, no doubt, been lost to the sea. For example, a number of midden beds, truncated by marine erosion, are exposed on coastal bluffs between Santa Cruz and Davenport. One, at the edge of an eroding cliff a little south of Davenport, has been reduced by recent wave action to a patch of only a few cubic meters.

The quantity of shell in the mounds and the presence of both mature and immature specimens of most common species suggest that parts of the shoreline were nearly stripped of mollusks at times. It seems likely that the Costanoans were a principal control of animal population sizes in the littoral zone, particularly of mollusks and pinnipeds, and that this control was maintained for centuries. On the other hand, the Indians' subsistence demands were spread over virtually the entire biotic spectrum, in contrast to those of later inhabitants, whose special and limited preferences (e.g., for the red abalone and sea otter) may have generated imbalances by making heavy demands on only a few species. Study of differences in shell size and maturity, and the relative abundance of species from different levels in the middens, may eventually make it possible to graph fluctuations of mollusk populations into the prehistoric past.

1.4. Plant Cover and Indian Burning before European Settlement

Although the Indians of California have been described as lacking the "torch technology" required for using fire with major and predictable ecological effect, early records do not support this view. The subject is discussed here in some detail because of its importance in interpreting present biogeographic circumstances and in determining the potential natural vegetation of the area.

At the time when European settlement began, the vegetation in parts of the Monterey Bay area had been considerably altered by fires set by the Costanoans, who found an increased supply of food plants and game in country opened by burning. The amount of burning done by the Indians is generally underestimated. Fire was their principal tool of land management. The historical and ethnographic evidence assembled in the following paragraphs suggests that their burning was done with considerable skill and foresight, that the successional consequences of burning were well known to them, and that when they were forced to discontinue the practice some of their main food sources were cut off.

The accounts also suggest that this system of managing the vegetation had been developed by the women who, although they gathered mussels, were strongly associated with the plant world under the Costanoan division of labor. According to an aged woman survivor of a small group known as "San Juans" who lived in the hills near Monterey, "The men had the animal part of the diet to hunt for, the women the vegetable. The women had to gather the acorns, the greens, the roots, the seeds, the nuts . . . . They also had to keep the camp supplied with wood" (Solarsano, 1930).

Fire was used by coastal Indians to encourage the growth of certain plants and to prepare others for harvest. Off Cape Mendocino in mid-September, 1818, while sailing southward to San Francisco, the French explorer de Roquefeuil saw fires on the coast several nights in succession, including one "which covered the greater part of the hill, from the seashore to the summit, and it appeared to extend to the other side . . . . The natives at this season set fire to the grass, *to dry the pods of a grain which they use for food, to render it more easy to gather*" (de Roquefeuil, 1823, p. 105). Such burning practices suggest considerable control.

Another expedition made a similar observation at San Francisco in 1816: "All night, great fires burned on the land at the back of the harbor; the natives are in the habit of burning the grass to further its growth" (Rudkin, 1954, p. 41).

In parts of the area, the seed of grasses or other herbaceous plants was a food staple. Exactly which plants these were is uncertain. It is unlikely that grass seeds were the only ones collected, as the yield of the native grasses was small. One plant that comes immediately to mind, because of its common use by California Indians, is the chia, a small, annual, purple-flowered plant of the mint family whose dark, glutinous seeds were an important food. Spanish travelers in the Costanoan area were frequently offered foods made of some small black seed, possibly chia, for example, "large tamales, kneaded of a dough made of very black wild seeds, resembling tar" (Bolton, 1926, pp. 277, 290).

California Indians also set fires to produce a needed supply of greens:

In all of New California from Fronteras northward the gentiles have the custom of burning brush so that with the first light rain or dew the shoots will come up . . . upon which they feed like cattle when the weather does not permit them to seek other food. (Simpson, 1961, p. 51)

These comments may refer to one of the several species of clover known to have been eaten by various California tribes.

Fire was used to fell individual trees: Costanoans near Santa Cruz "made their huts of branches of *trees, which they cut down by firing* and then using sharp stones" (Williams, 1892, p. 47). Such fire rings, burned in the bases of tree trunks, were also used in harvesting pine nuts in the vicinity of Carmel Mission:

The cones of the pine tree are small, and the nuts are extremely so, but very good and pleasing to the taste. The method of gathering them is to build a fire at the foot of the tree, which in a few hours falls, making the fruit available without difficulty. (Fages, 1937, p. 68)

Which pine species this may have been is uncertain. The most important food species in this part of California was the digger pine, but, at least nowadays, the tree does not grow on the Monterey Peninsula itself. The reference may be to a small area of digger pines in Pine Canyon a few kilometers eastward, near the north base of Mt. Toro.

Early accounts of Indian actions are sometimes difficult to interpret—not necessarily because the accounts themselves are inaccurate, but because knowledge of Costanoan custom is limited.

Hazel was so abundant between Pinto Lake and Corralitos Lagoon that, in 1769, missionary Father Juan Crespi named this area the land of "lakes and hazelnuts," noting that a little to the north were ". . . many hills covered with hazelnut thickets." The Costanoans periodically burned these thickets. Why was hazel desired in such quantities? Apparently not solely for its edible nuts, because Crespi noted that the ". . . thickets had been burned off . . . when the trees were in flower . . . " (Stanger, pp. 79, 80-81). An explanation of the Costanoan demand for hazel may come from ethnographic accounts of other north-Californian tribes: Although hazel withes had a variety of uses (e.g., as binding material, for making traps, etc.), they were employed above all in the making of baskets—the principal Indian utensil. For example, Hupa women sought out regrowth patches of hazel (during the second and third year after they had been burned-over) to gather shoots for the manufacture of large baskets (Goddard, 1903, p. 38). Probably the Costanoan purpose in burning hazel thickets was to keep the plants small, and their withes of a uniform size: "They grow in thickets the highest of which are a yard and a half or a yard and three-fourths tall"—that is, considerably shorter than full-size hazels.

A Spanish captain, writing at the presidio in Monterey on October 3, 1774, spoke of a "bad habit of the heathens. *Having harvested their seeds, they set fires . . . so that new 'yerbas'* [grasses or other herbs] *will come up; also to catch the rabbits which get confused by the smoke"* (Rivera y Moncada, 1774, I, pp. 57-58). The practice was noted elsewhere in the vicinity of the Monterey Peninsula. On July 5 of the same year, the captain wrote of smoke from the fires set by the Indians in the country "to the south" being visible from the presidio. The party sent that afternoon to investigate did not return until dusk, reporting that the fires were farther away than had been supposed (Rivera y Moncada, 1774, I, p. 34), probably in the Carmel Valley.

According to a Spanish report of 1792, the hunting of small game with fire, as described in the foregoing account, was widespread: "the gentiles [i.e., the natives] have the custom of burning the brush . . . for hunting rabbits and hares" (Simpson, 1961, p. 51). On the other hand, a Spanish account of an Indian antelope hunt near Chualar describes fire driving of large game as well, a custom not generally associated with this area (Fages, 1911, p. 61: Crespi's diary, cited in Bolton, 1927, p. 300).

Indian burning was still widespread after several decades of Spanish settlement, and a nuisance to cattlemen. The Spanish, themselves, continued the practice of burning unwanted plant cover, but they punished the Indians (who used other methods and had other reasons) for doing so. Official proclamations were issued asking mission authorities up and down the coast to warn offenders "against this very harmful practice of setting fires to pasture lands." Governor Arrillaga wrote from Santa Barbara to the Father President of the Missions on May 31, 1793:

> Because of . . . the serious damage that results from the fires that are set each year in the pastures by Christian and Gentile Indians . . . [the mission fathers should warn] the Christian Indians, and *particularly the old women* . . . threatening them with the rigors of the law . . . . (Clar, 1957, pp. 6, 8 and 10).

Mission Santa Cruz and the "other two missions of the north," i.e., Santa Clara and San Francisco (all within Costanoan territory) are specifically mentioned as having received the warning immediately.

Burning was commonly done in the fall, after the seed harvest, when the grass was dry. The most persistently fired areas were close to the shore itself; there the additional harvest acquired as a result of such burning was conveniently near the intertidal food supply. Onshore winds tended to drive fires inland, away from the coastal villages.

During the wet season, the Costanoans sometimes carried lighted firebrands as they traveled about. The following Spanish account of this Costanoan custom was recorded south of San Francisco in December 1774: "A heavy fog came up . . . . *Taking up their lighted firebrands with which to warm themselves on the way*, they took themselves off." And some days later, between the San Lorenzo and Pajaro rivers, the Spanish came upon "*an old woman* who received us with cries and *a firebrand in her hand* . . . which I accepted in order not to offend her" (Bolton, 1926, pp. 274, 302-303). Far from having a primitive torch technology, the Costanoans were adept in the use of fire; for example, they roasted seeds by tossing them with live coals in basketry trays, and even used flames to trim their hair and beards: "The Indians of the *rancherias* [i.e., the independent Indian villages, away from the missions] having no instruments of iron, perform this operation with lighted firebrands" (La Pérouse, 1789, p. 453).

When Father Juan Crespi, coming from the south with the Portola expedition, entered the Salinas Valley near the present site of King City, he wrote an account of plant cover and Indian burning. Traveling northwestward along the Salinas River on September 28, 1769, in the vicinity of Greenfield, his party "followed the same valley and river by a level road, *the grass all burned.*" In the evening the party "halted in the same plain of the valley *in the midst of a grove of live oaks* which had a *little pasture that had not been burned.*" Proceeding northwestward the next day, September 29, between Soledad and Chualar, the party followed "the course of the river by a level road like the preceding, *although it was more abundant in unburned pasture.*" Near Chualar, the party passed along "the wood formed by the trees of the river which must be more than four hundred varas [that is, more than 365 m] wide." On the next day, September 30, traveling northward from Chualar, Crespi again noted that "The soil is whitish and *short of pasture on account of the fires set by the heathen*" (Bolton, 1927, pp. 199-201). Thus, Fr. Crespi saw mainly newly burned grassland on the floor of the Salinas Valley between the present sites of Greenfield and Spreckels, with at least one isolated grove of live oaks and a broad strip of riparian forest along the river itself.

Fr. Crespi's diary goes on to describe the neighborhood of an Indian village in the lower Pajaro Valley near the present site of Watsonville. On October 8, "We halted on the bank of the river . . . which was near its very verdant and pleasant plain, *full of cottonwoods, alders, tall oaks, live oaks*, and other species not known to us . . . . The soldiers called the stream Rio del Pajaro" (Bolton, 1927, p. 211). This floodplain forest of the lower Pajaro Valley has disappeared; today the land is used for intensive culture of field crops.

The diary next describes the country between Watsonville and Pinto Lake: On October 10, "we must have traveled but little more than one league [about 5 km], *over plains and low hills, well forested* with very high trees of a red color, not known to us. They have a very different leaf from cedars . . . . We stopped near a lagoon" (Bolton, 1927, p. 211). These notes are the first historical account of the California redwood. The land between the Pajaro River and Pinto Lake is now planted to orchard and truck crops.

Early historical records are sometimes discounted as being simply the careless, general observations of missionaries and fortune hunters who had little real interest in natural history. This mistaken impression arises mainly from difficulties in translating the early journals accurately in terms of the local setting and the knowledge available at the time. The first Spanish journals are filled with sound comment on plant and animal life, but since the California flora contains many genera completely lacking in Europe, the Spanish language contained no relevant names for much of it. The old diaries show that in coming upon the plants of their homeland here, the wild roses, oaks, alders, and pines, the homesick explorers, plainly delighted, greeted the "flowers of Castille" as so many familiar faces. The diaries also show the travelers, both soldiers and priests, debating the botanical relationships of conspicuous species new to them—for instance, arguing about whether the redwood was actually more like a cedar or a fir.

On October 16, 1769, Crespi's party, coming from the neighborhood of Corralitos, traveled "very near the beach, and the range of hills which follows, which has *good pasture, although it has just been burned by the heathen.*" On October 17, they came to the San Lorenzo River. "Not far from the stream *we found a patch of ground that is not burned*, and it is a pleasure to see the grass and the variety of herbs . . . ." On October 18, they moved from what is now the site of Santa Cruz along the coast toward Año Nuevo: "we descended and ascended four deep watercourses [these would include Wilder, Laguna, and Scott creeks] . . . . *Only in the watercourses are any trees to be seen; elsewhere we saw nothing but grass that was burned"* (Bolton, 1927, pp. 214-216).

The early Spanish accounts of their travels repeatedly mention tree growth: pines, oaks, sycamores, cottonwoods, and so on. Mindful both of the needs of their horses and prospects for the area's settlement, the Spanish conscientiously noted the occurrence of timber, grass, and water. There can be little question that except for the Salinas Valley, their impression was one of a well-wooded area. Nevertheless, parts of the country were plainly already open grassland in 1769, and the association of this grassland with Indian burning (done just before the beginning of the rainy season) is explicit. Thus, when the Spanish first saw the Monterey Bay area, its potential natural vegetation was not everywhere in existence and manmade fires had long been an important ecological factor.

Thus, the surfaces of the lower marine terraces upcoast from Santa Cruz, like parts of the lower Salinas Valley, were kept in grass cover by Indian burning. The same is probably true of many smaller tracts around Costanoan villages scattered throughout the area, and perhaps of the grassy "balds" on hills in the south (e.g., those on the northern slopes of Mr. Toro). It is true that the minimal invasion of woody plants in these balds suggests that their potential natural vegetation is, in fact, herbaceous. But there is no edaphic or climatic explanation for the absence of woody growth in most. Prolonged burning and, in more recent times, cattle grazing coupled with increased deer populations probably explain the absence of woody plants.

On the other hand, in the hinterlands beyond areas repeatedly burned, plant communities were probably but slightly disturbed when first seen by the Spanish—except by the occasional escape of an Indian fire.

Few alien species had been introduced. The plants and animals present in Indian times were native to this region, with but few exceptions. The domesticated dog and a few household pests (e.g., fleas and lice) had arrived long before, with the first immigrants to the Americas. On the other hand, seeds of Indian hemp, the most widely used North American aboriginal fiber plant, may have reached California from east of the Sierra, in trade.

Some plants known to have been used by the Costanoans still grow in the neighborhood of midden sites. In places, for example, the buckeye has a peculiar distribution, growing as it does in small groves both along stream courses and in isolated clusters well up on the slopes. How its heavy fruits were disseminated to give such a spotty distribution is something of a puzzle. It has been suggested (Jepson, 1923, p. 167) that this distribution is partly artificial—the result of the Indians' transporting the fruit for food and dropping some of it by their campsites. Collecting and carrying around large quantities of acorns and islay prunes as they did, the Costanoans no doubt also influenced the numbers of oak and prune trees and perhaps, here and there, the geographical range of species.

2. Spanish-Mexican Land Use: Environmental Effects

More than a century and a half passed between the Spanish discovery of Monterey Bay and the establishment of the first settlements in 1770, shortly after the arrival of Portola's expedition. Settlement brought about sweeping changes in landscape and ecology. New plants and animals, especially horses and cattle, were introduced.

In Spain, where the horse, or *caballo*, has long been associated with gentry, a gentleman is called a *caballero*—that is, one who rides horseback. On the spacious frontiers of New Spain, the enviable life of horseman and cattle rancher was open to many. This pastoral manner of living flowered late, but strongly, in the Monterey Bay area. The traditional equestrian emphasis appeared in folk terms and names on the land: An early Spanish land measure was the *caballeria* (the area needed to feed one horse). Similarly, patches of grassland (pictured as suited to the rearing of colts, or *potros*) were called *potreros*, a word still common in California place names: Potrero Canyon, in the Carmel Valley; the Bolsa de Potrero land grant, in the Salinas Valley; Potrero Hill, in San Francisco, etc.

Squaw grass (known also as bear grass, fire-lily, and Indian basket grass) and gowen cypress on Monterey Peninsula. Northern California Indians wove baskets from the fibrous leaves, and ate the bulbous roots. Before gathering their leaf supply, the Indians reburned tracts of squaw grass to destroy the old, dry leaves. The plant flowers strongly only after fires (Maule, 1959).

Rather than surviving in areas that have had minimal human influence, several endemic species grow in areas of formerly dense Indian settlement. For example, Huckleberry Hill (where such fire-favored species as squaw grass, Monterey pine, and Bishop pine grow close to each other) is surrounded by archaeological sites. Año Nuevo and Waddell Creek are also in an area of dense prehistoric settlement. There, the fertile hybrid species, Monterey pine x knobcone pine, may be the result of repeated burning, in Indian times and later. Knobcone grows nearby, and somewhat inland from, the stands of Monterey pine; since both species colonize burned spots, fire brings the two together.

It is difficult to explain the distribution of a number of native plants solely in terms of natural environmental factors. Special edaphic circumstances are, at best, only a necessary, not a sufficient, condition for their successful

reproduction. It is unlikely that lightning-caused fires have burned with sufficient frequency to maintain these plants since the mid-Holocene period, when modern climatic conditions developed.

Thus, manmade fire may well have been a critical factor in their survival over a period of several thousand years. Without fire most closed-cone conifers lose ground to other species, e.g., to the live oak and Douglas fir. Controlled burning, and other kinds of human disturbance of the terrain, may be required to save several rare plant species in the Monterey Bay area. (Photo B. Gordon)

Buckeye grove near archaeological site on Laguna Creek. Buckeyes prefer streamsides; so did the Costanoans. But along streams in some areas, archaeological sites and buckeye groves are so frequently together that a more-than-coincidental association is probable. Buckeyes are strung along Año Nuevo Creek, where another principal Costanoan village was located. They also grow near shell mounds on Elliot and Scott creeks. And near Laguna Creek, the thickly clustered buckeyes shown above extend some 200 m along a midden site, forming a veritable orchard. (Photo B. Gordon)

Areas suitable for grazing cattle already existed, particularly in the lower Salinas Valley, but such grassland was extended by the burning of woody plant cover in lowlands and on the lower slopes. Cattle, horses, and sheep were soon being raised in large numbers to support a Spanish colonial economy based mainly on grazing.

In association with the cattle industry, exotic plants and animals were introduced, particularly from the Mediterranean area, and the new species spread to other parts of the West Coast from Monterey, the main site of Spanish activity in northern California. Some of the grasses and weeds are now among the most characteristic plants of rural California: wild oat, for instance, and filaree, mustard, wild radish, foxtail, and bur clover.

Soap plant (*Chorogalum pomeridianum*) growing on an archaeological site in the dunes south of Moss Landing. The shell fragments are from pismo clams, the principal shell in this midden. Note the four bulbs placed between the soap plants. The Costanoans made brushes from the coarse brown fibers that envelop the bulbs, to be used, for example, in sweeping ground meal from stone mortars. Crushed bulbs were strewn in slow-flowing streams to stupefy fish so they could be easily caught. The bulbs were also used as soap.

Inland, the soap plant grows scattered throughout grasslands, but its occurrence in dunes is unusual. Elsewhere in California, various plants used by native tribes can still be found clustered around former Indian habitation sites. (In addition to the buckeye, such plants include the California black walnut around Walnut Creek and Round Valley, Indian hemp and chia in Sonoma County, and squaw bush in Tehama County.) Although in general this association with Costanoan sites does not apply to the soap plant's distribution, the plants shown here probably grew from bulbs carried to this dune site by Costanoan inhabitants, since the species is found nowhere else in the immediate vicinity. With increasing agricultural and other economic development of the area, the association between plant distribution and Costanoan sites—still visible in the 1940s—has almost disappeared. (Indian hemp was especially common around archaeological sites.) The photograph was taken in 1975; since then part of the site, and the soap plant, have been scattered by farm equipment. (Photo B. Gordon)

An ingenious method of determining the time of introduction of weed species involves ascertaining the presence or absence of their seeds in adobe samples taken from the Spanish mission buildings whose construction dates are known (see Hendry's publications). For example, both the wild oat and the red-stem filaree are present in the bricks of the mission of San Juan Bautista, constructed in 1797. Exactly how such plants got into the area is not known. No doubt the seeds of some arrived intermixed with crop seed and in the fleeces and pelts of domestic animals. Hay, carried by mule train to the mines in the Santa Lucia Mountains and eastward to Idria and New Almaden, probably included some of the first exotic weeds and insects imported to the hinterland.

Livestock raising was the Spanish activity that had the greatest influence on the landscape. Accounts written during the Spanish-Mexican period agree on the great numbers of cattle. A description of the Pajaro Valley as it was in mid-nineteenth century stated: "There were no fences in the valley. Hundreds of Spanish cattle were here at that time. We went on horseback to keep from being chased by them" (Kitchen, writing in 1852, unpaginated).

A report by John C. Fremont written in 1846 shows that by this time parts of the original woodland and forest in the northern part of the bay area had been cleared, and that the wild oat, introduced about half a century earlier, had become well established:

In the country between Santa Cruz and Monterey and around the plains of St. John [that is, around San Juan Bautista] the grass, which had been eaten down by the *large herds of cattle*, was now everywhere springing up . . . in the valleys of the mountains bordering the Salinas plains . . . *wild oats* were three feet high, and well headed, by the 6th of March. (Fremont, 1849, p. 68)

In comparison with the cattle industry, tilling the soil was a minor Spanish activity. Tillage and irrigation were localized mainly around the missions, where Old World plants, whose cultivation in California began with the Spanish, included the wine grape, olive, fig, apple, pear, and English walnut. The pepper tree was also carried here by the Spanish, from their colonies in the Andes.

The Spanish did so little gardening that a British naturalist visiting Monterey in 1792 reproached the inhabitants there for "not rearing, in country like this where the soil is so very productive, a sufficient quantity of vegetables for their own consumption" (Menzies, 1924, p. 287; Simpson, 1930, p. 90). Americans arriving in the Salinas and Pajaro valleys in the mid-nineteenth century remarked similarly on the characteristic Spanish land use: only a few tiny gardens, multitudes of cattle, and no fences or barns (Leonard, 1934, p. 168; Kitchen, 1952). Marine resourses were similarly unused: The Spanish settlers, coming mainly from cattle-country in Mexico, rarely ate fish and made no boats (Simpson, 1930, p. 105).

The far-reaching ecological effect of Spanish cattle raising was out of proportion to the number of settlers. Even during the latter part of the Spanish-Mexican period, population was sparse over most of the bay area. As late as 1847, the Pajaro Valley, now outstanding for its agricultural productivity, "contained only about forty inhabitants, and was a great pasture ground for their herds" (*Overland Monthly*, 1887, p. 6). This early census disregards the few surviving Costanoans.

During the Mexican period many land grants, called *ranchos*, were awarded to Spanish-speaking settlers. Although most of the grants had been in existence scarcely 20 years when California became an American possession, they indelibly marked the landscape by establishing a framework within which future subdivisions of the land were made. The framework can still be seen from the air (see photo, pp. 112-113). In the country between the Salinas and Pajaro rivers grant boundaries act as property divisions throughout almost 80% of their lengths (Foster, 1968, p. 88). Where not bounded by natural features the grants are nowadays almost everywhere marked by fences and roads. On aerial photographs the old grant boundaries often stand out strongly because field strips, furrows, and plant rows abut against them at differing angles on opposite sides. In hilly country, they may mark the edges of chaparral tracts. Different grazing stages frequently appear on opposite sides of their now-fenced boundaries. Thus they commonly demarcate contrasting animal habitats as well.

Although the Spanish did not fence their rangeland here, they began the planting of tree rows, or living fences, near settlements—a practice that they had established over most of their cattle country in Central America. Along roads, twin fences of trees were sometimes extended into towns, forming shaded driveways, or *alamedas*. In California, e.g., at San Juan Bautista, willows were often used because pieces of their roots, stuck in the ground, readily strike root (Mylar, 1970, p. 48; Robinson, 1891, p. 118). Tree rows appear in several drawings and paintings made of the Monterey Peninsula in the 1840s (Van Nostrand, 1968, plates 26 and 40); and beyond the Monterey Bay area, at San Jose, "a beautiful avenue of trees, nearly three miles in length, leads from the mission to the pueblo" (Beechey, 1831, v. 2, p. 47); such tree rows were given official protection from woodcutters in 1833. Unfortunately, both from the standpoint of beautifying the countryside and maintaining its wildlife, the practice was discontinued within a few years after American occupancy began.

Within a century following the beginnings of Spanish settlement, coastal California had experienced a botanical transformation comparable in magnitude to that undergone gradually by Europe in its long transition from a paleolithic (hunting and gathering) to a neolithic (agricultural) economy.

3. Changes Attending American Occupancy

For a period of 50 years after European settlement practically the only commerce on the California coast had to do with the hunting of marine animals. The principal commercial items were sea otter, fur seal, sea lion, and whale (Evermann, 1923, pp. 522, 526). Monterey was a major center.

The sea otter was a major economic factor in the exploration and settlement of the California coast. Its pelt was highly prized in both Asia and Europe. The animal was hunted along the West Coast of North America by the Spanish, Russians, and Americans.

Actually, there are two geographical races of the sea otter, a northern and a southern. In 1804, the Russians brought about a hundred Aleutian Indians to the California coast to hunt the southern, or California, sea otter. The following account describes the hunting of sea otter in the Monterey Bay area:

> About 1823 was organized a company of otter hunters. They were Kadiaks [Kodiaks] from Alaska. Their way was to pursue in their boats the otter in the bay of Monterey, and when the latter became tired out, kill them with arrows. The otter used to sleep on a bed of seaweed opposite the sand banks of the bay. The Kadiak skin boats would take positions in line; then from a large boat several shots were fired; the frightened otter would start on a run, and the boats pursued them with the utmost speed. Their boats were made of seal-skin, the hair having been removed . . . . In this manner were destroyed all the otter on that part of the coast and further down. (Bancroft, 1888, pp. 470-471)

Thus, by the middle of the nineteenth century (ironically, about the same time Darwin was writing *The Origin of Species*), the California sea otter had almost disappeared.

The masses of shell in the middens of the Monterey Peninsula show that it has been thousands of years since abalone populations here were an expression of purely natural environmental controls. Excessive use is by no means a phenomenon of recent times only. Almost from their beginnings, historical records evidence periods of severe depletion (with harvest of immature specimens) and intervening times of at least partial recovery. At about the same time that the Russian otter hunting described above was going on (and while the Monterey Bay area was still Spanish territory), an American commerce in abalone began; in abalone shell, not flesh. There was no meeting the demand for otter skins at the time, and shells were carried northward to trade for skins. When Camille de Roquefeuil visited this coast in 1817, he stated,

> I obtained some information concerning the abalone (*Haliotis*) . . . an object much sought after by the tribes from whom the otter skins are obtained. [The

reference is to the tribes of the northwest coast, and to the northern sea otter.] In fact this shell has brought a high price on the northwest coast but it is much less highly valued since the *Americans from the United States have introduced whole shiploads which they came to Monterey to get*; at the same time *it has become rare in California*, as much because of this immense exploitation as because of their consumption on the spot. *For several years, the Indians have been eating the shellfish avidly before they reach full growth*, and the Spanish burn the shells to make lime. (Rudkin, 1954, p. 15)

The Spanish likewise exported the shells of *Haliotis rufescens* from Monterey in trade with the Indians of the northwest coast (Leechman, 1942, p. 160; Heizer, 1940, p. 399). And the Americans shipped some home to the East Coast. In 1836, Richard Dana described a fishing trip along Point Pinos with several shipmates: one "... of our numbers brought up on his hook a large and beautiful pearl-oyster shell. *We afterwards learned that a small schooner had made a good voyage by carrying a cargo of them to the United States*" (Dana, 1911, p. 78).

As American occupation of the coast began, commercial harvest of marine products intensified.

3.1. Early American Exploitation of Marine Resources

Oceanic explorers, certainly experienced observers of marine life, were surprised by the number of whales in Monterey Bay: La Pérouse, in 1786, wrote, "It is impossible to describe either the number of whales with which we were surrounded, or their familiarity. They blowed every half minute within half a pistol shot from our frigates" (La Pérouse, 1799, vol. 2, p. 178). The leader of another French expedition, visiting California in 1837, complained

The roadstead of Monterey is frequented by an innumerable school of hump-backed whales which get very familiar. They come in among the ships anchored in the road where they infect the air . . . by the penetrating and nauseating odor which they give off. (Petit-Thouars, 1956, p. 76)

According to Sir George Simpson, when he visited Monterey in 1841-1842, "Several whale were spouting near our vessel, the Bay of

Monterey being a favorite resort of the fish" (Simpson, 1930, p. 105).

In the late eighteenth and early nineteenth centuries, New England whalers often hunted the waters off northern California, flensing the whale carcasses by rolling them in the water alongside their ships and rendering the blubber in kettles on board. Although the New Englanders killed whale far out in the Pacific, they hunted in coastal bays as well. Monterey and San Francisco were principal supply ports.

About 1851, an old European (and very different) method of whaling—called "shore whaling"—had its California beginnings at Monterey. The whalers selected a beach and established a settlement nearby. Whales were sighted from hilly vantage points along the coast, whence signals were flagged to small boats at sea. Harpooned from the boats, the whales were towed ashore, rolled on the beach for flensing, and their blubber rendered in open-air kettles. The whaling boats seldom ventured more than 16 km from shore (Scammon, 1968, p. 248). The industry, mainly in the hands of Portuguese immigrants from the Azores, was based almost entirely on two species common in near-shore waters, the gray whale and the humpback. In the first few seasons the whales taken were mostly humpbacks, but by 1858 shore whalers were concentrating their efforts on the grays, avoided earlier because of their "*savage disposition* and the shoalness of the water into which they are followed" (Goode, 1884, p. 32); these quickly became the mainstay of the industry. According to the famous whaler, C. M. Scammon, bones of the gray whale were soon "scattered along the broken coasts from Siberia to the Gulf of California." (Irritable with good reason, the whale sometimes attempted to defend itself. Nowadays, gray whales are so placid that boating parties have approached them within a few feet.)

Settlements were established up and down the coast—for example, at Half Moon Bay, Pigeon Point, Davenport, Santa Cruz, Moss Landing, Monterey itself (there were three whaling stations in the vicinity), Carmel Bay (a hill on nearby Point Lobos, once a lookout and signal station, is still known as "Whaler's Knoll" and a small bight below as "Whaler's Cove"), and at Big Sur.

Shore-whaling station on Carmel Bay. This settlement (established in 1862 by Portuguese who had come to Monterey from the Azores) was located in Whaler's Cove east of Point Lobos. On the hill, "...are the neatly whitewashed cabins of the whalers ... upon a stone-laid quay, is erected the whole establishment of cutting-in and trying out the blubber of the whales. Instead of rolling them upon the beach, as is usually done, the cutting tackles are suspended from an elevated beam, whereby the carcass is rolled over in the water—when undergoing the process of flensing. Near by are the try-works, sending forth volumes of thick, black smoke from the scrap-fire under the steaming cauldrons of boiling oil .... on the crest of a cone-shaped hill, stands the signal-pole of the lookout station" (Scammon, 1874, p. 250). (Courtesy of the San Francisco Maritime Museum).

Abandoned shore-whaling station at Pigeon Point in the 1890s. At one time, when a company of Portuguese operated the station, the point was called "Punta Ballenas," meaning *whale point*. A lighthouse has been built near the site, which was officially renamed Pigeon Point after the clipper ship "Carrier Pigeon," wrecked nearby in 1863. In 1872, a visitor arriving at this station in the fall, several months before the gray-whale season, reported, "They had cut up 12 whales already, and killed and lost 10 more"; all were humpbacks (Evans, 1973, p. 46). In 1867 alone, Pigeon Point exported "nine hundred barrels of whale oil" (Cronise, 1868, p. 128). (Photo courtesy of the San Francisco Maritime Museum)

By 1861, Monterey was described as a great whaling port: "The number of whale bones on the sandy beach is astonishing—the beach is white with them" (Brewer, 1949, p. 105).

During the same years in which shore whaling began, the gray whale population received what was probably an even more critical blow: American whaling ships began hunting the females in the lagoons of Baja California. In the winter, the gray whale migrates southward from the North Pacific, passing near the shore along the California coast. The females congregate in the embayments of northwestern Mexico, where the young are born. In the spring, again following the

Whale bones, mainly those of humpback whales, accumulated at Moss Landing in the 1920s, during the last years of the whaling industry there. (Photo courtesy of the San Francisco Maritime Museum)

coast, the whales return to Arctic waters. Suffering from both the depredations by shore-whaling stations and the destruction of females at the calving sites, the gray whale population was rapidly depleted.

Within little more than two decades, the supply of gray whales (and the littoral population of humpbacks) was nearing exhaustion. In Monterey Bay, the killing of gray whales probably reached its peak between 1865 and 1871:

> Though many whale were killed during my visit, chiefly the "California Gray" (*Rachianectes glaucus* Cope), it was impossible to obtain measurements and drawings of them as they were always being cut up while floating [In the protection of Monterey harbor, shore whalers were able to begin processing the bodies while they were still afloat], and the mutilated carcasses when washed ashore were deprived of "flukes" and other essential parts, besides smelling so strong that the odor for miles was almost unbearable. (J. G. Cooper, 1871, pp. 757-758)

The fact that whale populations along this coast were being threatened was well known to Californians:

> The whale fishery, which for the last twenty-five years has constituted one of the most important of our local industries, is likely soon to become a thing of the past. The whales are gradually becoming scarcer . . . . Many years ago, while

California was yet a province of Mexico, the New Bedford whaling ships caught large numbers of Sperm and Right whales along this coast; but these species have now almost disappeared, and our whalers have to content themselves with the more numerous but less valuable California Greys and Humpbacks. (Walton and Curtis, 1875, p. 44)

Actually, by this date (1875), even grays and humpbacks were becoming scarce in the Monterey Bay area. And the shore-whaling industry began to decline. By 1888, it had virtually disappeared, though an occasional whale was still taken at Pigeon Point. As the industry failed, most of the whaler settlements disappeared.

In the twentieth century, well after the decline of shore whaling, yet another—and a very effective—method of taking whales was perfected: The crews of large boats killed whales of various species well out at sea. The bodies were inflated with air and towed to mechanized factories on land. One of the three such factories in California was located in Moss Landing. It was in operation from 1919 until 1926, processing chiefly humpbacks (Scofield, 1954, p. 16).

A more generalized use of marine resources was made by Chinese settlers. Having had long experience with the resources of the Pacific, the Chinese knew them better than did immigrants from the eastern United States.

Starting around the bays of San Francisco and Monterey in the 1850s, the Chinese developed a thriving industry based on shipment of dried sea products, mainly back to China. A climatic factor partly explains the success of the industry: The dependably rainless summers of the central California coast are ideal for such drying operations.

In the spring of 1853, a few Chinese came to Monterey from San Francisco and began collecting and drying abalone. They settled at Mussel Point (that is, in the Cabrillo Point-Point Alones area), close to where Hopkins Marine Station is now located. By summer, several hundred had arrived.

Chinese customs were introduced, with but slight modification to suit local conditions. The villagers were engaged in gathering the conchas nacar [i.e., *conchas de nacar*, the Spanish name here for abalone] and drying and packing the meat . . . . Their evenings are devoted to opening and spreading or hanging out the meat to dry. The sides and roofs of their cabins are covered with this species . . . . The conchas nacar when dried are packed in barrels and sent to this place [San Francisco] for shipment to China. (*Daily Alta Californian*, May 20, 1853)

Old descriptions of life there bring to mind scenes from coasts of the Far East: "sampan-like skiffs with bamboo-rigged sails" and peddlers carrying fish "in two large plaited baskets hanging from the tips of the carrying pole" (Scofield, 1954, p. 97).

Squids were laid out in the fields to dry. At night, skiffs were rowed about in the bay with torches burning at the bows, or pine pitch burning in a wire basket, to attract schools of squids, which were caught in small seine nets.

Thus, the Chinese harvested marine products whose uses were but little known among other American settlers at the time—for example, abalone, squid, seaweed, and shark fin were sun dried, along with various species of fishes. Although the Chinese harvested squids and seaweed here for years, other Americans never took to these products as they did to abalone (even recently the squid canned at Monterey has been for foreign markets).

Soon Chinese fishing camps were scattered around the bay and along the coast to the north and south. In 1868, a large Chinese camp for drying abalone was operating at Pebble Beach, on the seaward side of the peninsula. A short time later fish were being dried at the present site of Capitola, for shipment to San Francisco (Scofield, 1954, p. 97). And marine algae were collected on the rocks around the Monterey peninsula for shipment to China (C. L. Anderson, 1891, p. 26); Californians of Chinese descent still harvest small amounts of these plants for local use.

Restrictive legislation, growing partly from conservational concern and partly from the efforts of rival fishing interests, brought about a decline in the Chinese industries. The Chinese sometimes suffered too from an unfriendly attitude on the part of their neighbors. (The settlement in Pacific Grove was destroyed by fire in 1906.) In 1900, commercial harvest of abalone in shallow water was made illegal, and in 1915, the commercial drying of abalone meat was prohibited. In the Monterey Bay area, the products sought by the Chinese were so varied that effects of their activities were probably relatively short-lived. On the other hand, the inshore abalone population was, no doubt, greatly diminished. It was also claimed at the time that the average size of flounder in the bay decreased markedly because of over fishing. (Populations of flatfish are often among the first to decline under fishing pressure.)

3.2. Other Events of Ecological Significance

Following are additional historical events that were important in the development of existing ecological conditions.

The Costanoan Indian population virtually disappeared during the first few decades of American settlement, and hard pressed Spanish-Mexicans survived mainly in poorer country, as described in the following account written by an American in May 1870:

> From this point [about 8 km up the Pajaro Valley from Watsonville, around Aromas] to San Juan, there is little to interest the traveler: the few secluded spots among the hills adapted to farming, being occupied by Mexicans; the hills, already parched and brown, occupied by sheep, horses, cattle, and the ubiquitous ground squirrel. (*The Overland Monthly*, 1870, p. 348)

The narrator, like most American settlers, and in contrast to the Spanish-Mexican cattlemen, appraised the area largely in terms of its farming potentialities. Large-scale commercial agriculture, with extensive plowing, drainage, and irrigation, began under the Americans. In the Salinas Valley, many of the first American settlers were, like the Spanish before them, cattlemen. Sheep were raised in great numbers in the southern part of the Monterey Bay area, and rangeland there was especially heavily grazed. In 1860, Monterey County "contained more sheep than any other county in the United

States . . . and 100,000 cattle" (Cronise, 1868, p. 122). In 1870, there were 290,000 sheep in Monterey County. The cattle and sheep shipped in large numbers from the area necessarily represented a considerable export of soil minerals as well; at that time there was virtually no restoration of nutrients in the form of mineral fertilizers. (Gradual chemical depletion of soils may partly explain some seemingly exaggerated references to luxuriant growth in the early literature: patches of mustard growing so tall that cattle hid in them, wild oats rising almost to the pommel of a horseman's saddle, etc.)

By 1870, tillage for commercial agriculture was well underway in the Salinas Valley and, by 1890, most of the cattle ranches in the valley had been subdivided into grain farms. In 1888, sugar beets were planted in the valley; by 1897, beet growing and dairying were replacing grain farming on the more fertile soils (Allen, 1935, p. 139).

The introduction of exotic species continued with the Americans, and such species now number in the hundreds. These fall mainly into a category of plants and animals sometimes called synanthropes, because of their close association with people; some, like the dwarf nettle, have been humankind's camp followers for thousands of years. In addition to the numerous agricultural and horticultural species that are planted in the area, many other foreign plants reproduce themselves here untended. By far the larger number of the alien plants growing outside cultivation in the area are herbaceous. More than half are composites, grasses, legumes, or crucifers. Although most were imported accidentally, many are now considered valuable additions to the flora, particularly as forage plants. In the early days came such common plants as poison hemlock, sweet fennel, bermuda grass, common groundsel, and eucalyptus. Pampas grass, which now thrives on roadcuts and badly eroded spots, is more recent (Costas Lippman, 1977. For a thorough discussion of alien plants established in California see Frenkel, 1970 and Robbins, 1940).

Almost one third (31%) of the total number of 553 species of vascular plants growing without cultivation in the Santa Cruz

Wild oat, one of the most common plants of the area, was introduced from Europe by the Spaniards. (Photo B. Gordon)

Fuller's teasel (*Dipsacus fullonum*), introduced into the Americas with the Spanish sheep industry, was formerly widely cultivated for use in raising nap on woolen fabrics. (In remote Guatemalan blanket-making villages, it is still cultivated for that purpose.) In the Monterey Bay area, feral teasel is often found near roadsides and other recently disturbed sites. (Photo B. Gordon)

Poison hemlock, a species introduced from Europe, is widespread here, especially in recently disturbed spots. For example, it commonly forms lines along roadsides where bulldozers have heaped up loose dirt. It is common, too, in untended yards and recently abandoned fields, especially on moist sandy soils. The plant is of slight value to wildlife; furthermore, it is, as the name indicates, dangerously toxic to people. Poison hemlock is an example of an alien species whose introduction was in all respects unfortunate. (Photo B. Gordon)

Hottentot ivy is also called German ivy—a misnomer, because it is actually from South Africa. The vine is common along streams, where it is conspicuous trailing from willows when they are leafless in winter. Hottentot ivy is one of our more intrusive weeds. At the edges of oak woodland, where the slanting rays of the sun penetrate far under the trees, it may almost entirely cover patches of native undergrowth. On sun-facing road banks, too, it is sometimes draped heavily over native plants. At Moss Landing the monarch butterfly can be seen feeding on its nectar in January. Honeybees are also attracted to its strongly scented flowers. (Photo B. Gordon)

Quaking grass (*Briza maxima*), an attractive species introduced from Europe, is common in spots along roadsides and in other disturbed places, but it does not cover extensive areas. It is sometimes called "rattlesnake grass" because the seed heads are shaped somewhat like that snake's rattles. The grass probably escaped from gardens, where it was occasionally cultivated as an ornamental; it was already present in this area in the nineteenth century (Harrison, 1892, p. 131).

Introduced weeds are not universally unpopular among conservationists. In Britain, for example, some weeds are approaching extinction as a result of the use of herbicides and seed disinfectants. Attempts are being made to preserve several for nostalgic and aesthetic reasons. Some alien species are so well established in British folklore as to be part of the regional identity. There, as in the Monterey Bay area, many introduced plants have been present longer than the ethnic groups they live amongst. (Photo Nancy Burnett)

Milk thistle, introduced from the Mediterranean area, takes its name from the white-spotted leaves. It is common on ranch land, especially where cattle bed down, around watering troughs, and so on. The plant is generally a nuisance in pastures: Its leaves are prickly and have little forage value. On the other hand, in the fall, when its seed heads are dry, milk thistle seeds feed flocks of native finches. Local farmers say that when squirrel-extermination programs are successful, milk thistle grows most abundantly—at which time some farmers even go about with hand sprayers, killing the plants individually. Such details suggest the total consequence of human-induced ecological change in the area, the ramifications of which remain, as yet, for the most part untraced. (Photo B. Gordon)

Mountains are introduced (Thomas, 1961, p. 25). But such facts alone do not completely reveal the sweeping changes in plant cover: Over the larger part of the Monterey Bay area, particularly in the lower and drier sections, introduced plants cover much more of the actual surface than do natives.

On the other hand, few foreign species can penetrate and establish themselves within the natural plant associations, except where the latter are broken by open patches or otherwise disturbed. In the Santa Cruz Mountains the yellow-flowered French broom has become established along road banks throughout redwood forest and chaparral. But the shrub is not found in the undisturbed interior of these associations. (Assertions of the contrary are usually based upon inadequate knowledge of past human trafficking at the sites in question.)

Whatever its shortcomings, French broom serves as a valuable indicator species—a sensitive marker and reminder of past human

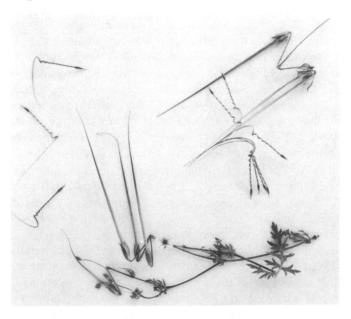

Long-beaked filaree (Storksbill, Clocks), a native of Europe, is common in annual grasslands, where it is valuable forage for sheep and cattle.

disturbance of the natural plant communities. The broom has been present in much of the area at least since the 1950s—both on Monterey Peninsula and in the Santa Cruz Mountains. It has benefitted greatly from the constant increase in landscaping, road building, felling of trees, making of forest paths, etc. In colonizing such disturbed terrain the plant has a competitive advantage over many native species. Though an ambitious eradication program, organized by concerned conservationists, began as early as 1979 (Mountjoy, 1979, p. 12), the shrub has become even more common since that time: Broom is only encouraged by the further disturbance of soil associated with such efforts—by people tramping to, through, and around its colonies as they undertake uprooting operations, etc. Nevertheless, in Santa Cruz County, "Parks and public works crews will be told to make yanking the pesky weeds out a priority whenever they are out on other jobs" (*The Santa Cruz Sentinel,* May 15, 1993). It is doubtful that these efforts can be sustained, or that they will have the desired effect in the long term. (It is, of course, pointless to rail against plants and animals— projecting on them the blame for past human misdeeds.) The problem is probably best solved by allowing natural succession to take its course. The shrub does not seriously retard the successional process: It is suppressed when thoroughly overshadowed by such native evergreens as Douglas fir and coast live oak. All human activity in the plant's vicinity should cease, with the possible exception of planting tree seedlings.

Near the Pajaro River at Watsonville—as along other streams— two vines, the periwinkle from Europe and Hottentot ivy from South Africa, intrude into the narrow strip of willow-cottonwood forest between the artificial levee and the river bank. But this riparian vegetation is subject to constant disturbance, both natural (by flooding) and artificial. Saline environments especially resist the intrusion of alien weeds. But there are exceptions: brass buttons, an African species, grows within the pickleweed area in salt marshes of Elkhorn Slough, and curly dock, of European origin, establishes itself on saline soils.

Relatively few Californian herbs have developed the weedy characteristics of the Eurasian immigrants and expanded their ranges into areas disturbed by tillage. Some that have done so are the telegraph weed, miner's lettuce (in shaded and moist spots), the turkey mullein (in drier parts of the area), and the California poppy.

Monterey pine cones. Distribution of the western gray squirrel is influenced by the planting of isolated groves of Monterey pines. Although usually described as associated with oaks, gray squirrels are rare in oak woodland near the coast, except where there is an admixture of conifers. In the Larkin Valley area, the squirrels travel from their preferred coniferous-tree cover, consisting of surviving patches of Douglas fir and redwood, through scattered live oaks and chaparral to find the pines and feed on their seeds. They gnaw apart the green, unopened cones like the one near the center of the photograph. (Note the gnawed cones, some with only the cores remaining, and the mature cone, open and undamaged.) The nearest naturally growing Monterey pines are located near Año Nuevo and on the Monterey Peninsula, where pine seeds are one of this squirrel's major foods. There, the gray squirrel is an important factor in forest reproduction. Beneath some pines at Año Nuevo, at least two-thirds of the cones have been gnawed apart. The squirrels also gnaw off many branchlets, letting whole clusters of soft green cones fall to the ground. By eating seeds and destroying immature cones, the squirrels help keep seedlings from growing too thickly around parent trees. And in carrying cones and seeds about, they disseminate trees to new sites. (Photo B. Gordon)

Among the native plants that have had their ranges extended through being planted are the Monterey cypress and the Monterey pine; both are much more abundant than formerly. Under natural conditions the Monterey cypress verged on extinction. When Europeans first arrived there were fewer than 11,000 of these trees, growing within a total area of some 50 acres, and all within several hundred meters of shoreline on the Monterey Peninsula and around Carmel Bay (Greene, 1929, p. 197). Perhaps in Spanish-Mexican times, and certainly in the 1870s, the cypress was being widely planted. A nursery for its propagation was located a few miles east of Monterey (*The Salinas City Index*, April 27, 1876). The Monterey pine, too, has been planted beyond its natural range in the Monterey Bay area, and especially abroad.

On the other hand, the ranges of most native species have been reduced. And in an area as rich in endemics as this one, burning, logging, clearing, and draining operations (and more recently housing developments) are particularly likely to result in extinctions.

Seasonal color changes in plant cover have likely been accentuated since European settlement began. The most conspicuous overall seasonal change in appearance of the landscape is largely the result of deforestation. Hills, originally covered with dark evergreen trees, now are covered with grasses which turn from yellow-tan in summer to light green in winter. The expanses of bright yellow colors produced from January to April by the blossoms of mustard, acacia, and Cape oxalis (all alien plants) were lacking aboriginally.

As emphasized earlier, fire has long been an important ecological factor in the area—not fires set by natural causes (these are rare here), but fires set purposely or accidentally by man. Much of the grassland in the Monterey Bay area was created by burning off woody plant cover. Intentional burning, begun during the period of Indian occupancy, was continued on a greater scale in association with the Spanish and American cattle industry. In later years the use of matches increased the number of accidentally set fires.

From the cattlemen's standpoint there was a strong temptation to burn chaparral: A spark could well turn a few hundred acres of worthless land into a profitable ranch. When woody cover is burned off, grass and forbs soon replace it. Grass-forb cover is maintained indefinitely under constant grazing. If grazing is discontinued, chaparral and forest begin to reclaim the land, rendering it useless to the cattleman. Intentional burning to improve grazing was frequently condemned, but "in many backward communities [of California], it was practically considered to be a duty on the part of some citizens to burn the woods, regardless of who owned them" (Clar, 1959, p. 300). Early cattlemen (and deer hunters, careless with their campfires) were inclined to report back-country fires as being set by lightning—an inclination so strong that it was once the subject of rural jokes. Despite restrictive legislation, the practice died slowly, and violations persisted in the area at least into the 1940s. In 1945, the California Division of Forestry began issuing burning permits.

Since that time more than 2.3 million acres [930 thousand hectares] of private lands have been burned . . . . The U.S. Forest Service and the Bureau of Land Management have also done considerable prescribed burning . . . . [Of the burning done under permit in California] *the majority has been done to improve grazing for livestock.* (Biswell, 1969, p. 439)

Statistics are not available for estimating what portion of this burning actually took place in the Monterey Bay area.

A mapping of historical fires shows that, besides grasslands, virtually the whole presently-wooded Monterey Bay area has been burned over since European settlement began—and a good part of it, repeatedly. (For ample documentation, see WPA; Greenlee and Langenheim, 1980; Greenlee and Moldenke, 1981). Wildlife has been subjected to frequent and drastic readjustment.

Since there can be no doubt that fire has been a major ecological factor throughout the area's history, an important (and controversial) question concerns the number of fires that are caused by nature itself—as opposed to those that are manmade. (Local fire departments respond to scores of grassland and brushland fires every year.) If no people were present, would naturally-caused fires occur with sufficient frequency to maintain the large areas of fire-dependent chaparral, knobcone pine, grassland, etc., which exist at present? Are lightning-sparked fires frequent enough to sustain the various endemic species which are partially dependent on fire for their reproduction? On an average over the centuries, how frequently will any specified hectare in the Monterey Bay area be burned-over by a lightning-sparked fire (i.e., one hectare out of the more than 250,000 total in the area)?

There being no active volcanoes in this area, lightning is virtually the only natural cause of fire. Most lightning flashes are associated with thunderstorms—and, according to a U.S. Weather Bureau report, coastal California has fewer thunderstorms than any other part of the United States. To the north and south of the Monterey Bay area, at San Francisco Airport and at Santa Maria, thunderstorms occur on an average one day a year or less (CSD, pp. 2, 22). Many lightning flashes move from cloud to cloud, and do not reach the ground; and of those that do strike ground, very few start fires. Of the fires started, most occur during the rainy season, and do not spread. Residents near the coast of Monterey Bay know that more than a year may pass without their hearing a single thunderclap. (The use of lightning-rods is almost unknown hereabouts.)

Along the coast, most lightning is associated with frontal storms, especially storms of late fall and winter. Inland, lightning is usually associated with summer thunderheads, produced by thermal convection. Eastward, toward and beyond the Gabilans, such convectional storms become increasingly frequent. Thus, in assessing lightning-fire periodicity through the years, records from the coast should not be mixed with those from east of the Gabilans, or from Mt. Diablo: Doing so greatly exaggerates the incidence of lightning-sparked fires in the Monterey Bay area itself. Although the incidence of such fires increases with distance inland, and with elevation above sea level, even in Pinnacles National Monument lightning has started only two fires in the entire period of record. (And both burned on the park's eastern slopes—that is, slightly to the east of the Monterey Bay area.) Similarly, the notorious Marble Cone fires of 1977, started by lightning high in the Santa Lucia Mountains, were to the south of the Monterey Bay area.

Although flammable materials in shingle roofs and weed-covered lots are dry almost half the year in this area, the chances that any specified building will be set aflame by lightning in a given year are minuscule (not to mention the chances that that building's replacement will also be burned by lightning within the following century). The same is true of a plant species whose total natural area may cover only a few square kilometers—for example, the bishop pine or Gowen cypress.

Estimating the number of hectares over which a lightning-sparked fire might spread under natural conditions (that is, in unaltered plant cover and without human interference) is a highly speculative procedure—and opinions differ sharply over which assumptions should be made. Having searched written records covering some 125 years (and consulted local park rangers and city fire departments), the writer concludes that it is impossible to extrapolate a credible natural re-burn cycle of less than 500 years for the coastal half of the Monterey Bay area—and for the inland half, less than 300 years. Neither of these is a dependable periodicity for those plants that are favored by (or in any way dependent upon) fire for their replenishment—unless, of course, the redwood is counted as a fire-favored species.

The combined incursions of American lumbermen and agriculturists into the forests of the area during the second half of the nineteenth century are illustrated in the following description of the San Lorenzo Valley north of Santa Cruz:

> The industries of this section are in the main the manufacture of lumber and the production of railroad ties, telegraph poles, shingles, shakes, barrel staves, etc. . . . As the axeman and the oxteam advance . . . the husbandman, the viniculturist, and the orchardist keep pace. (*The Resources of California*, June 1883, p. 6)

Most of the numerous openings scattered over the San Lorenzo Valley, now tilled, grazed, or in various stages of regrowth, date from this period, as do most of the valley's introduced plant and animal species.

In 1871, the Southern Pacific Railroad joined the Pajaro Valley to the Santa Clara Valley with a line that ran through Pajaro Gap. After the arrival of the railroad, quantities of grain, cattle, firewood, and household goods were hauled into and out of the area. Weed and insect species were no doubt introduced repeatedly as the railroads provided continuous routes of dissemination from the East Coast.

Although Spanish cattlemen had made little use of enclosures, except for corrals, American ranchers put up wooden fences. These, however, were replaced almost entirely with barbwire in the early 1870s.

Lumbering was started by the mission fathers, using Indian laborers, but the scale was so small that ecological consequences were slight. Under the Americans, operations were conducted on a grand scale, particularly the lumbering of redwood trees. Lumber companies penetrated virtually the whole redwood area, leaving almost no virgin stands. Old photographs show scenes of devastating and slovenly operations. The giant trees in the unharvested grove in Big Basin State Park give some impression of the original redwood forests as seen by the Spanish. Unlike most conifers, redwood sprouts from the stump, or root crown, when felled; thus it has great regenerative powers. When the trees are sawed, saplings sprout, forming circles around the parent stumps. In the 1880s and 1890s, the period during which most trees were sawed, many such circles were formed. Today a circular grove pattern of trees a little under a century in age is common throughout existing forests. Good examples can be seen at Henry Cowell Redwoods State Park and at Mount Madonna County Park. At one time there were 25 sawmills within an 8-km radius of Boulder Creek alone, and the town was the leading lumber center of the Pacific coast (Wilson, 1937, pp. 481, 510).

Tanbark oak is an example of a hardy species that has survived very intensive disturbance by man. With the disappearance of the Indian population, the tanbark oak ceased to be a source of human food;

Logging redwood between Corralitos and Loma Prieta in the 1880s. Redwood lumbering began in the northern part of the Monterey Bay area. In early days, the logs were dragged out of the forest on skid trails, originally by ox teams and later by steam power. The slash in the area photographed has been burned: note the charred trunks on the left. On flatter land, deep gulches were gouged out: Some can still be seen, although most are now overgrown. Soil erosion was greatly accelerated.

Similar lumbering methods were practiced upcoast toward San Francisco. In 1890 conditions at Purissima Creek, north of Año Nuevo, were described as follows: "The sawdust and blocks of redwood are thrown into the stream, which turns the water to a dark red, and in some places, to an inky black . . . . This is poisonous, and kills the fish in half an hour . . . . Cattle along the stream are walking skeletons. I saw several carcasses of dead animals lying along the bank, notwithstanding there is plenty of grass . . . . " (BRCF).

Except for a few patches (e.g., Big Basin State Park), all redwood and Douglas-fir forest in the Monterey Bay area has been logged—parts of it several times. Were it not for the processes of natural plant succession and the strong regenerative powers of the redwood, the scene would be one of utter desolation—for example, on what is now the University of California campus or at Nisene Marks State Park. (Photo courtesy of the Pajaro Valley Historical Association) but, beginning with American settlement, a completely new use for the tree was found: the use of its bark in tanning hides.

Santa Cruz County was one of the largest tanning centers in California. The bark of the tanbark oak was first used near Santa Cruz (Jepson, 1911, p. 8), and the industry was concentrated there because of the large number of these trees in the area. The first tannery was built in Scott's Valley in 1843. By 1868, tanning was a major industry: "There are at present seven tanneries in Santa Cruz which consume monthly about three hundred tons of this bark" (Cronise, 1868, p. 131). In 1870, there were ten tanneries in the county. Great quantities of tanbark were hauled out of the Santa Cruz Mountains on mule back. More than 5000 cords of bark were harvested in 1886 alone. Within a few decades the tanning industry was threatening the existence of the oak, and the industry began its decline because of a dwindling supply of bark. In 1918, it was estimated that three quarters of the tanbark oak of Santa Cruz County had been peeled (*Timberman*, June 15, 1918). Large quantities of tanbark were collected in the Santa Lucia Mountains, as well.

Under natural conditions, tanbark oak does not form extensive pure stands. Since it is successional in areas where coniferous forest has been logged, today the tree is again plentiful. Dense, evenly-aged regrowth stands are found throughout the west slopes of the Santa Cruz Mountains—for example, in Nisene Marks State Park.

As noted earlier, in the northern part of the Monterey Bay area, large tracts of hazel thicket were once managed by Costanoans. These thickets were soon put to use by the Spanish, and then by the Americans. Around Mission Santa Cruz, the Spanish fences (built to protect gardens from free-ranging cattle) were made of ". . . posts driven in the ground and tied with hazel bark . . ." (Harrison, 1892, p. 47). The Americans used the hazel for barrel hoops. Until they came under agricultural use, the lower hills of the Santa Cruz Mountains still supported ". . . a great quantity of hazel bushes, from which nearly all hoops used by the powder works and lime-makers are made. The powder company uses 1,700,000 and the lime-works over 300,000 of these hoops annually, and large quantities are also exported to other places . . ." (Cronise, 1868, p. 131). Although hazel is still common in the area, nothing like the great hazel copses needed to support such an industry survives. (The hazel is absent from the southern part of the Monterey Bay area. Hall and Garin roads in the upper drainage of Elkhorn Slough are at its approximate southern limit.)

By the time the Americans reached California, commercial hunting had become part of their way of life. For several decades after their arrival, hunters, unrestrained by laws, ravished the wildlife of the Monterey Bay area. Old editions of the Salinas newspapers record both the sale of game at local markets and its shipment to San Francisco. The establishment of the California Board of Fish Commissioners (forerunner of the California Fish and Game Department) in 1870 led to the termination of commercial hunting and the legal regulation of hunting and fishing. These events were of major ecological importance, as were the building of fish hatcheries and the introduction of game animals.

Another form of regulation of animal numbers long practiced on a sweeping scale is pest control. State pest-control (e.g., mosquito-abatement) agencies are concerned with public hygiene. County agricultural commissioners work with local farmers to protect crops (e.g., from the California ground squirrel). The year 1888 marks the beginnings of a biological-control program in California. Biological control has been studied and applied in the Monterey Bay area on a limited scale but so far it has been deemed inadequate. As a result, controls commonly involve an onslaught with pesticides, herbicides, and the like—a negative form of regulation compared with game laws and stocking programs, albeit necessary under present conditions of land use. These two approaches represent about all that exists in the way of planned regulation of animal numbers.

The protection of large tracts of native plant cover and associated animal life with the establishment of the state parks and beaches and the county parks is also of major ecological significance. In 1927, the

State Division of Beaches and Parks was organized. More than a dozen beaches were made available for public use in the area. Año Nuevo Island was purchased by the State in 1955, and soon thereafter was made a scientific reserve, closed to the public in order to reestablish the pinniped population there. Similarly significant was the founding of the State Department of Forestry, with its regulation of logging and burning.

Technological innovations have profoundly affected plant and animal life. The introduction of turbine pumps between 1910 and 1920 lowered groundwater tables throughout the area, and greatly increased the redistribution of water and irrigation, especially in the Salinas Valley. Automobile transport, begun in the early years of the twentieth century, produced a denser road network and contributed to air pollution.

The widespread use of petrochemical fertilizers and herbicides, and chemical changes in insecticides (e.g., the use of chlorinated hydrocarbons following World War II), are among the stronger human influences recently exerted on life in the area. The larger part of the pesticide and herbicide chemicals is used for purposes of eradicating *alien* plants and animals, since most of the worst agricultural pests in the area arrived with agriculture itself.

Following construction in Moss Landing in 1942, the Kaiser Refractories factory began hauling dolomite from Natividad in the Gabilans, extracting magnesium from seawater, and emptying tailings along Moro Cojo slough. Local thermal alterations of the bay's water began when the Pacific Gas and Electric plant at Moss Landing started operating in 1952. Seawater is used as a coolant, and the heated water is discharged partly into the slough and partly into the bay.

3.3. The Rural and Urban Biotic Associations

The total area of the natural plant associations in the Monterey Bay area has been greatly reduced. The replacement has been an extensive cultural landscape within which two culturally induced biotic associations can be distinguished. These may be added to the twelve natural associations listed earlier. (See Table on pages 28-29.)

(13) Rural Bio-association. The rural bio-association covers most of the lowlands, where the original floodplain association has been largely removed for agricultural use, and the smoother parts of the hill country, which have been cleared for grazing. It includes pastures, hayfields, orchards, and eucalyptus groves; fields of lettuce, artichokes, brussels sprouts, etc.; irrigation ponds; and farmyards. Although grassland vegetation here is composed mainly of introduced species (e.g., wild oats and many other grasses, filarees, and bur clover), natives are numerous too, including many wildflowers, as well as turpentine weed, turkey mullein, etc.

(14) Urban Bio-association. This biotic community includes parks, street sides, lawns, flower gardens, freeway landscaping, and golf courses. In urban areas, an even larger proportion of the plants is foreign and dependent on man for survival. Many depend on irrigation and are unable to reproduce themselves untended. Australian trees and shrubs are especially well represented (e.g., species of *Pittosporum, Acacia, Eucalyptus*, and *Eugenia*).

3.4. Replacement of Natural Plant Cover by an Alien Species: Ecology of Eucalyptus Groves

The eucalypts, all native to Australia and its vicinity, have been introduced into many areas. In California, eucalyptus is so conspicuous that it has become something of a symbol of human alteration of the natural landscape. There is much discussion of its merits, esthetic and utilitarian.

By far the most plentiful eucalypt in California is the blue gum, but a large number of other species have been introduced at different times, in various parts of the state, for a variety of reasons. Few other introduced plants have been subject to such publicity. Eucalypts were being sold as ornamentals in San Francisco as early as 1850. A short time later great interest developed in the trees as a source of fine

Walnut orchard, a part of the rural bio-association. The ground cover is made up entirely of Eurasian herbs. The trees symbolize the changed California landscape: English walnuts, native to Mediterranean Eurasia, are grafted on native California black walnuts, *Juglans californica* var. *hindsii*—brought here from Contra Costa County. (Roots of the native walnut are more tolerant of local soil conditions.) The two frequently hybridize. Curiously, the total original population of the native variety consisted of only a few hundred trees growing more or less in association with Indian villages around Walnut Creek, and northward (R.E. Smith, 1949, p. 12).

hardwood for furniture making and the like. Blue gum was brought to San Jose in 1858, and by the 1860s it was widely planted for hardwood.

In the second half of the nineteenth century, culminating around 1880, malaria was a major cause of illness in California. A segment of medical opinion favored the belief that malaria was caused by "miasma," or "bad air"; that the eucalyptus, its leaves introducing pungent, antiseptic, volatile oils into the air, was "the fever destroying tree" (Thompson, 1970, p. 236); and that if it was simply planted in

Map of the Monterey Peninsula, published in 1884 (Chittenden, 1884, p. 109). Note the whale "fisheries" at Monterey and at the base of Point Lobos, and the two Chinese fishing settlements on opposite sides of the peninsula: China Town and Chinese Cove (now Stillwater Cove).

The map suggests uses of land at the time; for example, dairies have replaced the Spanish cattle ranches. The sparse settlement of most of the peninsula accounts for such markings as "cabin," "water trough," and "bridle path." The "Sand Hills" shown have since been mined and much of the sand hauled away. The word *aulone,* as in Points Aulon and Alones on the map, is one of the early varying spellings of "abalone"; an original name for the Costanoans, applied by their inland neighbors, was "Ohlone"—i.e., *abalone people.* (Point Aulon is now called Lovers Point.) The Peninsula is fringed with shell middens (Raskin, 1972). Inland archaeological remains include habitation sites, bedrock mortars, and other artifacts.

Huckleberry Hill is named for the evergreen huckleberry, associated on the north slope of the hill with a remarkable patch of coniferous forest. This is the only place where Monterey pine and bishop pine, both of limited coastal distribution, can be found growing naturally together. They are joined on the hill by the Gowen cypress, which exists nowhere else. The "young cypresses" shown on the map are probably Gowen cypresses; the trees grow in a naturally stunted form. They are now included in the S.F.B. Morse Botanical Reserve, along with several other rare plants. The area was repeatedly burned over by Indians; it has been burned accidentally by Americans, as well, e.g., in 1901 (*The Record Union*), in 1940, and in the drought year 1987.

Cypress Point is named for yet another geographically restricted species, the Monterey cypress; note the label "Cypress Grove" nearby. Monterey cypresses grow naturally only in a short, interrupted coastal fringe extending from Cypress Point to Pescadero Point, and on parts of Point Lobos. Point Lobos was so named by the Spanish because of the many "sea wolves" they saw there—the animals that we call "sea lions."

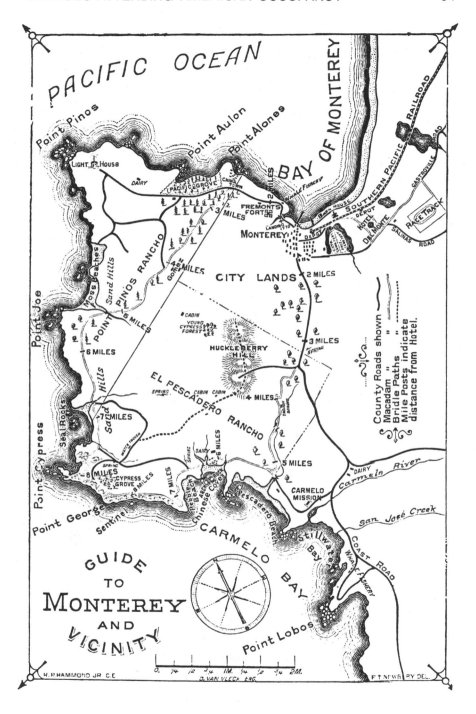

an area, malaria was driven out. Beginning around 1870, belief in the hygienic merits of the trees led to their being planted on an unprecedented scale. Both the U.S. Department of Forestry and the California Board of Forestry propagated and distributed eucalyptus, mainly the blue gum. At the beginning of 1874, it was officially estimated that at least one million trees had been planted in California (Thompson, 1970, p. 235).

Even though the connection between mosquitoes and malaria became known in the 1890s, blue gum planting continued, because the tree was still thought to have a great potential for hardwood. However, difficulties in curing and marketing the wood being present from the outset, it did not live up to this promise. Instead, the trees came to have a very important role as a source of household fuel in areas where the original plant cover had been cleared. Natural gas began to replace firewood in the cities at the beginning of the twentieth century. By the beginning of World War II, tanked butane gas was burned in many country households as well, and few new eucalyptus groves were planted. Woodlots mostly disappeared from the towns, and the grove that had once provided the farmer with a good supplementary income became a nuisance, but costly to remove. As a result, groves planted in the first half of the twentieth century now contain towering specimens, and their total acreage in the Monterey Bay area is still considerable. At present eucalypts are of only minor economic importance as firewood. Their principal worth is as food for honeybees, as ornamentals for landscaping, and as shelter for Monarch butterflies.

Ecological conditions in eucalyptus groves contrast strongly with those in neighboring live-oak woodland and redwood groves. The contrast is not so noticeable where eucalyptus trees are well separated and develop a branched and spreading form. Nevertheless, eucalyptus groves in general seem sterile compared to neighboring oak woodland.

Eucalyptus trees have usually been planted close together to better utilize space and to encourage growth of long straight boles and few lower branches, which makes them more manageable for woodcutters.

Closely spaced, the trees probably use much of the available soil nutrients and water. Where abundant groundwater rises to the surface in the groves, the amount of undergrowth increases. Where the trees are widely spaced, there may be a light undergrowth of coyote brush, poison oak, and toyon. (Scanty undergrowth can hardly be attributed to shading alone; in redwood groves, which are even more deeply shaded, there may be a rich ground flora—sword fern, redwood sorrel, etc.) It is also claimed that the terpenes present in decaying eucalyptus leaves retard germination of other plants. Eucalyptus leaves usually do not weather to a thick mold like that beneath live-oak stands, probably because the soil-forming bacteria present in the eucalypt's homeland are absent here.

In Australia itself, eucalypts have a rich associated biota including birds, insects, and mammals that feed on their leaves. Perhaps fortunately, none of these arrived in California, because the eucalyptus was disseminated by seeds alone. The fauna associated with the groves in the Monterey Bay area is poor. A number of introduced insects are present, but native insects find little food there. Insects found under the tree bark are mainly predators that fly out of the groves to feed (Professor Larry Swan, personal communication). The leaves rarely show insect damage, and insects seem not to eat the seed capsules. As there is little grass in most of the groves, there is little food for grazing or seed-eating mammals. Wood rats sometimes build nests in the groves, but they forage beyond the limits of the groves. At Mount Madonna County Park, western gray squirrels, present in the tanbark oaks and redwoods, avoid the eucalyptus trees.

Eucalyptus trees are poor sources of food for native birds. They may also be unattractive to some birds because of their smooth bark and vertical growth habit, providing less purchase for roosting and nest building. Nevertheless, eucalyptus groves are used for roosting by shrikes, hawks, and other birds; the monarch butterfly swarms in several groves along the coast; honeybees feed on eucalyptus blossoms, and hummingbirds take nectar from the flowers.

Although the subject is debated, it appears that the eucalyptus is not well adapted for self-propagation here. It cannot be regarded as having become a permanent part of the flora, independent of human activities, despite its remarkable growth rate and drought resistance and despite the fact that even on poor, sandy soils it soon rises above the native live oak. True, its seeds germinate readily where soil in and around the groves has been bared by burning or scraping, but the total area of eucalyptus groves is not increasing. Seedlings rarely appear in, and even more rarely survive in, areas already covered with other woody growth. (Adventive shoots from the root systems of sawed trees are sometimes mistaken for seedlings.)

Eucalyptus trees were planted along several bridle paths in the redwood forest at Mount Madonna County Park. Most of these trees are now closely crowded by redwood and tanbark oaks. They are producing large numbers of seeds but no seedlings, and will no doubt be replaced as they die off by native trees.

One reason that the eucalyptus does not spread far, even on disturbed land, is that it is almost totally dependent on gravity for dissemination. Its fruit capsules are not eaten by native birds or mammals. There are also climatic reasons for concluding that the eucalyptus cannot thrive here under natural conditions: During the winter of 1972-73, and again in late December, 1990, eucalypts were much more severely damaged by the unusually low temperatures than were native trees.

The ecotone that develops at the margins of native forest, with its rich bird and mammal life, is absent from the edges of eucalyptus groves. From the standpoint of wildlife preservation, eucalyptus is not the ideal woodlot tree.

There is said to be a correlation between the length of time an introduced plant has been established in California and the number of native insect species that feed on it. The percentage of native insects on introduced plants tends to reach a level comparable to their occurrence on native plants within about 200 years (Azevedo, 1965, p. 70). These conclusions suggest rapid evolution of insect populations

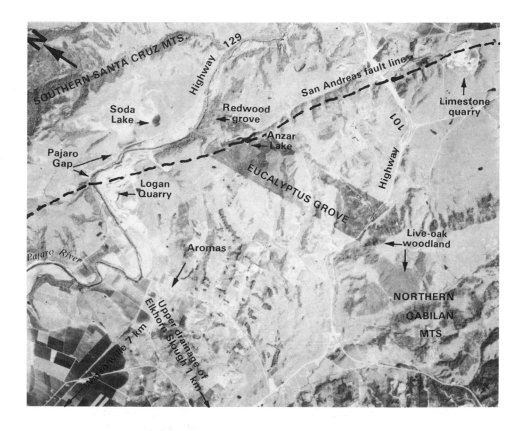

Labels on image: SOUTHERN SANTA CRUZ MTS., Highway 129, San Andreas fault line, Limestone quarry, Soda Lake, Redwood grove, Anzar Lake, 101, Highway, Pajaro Gap, Logan Quarry, EUCALYPTUS GROVE, Live-oak woodland, Pajaro River, Aromas, NORTHERN GABILAN MTS., Upper drainage of Elkhorn Slough 7 km, Watsonville 7 km

Large eucalyptus grove east of Aromas between Highways 101 and 129—
near School Road, east of Aromas. (The San Andreas fault passes through the
grove; Anzar Lake lies in the fault rift.) This is a good place to compare the
ecological conditions under eucalyptus trees with those under native tree cover:
Here eucalyptus groves and live-oak woodland come together. The grove, covering
some 364 hectares, is one of the largest in North America. It extends from San
Juan Rocks on Highway 101 northward, on the old Las Aromitas y Aguas Calientes
grant, toward Soda Lake. Planted between 1911 and 1920, the grove is said to
have been intended as a supply of furniture wood. It has been harvested repeatedly
for firewood and for the manufacture of cardboard. At present, the trees are mainly
regrowth from root shoots.

Eucalyptus does not spread far beyond where it is planted: after more than 70
years the grove maintains its original sharp outline. (NASA photo, 1971)

in terms of food tolerances and preferences, all in response to certain consequences of human occupancy. However, as noted above, few native insects feed on the eucalyptus, despite the fact that it has been in California for more than a century.

3.5. Regrowth and Succession in Old Fields

Succession has correctly been called the most informative ecological process. Successional studies on sites of human disturbance are particularly relevant for planning purposes. Each successional stage (sere) has its potential both for creating maximum biological diversity in the area and for beautifying the cultural landscape; "as an instrument for the control of the entire range of human uses of the vegetation and the land, succession is wholly unrivaled" (Clements, 1935, p. 345).

Most of the Monterey Bay area, subjected as it has been to thoroughgoing human change, exists in an intermediate stage between a disturbed and a climax condition. Scores of exotic species have been intermixed with the native biota. Although the overall successional trend is toward elimination of these foreigners and the reestablishment of native species directly under natural climatic and edaphic controls, the stages in the return are varied and poorly known.

> The natural process [of succession] once thoroughly understood, it becomes possible to retard or accelerate it, to "telescope" it or hold it more or less definitely in one stage, or deflect it in any one of several possible directions . . . . (Clements, 1935, p. 345)

The considerable phenological information for the area must be compiled and its interrelationships studied. A comprehensive ecological almanac is needed, synchronizing the flowering and fruiting seasons of regrowth plants with food demands and reproductive cycles in the animal world. Were this done, it might be possible to discover components that are critical to the ecological balance of each successional stage and to determine the points in time at which such a balance can most easily be tipped. With such information at hand, future landscapes can be planned to include people in more harmonious relationships with their biotic environment.

Regrowth and succession in several native plant associations are discussed below.

3.5.1. Live-Oak Woodland

The coast live oak is the oak species most widely distributed in the area and the only species common along the coast. The Spanish made charcoal from its wood for use as household fuel. The tree became a major source of firewood for later immigrants as the population of the area increased, partly because of its easy accessibility. The limits of the coast live oak's distribution include some of the most attractive areas for human settlement. As lumber the wood is inferior, and it has been but little used in building and tool making. On the other hand, the coast live oak is one of the easiest oak species to plant and put to horticultural uses. And probably no other tree in the area supports so great a variety of birds and other wildlife.

The primary seed sources for woody-plant succession in the orchards in the Larkin Valley area are scattered tracts of live-oak woodland with poison oak, coffee berry, coyote brush, *Ceanothus,* etc., growing at its margins and in open spaces between the oaks. These adventive plants congregating at the sunny margins of orchard clearings in oak woodland exemplify the special importance of ecotone content in succession studies.

Historical sources cited indicate that oak woodland was not the only tree cover in Larkin Valley at one time. In pre-European times groves of redwood were scattered around, especially on north slopes. A few clusters of redwood still grow in the valley. Large Douglas fir are growing near the junction of Larkin Valley Road and Highway 1 and, although the firs are reseeding poorly (for some unknown reason), an occasional seedling can be found among the oaks as far south as Fiesta Road. Given time and without human disturbance of the land, coniferous growth would reestablish itself in parts of the oak-woodland area, despite the fact that most local seed sources have been eradicated by overclearing.

In the early American period of settlement, sizable coast live oaks grew scattered between the small lakes north of Salinas, over the lands to the east of Castroville around Moro Cojo Slough, to the east and north of Moss Landing on all sides of Elkhorn Slough, and northward to the floodplain of the Pajaro River. The region is now mainly open grassland or planted to such crops as artichokes and strawberries.

The oaks were cleared by American settlers, partly for use as firewood and partly to make the land available for tillage. Until the middle of the nineteenth century this country, divided into the Spanish-Mexican land grants, was used for cattle raising. We read in the field notes of J.E. Terrell, surveying under instruction of the U.S. Surveyor General in 1859, that the east boundary of the Bolsa de San Cayetano grant, as it ran from the uppermost end of Elkhorn Slough northeastward toward Watsonville, extended from an "oak tree 2½ feet [0.8 m] in diameter, thence to an oak tree 3 feet [0.9 m] in diameter . . . to an oak tree 2½ feet in diameter, on the edge of the estero [that is, on Elkhorn Slough itself, near the site of Hudson Landing]."

Since today's fuel comes mainly from mineral sources, the quantities of trees that were once consumed as firewood are easily underestimated. The following account refers to oak woodland that extended to the east of Castroville in 1881:

> On the uplands and low hills east of town there is an almost inexhaustible supply of good oak cordwood, a large trade in which with San Jose and other points is carried on by the medium of the Southern Pacific Railroad. (*The Resources of California*, April 1881, p. 93)

Although today only a few tracts of oak woodland remain immediately east of Castroville, to the northeast, in the higher lands of the Prunedale district, many patches survive on the Aromas Red Sands. Most of these trees are much smaller, being recent regrowth which has developed since the Depression of the 1930s, a time when agricultural use of the Prunedale district reached a maximum. The appearance of this regrowth indicates the persistence of undiminished regenerative powers.

Oak woodland also covered parts of the Salinas Valley. The following note describes this growth on the southwest side of the river:

> Lands [i.e., potential agricultural land] south and west of the Salinas River are not so great in quantity as on the north and east. They are *mostly covered with oak timber which is being chopped into stove wood* for market, and apparently for the purpose of clearing the land for cultivation. The Guadalupe Rancho is mostly covered with a growth of small oak timber. (*The Salinas City Index*, Nov. 25, 1875)

Valuable evidence of the historical plant cover of the lower Salinas Valley to the north of the river is provided by a grove of large live

Coast live oak in pasture near Elkhorn Slough Road. (Photo B. Gordon)

Douglas fir near Highway 1 and San Andreas Road. (Photo B. Gordon)

oaks which still grow on the valley floor, northeast of Salinas near the foot of the Gabilan Mountains. This grove is made up of 75 or 80 trees on several acres near the junction of Williams and Old Stage roads—an area of intensive culture of truck crops. The trees, among the largest live oaks in the Monterey Bay area, have trunks 1.2 to 1.5 m in diameter. They are said to have been growing here in the 1850s. The grove is especially significant since it shows that oak woodland is part of the potential natural vegetation of the lower Salinas Valley, along with bunchgrass, tule marsh, and riparian forest.

The interior live oak has, as its name suggests, a more inland distribution than does coast live oak, and tends to favor higher slopes. Nevertheless, interior live oak does come within a few miles of the coast in such places as the University of California campus at Santa Cruz and between Aptos and Larkin Valley. The two species do not usually grow intermixed with each other. Interior live oak, reputedly the best fuel of any California oak, was much sought by woodcutters at one time.

Although its total expanse in coastal parts of the Monterey Bay area has plainly been much decreased since European settlement began, oak woodland has been extended into coniferous forest areas on higher, wetter lands.

> More than half of its 97,190 acres [39,333 hectares; i.e., the oak-woodland area in the Santa Cruz Mountains as a whole] are potential redwood and Douglas fir lands, having taken over the areas following removal of the conifers either by logging and fire or by fire alone. (Jensen, 1939, p. 16)

(Most of these 39,333 hectares are within the Monterey Bay area as defined here.)

3.5.2. Succession in Old Orchards

During the first half of the twentieth century, large parts of the northern Monterey Bay area were in use for farming and orcharding. By 1950, most of the fields and orchards were abandoned and being taken over by regrowth. Residential landscaping is now removing their last traces. The process of plant succession in the abandoned orchards and neighboring farmland is described below in some detail—because of its significance for maintaining and restoring native vegetation and wildlife.

Before discussing plant succession at these sites, a preliminary comment is needed on a type of farm common before the mid-nineteenth century, but now a rarity: This was a diversified, partly subsistence-type farm—often with a dozen acres of orchard or truck crops, a team of horses, a few milk cows, and a couple hundred chickens. Farm operation busied the whole family with such chores as pruning trees, hoeing weeds, milking cows, chopping wood, and canning fruit. Milk, fruit, eggs, and vegetables were sold in Watsonville and Santa Cruz. Dozens of such small farms were scattered over hilly country from the Prunedale district and Elkhorn Slough to Aromas, Corralitos, and Larkin Valley.

Shortly before World War II this type of family farming began to break up: The Great Depression was ending; good wages and the war drew young people away. Many farmers, unable to afford outside labor, were forced either to sell out, or to rent their farms to indigent families—then called "Okies"—coming from the southeastern United States. The Okies continued here on the rented farms a livelihood similar to that they had known back home. These were also difficult times for the landowners—some of whom had once prided themselves on being "landed gentry." (Later, those who had managed to keep their holdings were able to reclaim this status when land prices rose in the 1970s—by selling parcels to residential developers.)

Coffee berry, *left*, an evergreen shrub or small tree. An ecotone species between chaparral and woodland, it is a common regrowth in old orchards.
Hairy honeysuckle, *right*, a vine-like shrub, common in sunny spots in live-oak woodland. (Photos B. Gordon)

Although barns and chicken houses have now fallen apart, many of the old farm houses still stand, freshly painted, and looking good as ever—but their present occupants are mainly employed in urban industries. Little agricultural use is made of the land, and a truly rural landscape has almost disappeared (The fertile alluvial flatland along the Pajaro and Salinas rivers is another matter: It supported a highly mechanized and specialized commercial agriculture—comparatively prosperous, then as now. Here, traditional farming had long since given way to the "factories of the field" seen today—serviced by immigrant laborers: At the time Filipinos and Okies, and now mainly Mexicans [see McWilliams, 1939].)

Much former crop and orchard land was left unused. In the hills around Aromas, where only a few stumps of apricot trees remain, the fields were once dappled orange in summer with trays of apricots set out to dry. In Larkin Valley and around Aptos, the principal orchard crop was apples.

In 1956, there were several dozen recently-abandoned apple orchards between Aptos and Watsonville (see aerial photo, pp. 112-113). The sites of several, clustered around Larkin Valley, have been inspected, and their approximate dates of abandonment established by examining old aerial photographs and by questioning longtime local residents. Based on such information the sequence of events that take place as regrowth plants establish themselves on abandoned farmland can be roughly predicted. An orchard on Mar Monte Avenue, just off Larkin Valley Road, is used as a prime example. The successional progression is divided here into three phases: initial, intermediate, and final:

3.5.2.1. The initial phase. In this first phase, the plant cover is almost entirely herbaceous. Under tillage the seeds of annual weeds are present in the soil. During the first two years after a field is abandoned, these weeds—mainly aliens (field mustard, bindweed, amaranth, mallow, etc.)—make up the predominant plant cover. During the next several years most of these are gradually replaced by other herbs (wild oat and various other alien grasses, filarees, plantains, bull thistle, etc.)—again mainly alien, but intermixed with such natives as lupines, California poppy, blue-eyed grass, and brodiaea. Amongst them, patches of bracken arise. On badly eroded spots deerweed is a likely pioneer.

Birds that feed on the seeds of grasses and thistles (lesser goldfinches, house finches, and mourning doves) are abundant, as are seed-eating rodents (meadow mice and ground squirrels). Pocket gophers burrow where the grass is short, and the soil moist. Meadowlarks nest in the tall grass. Various sun-loving animals thrive: The black stink beetle (which does a headstand on bare, sandy spots and emits a foul smell when approached), western fence lizards, alligator lizards, and buckeye butterflies.

3.5.2.2. The intermediate phase. Within five years after the abandonment parts of the land are covered with shrubs. Usually the first woody plant to appear is the native coyote brush. From a conservationist's standpoint this shrub is a godsend, taking as it does the first step toward reestablishment of the woody cover that existed before agriculture began. Most agriculturalists don't see it that way. The coyote brush is an aggressive invader of pastures and difficult to eradicate. A composite, it produces wind-borne seeds in profusion. And the shrub's ability to flower and seed over a long season is hardly rivaled by other woody species here. If broken off, new plants sprout from the roots; if chopped up by disk harrows, the shrub may reproduce vegetatively from the cuttings. On the other hand, its seedlings are very susceptible to damage from grazing and burning (McBride and Heady, 1968, p. 106). During the rainy season, in December, multitudes of coyote brush seedlings are often intermixed with sprouting grass and forbs. Although they rarely browse on the mature coyote brush, cattle eat these non-woody seedlings along with the herbs. (Thus, heavy grazing may arrest plant succession in the initial, herbaceous stage, indefinitely.)

Blue blossom and scattered oak seedlings appear shortly after the coyote brush. Within twelve years, these plants may have spread to cover most of the surface. In abandoned orchards, violet-green swallows nest in holes drilled by downy woodpeckers in dying fruit trees. Many animals from neighboring areas visit the old orchards and fields: Quail, mourning doves, and red-shafted flickers come and go; deer browse frequently; and the many small rodents attract red-tailed hawks, great horned owls, and coyotes.

As plant succession proceeds, animal life varies accordingly. Thus, when old fruit trees die, so do their pests (coddling moths, etc.); as coyote brush disappears, so do the numerous insects it supports. Soon live oak seedlings are scattered about—some rising only a foot or two above the grass; in some summers, a thin cloud of oak moths can be seen hanging over each—a conspicuous example of animal life following plant succession.

Chipmunks may appear as the orchards become shrub-covered. (Occasionally chipmunks can be seen in March perched in branches of the flowering currant—nibbling on clusters of blossoms grasped in their forepaws.) In old fields where oak woodland with admixed Douglas fir or Monterey pine is the potential natural vegetation, the squirrel-family sequence is:

$$\left.\begin{array}{l}\text{ground squirrel}\\\text{grassland}\end{array}\right\} \longrightarrow \left\{\begin{array}{l}\text{chipmunk}\\\text{regrowth shrubs}\\\text{and chaparral}\end{array}\right\} \longrightarrow \left\{\begin{array}{l}\text{western gray squirrel}\\\text{oak woodland with}\\\text{admixed conifers}\end{array}\right.$$

As the oak seedlings become trees, dusky-footed wood rats build piles of twigs for nests against the tree trunks (especially, in old orchards, around the trunks of dead fruit trees). Hazelnut shells and the husks of wild cucumber seeds may litter the ground around the nests; sometimes, wild cucumber vines grow out of the nests themselves. (Although mature nuts can rarely be found on hazelnut bushes hereabouts, wood-rat nests, if opened, often supply pocketfuls.)

Ten or twelve years after abandonment, the land is richer in animal species than during either the initial or final phases of succession. There are probably two reasons for this diversity: The plant cover is at its patchiest and a number of alien herbs are usually still present;

thus, a great variety of animal habitats and food sources is available.

The rate of regrowth varies from spot to spot and, up to twenty years after abandonment, an old field may remain a patchwork of different vegetation types—depending on a variety of factors; for instance, on whether the land was later used for grazing cattle; on the size of the local deer population; on differences in slope and the amount of soil moisture; on how badly the surface was eroded while in agricultural use; and so on. (Thus, the different patches of vegetation shown at Mar Monte in 1974; see figure on p. 108.) But by this time the number of alien plants has been sharply reduced.

Although regrowth plant cover is described here as mainly determining the kinds of animals present, the influences are actually reciprocal, with animal life itself playing a significant part in successional trends. Wind is a major disseminating agency for many of the first plant colonists (e.g., for coyote brush and other composites). Birds whose diets are largely herb seeds are plentiful in the initial phase of succession, while birds that eat berries and nuts become more numerous later on. The importance of berry-eating birds in plant succession is readily seen in abandoned orchards where the branches of old fruit trees serve as perches. Seeds in bird droppings accumulate on the ground beneath, and the seedlings of various woody plants spring up—their growth probably stimulated by nitrates in the bird excrement. Seedlings of coffee berry, poison oak, hairy honeysuckle, and California blackberry (all of which bear fleshy fruit and are disseminated by birds) appear, and the progression to woody plant cover is speeded. Of importance in the reestablishment of oak trees are those birds and other animals that carry acorns about; for instance, jays, woodpeckers, packrats, and squirrels. Although the California woodpecker is well known for its transport of acorns, the scrub jay may be more important in oak dissemination—because the jay sometimes actually buries the acorns (Davis and Baldridge, 1980; p. 94). No doubt the general deforestation of the area as a whole and the community jay hunts held in the early twentieth century had

Mima mounds on marine terraces west of Santa Cruz between Empire Grade and Highway 1, partly on the property of the University of California. The origin of such knoll and swale microrelief is still disputed. A favorite theory is that the mounds are built up by pocket gophers (Scheffer, 1984). Usually oval in outline and some 10 to 20 m in length, the mounds are made up mainly of sandy loam, between 1 and 2 m in thickness, resting on a less permeable clayey sublayer (Avey, 1970). At times the mounds stand out sharply: in 1967 the area was not so heavily grazed as now; viewed from the air, the mounds then looked like so many bouquets because of the lupines blooming on them.

A high proportion of alien species (for example, wild oats and plantains) grows on the mounds themselves. If part of the area were to be fenced off, the rarer vernal-marsh species that grow in the poorly drained swales might become more abundant. (The geographical extent of the vernal-marsh association is constantly declining in California [Stebbins, 1976, p. 15]). The area was especially closely grazed in 1976.

Natural grassland was of small extent in the Monterey Bay area, particularly here in the north: A few poorly drained areas such as this, and possibly some spots with soils derived from limestone, were probably the only natural meadows that existed in the area. It would be of interest to see how far woody vegetation, such as the madrones and redwoods shown at the top of the photograph and the live oaks shown at the bottom, would encroach on the mound area if it were left undisturbed. (Photo B. Gordon and D. Hawley) lingering effects on plant succession: Those cleared areas most distant from oak groves are slowest to regenerate oak woodland. Thus, the events of human history enter into the successional process at every stage.

As tree cover becomes more extensive, the following birds become more common: Hutton's vireo, black-headed grosbeak, chestnut-backed chickadee, common bushtit, and rufous-sided towhee—all are present in May.

The following figure shows the vegetation that developed as a result of plant succession in an abandoned orchard over an approximately 18-year period. The site covers several hectares on a north-facing slope along the south side of Mar Monte Avenue.

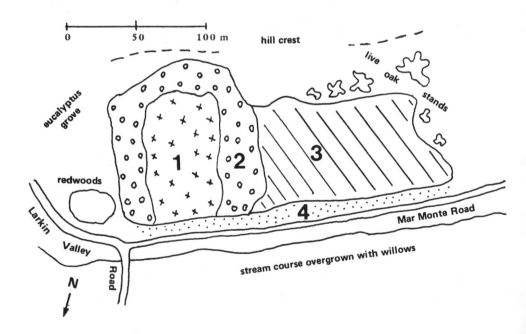

Plant succession in an abandoned orchard on Mar Monte Avenue 1956-1974 (see facing page): This orchard was one of the first in the area to be abandoned. It has not been tilled since about 1940—but its apples were occasionally picked and its regrowth grazed during the following decade. An aerial photograph taken in July 1952 shows the orchard with all of the apple trees in full leaf and the ground between the trees covered with grass. Grazing was discontinued about this time. Another aerial photograph taken in June 1956 (see p. 112-113) shows the apple trees still living but with what appear to be shrubs, probably coyote brush, growing in the grassy spaces between the trees. By 1974, the apple trees were dead. The orchard was overgrown and in a later stage of succession than most old orchards in the area.

Plant-cover categories at the site in 1974:

Area 1. Coyote brush, California buckeye, and bracken made up about 95% of the ground cover, with coyote brush predominating. Coast live-oak saplings were very sparsely scattered through this plant cover; there were only about a dozen in the entire tract. There was no blue blossom and only a few small coffee berry bushes. About 5% of this area was covered with grass and other herbs.

Area 2. Almost the whole area was covered with woody growth. As in area 1, mature coyote brush was the dominant plant. Next to coyote brush, blue blossom was the most extensive species, forming close to 30% of the ground cover. The blue blossom formed a dense canopy, shading the ground so completely that there was little undergrowth except yerba buena. Although the blue blossom had not attained maximum size, it was apparently excluding coyote brush.

Area 3. In the upper, western part of the orchard, tree-sized coast live oak, coffee berry, and wax myrtle made up about 45% of the plant cover. Another 45% was made up of low-growing coyote brush and blackberry, intermixed with young oak saplings and small coffee berries. The remaining 10% of the category, on especially steep slope, was bare ground or covered with mosses and scattered herbs.

The live oaks were branched and rose to heights of 6 m, with trunks about 20 cm in diameter at the base. Coffee berry and wax myrtle grew to almost the same heights as the live oak. Blue blossom made up a small percentage of the cover, as compared to its occurrence in category 2. Young wax myrtles were numerous, but the most vigorously reseeding woody plants were coast live oak and coffee berry. These were present in many stages of growth. Wax myrtle's presence was partly explained by its preference in this general area for moist, north-facing slopes.

Area 4. Poison oak and hazelnut formed a dense cover along the lower edge of the orchard near the road. Intermixed were a few flowering currants. Actually poison oak grew plentifully throughout the entire orchard, but it was easy to underestimate its total area because it often grows intertwined with other plants.

3.5.2.3. The final phase. In the final phase, almost the whole area is densely covered by woody species, mainly live oak—and the total biomass (standing crop) is at a maximum. Whether annual biomass productivity is greatest in the initial or in the final phase is an open question. Throughout the successional process, the vegetation becomes progressively more stable—that is to say, the plant cover changes at a reduced rate.

There is little herbaceous growth, and all alien plants have been excluded. The field mice, ground squirrels, western fence lizards, etc. of the initial phase have disappeared. All stumps of dead fruit trees having rotted away, the hole-nesting swallows have departed; the meadowlarks are gone. The buckeye butterflies have been replaced by California sisters, the fence lizards by slender salamanders, and so on.

At Mar Monte Avenue, by 1994, the distinction between the four categories shown in the above figure had blurred. The tallest plants were live oak (some over 9 m tall). Spindly wax myrtles and coffee berries rose to almost the same height. In their shade lay an almost impenetrable tangle of dead blue blossom and coyote brush. Aside from a few specimens at the edge of Mar Monte road itself, no living coyote brush, bracken, or blackberry remained. Except for honeybees, no introduced animals were present (though feral pigs had been rooting under some oak trees).

There were few oak seedlings, but if all of the young oaks already present were fully grown, their canopy would cover most of the area. This one remaining successional step will probably reduce the amount of coffee berry and poison oak (Seeds of these two plants still sprout in great numbers throughout the whole area.) Clearly, the potential vegetation on most of this old orchard site is live oak woodland—though, given sufficient time, the redwoods at the east of the former orchard may colonize parts of the site.

Though some of these old orchards and fields remain covered by regrowth, most are being landscaped for residential housing. Sites that have been left undisturbed long enough for climax vegetation to

On the right, mound-like stands of Hooker's manzanita, a subspecies confined to the Monterey Bay area. Hooker's manzanita shows a considerable ability to survive habitat disruption. These stands are located along Trabing Road, 2 km northwest of the Watsonville airport, in an area that has been much disturbed over a long period. Here the manzanita grows with pampas grass on the soil-less highway cut—and northward, a few manzanita even colonize the edges of eucalyptus groves such as the one shown in the background—an unattractive environment for most other plants.

Disregarding, of course, long-term evolutionary processes—human activities are the only threats to the survival of most native plants. On the other hand, some obviously benefit from those same activities; for example, the many wildflowers that spring up in manmade grasslands. Others may now be dependent on certain kinds of human disturbance. The endangered Santa Cruz tar plant, another native species confined to the Monterey Bay area, often grows in manmade grasslands and other disturbed areas—areas where historically there is scarcely a square meter that has not been repeatedly grazed, cleared, or burned—for example, within the city limits of Watsonville itself. From the standpoint of conservation, the problem is to identify which types of human action are beneficial. In order to protect some natives from being overshadowed by woody growth, natural succession will have to be kept in an arrested stage.

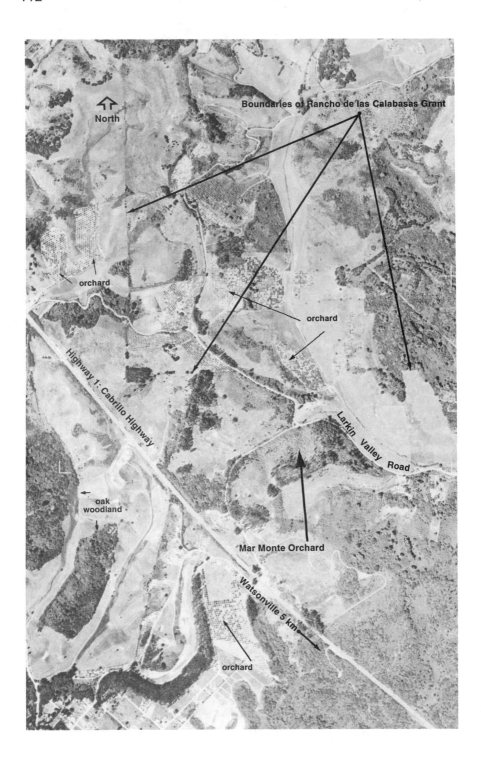

North

Boundaries of Rancho de las Calabasas Grant

orchard

orchard

Highway 1: Cabrillo Highway

Larkin Valley Road

oak woodland

Mar Monte Orchard

Watsonville 5 km

orchard

Aerial photo (June 1956) shows plant cover on hill country south of Aptos. One of the largest remaining tracts of live-oak woodland in the area is shown in the lower left of the picture. Woodcutters have long harvested firewood in these hills for sale in Watsonville. In the 1940s, manzanita burls were dug up in parts of the woodland for making pipe bowls. Openings in the woodland have been grazed for over a century.

Several apple orchards appear. Mar Monte Orchard, near the center of the photo, has been the site of a study of plant succession (pp. 103-116). The rate of reestablishment of native trees in orchards here is not exceptionally rapid, this hill country being edaphically less favorable for plant growth than neighboring lowlands. The hills, 30 to 60 m above sea level (largely very soft sandstone of the Aromas Red Sands) have low water-holding capacity and ready erodibility. These characteristics were demonstrated here by severe erosion and slumping on the roadcuts made in the process of widening Highway 1 which extends through the area. In oak woodland a loamy sand, covered with deep leaf mold, develops, but this soil horizon is lacking over much of the area, profiles having been greatly modified by grazing and tillage.

Boundaries of the Rancho de las Calabasas (granted by the Mexican government to Felipe Hernandez in 1833) are shown. Such boundaries are likely sites for "archival, or benchmark" soils—so called because they sometimes preserve earlier environmental conditions; for instance, soil profiles and soil fauna that were widespread before ploughing, petrochemical fertilizers, etc.

Except where cleared for residential development, live oaks cover the woodland tracts more thickly now than in 1956. Coniferous growth is reestablishing itself slowly: There are more than a dozen circular groves of redwood in the area, growing from old stumps, but the tree is not spreading. And seeds from the scattered Douglas fir trees west of Highway 1 seldom germinate. Perhaps recovery of redwood and Douglas fir is slow because the area is a natural zone of transition from coniferous forest to oak woodland: This is now the southwest boundary of redwood and Douglas fir in the Monterey Bay area.

An old barn on Aromas Road—among the last of hundreds that were present in the first half of the twentieth century. Existence of such barns led to the redistribution of many native animals—attracting barn owls, barn swallows, and others; the associated haystacks and granaries drew seed-eating birds, deer mice, etc. All such changes greatly influence the inter-relationships of species: relative abundance, competition, predator-prey relationships, etc. In the upper left is a grove of large eucalyptus trees. (This grove, which had previously produced firewood, was harvested for pulp around 1950.) Shown in the upper right is live-oak woodland, reestablished on slopes where an apricot orchard stood in the 1930s. Dairying and the practice of manuring fields were responsible for the dissemination (here and throughout most temperate regions) of various nitrophilous foreign weeds, e.g., the white goosefoot. The field in the foreground, recently ploughed, is covered mainly with mustard and wild radish.

An urban bio-community (for much of the area, the habitat of the future), in which plant and animal life are spaced within a characteristic checkerboard pattern (Photo J. Christenson)

develop are becoming hard to find: The Mar Monte site is, itself, scheduled to be cleared.

This review of the successional process shows not only that natural successional tendencies strongly favor the reestablishment of native species, but that this benefit to wildlife can be enhanced by keeping parts of the regrowth in a state of arrested succession.

In other parts of the Monterey Bay area, development of the potential natural vegetation proceeds at different rates—depending on a variety of factors; for instance, depending on differences in rainfall, on how badly the soil was degraded while in use, on the incidence of fires, and on the abundance of seed dispersing animals. Large numbers of browsing deer and grazing cattle may also suspend regrowth. Yet unexplained anomalies exist: In a remarkable case of retarded succession, a field at Hastings Reservation in the upper Carmel Valley was still in annual grasses forty years after grazing had been discontinued (Davis and Baldridge, 1980, p. 117)—thus raising a question as to whether severe degradation of the natural plant cover may not, in at least rare cases, be irreversible.

The animal inhabitants of old barns, deserted houses and their dooryards themselves pass through successional stages after people leave: Along with its human residents, the typical house has from time to time a surprisingly large number of other occupants—especially insects. The following are but a few: argentine ant, clothes moth, drywood termite (which under natural conditions infests dead branches in native trees), earwigs, house cricket, house fly, house mosquito, subterranean termite, vinegar (fruit) fly.

When a house is long uncared for, alien insects (which include all of the above, except for the termites) begin to disappear. The termites remain and assist greatly in the house's collapse and decomposition—drywood termites attacking from above, and subterranean termites from below.

A few more examples of these changing imprints on the landscape: In the fall of 1969, an abandoned two-story wooden-frame house stood overlooking Elkhorn Slough—a little south of Hudson Landing.

When visited by the author, several ring-necked pheasants flew out of the shrubbery behind the house. From a top-story window there was a fine view over the slough, covered with pink pickleweed and dotted with marsh birds. The house (now gone) was built in the style common in the 1930s, its many rooms small, and separated by doors. Honeybees nested in the wall. Scattered around the doorstep were a few broken fruit jars of a brand once kept by the dozens for canning, along with an old ironing board and a window sash weight. A pair of harness hames lay in the weeds. A bellefleur apple tree and garden flowers grew among the weeds around the front steps—the varieties, those favored by an earlier generation: hollyhock, periwinkle, foxglove, calla lily, and valerian.

The backyard was overgrown with Himalayan blackberries—an old standby around California farmhouses. Its berries have a tangy, wild flavor. Like the bellefleur apple, it was once widely grown hereabouts; although loganberries and boysenberries have replaced it commercially, the berry is still common along roadways and drainage ditches—its thick, tough canes making a formidable bramble. Note: The transoceanic pheasants, honeybees, berries, garden flowers, and apples linger on here, growing alongside native marsh birds, willows, live oaks, and pickleweed. The house is now gone; live oaks shade the ground where it stood. Water from the spring that supplied the household now seeps through the yard, making a soggy patch pretty well taken over by native willows. These homesites are now covered by live oaks.

One warm summer afternoon, the author visited an old barn standing behind an abandoned house in the Carneros district. About a dozen alarmed ground squirrels scurried toward the building, making for nests under the rotting floorboards. Inside there was a sweet odor of moldy hay. A few pigeons still nested in the barn—evidence that the house in front had probably been vacant only a short time. Pigeons usually don't stay long after people have gone.

The barn was still used as a shelter for horses, and the barnyard was trampled and dusty—with gray-green clumps of hoarhound scattered around. White-faced hornets had built their large, papery nests under the eaves. Numerous linnets fluttered in and out of the weedy growth around the corral. Nothing could be more typical than the lone phoebe, perched on the watering trough. The path leading from barn to house was covered with periwinkle—like ivy and valerian steadfast markers of old dooryards. Note: The squirrels, hornets, linnets, and phoebes are natives, drawn here to a human habitat. The horses and pigeons were introduced purposely from the Old World, whence came by chance the hoarhound and the other corral weeds.

With each such change in land use, new inter-relationships between species appear—and new selective pressures are brought to bear on local plant and animal life.

3.5.3. Foothill Woodland

The general setting of foothill woodland is climatically and floristically different from that of the live-oak woodland, discussed above. Here, too, oaks make up most of the tree cover—but the principal oaks are blue oak, black oak, valley oak, and maul oak: In most of the area coast live oak, though common, is not dominant. Scattered digger pines are the principal coniferous growth. An isolated stand of Coulter pines grows on Fremont Peak, and patches of the trees are scattered along the crest of the Gabilans southward to Gloria Road. California juniper is present at Pinnacles National Monument. Coyote brush, the aggressive colonist of old fields in northern parts of the Monterey Bay area, is rare here and plays but a small part in succession.

Coast live oaks are numerous on the lower slopes of the northern Gabilans east of Natividad and Old Stage Road—but as the rainfall decreases southward, they give way to blue oak. This is seen to the east of Soledad, where blue oak is often the most common tree, followed by coast live oak and digger pine. Blue oak is also common, intermixed with other oaks, at middle elevations in the eastern Sierra de Salinas. The blue oak is outstanding among native oaks for its drought resistance. It is adapted to the driest slopes and so intolerant of excessive water that it is actually killed by irrigation (Jepson, 1910,

p. 216). Thus the tree is absent from the wetter, northern parts of the Monterey Bay area.

The black oak is found mainly in the southern half of the Monterey Bay area. The state park on Fremont Peak includes a grove of large trees. The black oak's response to fire partly explains its distribution in scattered groves: "Of all our oaks, fire is the most destructive to this one" (Jepson, 1910, p. 233). (On the other hand, coast live oak is among those most tolerant of fire.) Although still common in parts of the Sierra de Salinas, black oaks are generally restricted to sites distant from the recent manmade forest fires that have swept the area. Further working to the black oak's disadvantage is the fact that its foliage is especially attractive to feeding cattle and deer—so much so that at one time the tree's propagation for forage was recommended.

The valley oak does not thrive in the immediate vicinity of the coast. This large, deciduous tree was once most common in interior valleys. Yet it grows high up on slopes as well, and can be found in both the Gabilans and the Sierra de Salinas; some large trees are growing near the entrance to Toro Regional Park. Like the blue and black oaks, valley oak is uncommon in the northern half of the Monterey Bay area. Although now rarely found on the west side of the Santa Cruz Mountains, in the early days of the twentieth century the valley oak grew in many places where it is absent today: "In Scott's Valley we find a kind of white oak *(Quercus lobata); it grows in moist, open valleys" (Santa Cruz Sentinel,* Aug. 12, 1871); there is still a sizable tract of valley oaks a few miles to the west, on Zayante Road. In pre-human times, the valley oak was no doubt a major component of the riparian vegetation, but it has suffered from the clearing of valley bottoms for agriculture. Deer and cattle have further limited its range: ". . . cows either eat the acorns or browse and trample the seedlings" (Griffin, 1973, p.8). (Historically, the effect of predator extermination programs and game laws has been to keep deer populations in the whole area at artificially high levels. As a result, the browsing of seedlings at the edges of clearings by deer is a major factor in slowing oak regeneration.)

By the 18th century, oak lumber was scarce in many parts of Europe. Arriving in their wooden ships and seeing California's extensive oak woodlands, some early explorers predicted a bright industrial future for the area, based on shipbuilding, Actually, most California oaks were not suitable for that purpose. Of all the western oaks, maul oak is one of the few that yields valuable lumber, but the species was never harvested enough to be seriously depleted. Maul oak is found scattered throughout the Santa Cruz Mountains, but is more abundant in the Santa Lucia Mountains and in the Sierra de Salinas.

Digger pine grows only in the southern part of the Monterey Bay area, southward in the Gabilans from Gloria Road east of Gonzales. (It is not found on the west slopes of the Santa Cruz Mountains.) Unlike the closed-cone pines, digger pine is intolerant of burning. In areas protected from fire, digger pine is reestablishing itself vigorously. Near the road leading from Soledad to the west entrance of Pinnacles National Monument, it descends the west slopes of the Gabilans almost to the floor of the Salinas Valley. The total area of digger pine (and perhaps that of the Coulter pine, as well) was once more extensive on the west slopes of the Gabilans than now: The U.S. government survey of the El Alisal grant, east of Salinas, in referring to the northeastern part of the grant extending from the valley toward the Gabilans, used the description "*pine timber*, low hills." The area was frequently swept by forest fire; in 1888, a local newspaper described a "fire in the Gabilan Hills west of Fremont's Peak . . . burning over thousands of acres of brush and field . . . . Considerable *pine timber* was destroyed" (*San Benito Advance*, August 10, 1888). As late as 1929, another paper reported a fire in the foothills of the Gabilans 16 km [10 miles] east of Salinas which " . . . leveled 30,000 acres [12,000 hectares] of timber, brush, and grassland" (*Gilroy Advocate*, Sept. 20, 1929).

A remarkable colony of digger pine is located in Pine Canyon in Toro Regional Park. In 1846, the botanist Hartweg returned to Monterey from the Rancho de Tularcitos, in the upper Carmel Valley, by way of El Toro Peak. He traveled "over El Toro, a high mountain destitute of trees or shrubs, but thickly covered with wild oats (Avenae species), [and] found, on the north side, in a ravine, a few small trees of *Pinus sabiniana*, the highest of them not exceeding 30 feet [9 meters]" (Hartweg, 1847, p. 188). The digger pine area in Pine Canyon now includes at least 400 hectares of mature trees. This area is of special interest because it is quite isolated from other areas of digger pine well to the southeast. The presence at the head of the canyon of bedrock mortars, surrounded by a large grove of buckeye and stands of islay prune (Ohlone food plants like the pine, and known to have been occasionally distributed by Indians) makes one suspect that the Ohlone may have established the pine at this location.

3.5.4. Chaparral

Four subdivisions are made here in the chaparral vegetation of the Monterey Bay area: Three inland and one coastal. These subdivisions intergrade, since all have species in common. The three inland subdivisions are timberland chaparral, hard broad-leaf chaparral, and chamise chaparral; in this order, the three occupy progressively drier and, as regards summer temperatures, hotter parts of the area. The coastal subdivision has been called maritime chaparral (Griffin, 1978).

Timberland chaparral is found mainly in the Santa Cruz Mountains. Its dominant species are blue blossom and coast whitethorn. It is sometimes classified as "subclimax brush of the coastal forest [because] . . . in most cases it is quite evident that these species occupy areas from which former timber stands have been removed by logging or fire" (Jensen, 1939, p. 15). Stands of timberland chaparral are dense and somewhat taller than other chaparral types, rising to heights of 2 to 4.6 m. Blue blossom is strongly associated with the coast redwood, and with the physical conditions favorable for the redwood's growth. Thus, blue blossom often serves as a rough marker of those areas that were formerly covered by redwoods. Under undisturbed conditions, the coast whitethorn is most common on stream banks, whence it, too, spreads over burned or logged slopes.

Characteristic species of the hard broad-leaf chaparral are

manzanitas, California scrub oak, and chaparral pea. These often grow with knobcone pine on old forest-fire burns—for example, between Mount Madonna County Park and Loma Prieta. Common here are several additional fire-favored shrubs—namely, two complex and varied species of manzanita (*Arctostaphylos glandulosa* and *A. tomentosa*), and buck brush. If old chaparral stands are burned, the two manzanitas soon reestablish themselves by sprouting new shoots from enlarged, half-buried burls at the base of their trunks. Buck brush, the most abundant and widespread ceanothus in California's chaparral, also stump sprouts after fires. Among non-sprouting chaparral plants the seeds of deerweed, and a number of others, germinate more freely after being exposed to fire. Some claim that with the possible exception of on a few cliffs, rattan's monkey flower can only be found on areas that have been burned or otherwise disturbed.

Chamise chaparral, in which the chamise shrub is strongly dominant, is most extensive in southern parts of the Monterey Bay area—but the shrub is a typical chaparral species, and appears in all four subdivisions. In the Gabilans, it is closely associated with foothill woodland. Northward, in the Santa Cruz Mountains, it is found mainly along ridges and on slopes with south and westerly exposures: "From such localities its spread to adjacent areas is favored by recurrent fires" (Jensen, 1939, p. 15). The chamise plant differs from most other chaparral shrubs in having thin, needle-like leaves.

In the Santa Cruz Mountains, timberland chaparral usually appears as an interruption of darker-hued coniferous forest or woodland—while chamise chaparral, farther south on the lower slopes of the Gabilans and Sierra de Salinas, commonly stands out as dark tracts adjoined by a lighter grassland. There, the sharp zigzag lines that usually mark the junction of chaparral and grassland rarely express climatic or edaphic contrasts, but rather the limits of burning and grazing. In places where the chaparral has recently been burned, old cattle-trail terraces are sometimes uncovered, indicating that the same slopes have been cleared previously for grazing purposes, and that the chaparral is of no great age.

Chamise-chaparral in the Gabilan foothills. *Above.* Several grazing stages in young chaparral; the oldest stage is in the center background. The scattered trees are coast live oaks. *Below.* Some 20 mi. farther south, along Gloria Road, an old chamise stand being colonized by digger (gray) pines. (Photos B. Gordon)

Plant Succession in the Gabilan Mts. west of Pinnacles National Monument off Highway 146. For over 150 years chaparral has been burned to produce grazing land. Here (in 1969) chaparral is being mechanically cleared to increase the deer population. Aging chamise, the dominant plant, is uprooted.

Succession begins with grasses and forbs, followed by California sage and wild buckwheat—and, on badly eroded slopes, deerweed. (Where the chaparral is burned rather than cleared mechanically, golden ear-drops becomes very plentiful.) After between 5 and 10 years chamise shrubs and seedlings become the dominant plant cover, and most herbaceous plants are excluded.

The scattered digger pines and oaks, *above* and *center*, are an indication of the successional trend: chaparral may survive some 30 years, gradually being invaded by pines and oaks. Eventually foothill woodland develops. Without knowledge of recent human disturbance, the remarkable plant boundaries shown above might be taken, mistakenly, for the result of natural processes alone.

Below, a clump of chamise, pulled up with much of its root system intact. For purposes of delaying the return of woody plant cover, this method of clearing is more effective than burning, because chamise sprouts vigorously from its burls after fires. Many such clumps have more than 10 stems, some 7 cm in diameter and 4.3 m long.

In 1974, in the first extensive tillage in this vicinity since the 1880s, a large tract of nearby cleared land was planted to safflower. Succession on such repeatedly-ploughed land will differ somewhat from that on either burned or mechanically-cleared sites. (Photos B. Gordon)

Cattle trail terraces near Soquel. Within the general human influence on landscape, different cultures leave distinctive imprints. Absent here before the introduction of cattle, this terracing is a specifically European contribution.

Unlike deer which move easily up and down slope, cows are ungainly on steep hills, and prefer walking nearly on the level. Following each other along closely-spaced contours, they gradually wear flat paths.

The cow's grazing habits determine the spacing of the terraces; while grazing on level land, the animal moves forward swinging its muzzle from side to side through an arc of only about 90°—thus cutting a narrow swath. On steep hills the paths must be closely spaced if plants from the whole surface are to be harvested. The cows feed mainly on their uphill side where they can reach herbage without kneeling. Thus, their hooves gradually undercut the slope along the inner edges of paths. Such terrace-making increases downslope soil creep—as is sometimes evidenced by tilted, or even displaced, fences. (Photo B. Gordon)

Chamise chaparral as a succession feature is well illustrated at Pinnacles National Monument, where it represents something of a management problem. The U.S. Forest Service has long advertised the Pinnacles as a prize example of the chaparral biotic community and has considerable interest in maintaining this plant cover. It has found this difficult to do. Much of the dense chaparral at the monument is now composed of old and weakened chamise plants, which yield inadequate supplies of food for some chaparral animals. For example, studies of deer population show that "sprouting chamise on a recent burn is far superior to old-growth chamise as forage" (Longhurst et al., 1952, p. 45).

If the chaparral community at the Pinnacles is to be maintained, it will probably have to renewed by periodic burning or clearing. This conflicts, of course, with the policy to date, which has been to protect the monument from the burning and clearing that have been commonplace on surrounding privately owned and Bureau of Land Management lands. Although leaving nature undisturbed has been an ideal of the Forest Service, to maintain only chaparral on parts of the monument is, in fact, to interfere with the natural plant succession.

In most tracts where chaparral is dying off, the successional trend is toward digger pine-blue oak forest, probably the climax vegetation of the area. The digger pine is particularly intolerant of burning. Since the government acquired this land, any fires that have occurred have been accidental and extinguished as soon as possible. Consequently, young digger pines are now very common, for example, around the gate at the east entrance to the monument and westward throughout the area of the visitors' center. Indeed, the most obvious change in the vegetation on parts of the monument during the second half of the twentieth century has been the increase in digger pines. (As noted earlier, a similar spread of digger pine, following reduced burning during the same time period, has occurred in Pine Canyon on the lands of Toro Regional Park.)

Maritime chaparral, which extends from south of Carmel Valley northward to Larkin Valley, lies in the coastal zone of summer fog. Large stands are found on Monterey Peninsula, at Fort Ord, and in the Prunedale district. The stump-sprouting manzanita, *Arctostaphylos tomentosa,* and chamise are dominant (Griffin, 1978, p. 73), but accompanied by such fire-favored species as Monterey ceanothus and deerweed. Though all of these are widespread chaparral shrubs, they are joined in the maritime chaparral by a number of endemic species— including the Monterey, Hooker's, Pajaro, and sandmat manzanitas.

Button sage (black sage) growing on the lower slopes of the Gabilan Mountains. Digger pine is shown in the far background at the left of the photo.

This is another example of successional trends deflected according to land use: On sandy soils, where the vegetation has been grazed longest and most intensively, button sage, rather than the usual chamise, covers the surface. Once the sage is established, succession goes on slowly and chamise is excluded: button sage inhibits the germination of chamise seeds beneath it (Went et al., 1952, p. 361). Button sage is similarly associated with arrested succession in the coastal chaparral, northeast of Monterey (Griffin, 1978, p. 77)

(Photo B. Gordon)

Maritime chaparral is associated geographically with coast live-oak woodland and closed-cone coniferous forest. Under plant succession, without fire or other disturbance, most areas of maritime chaparral will, like the closed-cone coniferous forest itself, revert to live-oak woodland.

3.5.5. Ponderosa Pine Forest

The ponderosa pine stands in the Santa Cruz Mountains are noted here both as an example of human modification of natural plant cover and as an example of the significance of potential natural vegetation in the planning of land use.

The very existence of ponderosa pine in the Santa Cruz Mountains is of considerable biogeographic interest; its total area here is small (at present covering some 247 hectares, or 610 acres) and quite isolated from other ponderosa pines. One particularly associates this pine with the great forests on the western slopes of the Sierra Nevada. The nearest naturally growing ponderosa pines to those of the Santa Cruz Mountains are located in Napa County to the north, on Mount Hamilton to the east, and in the Santa Lucia Mountains to the south. There are actually two stands of the pine in the Santa Cruz Mountains, separated from each other by a short distance and both growing within 16 km (10 miles) of Santa Cruz itself. The larger stand extends from the Henry Cowell Redwood State Park east of Felton northeastward for a distance of about 5 km. The other stand is located in the Bonny Doon area, along Martin Road. In the Santa Cruz Mountains the distribution of ponderosa pine is limited by edaphic factors. The tree is found on certain light-colored, sandy soils, derived from old marine sandstones, and on relatively smooth terrain. This edaphic limitation is not characteristic of the species in its other areas of growth. At the same time, certain other tree species are excluded from the ponderosa pine stands, presumably by these same edaphic factors: For instance, redwood and Douglas fir, which grow in the neighborhood, do not grow on these sandy soils. Soils of these old marine sands are of little agricultural value; various attempts to use them agriculturally have failed (Griffin, 1964, p. 410).

These unusual groves of ponderosa pine were discovered by the botanist Hartweg in 1846. He noted that "the trees rise to a height of 100 feet [30 m], with a stem of 3 or 4 feet [91 or 122 cm] in diameter" (Hartweg, 1847, p. 189). The groves have been changed considerably since American settlement in the area began. Only about 60 hectares (150 acres) of the total area are classified as virgin growth (Jensen, 1939, p. 23). According to an account of an old resident, the best ponderosa pine trees were cut long ago. Around 1890, part of the area was logged to supply the local market for box-making lumber. Ponderosa pine has reestablished itself on parts of the logged area, and grows there now to heights of over 30 m (100 feet) (Jensen, 1939, p. 23). Elsewhere in the vicinity, the presence of ponderosa pine stumps is evidence that the pine once covered a larger part of this area of distinctive, sandy soils than it does now; chaparral and knobcone pine, a successional stage, now cover a considerable part of it. As we have seen, chaparral and knobcone pine commonly come together in areas that have been cleared and burned. This is followed by the potential natural vegetation: ponderosa pine. It is estimated that ponderosa pine could reestablish itself upon some 400 additional hectares. The young pines appear and grow vigorously "wherever the soils have not been badly depleted" (Jensen, 1939, p. 23). Near the east entrance to Henry Cowell Redwood State Park, an area now protected from disturbance, there is a fine growth of young ponderosa pine.

This ponderosa pine-marine sands area is a repository of rare or endangered species—including as it does, the Bonny Doon manzanita, Hartweg's spine flower, and Santa Cruz wallflower. Recent studies have also revealed the presence of a number of rare insects. Some of the original components of this plant community may already have been lost—taking into account the destructive effects of logging and agriculture in the past, and the ongoing sand-quarrying in parts of the area.

3.5.6. Closed-Cone Conifer Forest

There are three closed-cone pines in the area (Monterey, knobcone and bishop), and three closed-cone cypresses (the Monterey, Gowen and Santa Cruz). They are called "closed-cone" because (unless exposed to unusually high temperatures) their cones do not open completely. The cones of some, e.g., the bishop and knobcone pine, seldom open fully enough to release seeds unless exposed to fire. During the Pleistocene, closed-cone conifers grew in many places along the California coast (Langenheim and Durham, 1963, p. 37), but they have steadily lost ground. (Presumably the favorable conditions for their growth which existed earlier included a somewhat different climate with more frequent natural fires than occur now).

As noted earlier, the knobcone pine is concentrated in burned areas. Since fire opens the cones and permits their seeds to scatter, burning not only tends to produce stands of increased density, but also facilitates the knobcone's spread into adjacent areas. Seeds are said to remain viable some 40 years if the cones don't rot. Stands are scattered but of frequent occurrence in the Santa Cruz Mountains. Most large stands are made up of even-aged trees dating back to recorded forest fires. The trees are commonly between 4.5 and 20 m tall, and the stands either dense or open. Interspaces are commonly taken up by manzanita, chamise, chinquapin, and chaparral pea. There are large tracts of knobcone-manzanita-chinquapin association in the Santa Cruz Mountains between Mount Madonna County Park and Loma Prieta and along Empire Grade Road near Bonny Doon. Most of the Empire Grade groves date from a fire of 1927, which started near Eagle Rock and burned toward Santa Cruz. In one younger stand on Empire Grade the pines are between 13 and 20 cm in diameter and some 8 m in height. The space between them is covered with low chaparral made up mainly of manzanita, with a scattering of chamise, interrupted by patches of bracken. In an older grove nearby, the knobcones are between 25 and 46 cm in diameter and some 18 m in height. These trees are aging and dying off. Growing among them are chinquapin, interior live oak, madrone, and blue blossom, rising to heights of some 6 to 10 m. The lower-growing chaparral species are present here too, but patches of dead manzanita and blue blossom can be seen, killed by the shade of oaks that have overtopped them. In neither grove are knobcone seedlings present. Young Douglas firs are scattered about. A few stumps of redwood that survived the fire have sprouted from the crowns. Roughly, the successional sequence here following forest fire is as follows, in overlapping stages: Knobcone and low chaparral→knobcone and broad-leaved evergreen trees→Douglas fir and redwood, the last stage (or in places, the last two stages) being the potential natural vegetation of the area.

Extensive stands of knobcone are a fire hazard because of the tree's high resin content. Thus, the knobcone (and to a lesser extent other closed-cone conifers) is, paradoxically, both especially vulnerable to, and especially dependent upon, forest fires. Furthermore, in densely crowded stands, many trees begin to die within 10 years of the time of sprouting. As surviving trees live only some 50 to 70 years longer, such stands may be half-filled with dead and dying trees. Although homes are being built in such fire-prone knobcone stands hereabouts, if the pines can be kept unburnt, residents may expect continually changing and eventually less-flammable surroundings.

Since all of the forest fires which have occurred in the Santa Cruz Mountains in the last 75 years (roughly, the average life-span of a knobcone pine) have been set by people, the extensive complex of knobcone-pine stands and interspace plants is largely a successional phase brought into existence through human action.

The knobcone has no commercial value. Even as firewood it is of poor quality, beginning to rot within a year of the time when the trees are cut. Under ideal conditions extensive stands of knobcone pine would not exist. The tree will, however, continue to have value as cover on patches of dry slope, too steep, rocky, or infertile for other conifers—this being probably its natural distribution.

Reference should be made here to the extensive closed-cone pine forest in the vicinity of Año Nuevo. Along Highway 1, between San Francisco and the Monterey Peninsula, there is only one small area in this whole stretch where coniferous forest still extends almost to the shore, and that is from a little north of Año Nuevo to a little south of Waddell Creek. Elsewhere along the coast forest either has been cleared or is excluded by edaphic conditions.

The persistence of an isolated forest along the shoreline near Año Nuevo is something of a puzzle. An attempt is made here to explain the circumstance in terms of human disturbance, plant succession, and certain characteristics of the Monterey and knobcone pines, the

Left, **Knobcone pine stand** on Empire Grade, northeast of Santa Cruz. These pines, all of nearly the same age and closely-spaced, date back to a single forest fire. Within the Monterey Bay area, knobcone is mainly found in the Santa Cruz Mountains: It is not found in the Gabilans or on the Monterey Peninsula (Photo B. Gordon).

Right, **Cones grow in whorls** and curve in toward the supporting branches and trunks. Knobcone takes its name from the pointed knobs formed by the enlarged scales at the outer base of the cone. (Photo C. Grube)

two dominant species. Across the bay on the Monterey Peninsula itself, another tract of forest approaches the shoreline, and there, too, Monterey pine is dominant. (Indeed, as defined here the Monterey Bay area is enclosed between two coastal forests dominated by this tree, named for the bay and known only from the California coast.)

Although pines alone appear in the shoreward parts of the forest at Año Nuevo, away from the shore they grow intermixed first with Douglas fir and then redwood groves, the latter becoming dominant farther inland. Monterey pine is not found more than about 1.6 km (1 mile) from the sea in the Año Nuevo area, nor at elevations of over

244 m (800 feet) (Forde, 1964, p. 61). The total area of its distribution is approximately 405 hectares (1000 acres).

The fact that forest survives near Año Nuevo cannot be explained on the basis of the area's being remote and little used. As noted earlier, the vicinity of Año Nuevo was something of an Indian population center. Spanish accounts of Indian burning are particularly numerous in this general area and leave the impression that much of it was well cleared before European settlement began. Clearing for grazing and agricultural purposes was continued by Spanish-Mexican and American settlers. Part of the area was included in the Mexican rancho Punto del Año Nuevo, known for its large herds of cattle. In the last half of the nineteenth century a dairy industry developed here; in 1867, there were 11 dairies in the vicinity of Año Nuevo. The area has long been a lumbering center; in the 1860s and 1870s, lumber was shipped from Waddell's Wharf, boards being brought from a sawmill 8 km (5 miles) inland on Waddell Creek (Stanger, 1968, pp. 8, 12).

Curiously, the Monterey pine has never been considered an attractive lumber tree here in its homeland. Very little commercial sawing of the tree has taken place in the Año Nuevo area. Knobcone pine has been used even less. The Monterey pine is exceptionally fast-growing and is widely planted in foreign sylviculture. Over 121,400 hectares (300,000 acres) of Monterey pine are grown in Australia and New Zealand alone—many times the total area of its natural distribution in coastal California. Seeds for the foreign plantations seem to have come in large part from the Año Nuevo area. One of the first lumbermen there had a

flourishing trade with Australian farmers in the nuts of the bullpine [a lumberman's name for species which produced inferior lumber, applied here to the Monterey pine]. A special retort was used to heat the pine cones to a temperature that caused them to burst and disgorge their seeds. (McHugh, 1959, p. 16)

Actually, cones of the Monterey pine usually open, at least partly, without fire—requiring less heat to do so than knobcones. On hot summer days so many cones may be opening that the whole tree crackles.

No doubt a principal reason for the neglect of Monterey pine by lumbermen has been the presence in the area of two superb lumber trees: the Douglas fir and the redwood. (A lumber mill located in pine forest near the highway south of Waddell Creek still operates, but it does not harvest local pine species.)

Several fires have occurred in the Año Nuevo forest within the twentieth century . Fire is more destructive of Douglas fir stands than of redwood stands: While the Douglas fir is completely killed off, the redwood regenerates by sprouting from surviving stumps. On the other hand, the reproduction of Monterey pine and knobcone pine is greatly stimulated by fire, especially the knobcone pine. (The two species intermix and hybridize near Waddell Creek; Stockwell and Righter, 1946, pp. 155-159.) Between Waddell Creek and Green Oaks Creek an edaphic factor also favors knobcone pine over other conifers: some crests and upper slopes of the rough hills there are made up of a crumbly, white, diatomaceous shale which is permeable and, in places, almost devoid of soil cover. The land is quite useless for agriculture or grazing. Within the last century, forest fires have burned parts of the area on several occasions—for example, around 1917. The hills are covered by chaparral made up of dwarf maul oak, manzanitas, chinquapin, etc. Knobcone, which tolerates thinner, poorer soils than do other conifers in the vicinity, is plentiful. During periods of intensive land-use in the surrounding areas, these surfaces probably served as seed beds for the knobcone pine.

In 1846, the botanist Hartweg sailed along the coast from Santa Cruz to San Francisco

. . . we sailed again, and . . . kept close inshore. *The whole of the coast is destitute of trees or shrubs,* with the exception of Point Año Nuevo, where some pines or cypresses seem to grow. (Hartweg, 1847, p. 189)

Hartweg was a careful observer, and his is an early description. But it should not be assumed that the conditions he described were natural.

Neither the present plant cover (a so-called "coastal prairie") nor that of Hartweg's time represents the potential natural vegetation of the area.

Although redwoods do not thrive at the shoreline itself because of their intolerance to salt in the air, the trees once approached the coast more closely than at present; those stands of redwood (and Douglas fir) there that survived Indian burning were harvested by lumbermen at an early date. Even today the redwood extends seaward along Coja Creek, about 8 km west of Santa Cruz, to within a kilometer of the shore. Its closest approach to the sea in the Monterey Bay area is along Aptos Creek. There, shielded by the slopes from offshore winds, redwoods grow within a few hundred meters of shoreline. Even this hardy tree was killed off by a burning program that continued for hundreds, if not thousands, of years. Many of the fires once set by Indian inhabitants in coastal land of grass and brush, burned inland unchecked—spending themselves at the seaward edges of redwood forest.

The closed-cone pines are not only better able to regenerate after burning than are Douglas fir and redwood, but after clearing operations as well: "When a mixed stand is logged, the opening-up leads to dense regeneration of pine seedlings" (Forde, 1964, p. 67). Where Monterey pine and Douglas fir grow intermixed, the pine grows more abundantly at the forest margin; examples can be seen along Scott Creek (Forde, 1964, p. 67). The pines are also faster growing than Douglas fir or redwood. When pastures that were made by clearing mixed forest are abandoned, the faster-growing pines take over in the earlier successional stages. The pines that are spreading south on seaward slopes in the vicinity of Swanton Road indicate that the potential natural vegetation of these slopes is coniferous forest.

Plant cover in the country along Cabrillo Highway from Santa Cruz past Davenport and Año Nuevo was burned by Indians annually, probably over a period of many centuries; the area was then heavily grazed by the herds of Spanish and American cattlemen. Within the twentieth century the flat land, mostly to the west of the highway on the lowest marine terrace, has been ploughed for field crops. Given enough time without human disturbance, forest would approach the shoreline much more closely than it does at present, both upcoast and down from Año Nuevo. The fact that trees planted along the coast thrive, shows that climatically and edaphically the area is suited to tree growth. During the recent years of reduced grazing and tilling of the hills, the amount of woody growth has increased. Old-time residents say that more such plant cover exists now than at any other time within the period they remember.

Because this coastal strip was almost without forest when first seen by Europeans, except around Año Nuevo, and has remained so throughout historic times, its ability to support tree growth has been underestimated. Some maps that attempt to reconstruct natural vegetation show the area as largely coastal shrub. Patches that have not been grazed or tilled for a five- or ten-year period do, in fact, develop a dense cover of shrubs (especially California sage). But, undisturbed, this shrub cover is later usually replaced by oaks—and this is true on both north and south exposures, and even on steep slopes. The wind-swept oak grove on the knoll facing the highway to the north of Laguna Creek is an example. The potential natural vegetation along most of this coast is live-oak woodland or coniferous forest.

Another major closed-cone pine forest is on the Monterey Peninsula, where Monterey pine covers an area of approximately 4860 hectares (12,000 acres). There is no knobcone pine here.

The distribution of tree species on the Monterey Peninsula has long been in a state of flux, vegetation there having been subjected for hundreds of years to constant disturbance. In reviewing the historical events, mentioned earlier, that have changed the plant cover of the area, it will be recalled that the Monterey Peninsula, like Año Nuevo, was a major Costanoan population center. Indians of the peninsula consciously used fire to produce a desired plant cover, and, at least to a limited extent, to capture game. Furthermore, the peninsula is the oldest center of Spanish settlement in northern California. The characteristic institutions of Spanish-Mexican colonization (mission, presidio, and *rancho*) were all present here, and their influence is stamped boldly on the landscape. In early Spanish times cattle-growing became the only major industry in the area. Thus, a specialized economy developed, based on the use, botanical transformation, and extension of grassland. Under the Spanish and Mexicans, the port of Monterey was both a shipping and a refueling center—the peninsula supplying firewood not only for local use but for ocean-going vessels as well. Later, American settlers continued the Spanish cattle-growing tradition—using badly overgrazed ranges into the late 1870s. During the twentieth century, as such uses of the land were gradually discontinued, the area of tree growth on the peninsula has greatly increased—despite several destructive forest fires and urban expansion —except, of course, in the cities themselves. *Tree cover on the peninsula is probably denser and more extensive now than at any other time in the historical period.*

In Indian times there appears to have been a considerable tree cover on the peninsula despite fires set by the Costanoans. Sebastián Vizcaíno, the first European explorer to enter and describe the Monterey Bay, landed in the vicinity of what is now Monterey Harbor in December 1602. He found pines and oaks near the shoreline there, in an area now partly covered by the city of Monterey (Mathes, 1965, I, pp. 375, 603). In 1770, Father Junipero Serra took possession of California for Spain, standing beneath an oak at the site of the Mission San Carlos in Monterey.

Within the first few decades of Spanish settlement, much of the forest had been cleared and the peninsula was heavily grazed. According to a traveler who crossed the peninsula in 1792, the country between Monterey and Carmel was grassland with tracts of chaparral and scattered pines:

Our ride was through a pleasing hilly country interspersed with pines thinly scattered, coppices of stiff scrubby brush wood and extensive spots of clear pasturage swarming with horses and cattle feeding in herds. (Menzies, 1924, p. 283)

The sparse tree cover of the Monterey Peninsula during the Spanish period, contrasting strongly with the abundant tree growth of the present, is shown in pictures made by visiting artists—for example, the drawings made in 1822 by John Sikes (see Van Nostrand, 1968, p. 32) and in 1827 by William Smyth.

According to an Englishman's account in 1837-1839, the country surrounding Monterey "resembles as near as possible a gentleman's park in England . . . the large knots of pine and oak were beautifully grouped . . . with rich pastures on which numerous herds were grazing" (Simpkinson, 1969, p. 29). A few years later, in 1841-1842, another British visitor drew much the same picture of the peninsula, describing it as "a succession of grassy slopes with a sufficient sprinkling of timber to relieve the monotony. The number of cattle that grazed on the rich pasturage was very considerable" (Simpson, 1930, p. 109).

By 1830, woodcutters had cleared so many trees around Monterey that the Provincial Assembly issued an ordinance (the Reglamento of August 17) regulating the felling of trees there. Wood from the trees remaining around Monterey in 1840 was much in demand:

> Housekeeping is very expensive in California. Oak fuel is $3.00 a carload and rough pine in billets $2.00 [oak is superior to pine as fuel] . . . . *There is no wood save a few scattered oaks and sycamores in the valleys, the only timber in the country being produced in the mountains.* Timber is in fact inconveniently scarce. (Douglas, 1929, p. 109)

Despite the above reports of good pasturage elsewhere on the peninsula, in 1840 the north side appears to have been overgrazed and almost devegetated, at least seasonally:

> This plane extending from Monterey to the Salinas River is covered with a low evergreen bush closely resembling wormwood [probably *Artemesia californica*, common on overgrazed surfaces] . . . . A few diminutive live oak trees grow in the hollows, but *not a blade of grass appears either on the ridges or in the intervening depressions.* At dusk we descended into the valley of the Salinas River; its banks are covered with willow of great size and the cottonwood tree. (Douglas, 1929, p. 109)

If the original plant cover on this northeast side of the peninsula was tree growth, it has never recovered. Evidence of Monterey pine forest here "in the very recent past is the finding of pine roots in the soil layers in the country to the north along Monterey Bay. It is probable that this forest may have occupied much of the region from Monterey to the Salinas River" (Mason,1934, p.124). Unfortunately, it is not known how old these pine roots actually are.

Former growth of conifers along the midbay shoreline is also suggested by the following historical note: The first European to see Monterey Bay was Juan Rodriguez Cabrillo, in November 1542. Unable to land because of high seas, he skirted the shores of the bay and finally anchored near the shore in approximately 80 m of water. He named the bay "Bahia de los Pinos." Although the bay's name was probably suggested by pine forests on Monterey Peninsula and Point Año Nuevo, coniferous trees may have grown on other parts of the Monterey Bay coastland as well. Cabrillo stated that he sighted pine trees (or at least trees with a similar outline—perhaps redwood or Douglas fir) from his anchorage: "the depth of water in which Cabrillo's ship was anchored close to the coast can only be found off Moss Landing in the submarine canyon" (Wagner, 1937, II, p. 398). Thus, the country within sight of Moss Landing, now almost treeless, except for planted groves, may have supported some coniferous growth at that time.

On the Monterey Peninsula itself, by 1913 a regrowth of chaparral covered southern parts, in what is now residential area or regrown to pines. North of Carmel, chaparral was described as extending between elevations of 30 m (100 feet) and 610 m (2000 feet) above sea level and approaching to within 1 km of the sea. Around Carmel itself, the chaparral was at that time being replaced by Monterey pine and coast live oak, "forming an open forest with the pine dominating" (Cannon, 1913, p. 36). Fire gives the pine, whose seeds are scattered by the wind, a temporary advantage over the oak: Though less easily damaged by fire than the pine, the oak (largely dependent on animals for seed dispersal) is slower to colonize newly-burned areas. Without fires,

"The Presidio and Pueblo of Monterrey, Upper California," by William Smyth,
1827. This watercolor sketch shows the Monterey Peninsula as Spanish-Mexican
cattle country. The view is from the presidio toward the southeast, with San Carlos
Church in the center, the crests of the peninsular hills in the right background,
and El Estero (then an estuary, now a lake) on the left. Note the scanty tree
growth on the hills, alignment of trees (in tree-fences or along alamedas), and
deeply eroded gullies in the stick-fence corrals. (Courtesy of the director, Bancroft
Library, University of California, Berkeley)

Monterey pine is gradually replaced by coast live oak—especially at
the inland edge of the pine's territory. But even on some coastal dunes,
replacement of pine by oak is likely, "provided the current fire
protection program is continued" (McBride and Stone, 1976, 130).

It is often assumed that the natural geographical limits of a species
are determined by its inanimate environment—say by a critical climatic
factor such as an isotherm, or by the presence of a certain chemical in
the soil. But, in temperate climates, the ranges of both plants and
animals are more commonly limited by inter-specific interactions such
as competition or predation (Walter, 1973, pp. 8-9). When human
activities interfere with these interactions, some species are given
competitive advantage over others, and their territories increase.

The three closed-cone cypresses of the Monterey Bay area are all
confined to small areas, and this limited distribution has often been
described as an example of "edaphic restriction." Nevertheless, though

their relationship to soil chemistry has been studied intensively, no unusual soil constituent has been found that is required for their growth. True, the soils upon which they grow naturally are generally sandy and infertile, but these conifers are limited to such soils mainly by competition from other species. Not only are all three "able to grow on other soils besides those to which they are geographically restricted" (McMillan, 1956, p. 207-208), but on more fertile soils the trees often grow *better*.

Not only do the Santa Cruz cypress and the knobcone pine quickly colonize the burned-over areas with better soils, they grow there to an unusual size. Neverthless, they gradually lose ground to other species during the successional process, and retreat to a refuge on barren sandstone exposures where few other trees follow. (For further examples of the successful, or even improved, growth of the three cypresses on fertile soils, see McMillan, 1956, pp. 186, 187-192; Greene, 1929, 197-199; and Hoover, 1957, p. 142.)

Prescribed burning (to improve grazing for cattle, to improve deer habitat, for research, etc.) is still practiced in the area, but most forest and grassland fires of the twentieth century, large and small, were set accidentally. (An uncertain number were set deliberately, in order to make false insurance claims—or simply for malicious pleasure.) Thus, the ecological effects of modern fires are largely unplanned and haphazard.

Consider, for example, the effects of fire on the distribution and populations of but one class of animals—the amphibians: Several species of salamander do not, as might be supposed, find refuge in streams and ponds since they rarely if ever enter water (Professor G. S. Myers, *Santa Cruz Sentinel*, Oct. 2, 1977). The slender salamander, for instance, is common in oak woodland, living in damp spots beneath decaying logs and leaves. Even prolonged drought takes a heavy toll on such animals; few will survive fire.

3.6. Dissipated or Threatened Plant Associations

Several of the area's natural plant associations have been virtually eliminated: For example, the native bunchgrass association and much of the riparian forest association.

3.6.1. Bunchgrass Association

The pre-European grasslands were occupied mainly by perennial bunchgrasses, particularly nodding needlegrass and purple needlegrass—and on moister land, slender hairgrass. Other grasses and forbs filled in spaces between the well-separated clumps of bunchgrass, but just which herbs these might have been is conjectural. Although no undisturbed remnants of the original association remain, there is no evidence that any of the grass species themselves have become extinct (Beetle, 1947, p. 343). Small patches of nodding needlegrass can still be found scattered over parts of the area, but generally only on rougher terrain, inaccessible for heavy grazing or cultivation. Larger tracts are found at Fort Ord, where only light grazing has been permitted.

As noted earlier, some of the bunchgrass association was itself probably the product of human action—a result of burning done by the Costanoan Indians and grazing by elk. With Spanish and American land use, grassland areas were enlarged and became more completely a human artifact. Although the native bunchgrasses sprout strongly after being burned over, making rapid recovery possible (Sweeney, 1967, p. 114), they cannot withstand heavy grazing. While light burning of clearings as practiced by the Indians favored their spread and persistence, under grazing and faced with the competition of annual plants, they were soon eliminated and replaced. Thus, only scattered patches of native bunchgrass survive, although the total area of grassland itself has increased.

When Europeans first settled the Monterey Bay area, the largest expanses of bunchgrass association were located in the Salinas Valley southward from Chualar and along the coast to the west and northwest of Santa Cruz. "Few places on earth, if any, have had such rapid wholesale replacement of native plants by introduced species," according to a specialist on California rangelands, speaking of the state as a whole (Burcham, 1957, p. 198). In Monterey County, more than one-third (71 species out of 162) of all grasses now growing are introduced (Howitt and Howell, 1964, p. 27). The aliens are overwhelmingly dominant.

Although generally classified as wild species, the populations of many of these Eurasian grasses have been genetically modified by the selective preferences of *domesticated* grazing animals—and by the range management customs of their shepherds—over several thousands of years. During this time new varieties evolved, especially among the annual species. This selective cultural influence has varied regionally: In the Mediterranean area, for example, "each civilization has introduced its own forage plants into cultivation" (Vavilov, 1949-50, p. 37). In more recent times, special strains of these herbs have been bred, and the seeds of some (for instance, the rye grasses and red fescue) are often sown in California, and grow as part of what appears to be a spontaneous natural plant cover.

In the Monterey Bay area it is hard to find large areas where grass cover can be shown to be natural vegetation. Most of the west slope of the northern Gabilans and the lower east slopes of the Sierra de Salinas, both now grasslands, were once wooded, as was the Moro Cojo-Elkhorn Slough area. Only cultural maintenance and grazing keeps the grass-covered hills east of Watsonville from experiencing successional change. Grasslands of the Prunedale hills are only now being recolonized by coast live oak (and, unfortunately, as quickly cleared again to make room for strawberry fields).

Although the perennial bunchgrass association and parts of several other plant associations were converted to annual grassland within the first century following European settlement, a good deal of this new grassland itself later disappeared. This occurred particularly in the flatter, lower country where tilled land and residential aggregations replaced it.

Top, **Santa Cruz cypress** growing on, and around, a sandstone outcrop near Bonny Doon. This is one of several small groves of the tree in the Santa Cruz Mountains—all on similar soils. Knobcone pines grow on the sandstone too. Squaw grass is also found nearby (growing here, as at Huckleberry Hill, in the company of closed-cone conifers).

Right, **Young cypresses** on nearly bare sandstone at Eagle Rock, about 11 km north of Bonny Doon.

At this Bonny Doon site, the largest Santa Cruz cypresses are found a few meters away from the sandstone exposure—on deeper and better soils. The writer visited the Bonny Doon site in 1979 and again in the autumn of 1993 to inspect a tract of cypresses growing on these better soils. In 1979, cypresses in this stand were already mature, of approximately the same height, and with diameters of up to 40 cm. Several knobcone pines were scattered through the stand. Patches of

3.6.2. Riparian and Floodplain Vegetation

A chain of shallow lakes and marshes once extended from a point 8 or 10 km to the southeast of Salinas northwestward almost to the bay: for example, Smith Lake, Heinz Lake, Carr Lake, Sausal Lagoon, Boronda Lake, and Espinosa Lake. Most have now disappeared. In 1854, the following description was given of the northern Salinas Valley: "Much of the land is swampy and overgrown with tule, rush, willows, and marsh vegetation" (Antisell, 1854-1855, pp. 38-39). In addition to willows, the local riparian forest probably included tracts of alder, as indicated by the Spanish rancho names: Rancho Sausal, or Willow Ranch, and Rancho Alisal, or Alder Ranch. (Possibly the reference is to the sycamore, which the Spanish in parts of California

large manzanitas, overtopped by the cypresses, were dying off in the shade. Beneath the cypress trees, many live oak and Douglas fir seedlings were coming up. Most were less than a foot tall, though a few fir saplings rose to a height of several feet.

By the fall of 1993, several cypresses had diameters of 44 cm. The undergrowth of manzanitas noted in 1979 had disappeared. Knobcone pines were still present, but aging. Great numbers of live oak and Douglas fir seedlings were still springing up, along with an occasional tanbark oak. (Oak colonization is no doubt aided by acorn woodpeckers which, judging from their outcry, are exceptionally numerous here). Some live oaks that had been only seedlings or small saplings in 1979 were now over 14 cm. in diameter. Some Douglas fir which were saplings in 1979, now had diameters ranging from 5 cm to over 13 cm; several had reached a height of 4.7 m—almost half the height of the cypress trees. (Before many years have passed firs will likely overtop and threaten the cypresses: The latter are, like most closed-cone conifers, intolerant of shade.) Since no cypress or knobcone seedlings were present, both species are plainly being replaced by the oak and fir.

Lying unshaded on bare sandstone the cones of the knobcone pine sometimes open partially without having been exposed to fire—further evidence that such infertile sites are its natural habitat.

Southward, across the bay on Huckleberry Hill, the circumstances are similar to those in the Santa Cruz Mountains: There too an endemic cypress and pine grow together on infertile soils. But Huckleberry Hill has a different endemic pair—namely Gowen cypress and bishop pine rather than Santa Cruz cypress and knobcone pine. And on Huckleberry Hill, the pair's principal competition comes from the Monterey pine and live oak rather than from Douglas fir and live oak. (Photo B. Gordon) also called "aliso." Neither tree grows along the river near Salinas today.)

The importance of these lakes and marshes to birdlife is indicated in an early newspaper account from Castroville:

> It is astonishing to see the number of wild fowl that have taken up their abode for the winter in this vicinity, and fly back and forth between the lakes and sloughs where they rest, and the fields and marshes where they feed. The air is sometimes positively alive with them for miles, and their clangor is almost deafening. All kinds are represented, from the useless and ugly mudhen to the coveted "honker." (*The Castroville Argus*, Dec. 4, 1869)

Mid-nineteenth-century residents of Monterey traveled to the "Salinas plains" to shoot wild geese (Hutton, 1961, p. 4). According to a description of wetlands at the outskirts of Salinas written in 1877, "the yellow-legged plover [perhaps the greater yellow-legs, a sandpiper now sometimes present in winter] are in the fields by the thousands and hunted along with ducks and geese" (*Overton Manuscript*, 1877, p. 15).

The variety of birdlife in freshwater marshes is not fully shown in such popular descriptions of large flocks of wildfowl. The "tule, rush, willows, and marsh vegetation" included a complex assemblage of hydrophytes and aquatic animals with a correspondingly varied birdlife, most of which disappeared when such areas were drained.

These wetlands slowed the expansion of agriculture. The site of Salinas was surveyed in their midst in 1862, and the town was incorporated in 1872. In 1871, a local newspaper referred to "the tule swamps on our Salinas Plains. They cover a large area, are shallow, . . . and could be reclaimed at a small cost" (*Santa Cruz Sentinel*, Nov. 11, 1871). A program of drainage operations began around 1877. Writing in 1922, a renowned naturalist stated, "The most serious adverse effect of the human occupancy of California upon birdlife thus far has, I believe, resulted from . . . reclamation of swamplands" (Grinnell, 1943, p. 671).

In 1876, angling enthusiasts were stocking the lakes with introduced fish.

One hundred of the young fish ["Schuylkill" catfish, or brown bullhead, originally from Pennsylvania, brought here by rail from Sacramento] were put in *Sausal Lagoon* . . . and the other hundred were placed in that fine body of water known as *Espinosa Lagoon, about six miles* [10 km] *northwest of Salinas City* . . . *the entire chain of lakes, from Sausal to the bay*, will, in a few years, be swarming with them. (*The Salinas City Index,* Aug. 31, 1876)

Catfish had also been planted in Carr Lake, (now disappeared) at the outskirts of Salinas, in 1876 (*Overton Manuscript*, 1887, p. 3); and in 1878, landlocked salmon were planted in Espinosa Lake (*Castroville Argus*, 1878, April 20). However, hopes that this chain of shallow lakes would be used for sport fishing were short-lived, as drainage operations began on the larger lakes within a few years.

Rancho Sausal included 216 hectares (533 acres) and was

covered with a dense growth of tules and having water to a depth of over two feet standing on it the year around . . . . Some fifty acres [20 hectares] adjoining the northeast boundary of the tract was covered with a dense growth of willows. (*The Salinas City Index*, Feb. 15, 1877)

By the end of the following year a private company had completed draining the lake to provide agricultural land.

The original pattern of lake distribution in the lower Salinas Valley was still recognizable until around 1916 (Hare, 1916, p. 3). Drainage operations continue to the present. Plans for more canals and pumping stations in the Lake Merritt area are described in the Monterey County Flood Control and Water Conservation District report for 1960, as is the agency's ongoing spraying program to control tules in wetlands and along drainage ditches west of Salinas.

During the heavy rains and general flooding of early 1995, the basins of several of these lakes unexpectedly filled with water—submerging the artichoke fields on their slopes.

Although little now remains of what appears to have been a well-developed freshwater-marsh biocommunity in the lower Salinas Valley, a number of the marsh species have been preserved and widely spread

View across the Pajaro Valley, showing the southern Santa Cruz Mountains east of Watsonville. In the foreground are berries growing on the tilled floodplain of the Pajaro River, once covered by riparian forest. When the Spanish arrived here, redwood forests grew on the remainder of the lowlands, and on the slopes seen in the background. There were also extensive redwood forests northward and westward around Pinto Lake, Corralitos, and in Larkin Valley. As noted earlier, it was in this vicinity (in 1769) that the tree was first discovered; and it was here that redwood lumbering began: "... within a year of their discovery the first trees were falling at 'Corral Camp' for the construction of Monterey" (Stanger, 1969, p. 10). By the 1840s, redwood lumber was being hauled by cart from Corralitos to Monterey for export. Nothing remains of these redwood forests except a few small second-growth clumps e.g., near Corralitos Road and in Larkin Valley. The redwood normally regenerates quickly from stumps, but virtually all stumps were removed by agriculturists: Long-time residents here state that as late as the 1880s, their parents grubbed and burned redwood stumps in preparing land for the plough. Sizable redwood groves are now to be found only in the hills to the east. (Note the isolated trees on the upper slope and skyline.)

Of the redwoods that once grew on the Pajaro floodplain, one isolated grove remains; it is located across the Pajaro River near the Logan Quarry, just to the south of the area photographed. (Photo B. Gordon) throughout the Monterey Bay area by the construction of irrigation ponds.

3.6.3. Coastal-Dune Vegetation

Coastal dunes are most extensive along the shores of the southern half of the bay. Much of their original plant cover has been destroyed by residential development, sand mining, and highway construction. Dune-buggies, military vehicles, and other traffic have damaged the remainder.

One of the larger and least disturbed tracts of coastal-dune vegetation lies between Moss Landing and Mulligan Hill. A brief description of dune vegetation in that vicinity is given below:

The distribution of dune plants has a zonal character (Bluestone, 1981), with the various species arranged roughly according to distance from shoreline. This spacing is controlled mainly by offshore winds which determine the intensity of sand-blast and the inland penetration of salt-spray. One strong contrast is that between the narrow band of foredunes, facing the sea, and the more extensive reardunes farther inland. At Salinas River State Beach, for example, near the end of Potrero Road, the reardunes rise some 60 ft. above mean sea level, while the foredunes are generally less than 20 ft. above the sea.

Vegetation on the foredunes is largely made up of herbs and diminutive shrubs; these include beach-bur, sea rocket, beach saltbush, beach primrose, beach morning glory, and sea fig.

Woody shrubs—such as mock heather and its common associate, the blue beach lupine—are mostly confined to reardune surfaces. Other typical reardune perennials are bluff lettuce, coast buckwheat, and lizard tail. Since some of these plants, especially mock heather, produce considerable litter, organic material is more abundant there than in the foredunes, and in places the development of a soil profile has begun. Coast cryptantha, seaside amsinckia, and other annuals grow scattered about where shrubs are absent. At the extreme inland edge of the reardunes is a narrow fringe-strip covered by wild roses,

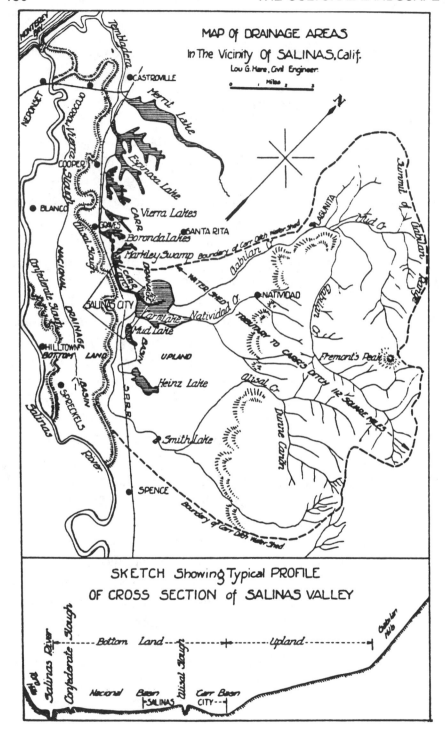

MAP of DRAINAGE AREAS
In The Vicinity Of SALINAS, Calif.
Lou G. Hare, Civil Engineer.

SKETCH Showing Typical PROFILE
OF CROSS SECTION of SALINAS VALLEY

Drainage area in the vicinity of Salinas in 1916, showing distribution of lakes in lower Salinas Valley. Before American settlement, a chain of lakes and marshes extended from Heinz Lake, south of Salinas, northward to the vicinity of Castroville, over 18 km; the lakes have since been drained. (This entire lake system is shown in excellent detail on Hare's earlier map, "Map of Survey for the Improvement of Gabilan Creek," 1906, scale 1 inch to 800 feet.)

Two broad catchment basins are distinguished on the map: The Carr Drainage Basin, in which most of the lakes were located (named after the former Carr Lake), and the Nacional Basin, between Alisal and Confederate sloughs. Physiographic evidence indicates considerable shifting of the Salinas River channel in past centuries. For example, Alisal Slough, which runs through Salinas, is the remains of one of the river's old channels (Hare, 1916, p. 4). Although the natural drainage pattern was still recognizable in 1916, it has been almost obliterated within the last half of the twentieth century by drainage operations, field leveling, and the building of artificial levees.

The history of a single small lake in the chain, one of the Vierra Lakes shown on the map between Lakes Espinosa and Boronda, indicates the magnitude of changes made throughout this lake area. The bed of the lake is on the Chinn Ranch, a little over 1 km north of San Jon Road and about 9 km from Monterey Bay. The surrounding terrain is low, the highest land being less than 20 m. The lake bed is 3-6 m above sea level. Pumps keep the bed dry during the rainy season. The area is now used for cultivation of artichokes and other vegetables. Coast live oaks survive on the southwest side—the only trees in the vicinity.

When the Costanoans lived here, shallow lakes, patches of tule and other marsh herbs, and broad willow thickets covered the lower parts of the county, surrounded on higher ground by oak woodland. The original marsh fauna is unknown.

There has been considerable earth moving in and around the lake bed to reduce slopes for cultivation. In 1967, in grading the west bank, which rises about 8 m above the lake bed, some 48 Indian graves were exposed. Later about a dozen more burials were uncovered. The skeletons were in a flexed. seated position, the heads of some capped with inverted, bowl-shaped stone mortars—implements that suggest the use of herb seeds or acorns. Mussel and clam shells and various mammal and bird bones intermixed with the dark soil scraped from the site indicate that a village was located on or near the burial grounds, the villagers drawing on the food resources of lake, woodland, marsh, and sea.

Left undisturbed, the area would gradually be reclaimed by native plant life, and the lake bed soon covered with water again. During very rainy weather as much as 100,000 liters (25,000 gallons) of water per minute are pumped from the bed, for as long as 15 days. There can be little subsurface drainage, as the peaty soil beneath the bed remains waterlogged throughout the year. Just one such pumping period removes enough water to produce a lake averaging 1.7 m deep.

In Costanoan times most of the water in the lake evaporated during the dry months. But since the bed was not originally flat, the depth varied, and water holes probably lasted through the summer. Since 1.7 m is too deep for tule and cattail, the original lake would have had areas of open water during the winter season which would have attracted migrant waterfowl.

blackberries, and willows; inland from the dunes, these meet salt-marsh vegetation.

Sand is moved along the coast by longshore drift, and carried to the swash zone by ocean waves. As beach sand dries, it is lifted by offshore winds and transported to the foredunes where its movement is slowed by plants. The foredunes are among the least stable of terrestrial environments, and plants growing there are adapted to constant change.

By far the most active plants in the formation and stabilization of the dune area as a whole come from the foredune zone. Some of these plants are actually dune-builders—that is, they not only slow the movement of sand, but trap it in place: As the sand accumulates over them, the plants—by constantly putting up shoots to reach the new surface—gradually form hillocks. Foredune plants extend the dune area seaward; for example, at Salinas River State Beach and to the north of Moss Landing, sea rocket and beach-bur form low sand mounds on the upper beach—generally less than a foot high. Most of these are washed away in winter storms, but on those that survive the sea rocket and beach-bur are joined then succeeded by beach morning glory, yellow sand verbena, and sea fig. Hillocks are formed which rise over 15 feet above mean sea level. Thus, dune plants—rather than simply reflecting edaphic conditions—play an important part in shaping the terrain.

Where the dune plant cover is broken by violent gusts, blowouts (wind-scoured depressions with bare sand exposed) may appear. A number of pioneer plants (plants able to quickly colonize bare sand) start the successional process and stop further erosion. Storm waves often reclaim parts of the dunes for the sea by eroding broad stretches of foredune (for example, north of the Salinas River mouth in early 1995). This, too, exposes bare sand. Thus dune vegetation is subject to frequent natural disturbance.

Not only do the foredune plants extend dunes seaward on to the beach—they also act in the reardunes. There, such foredune pioneers as beach-bur, coastal sagewort, and yellow sand verbena colonize blowouts and stabilize surfaces. (Beach-bur and sea rocket follow footpaths all the way from the beach to the inland edge of the dunes— growing on the churned sand.) In contrast, reardune species rarely colonize the foredune area.

Dune life is a complex and interacting assemblage of species, with the natural vegetation supporting a characteristic fauna. Dune herbivores vary widely in their subsistence needs. Because the food needs of some (including native butterflies and many other insects) are quite specific and cannot be met by alien species, elimination of native plants results in local extinction of the dependent animals as well.

The vulnerability of dune life along the California coast, as well as the dependence of dune animals on native plants, is well illustrated in the fate of three butterflies—one extinct, and two endangered: (1) The Xerces blue was last seen in 1944 in the dunes near San Francisco—the "only species of butterfly known to have become extinct during recorded U.S. history" (Powell and Hogue, 1979, p. 242); the butterfly is believed to have fed on a species of lotus; (2) Smith's blue, which feeds on two species of wild buckwheat in dunes of the Monterey Bay area, is an endangered species; and (3) the Moro blue near Morro Bay, whose host plant appears to be the blue beach lupine (Emmel and Emmel, 1973, p. 67). The dune habitat of the Moro blue, partly destroyed by dune buggies, is now threatened by residential development. Other rare or distinctive animals present in these coastal dunes include the black legless lizard, the coast horned lizard, and the globose dune beetle (*Sandpaper*, October, 1944, p. 3) —and, on neighboring beaches, the snowy plover.

Dunes in the southern part of the Monterey Bay area appear to be richer in species than those in the north—perhaps because dunes cover a larger area there, and the dune sands are more varied: Tidestrom's lupine, Menzies' wallflower, sandmat manzanita, sand gilia, and others, present on dunes in the southern part of the bay, are rare or absent north of the Salinas River.

Dune-building plants forming a hillock in the foredunes. Beach morning glory on slopes and sea fig on the crest. (Photo B. Gordon)

Beach sagewort and yellow sand verbena on inner foredunes near Moss Landing Marine laboratories. (Photo B. Gordon)

Marram grass (also known in America as European beach grass or Holland dune grass), was brought to San Francisco in 1869, and used there to stabilize the shifting dunes which later became Golden Gate Park. In 1919, marram grass was planted on dunes near the mouth of the Pajaro River (Locke-Paddon, 1964). This is the earliest known reference to its use in the Monterey Bay area. Marram grass spreads mainly by growth of its long horizontal rhizomes. Hillocks formed by marram grass are often higher and steeper-sloped than those formed by native dune builders.

The vegetation of coastal dunes is notoriously fragile. In addition to ecological considerations, the protection of this plant cover is important simply from an engineering standpoint. Where broad surfaces are denuded, sand is blown inland onto farmland and highways. In places the dunes are essential protection against marine flooding. Parts of the alluvial plain inland from the dunes at Salinas River State Park are less than 2 m (6 feet) above mean sea level, an elevation almost within the range of highest tides. (Estimated highest possible waters along this coast are 2.4 m [8 feet] above mean lower low water—that is, about 1.6 m [5.2 feet]—above mean sea level. Removal of the dunes would certainly expose fields inland from the dunes to ocean wave action. At the end of Potrero Road, foot traffic has already reduced the dunes to dangerously low levels. In areas where the natural plant cover has been completely destroyed, marram grass has been used to prevent the migration of dunes inland.

Hottentot fig, another introduced species, has spread in parts of the dune area, suppressing the growth of other plants; as is the case with marram grass, the number of native animals living in areas covered with Hottentot fig is also sharply reduced. In places, pampas grass has also invaded the dunes, but the most universally distributed of all introduced sand plants is the sea rocket, a European species now found on almost every beach and dune in the area.

Because coastal dunes are subject to natural disturbance frequently—and the process of plant succession, constantly interrupted—introduced foreign plants are not crowded-out so readily by natives there as in more stable environments.

3.7. Potential Natural Vegetation

Taking into account the many natural changes in relief and sea level known to have occurred along this coast in the geologic past, one may well ask whether the potential natural vegetation itself is not so variable as to make the concept useless for land-use planning. In answer, brief comment is made here upon the rate and magnitude of environmental change in the Monterey Bay area as it relates to a planner's time scale.

Admittedly, environmental history before European settlement is poorly known. But available evidence indicates that the area has long had a mild and foggy maritime climate, and did not experience such drastic climatic oscillations during the Pleistocene Period as are known to have occurred elsewhere, for instance in the northeastern United States. Abrupt changes in relief and drainage may occur with little corresponding local climatic change: Thus, the changes in sea level that produced the spectacular marine terraces of the Monterey Bay area (especially clearly marked as one looks northward from Natural Bridges State Park) were a response both to local tectonic activities and to worldwide climatic changes not strongly expressed here. In fact, paleobotanical evidence indicates that despite all such fluctuations, most of the native trees and shrubs mentioned in this text have survived in the area at least since mid-Pleistocene times—that is, for hundreds of thousands of years—grouped in plant associations very like those that exist today (Mason, 1934, p. 120). If we make the reasonable assumption that all these plants have not synchronously experienced marked and parallel changes in their physiologic requirements, and studies elsewhere indicate that this is unlikely (Whittaker, 1969)— such evidence suggests past climatic conditions not dissimilar to those of the present. Small post-Pleistocene climatic changes may have produced some redistribution of the natural plant associations in the

Although marram grass is unequaled as a dune stabilizer, its great shortcoming is that it excludes native species. The vegetation in the old mouth of Elkhorn Slough is a good example: In 1946 the effluent of Elkhorn Slough was displaced southward to its present location near Moss Landing, and dunes began to form in the 0.5-km stretch that marks the slough's old mouth. By 1977, this stretch of dunes was more or less vegetated. A patch of marram grass had been planted at the extreme north end of the stretch a short time earlier. (The straight rows of the planted grass were still visible, with a few coastal sagewort plants growing between.) Elsewhere the knolls were covered with intermixtures of beach-bur, sea fig, beach morning glory, yellow sand verbena, and sea rocket. In the swales there was much bare sand and considerable sand movement. Mock heather (characteristic of stabilized reardunes), though present immediately to the north and south of the stretch, was absent. By 1995, the plant cover had changed little, except that beneath the patch of marram grass, the dunes were higher and more stable than elsewhere in the stretch. Dunes formed by marram grass (shown in the center background) are also steeper-sloped and more pointed than those formed by other dune-building plants.Despite the passage of almost twenty years, no native pioneer species grew with the marram grass—the coastal sagewort having entirely disappeared.

Monterey Bay area. But despite the prolonged and irregular fluctuations (especially droughts) that appear in historical records, there is little evidence of a significant climatic trend during the last two thousand years. All in all, it is reasonable to assume that well into the future human inhabitants of the Monterey Bay area will be dealing with the same native plant species (barring their extinction by misuse of the land), and that natural environmental controls similar to those of the present will continue their potent molding action.

How similar is the present potential natural vegetation of the area to that of some two centuries ago when the first Spanish settlers arrived—taking into account the many man-made changes in plant cover? Have not so many irreversible changes been made that the two potentials are quite different? Plant successional study indicates that this is not the case. Granted, the actual extinction of a species is indeed an irreversible act, but the number of Monterey Bay area species known to have been completely exterminated is as yet relatively small. Although man-induced genetic changes have been made in some native species, most of the environmental changes made, sweeping though they may have been, are by no means so fundamental. For example, pumping of water from the many wells in the area has lowered the water table, and in places this no doubt slows reestablishment of natural vegetation. But groundwater tables would soon rise if pumping were discontinued. On the other hand, soil formation proceeds slowly, and erosion of the A-horizon long delays revival of the original plant cover.

Aware of the extermination of native species by aliens that is taking place in such island biotas as those of Hawaii and New Zealand, local conservationists are understandably concerned about the effects of foreign species in the Monterey Bay area. The subject is controversial, and generalization is difficult. In 1994, the Bureau of Land Management reported a widespread invasion of western rangelands by Eurasian weeds (*Science*, 265:1178-1179, 1994). That this has happened is not surprising—considering the fact that those rangelands have been grazed (often overgrazed) for more than a century by domesticated Eurasian sheep, bovine cattle, feral horses, and donkeys:

Before their arrival, most of these weeds had the advantage of several thousand years of selection for an ability to survive grazing by these animals—and for the ability to thrive on soils churned by their hooves. There is little evidence that these introduced plants displace native species on truly undisturbed sites. If such displacement occurs, probably little can now be done about it. Certainly, paleobotanical records show that, under natural conditions, the floras of different areas have intermixed considerably over the ages. Nevertheless, there is a large literature demonstrating that in most of the world successional processes tend to exclude the plants and animals that humans have transported—either deliberately or inadvertently—from place to place. This is the case even in areas like Europe where people have been disturbing the terrain for tens of millennia. Generally, the introduced plants of the Monterey Bay area are a threat to native species not because of their direct competition, but rather because persistent human disturbance of natural habitats creates new environmental conditions which favor aliens over natives.

Some plants and animals have greater roles in ecological processes than do others. Some have even been designated "keystone species" (defined as a "species whose removal may lead to a series of extinctions in an ecosystem"). Of the native plants hereabouts, coyote brush and live oak are clearly among the most bountiful providers for native animal life. Introduced plant species vary similarly: Many native herbivores feed to some extent on introduced plants—among which they often show distinct preferences. Thus, in considering their benefits to the total ecology of the Monterey Bay area, introduced decorative and weedy plants should (rather than coming under a blanket condemnation) be evaluated on the basis of how much support each gives to native animal life, and to which animal species. Other factors should be considered as well, such as the differing contributions the various introduced plants (e.g., those of the legume family) make to soil quality, and so on.

What would the successional chain of events be were the Monterey Bay area suddenly depopulated? Plant growth in abandoned orchards and farms suggests a rough outline: Truckcrop species would disappear forthwith. Most of the weeds now associated with tilled land would follow. Grasses and forbs, partly exotic and partly native species, would replace them. Exotic plants would disappear in an order scarcely related to their historical order of arrival: Some of the first to arrive (e.g., the wild radish) would be among the first losers in successional competition, whereas the wild oat, introduced at about the same time, might even find a permanent niche for itself (perhaps within a reestablished grassland of native perennials)—but within a much restricted area.

Several other introduced plants might persist on sites subject to constant *natural* disturbance, such as stream margins and coastal dunes (sites which are very similar to those they occupy in their homelands): Tree tobacco, an early arrival, is one of the few introduced woody plants that might remain; it is firmly established along rocky stream courses in the Gabilans and elsewhere. Forget-me-not, a more recent introduction, thrives on sand bars along the streams deep in the redwood forest of the Santa Cruz Mountains. The sea rocket would no doubt survive. Marram grass and Hottentot fig might persist for some time, replacing natural vegetation in parts of the dunes. Whether they would survive in the long term is difficult to say, since both owe their overall distribution largely to recent planting programs. Furthermore, the Hottentot fig is cold-sensitive; for instance it lost territory during the freeze of December, 1990. In the Monterey Bay area, there are few cases in which introduced plants can be said to threaten native plants directly—that is to say, without prior human disturbance of the environment.

Narrow strips of shrubby ecotone vegetation would broaden into wide transitional belts and, for a time, such plants as coyote brush, poison oak, Pacific blackberry, and coffee berry would flourish. In orchards, for instance, this shrubby undergrowth would grow taller and, aided by invading live oak, suppress the orchard trees within a few decades. Thus, grassland and pasture areas would shrink—grasses, filarees, etc., dying off beneath overgrowing shrubs. The ecotone shrub phase would be followed in parts of the area by a long oak-woodland phase. Slowly, Douglas fir would intermix in moister parts of the oak woodland, and redwood would somewhat extend its range toward the coast in valley bottoms. Oak woodland without admixed conifers would remain and spread on thin soils and exposed hilltops—areas such as the Aromas Red Sands. Probably within a century the plant cover of the Monterey Bay area would be similar to that seen by Vizcaíno and Fages: Oak woodland, Douglas fir, and redwood groves covering the lower parts of the northern bay area; oak woodland and perennial grasses in the Salinas Valley; blue oak and digger pine on the upper slopes and chaparral covering the lower slopes of the Gabilans; broad strips of riparian forest and freshwater marshes on the floodplains of the Salinas and Pajaro rivers; and so on.

Granted, the present trend in the Monterey Bay area is definitely not toward depopulation. Nevertheless, the concept of potential natural vegetation and the principles of plant succession can be usefully applied as the rural and urban biocommunities expand.

4

Faunal Changes

FEW NATIVE ANIMALS are unaffected by human-made environmental change. Native species unable to adjust to human activities have suffered either extinction, or a decline in population numbers. Others, more adaptable to human presence, thrive. Many foreign species have been introduced—but, for the most part, they flourish only in the cultural landscape.

1. Mammals

1.1. Extinct Mammals

Off Monterey, an approximately 19,000-year-old skull fragment of Steller's sea cow was dredged from the seafloor (Jones, 1967, p. 143): Presumably, sea cows once foraged along the shores of Monterey Bay. These gigantic kelp-eaters, which are claimed to have been as much as 26 feet (8 m) long and to have weighed up to 10 metric tons (Scheffer, 1972), survived on the Commander Islands in the Bering Sea until the mid-eighteenth century—when the last was exterminated by hunters. Trophic relationships in Monterey Bay's kelp beds would have been quite different when sea cows competed for food with invertebrate herbivores such as the sea urchin. Another major difference: There seem to have been no abalone in the area at that time (Addicott, 1966, p. C2). Whether sea cows were still present in the Monterey Bay area when the first human settlers arrived is unknown.

A number of large land mammals (horses, camels, ground sloths, etc.) became extinct in western North America about the time that humans arrived, or shortly thereafter. Probably the earliest human inhabitants of coastal California were, like their contemporaries farther inland, hunters of large land mammals—including the mammoth (Meighan, 1965, p. 718). According to many authorities, mammoths survived along California's coast until well after the maximum lowering of sea level at the close of the Pleistocene. Thus, the animals once ranged beyond the present shoreline into lands that are now deep beneath water: On the Channel Islands the remains of several hundred mammoths have been found in sea cliffs, exposed by wave erosion (Orr, 1969, p. 31, 35); mammoth remains have also been found at, or near, the present shoreline in other parts of coastal California. Among the last to disappear was a population of dwarf mammoths (some no more than 4-6 ft. tall) on Santa Rosa Island. These may have survived until 8000 years ago (Meighan, 1969, p. 711); according to some, human hunters were responsible for their extinction (Orr, 1969, pp. 79-85).

Porcupine bones have been found in the Santa Lucia mountains in middens that are some 3000 years old; thus the porcupine may have existed at that time in the Carmel Valley (Morejohn, 1976b, pp. 77, 79). The porcupine seems to have survived into historical times in this part of California. Between 1825 and 1828, the naturalists of a British expedition wrote the following description of Indian handicrafts: "They embroidered belts very beautifully with feathers . . . making use of the *young quills of the porcupine*" (Beechey, 1831, p. 76).

Some historical evidence suggests that the jaguar once ranged northward into California: In the early nineteenth century, several scientific expeditions collected descriptions of a cat, larger than and otherwise different from the mountain lion, living near Monterey Bay (Merriam, 1919, pp. 38-39). If the jaguar was once present here, it disappeared before American settlement began.

The first account of the California grizzly comes from the Vizcaíno party at Monterey in 1602. The bears were seen feeding on a whale carcass that had drifted onto the beach. The California grizzly was a remarkably omnivorous animal, and the bear was offered a great new food supply when Spanish settlers established the cattle industry in the last part of the eighteenth century. Only hides and tallow were marketed; only choice cuts were eaten. Horses became so numerous that they threatened the range and had to be killed by the thousands. Herds were driven into the sea at Monterey in 1810 (Vallejo, 1890, p. 189). "With so many dead bodies of domestic animals to be had without effort, grizzlies . . . multiplied as they had never done before" (Storer, 1955, p. 130).

Grizzlies were so numerous that, in 1792, soldiers at Mission Santa Cruz were sent out to hunt them (Torchiana, 1933, p. 193); near Monterey during the decade 1801-1810, bears often ate cattle before the eyes of the herdsmen (Bancroft, 1888, II, pp. 142-143). In December 1802, the *Provincial State Papers of Monterey* reported that bears, mountain lions, wolves, and coyotes had killed 207 cattle of the government hacienda's herd of 2284 during the year. Bull-and-bear fights became common entertainment during the Spanish-Mexican period and lasted over into the early American period. Bear-and-bull fights were held at Monterey, Carmel, Castroville, and elsewhere. A pioneer American in Watsonville in 1852 recalls that "here at First and Main Streets we would have bullfights and occasionally a grizzly bear and bullfight" (Kitchen, 1952, unpaginated).

As noted above, the first account of bear in the Monterey Bay area (no doubt a grizzly, since the black bear is not native along the coast south of San Francisco) describes it as feeding on a whale carcass lying on the beach. This food supply was later augmented by the whaling industry: "the grizzlies fed on the offal that floated ashore" (Storer, 1955, p. 58).

The California grizzly appears to have been especially gregarious; several accounts refer to its congregating on beaches. In September

1846, John C. Fremont's party, traveling in the Salinas Valley, came upon a number of grizzlies in the oaks; the party killed 12, and others escaped (Fremont, 1887, p. 571). In the 1870s and 1880s, grizzlies were still frequently reported in the Monterey Bay area. A rancher named Waddell was killed by a grizzly on the Rancho del Oso (Bear Ranch), near a stream now called Waddell Creek. In 1878, the sheriff of Salinas and his party "while hunting back of Tassajara Springs saw a huge grizzly bear. Pine Valley is full of grizzly at present" (*Overton Manuscript*, 1877, p. 18).

The Americans adopted the grizzly as a symbol on the California State flag. Nevertheless, as large steel traps, strychnine and, in later years, the repeating rifle came into use, the bear population decreased. The last recorded killing of a grizzly in Santa Cruz County was in 1885. Farther south, grizzlies were seen in the Santa Lucia Mountains as late as 1896 (von Bloeker, 1938, p. 158). Although the grizzly was probably extinct in the Monterey Bay area itself before the turn of the century, the animal survived into the twentieth century elsewhere. (The last California grizzly was seen in Sequoia National Park in 1924.)

The outstanding authority on the California grizzly suggests that a graph of its population numbers

would have shown a long plateau through the centuries with minor ups and downs, then a rise in numbers—particularly in the coastal regions adjacent to the missions where cattle were abundant—that reached a peak about the time of the American occupation. This was followed by a quick descent—a half century or less . . . to the base line, extinction. (Storer, 1955, p. 26)

The gray wolf became extinct in California at about the same time as the grizzly (Ingles, 1954, p. 122)—and in the Monterey Bay area, much earlier. But little is known about its former range. Spanish cattlemen at Monterey annually imported a vegetable poison known as *hierba de Puebla* from Mexico to reduce the wolf population. When shipments were not forthcoming, the industry reportedly suffered (Roquefeuil, 1923, p. 75).

Before American settlement, tule elk were plentiful in the lowlands of the Monterey Bay area, especially in and around the marshes of the lower Salinas and Pajaro valleys. Although it has been known by several names, Elkhorn Slough probably got its present name from the elk, antlers having often been found there and in the neighboring Pajaro Valley (Hans Struve, personal communication; also Reid, 1963, p. 13).

Actually, the largest herds of tule elk were in the bulrush, or tule, marshes of California's Central Valley. There, as in the Monterey Bay area, the elk survived throughout the period of Spanish settlement. Several early accounts show that the Spanish treated the elk pretty much like cattle:

The reindeer [tule elk] is found inland, particularly upon a plain called Tularayos [Tulare Basin in the San Joaquin Valley], on account of the large number of bulrushes growing there . . . . *The Spanish resort to this plain with their lassos,* and take as many of these animals as they can ensnare, for the sake of their fat . . . . (Beechey, 1831, pp. 79-80)

The great tracts of marshland in the San Joaquin Valley were drained by the Americans for agricultural use, and the animals were hunted, there and in various parts of central California, for shipment to San Francisco markets. By the early 1870s the elk herds of the Sacramento-San Joaquin Valley were reduced to a few individuals (Evermann, 1916, pp. 70-71).

As noted earlier, bones of the elk have been found in Costanoan middens. In 1602, the explorer Viscaíno mentioned the presence of elk near the southern shore of Monterey Bay: "Among the animals there are large fierce bears, and other animals called elks, from which they [the Indians] make elkleather jackets." The animal was reported by other early explorers of the area, and it survived here throughout the period of the Spanish cattle industry.

One American settler whose childhood was spent at Gilroy, remembered his family's going "over the mountains to the Pajaro Valley to hunt elk and returning with wagon loaded. At times the trip extended down to the Salinas plains" (Evermann, 1915, pp. 89-90). A French acquaintance of this settler, who had come to California in either 1843 or 1846 and lived in the vicinity of what is now Pajaro Junction, "often spoke of the sport he had killing elk here, saying that on occasions the vaqueros would ride *among them and the cattle*, single one out, ride him down and hamstring him with a machete." He also spoke "rather bitterly of the Americans' killing them so wastefully" (Evermann, 1915, pp. 89-90). Another settler, writing of the year 1852, said, "There were plenty of elk in the Castroville hills" (Kitchen, 1952, unpaginated). Elk are said to have survived nearby in San Benito County until 1864.

In 1977 there were some six or seven hundred tule elk in existence; there are now about 2900, none in the Monterey Bay area. The largest herds are in San Luis Obispo County.

Is it possible to reestablish the elk in the Monterey Bay area? Actually, an attempt was made earlier in this century. But the animals did not flourish here—possibly because of poor selection of sites: Elk were transported to enclosures at Big Basin, an area of redwood forest and never elk country; elk were also brought to Seventeen Mile Drive, an area of Monterey pine and sand dunes (about 15 descendants survived there as late as 1936); and a few elk were brought to Laveaga Park at Santa Cruz (Evermann, 1915, pp. 73, 76), another wooded area and by no means natural tule elk habitat. Probably the most promising area for reestablishment attempts in the Monterey Bay area is around Elkhorn Slough itself, if a large enough parcel of land were available there.

The fact that tule elk shared rangeland with cattle in Spanish times suggests research on the possibility of running elk and cattle together again. It has been claimed that in some areas increasing the number of herbivore species on rangeland helps to maintain vegetative diversity, and that the carrying capacity of rangeland under shared use may be greater than under use by one species alone.

To the south of the Monterey Bay area some Rocky Mountain elk were brought to San Simeon and released on the William R. Hearst Ranch. Some of these animals escaped into the wild and their descendants make up the existing Santa Lucia Mountain herd (Dasmann, 1965, p. 22). The Rocky Mountain race of elk, however, prefers a mountainous and forested habitat and cannot be thought of as a replacement for the native tule elk, in terms of restoring the natural setting.

Pronghorn antelope also ranged over the grass-covered parts of the Salinas Valley when the Spanish arrived. The explorers repeatedly mention the animal. For example, on September 27, 1769, Father Crespi reported from the area between King City and Greenfield, "We saw in this day's march two bands of antelope some distance from us." And the next day, from around the present site of Greenfield itself, "some bands of antelope were seen but not within gunshot" (Bolton, 1927 p. 199). In the year 1770, Pedro Fages reported from the vicinity of Chualar "seeing many herds of antelopes, some of them exceeding 50" (1911, p. 149). The antelope seems to have been most numerous in the drier country to the south of Salinas (while the tule elk was mainly in the swampier area to the north). The antelope appears to have become almost extinct here within a short time after the Spanish cattle industry began; there seem to be no records of them in the nineteenth century except for the following notes: According to an old-timer's account of an excursion made in January 1852, "We rode along the hills on the east and northeast side of the Salinas Plains [that is, along the west base of the northern Gabilans] . . . . We saw several bear and plenty of deer and *antelope*" (*The Salinas City Index*, Feb. 15, 1877). And "older settlers can remember the time in the Hildreth and Dunphy herding days when *antelope were not uncommon on the Salinas plains from Gonzales southward*" (*Monterey Democrat*, June 30, 1888, p. 6). There were also antelope in the upper drainage of the Pajaro River in the Santa Clara Valley (Robinson, 1947, p. 69). Probably the antelope's grassland haunts were quickly taken over by cattle, while the tule elk survived a little longer in marshier, hence for cattlemen less usable, areas downriver.

The ranges of two fur seals, the northern (Pribilof) fur seal and the Guadalupe fur seal, once overlapped along the California coast.

The bones of both have been found in Indian middens in the Monterey Bay area. The fact that bones of *young* northern fur seal pups have been found in middens at Año Nuevo suggests that the animal formerly bred in this general area (Rice, 1977, p. 3).

In the early nineteenth century, fur seals were killed for their skins in great numbers on the Farallon Islands. According to one estimate, the total number of fur seals killed along the California coast "must have exceeded 400,000" (Evermann, 1923, p. 524). The identity of these seals has long been in question, but in the Monterey Bay area and northward, the great majority were probably northern fur seals.

The northern fur seal, protected by international treaty since 1911, is numerous on the islands of the north Pacific. In addition to the Farallons (where its rookery had been wiped out by 1846) and the Monterey Bay area, the seal probably once bred in a number of places between Alaska and southern California. (An isolated southern rookery still exists on San Miguel Island.) Northern fur seals pass along this coast in winter and spring, but they now keep well offshore.

The Guadalupe fur seal was already rare by the mid-nineteenth century. In 1892 it survived only on Guadalupe Island off northern Baja California; even there an investigator was able to find "only 7 animals in 11 days of search" (Repinning et al., 1971, p. 27). Although it was believed to be extinct during the first years of the twentieth century, the seal was rediscovered on the island in 1926. Two hundred and forty were counted on Guadalupe Island in 1964 (Dougherty, 1965, p. 57). Under protection by the Mexican government, the Guadalupe fur seal population is slowly growing; nevertheless, the animal is still precariously close to extinction. None have returned to the Monterey Bay area.

1.2. Native Mammals That Have Been Reduced in Numbers

In the first years of shore whaling, gray whales were so abundant near the coast "that towing them more than two or three miles was not necessary" (Scofield, 1954, p. 88). The whales came close inshore: They swam through kelp beds, and were even "often seen among the breakers, where they were tossed about by the groundswell, and where the water is hardly deep enough to float them" (Goode, 1884, pp. 31-32).

When shore whaling began, some 30,000 gray whales were estimated to have passed southward along the coast each season, though some consider this to be in excess of the actual number. In 1874, the number was thought to be less than 8000 to 10,000 (Goode [quoting Scammon], 1884, pp. 31-32). In 1900, the total gray whale population was probably considerably less than 2000, few of which came south along the California coast. The reduction in local whale numbers is evidenced in whale-company records: At Moss Landing during three seasons, 1919-1921, 734 whales were landed; only 3 were gray whales (Starks, 1922, p. 16).

Considering the volume of zooplankton and other food animals consumed by these large mammals, such fluctuations in their numbers must considerably alter trophic relationships in coastal waters though, actually, this effect may have been less marked in the Monterey Bay area than northward, since the gray whale appears to do its heaviest feeding while in higher latitudes. Taking into account similar exploitation of other marine animals here, it is clear that population ratios between species are generally unstable, the near-shore ecosystem as a whole being constantly in a state of adjustment to human interference.

The gray whale was declared an endangered species and protected by law in 1938. In 1961, there were thought to be about 6000 (Dougherty, 1965, p. 24). The 1976 population was estimated at over 11,000—an unusually rapid recovery rate among depleted whale populations. Each year more are seen passing coastal headlands in the Monterey Bay area, and the animal is no longer considered endangered.

The northern sea otter, protected by international agreement, is relatively numerous from the Alaskan coast to the Commander Islands of the western Bering Sea, with the total population there estimated at between 120,000 and 130,000. The southern sea otter, on the other hand, was thought to be extinct during the first decades of the twentieth century. Then, in 1938, a herd of about 100 was discovered south of Carmel in Monterey County. Since that time it has become one of the most closely guarded and intensively studied wild animals. In June 1969, in a census made by California Fish and Game, 1014 sea otters were counted between Monterey Bay and Morro Bay. About 250 of these were in the Monterey-Carmel area. By 1976, the total population had grown to 1561. In 1977, the southern sea otter was officially declared a "threatened species." In 1995, the total number living within the limits of the Monterey Bay National Marine Sanctuary was some 1277. Thus, the population has grown slowly. On the other hand, the animal's range has increased, and it has become much less fearful of people: Sea otters are now found well to the north of Pigeon Point. Within the bay proper, sea otters are common near Hopkins Marine Station and near Natural Bridges State Park in Santa Cruz. They frequently enter Elkhorn Slough and are even occasionally seen in Moss Landing Harbor itself—near Sandholdt Bridge.

The sea otter's principal foods are mussels, sea urchins, and abalone —animals found on rocky shores and among kelp beds in shallow offshore waters. Thus its habitat is restricted; it is generally situated less than 1.6 km (1 mile) from shoreline and in water less than 30 m (100 feet) deep; in short, within that part of the sea which is today subject to the most garbage accumulation and pollution. Even with the legal protection that it enjoys, the sea otter probably will not reestablish itself in great numbers.

The elephant seal, a huge animal carrying a large mass of blubber, once ranged from Baja California northward to Point Reyes. Males reach a length of over 4 m (13 feet) and may weigh some 1814 kg (4000 pounds). The animal, which shows little fear of man, had been almost exterminated for its oil in 1869 (Scammon, 1968). By the end of the nineteenth century the estimated population was less than 100 (Radford et al., 1965, p. 602), living mainly on Guadalupe Island, off Baja California. As a result of protective measures the elephant seal has made a remarkable recovery. In 1911, the Mexican government prohibited killing it on Guadalupe Island; by 1930, the population there had built up to about 500, estimated then to be one-third of the total number. In 1937, elephant seals were occasionally seen north of the Mexican boundary, but they did not appear as far north as the Monterey Bay area (von Bloeker, 1937, p. 207). Since then, the elephant seal has spread northward and recovered a large part of its original range. In 1955, several were discovered on Año Nuevo Island. The island has become an important breeding ground; 483 were counted on the island in 1963 (Orr and Poulter, 1965, p. 400). In 1995, there were approximately 4000 elephant seal at Año Nuevo State Reserve during the breeding season. The total population is estimated at over 30,000, with the center still in the Guadalupe Island area.

The mountain lion lives mainly in remote and mountainous country. It was hunted relentlessly during the first half of the twentieth century: In California, "A total of 5811 lions was submitted for bounties from 1907 to 1929 inclusive; the annual total is now [i.e. in 1931] 300" (Storer, 1932, p. 173). Legislation removed the bounty on the animal in 1967. Since then growth in the animal's population and increased human use of its favored habitats have resulted in its being more commonly sighted. In the 1990s several sightings not far from suburban parts of the Monterey Bay area were reported. In December, 1994, a woman was killed in Cuyamaca Rancho State Park in Southern California by a mountain lion. Unfortunately, such tragic, but most unusual, events may be used to justify some sort of extermination program. Regarding the danger that native predators like the mountain lion and great white shark pose for humans, this much can be said from a statistical standpoint: More people have been injured or killed while driving to see a popular horror movie *about* the shark, than by the shark itself. And many more people have been injured or killed by by pet dogs (indeed, by pit bulls alone) than by mountain lions. Ought we ban dogs, cars, and movies? Policy should be based on realistic threats to human safety.

Trapped and hunted for its fur—and earlier because of its occasional raids of farmers' poultry—bobcat numbers have been kept down. During the first half of the twentieth century, when more of the area was rural, special efforts were made to destroy the animals: "One hundred and seventeen bobcats were killed in this county [Monterey] by members of the Salinas Rod and Gun Club between January 1 and October 1, 1937" (von Bloeker, 1938, p. 199).

1.3. Native Mammals That Are Now More Numerous than in Aboriginal Times

Before the arrival of American settlers, black-tailed deer were very plentiful in parts of the coastal country that had been cleared by the Indians and Spanish. The following is a note from a record kept by a visiting party of Americans traveling between Año Nuevo and

Black-tailed deer, near Corral de Tierra Road. The animals find ideal habitat where oak woodland, chaparral, and grassland come together. (Photo Kira Corser)

Monterey in 1833: "In the evening the hunters all returned to camp with the tongues of 93 deer and some of the hides" (Leonard, 1934, p. 156). This suggests a surprising abundance of deer. It also recalls the hunting habits of early Anglo-Americans—soon to be demonstrated, and more tellingly, on the elk and other mammals in this area, as they had been on the bison and passenger pigeon east of the Rockies. Nevertheless, considering the area as a whole, deer may be more numerous now than they ever were.

Deer both graze and browse and have a varied appetite. In the Santa Cruz Mountains the animals damage orchards by feeding on the bark of prune and pear trees. They are often found near the edges of openings; the grassy clearings along the crests of the Santa Cruz Mountains are favorite spots for deer hunters to wait while their hunting companions flush the animals upslope out of forest margins below. "The clearing of foothill and mountain homesteads, the cutting of timber, forest fires, and other events that created openings and led to the spread of palatable herbs and browses have actually improved the deer habitat" (Dasmann, 1965, p. 4).

As noted earlier, limited human settlement does not necessarily lead to an impoverishment of wildlife. In fact, with suitable planning, such settlement may be accompanied by increased variety and abundance. For instance, the following comment bears on the importance for animal life of generating new successional cycles in the plant cover: "influences which tend to keep woody vegetation in a subclimax stage increase the carrying capacity for deer" (Longhurst et al., 1952, p. 45). The main such renewing influence is human activity. Granted, the above comments refer only to deer (which in places are actually already overly plentiful because of the official encouragement they get as a favored game animal), but with a stable human population the principle might apply to other species as well—for example, to deer predators and avifauna.

Sea lion populations have fluctuated greatly because of commercial hunting. During the nineteenth century the animals were killed on a large scale for their oil and for their hides, the latter used in the

California sea lions on the Monterey Harbor breakwater in June 1974. Approximately 200 were in sight when the photo was taken. Observers walk to within a few meters of the resting animals. Note the abundant growth of marine algae on the imported rocks. (Photo B. Gordon)

manufacture of glue. In 1872, sportsmen traveling along the coast shot them for target practice (Evans, 1873). There was also a persistent hunting of sea lions for "trimmings," this being a collective name in the trade for pinniped genitalia; these were dried and sold to the Chinese, "who manufacture from them a preparation for the rejuvenation of the aged" (Bonnot, 1928, p. 15). In 1909, several conservation groups concerned about the survival of the California sea lion sponsored a bill for its protection. Nowadays, a great herd of California sea lions appears seasonally at Año Nuevo Island. They bark almost incessantly (in contrast to the rather quiet Steller's sea lion) making one of the characteristic sounds along rocky stretches of shoreline. A small herd, made up of ever-changing individuals, stays much of the year at Seal Rock near Lighthouse Point, Santa Cruz. The larger herd on the breakwater at Monterey Harbor shows how adaptable the animals are to human presence and activity: The breakwater was not built until 1932.

On sunny mornings they can often be seen assembled closely in groups off Moss Landing. There they float in the water, holding their flippers vertically in the air, and looking in the distance something like rafts drifting at sea.

Thus the animals are numerous in the area now, but that this has only recently been the case can be seen from the following statement made in 1938: "In former times the California sea lion seems to have been fairly abundant as far north as San Francisco, *but at the present time it is rare north of Point Carmel*" (Bonnot, 1928, p. 10). In 1961, 18,400 California sea lions were counted, more than three-quarters of these being in the southern part of the state where the animal breeds. Año Nuevo Island had the largest colony of Steller's sea lions in California: 2300 of the total of 7300 animals in the state were counted there in 1961. The California sea lion is probably at least as common now as it was in aboriginal times, whereas the population of Steller's sea lion has suffered a severe decline.

Note may be made here on the large pinniped herds at Año Nuevo Island Scientific Reserve: It appears that the large numbers there represent more than a renewal at an old center. The population probably was never so large in the past, mainly because of the legal protective measures taken recently, but also because of natural changes: In prehistoric times pinnipeds probably did not enjoy a protected insular rookery because, as noted earlier, it is unlikely that the island of Año Nuevo existed as such—that instead there was only a long, narrow peninsula there—terminating in Point Año Nuevo, and fringed with a few offshore stacks. The Costanoans made this neighborhood something of a population center; there is a concentration of midden sites in the vicinity. Considering the nature of Costanoan foodstuffs, Año Nuevo Point would have been a precarious location for a pinniped rookery, compared to the island as it exists today.

The pocket gopher, historically much favored by the development of agriculture, is one of the foremost mammalian crop pests. Though a native itself, it shows no dietary preference for native over introduced plants. Indeed, introduced plants are probably the principal support of today's large gopher populations. The animal is in no way threatened by the present expansion of suburbs—lawns, flower gardens, and golf courses being amongst its favorite habitats.

The cottontail rabbit is another animal that probably has spread with the extension of its favorite habitat, the ecotone vegetation.

The coyote is often given as an example of an animal that tolerates human presence. It is thought to have been largely a plains animal at one time and to have spread almost throughout the continental United States since European settlement began. It was, however, present in aboriginal California: Coyote bones are a common item in Costanoan middens. In the Monterey Bay area coyote were especially numerous in the days of the Spanish cattle and sheep industries. Spanish accounts refer to them as a nuisance. Naturalists of a British expedition, visiting the Monterey Bay area between 1825 and 1828 reported, "Wolves and foxes are numerous, and *cuiotas*, or jackalls [i.e. coyotes] range about the plains at night, and prove very destructive of sheep" (Beechey, 1831, p. 79; see also p. 56). When the naturalist Nuttall visited Monterey in 1836, he noted that "the prowling wolves, well-fed, were as tame as dogs, and every night yelled familiarly through the village" (Graustein, 1967, p. 314). Nuttall is almost certainly referring here to coyotes.

The raccoon, likewise, tolerates human presence, obtaining part of its food from orchard fruits, like cherries, apricots, prunes, and apples. Food is put out for them around some residences in wooded areas such as the San Lorenzo and Carmel valleys.

Meadow-mouse (vole) populations are known to experience remarkable fluctuations, both under natural conditions and under conditions of human land use. The lower Salinas Valley is California's major artichoke-growing center. The industry was established here in 1922, and by 1925, 1620 hectares (4000 acres) were under cultivation (Jones, 1949, p. 542). In 1994, approximately 2676 hectares (6680 acres) were under cultivation, furnishing over 90% of the U.S. supply of artichokes. The growers' three worst environmental problems here are depredations made on artichoke plants by the meadow mouse and the plume-moth larva and the intrusion of marine salt water. All three problems are closely linked to environmental changes resulting from human activities, present or in the recent past. Unlike many agricultural pests in this part of California, the plume moth and the meadow mouse are native species.

Meadow mice are always pests in the artichoke fields, but during the 1960s they sometimes became a veritable plague. The worst such infestation occurred in 1968, and a lesser one was in progress in 1971. In the summer of 1968, their effect was disastrous. Some growers lost nearly 50% of their crops. The infestation was finally brought under control, in mid-July, by an aerial broadcast of some 9072 kg (20,000 pounds) of rolled oats treated with zinc phosphide, spread over 2830 hectares (7000 acres).

From time to time, caterpillar tractors are used to pull long cutter blades through the fields, severing artichoke stalks from the roots—thus starting the plants on a new growth cycle. Because the mice build their nests among the artichoke stalks slightly below the ground level, most of the nests are exposed by the cutter: Thousands of mice are either mangled or scurry for cover. The mouse population in the fields at such times appears to fall into three age groups: Full-grown adults; animals a little less than half grown, but already covered with hair and with their eyes opened; and hairless newborn with eyes unopened. During its peak reproductive season, the meadow mouse is said to produce up to 12 or even 15 young every 28 days. Litters are produced throughout the year, the average being two to six per year, with 6 to 13 young being born at a time.

Vultures and seagulls swoop in to gorge on mice killed by the cutter blade. The gulls, largely California gulls, catch live young mice for the most part, but some also make off with adults in their beaks. A few crows have been observed to attempt to join the melee, but they are roughly treated by the gulls, often being forced to drop their prey despite the fact that mice are not in short supply. Other predator species, such as red-tailed hawks and kites, have been reported hunting over the fields but in much smaller numbers.

The meadow mouse is the most common rodent in these fields because of its food habits. Although the mouse will eat seeds, it feeds mainly on plant leaves and stems, whereas other mouse species in the vicinity—the deer mouse and the western harvest mouse—are primarily seed eaters, and seed-producing weeds are scarce in the artichoke fields. But reasons for occasional outbursts in the meadow-mouse population are unclear.

Even in untilled areas meadow-mouse populations have been observed to be higher than those of the western harvest mouse and the deer mouse (Brant, 1962, p. 167). And when the land is cultivated, the resulting vegetation favors the meadow mouse more strongly still over other species.

No censuses of the meadow mouse in the Castroville area have been published. However, as a basis of comparison, in one study of an uncultivated field near Berkeley, the widely fluctuating meadow-mouse population was estimated to range, over a period of several years, from less than 2 to 62 per hectare (1 to around 25 per acre) (Brant, 1962, p. 144). Another study near Berkeley detected densities varying between less than 1 to at least 800 per hectare (325 per acre) on one area within a period of three or four years (Krebs, 1966, p. 270). Granted, these counts were themselves not made under natural conditions: The fields studied are overgrown with dominantly alien plants—wild oats, soft chess, wild mustard, etc. Nevertheless, there is an obvious contrast between these Berkeley populations and those of the Castroville artichoke fields. During the Castroville population outburst of May 1971, the number of mice in each artichoke plant cluster averaged at least 6. As the number of plant clusters on a hectare averages 1285 (520 on an acre), the mouse population was at least 7700 per hectare (3120 per acre). In mid-January 1973, the average was slightly less than one mouse per plant cluster; that is, it was still some 1285 mice per hectare (520 per acre). (At that time only about 10% of the nests contained young, and the litters were small—only 2 or 3.) In the Berkeley area it was observed that the meadow mouse avoids riparian vegetation (Brant, 1962, p. 108), which was probably the original cover of the Castroville artichoke fields. This suggests that the species was not nearly so common here under natural conditions and that human-made changes in plant cover were responsible for its increased numbers.

Plainly, raptors and other native predators are now not numerous enough to control the meadow mouse population. Most are discouraged by agricultural activities. As practically all tree growth has been removed from fields under cultivation, roosting places for bird predators such as kites, hawks, and owls have been eliminated.

High meadow mouse populations are by no means confined to artichoke fields; for instance, the mice are sometimes present in great numbers in alfalfa fields. Artichoke growers say that a latent meadow mouse problem remains—that, were the mice not controlled as they now are by improving pesticides, destructive infestations would occur again.

This is yet another instance of the thoroughgoing influence of human action on ecological conditions. People have removed the native riparian plant cover here and introduced exotic plants such as the artichoke and its field weeds, the mustard and oat, thus altering the food base of a native mammal, the meadow mouse. The numbers of most native predators (hawks, owls, etc.) have been reduced, but another, more adaptable species, the gull, has multiplied.

Probably the most commonly seen native mammal in the state is the California (Beechey) ground squirrel. And few animals in the Monterey Bay area better illustrate the control problems created by changing land use and human food habits. Of native mammals the ground squirrel is by far the most costly pest, both in the Monterey Bay area and in the state as a whole. Federal, state, and county agencies have been enlisted in programs for its extermination; millions of dollars have been spent. Only through the use of all manner of poisons, trapping programs, and the payment of bounties has it been possible to keep squirrel numbers in check.

Under natural conditions the ground squirrel probably inhabited the grassy interspaces in oak and foothill woodland. It was no doubt

California ground squirrel. Some of the measures taken to reduce the ground-squirrel population had limited success. In 1891, the County of Monterey published Ordinance 205, requiring the County Clerk to pay "For each and every squirrel killed . . . a bounty of three cents . . . . the scalp of each squirrel with the ears thereon . . . securely strung on a string . . . ." Furthermore, the clerk "shall enter in a book, to be kept for the purpose and designated 'Record of Squirrel Scalps,' the date of the receipt and the number of such scalps . . . ." In 1898, in Ordinance 288, the wording was amended to have the bounty paid "on lots of at least 25 squirrel tails" and the payment noted in a book, "Record of Squirrel Tails." Actually, ground-squirrel numbers were of magnitudes beyond significant influence by bounty hunters. Then, too, 3 cents per squirrel, even in those days, hardly bought traps or ammunition. The ground squirrel is one of several native species that sometimes concentrate at campsites in public parks. For example, a concentration of abnormally plump squirrels, with picnickers' food scraps, scurry between lunch tables and parked cars at Point Lobos State Park. (Photo R. Buchsbaum)

already plentiful before Spanish settlement began; it was a common
food item among the Costanoans. California Indians fanned smoke
into ground-squirrel burrows, catching the animals as they emerged;
in places, squirrel bones are common in kitchen middens. Father Palou,
reporting on Indian foods at Mission San Antonio in the Salinas Valley,
described the squirrels as being "as savory as hares." According to
Europeans traveling later in California, ground squirrels were good
to eat (Beechey, 1831, p. 80). One writer, basing his forecast on
experience in the Atlantic states, predicted that immigrants from the
East, where tree squirrels are hunted for food, would soon do away
with excess ground squirrels here in California:

The Grey Ground-squirrels are so numerous and destructive . . . one of the most
serious pests . . . making their dwelling in the ground, which in many places is
full of their burrows for miles together. Although difficult to exterminate, *they
will probably in a few years become as scarce in the settled districts as the Eastern
squirrels now are* . . . . Our species are *considered pretty good eating when
properly prepared.* (Cronise, 1868, p. 443)

But for some reason, ground squirrels came to be thought of as
unsatisfactory for human food—certainly a turning point in terms of
control prospects.

    After the introduction of cattle and the associated changes in
grasslands, the ground squirrel became even more numerous than it
had been in aboriginal times. And its range was extended by the increase
made in the total area of grassland. Ground squirrels thrive on
overgrazed range. And periods of intensive livestock industry are
associated with increases in squirrel populations. Ranges in the
southern part of the Monterey Bay area were especially heavily grazed
in the 1860s and 1870s. From all accounts, ground squirrels swarmed
over the area during this period of maximum use and extension of
grassland.

    The abundance of squirrels at sites of human disturbance,
particularly where woody plant cover has been removed (on
overgrazed ranges, around abandoned ranch buildings, etc.) is
characteristic. In 1792, a naturalist describing the Monterey Peninsula

wrote of the ground squirrel, "a large, variegated squirrel which burrowed in dry sands were very abundant, *particularly about the Presidio*" (Menzies, 1924, p. 287). In 1861, a visitor to the ruins of Carmel Mission wrote, "the number of ground squirrels burrowing in the old mounds made by the crumbling adobe houses was incredible—we must have seen *thousands* in the aggregate. This seems a big story, but hundreds were in sight at once" (Brewer, 1949, p. 107). In such numbers the squirrel is associated only with the earlier stages of plant succession.

After extensive study of ground-squirrel habitats, a well known California naturalist concluded:

Squirrels in large numbers may be a symptom of unsuitable use of the land and they may become reduced after the misuse is corrected. The more nearly natural the cover of vegetation the less likely it is that squirrels can be unduly numerous and therefore injurious. This animal responds to disturbance of the soil in much the same manner as do some kinds of weedy plants. (Linsdale, 1946, p. 457)

In 1869-1870, the state legislature authorized payment of bounties on the squirrel, permitting the counties to levy an assessment on taxable property. One poison commonly applied down to the present day was sold in 1878, for private use: "J. A. Malloy has just received a large supply of bisulphide carbon [CS_2], a preparation said to be unexcelled for the extermination of squirrels. For sale at the drugstore" (*Castroville Argus*, April 12, 1878).

With agricultural development, squirrels continued to be a problem on grain farms. Cultivation and irrigation reduced their populations only locally.

In 1908, it was discovered that the ground-squirrel flea sometimes harbors the bubonic plague bacillus, and that plague exists endemically among ground squirrels. Between 1908 and 1914, a concerted, but unsuccessful, effort was made to exterminate the animals, with federal, state, and local agencies participating. (The California State Department of Public Health still periodically inspects the animals for evidence of the disease.)

In 1908-1909, the U.S. Bureau of Biological Survey began a program of squirrel poisoning using strychnine-coated barley. In 1917, the state legislature assigned the duties of rodent control to the County Agricultural Commissioners, where it remains. By 1930, a formidable assortment of poisons was in use, including strychnine, carbon bisulphide, cyanide salts, sulphur dioxide, chlorine gas, and thallium sulphate. The effects of thallium sulphate, which had but recently become a common poison (the federal government printed directions for applying it to grain bait in 1931), were so far-reaching that a number of articles were written objecting strongly to its use. In 1930, when squirrel poisoning with thallium sulphate was in progress in the Gabilans, quails, doves, blackbirds, larks, woodpeckers, house finches, rabbits, deer, jays, and magpies were poisoned as well (Linsdale, 1931, p. 98). Squirrel-poisoning programs also destroyed many of the principal predators capable of naturally limiting squirrel populations, such as bobcats, coyotes, and gray fox, because these carnivores ate the bodies of animals killed by the poison (Grinnell, Dixon, and Linsdale, 1937, p. 29). But even throughout this period squirrel populations were often high:

> On July 21, 1936, on an excursion from Soledad to The Indians, through an area in which poisoning had been carried on in the past, we saw an estimated average of *ten ground squirrels per acre* [25 per hectare] along either side of the road. (von Bloecker, 1937, p. 210)

The use of thallium sulphate has been discontinued. In recent years, the most commonly used poison has again been carbon bisulphide— one of the oldest in use. Anticoagulants are also used.

The overabundance of ground squirrels in the area results from clearing the woody plant cover. The squirrel avoids dense forests, both because most of its favored foods are in short supply there and because its principal predators are common. It also avoids thick chaparral and marshy or frequently flooded ground. But a detailed listing of environmental conditions unattractive to the animal would be of great use in planning a regional program to limit its numbers.

The ground squirrel feeds on many introduced plants of the annual grasslands, such as the filarees, soft chess, and ripgut grass. The more extensive the grassland, the farther removed are the squirrels' predators—most of which, including most hawks and owls, need some woody cover. An exception is the badger, which also lives in open country; but it is itself often destroyed. (Badgers were once trapped here for their coarse hair, used for shaving-brush bristles.) Ground squirrels are not common at Toro Regional Park, Royal Oaks County Park, or Mount Madonna County Park, where no poisoning is done and where woody cover has been encouraged and predators protected. The squirrels are very numerous at Fremont Peak State Park, on parts of which the tree cover is still sparse and which adjoins large tracts of grazing land. The ground-squirrel population of Larkin Valley and the Prunedale district, both sites of woody regrowth, was much diminished during the latter decades of the twentieth century.

Of course, cattle growing and agriculture are only possible when the land is cleared of much of its woody plant cover. Ranches and farmers cannot be expected to permit large tracts of this land to revert to its natural vegetation simply to reduce the squirrel population. On the other hand, the total cost of controlling ground squirrels in the Monterey Bay area has been a major economic factor, millions having been spent on this program in California. It does seem that in the long run there would be economic advantage in supplementing a squirrel control program based on the use of some of the less noxious poisons with a program of limited revegetation and the protection of predators.

The significance of predators in regulating animal numbers goes beyond their promise for the control of ground squirrels, to a more general biological role. Studies in other ecosystems suggest that "local animal species diversity is related to the number of predators in the system and their efficiency in preventing single species from monopolizing some important, limiting requisite"; that, in fact, predation may be capable of preventing extinction in competitive situations (Paine, 1966, pp. 65, 73).

1.4. Introduced Mammals

In addition to the strictly domesticated animals such as livestock and poultry, which are cared for by people, the following
mammals have been introduced into the area—some purposely, some
accidentally.

The house mouse, which is of central Asiatic origin, was brought
into California by the earliest Spanish settlers, probably in food cases,
barrels, and the like. It is now common not only in human dwellings
but in neighboring fields and weed patches as well, where it comes
into competition with native mice. Although it may be found at some
distance from human habitations, the house mouse does not go beyond
the urban-rural habitat created by human settlement. Two varieties
have been distinguished; one is commensal with man, and the other is
a feral variety adapted to living in old fields. When it ventures into
less altered country, it is kept in check by native predators such as
hawks, owls, weasels, skunks, and snakes. And even in areas where
plant cover is made up largely of alien herbs, the house mouse may be
kept in check by interaction with native mouse species. Study of a
dense feral-house-mouse population on an island in San Francisco
Bay showed a remarkably rapid decline of the population to extinction
when the native meadow mouse colonized the island (Lidicker, 1966,
p. 49).

The gray-brown Norway rat and the black rat are both found in
the Monterey Bay area. (The roof rat, also present, and the black rat
are races of a single species.) Just as the ground squirrel is the worst
native mammalian pest, the Norway rat is the worst introduced
mammalian pest in the state. It is more aggressive and destructive,
larger, and more prolific than the black rat. Where it is numerous,
black rats are likely to be scarce.

The Norway rat, probably native to western China, is thought to
have arrived in the eastern United States during the Revolutionary
War. In any case, it has been introduced into the country many times
by ship and probably arrived first in California with the Spanish. It is

a good climber, digger, and gnawer, and ideally suited by its food habits to a life commensal with people. As it seems unable to protect itself from native predators in the wilds, it does not range beyond urban areas and the vicinity of rural dwellings. By spreading the rat, people have produced a variety of new interspecific contacts. Bubonic plague, carried by fleas infesting rats, has occasionally been brought to port cities. Humans have been infected with trichinosis by eating pigs that have eaten infected rats.

Few land mammals thrive better in the marine shoreline environment than do rats. For example, they sometimes infest rock rubble, placed to protect the cliffs from waves, living there on food scraps dropped on the beaches by picnickers.

Five Virginia opossums that had been brought from Missouri were released near San Jose in 1900 (Koppel, 1915, p. 195). In 1910, at least five more escaped from cages in San Jose. By 1915, opossums were established in the Monterey Bay area; several were captured that year near Boulder Creek. The opossum has since established itself, with great success, not only around Monterey Bay but well beyond. Although limited to settled areas, it is now found in remote, sparsely settled parts—for example, at Mount Madonna County Park. Because it is nocturnal, and apparently easily confused by headlights, it is one of the wild animals most commonly seen dead on the roadside.

The aboreal native western gray squirrel is common throughout forests of the Santa Cruz and Santa Lucia mountains, although its area has been reduced by forest clearing and lumbering. It rarely ventures far beyond the boundaries of coniferous forest. In the Santa Cruz Mountains it has been joined by two introduced species that escaped or were released from around Menlo Park. The eastern fox squirrel is now well distributed throughout the Santa Cruz Mountains and even approaches the shoreline, with the western gray squirrel, in the pine forest near Año Nuevo. In the Santa Cruz Mountains, western gray squirrels and eastern fox squirrels have been seen feeding together in the same trees (McClean, 1958, p. 39). Whether or not one has a competitive advantage over the other is not known. Eastern fox squirrel has been planted, apparently recently, near Aptos in oak woodland—beyond the present range of the western gray squirrel. (Four were seen in November 1973 east of Valencia Lake along Encino Drive.)

The eastern gray squirrel has spread more slowly than has the eastern fox squirrel, having only recently crossed the crest to the seaward slopes of the Santa Cruz Mountains (McClean, 1958, p. 35). The squirrel commonly seen in city parks is likely to be the eastern gray squirrel, as the native western gray squirrel rarely reproduces under these conditions.

Of all introduced mammals here, feral pigs pose the greatest direct threat to native plants: The pig is one of the few domesticated species that can forage in undisturbed plant associations. The animal not only roots up many herbaceous plants but, being an omnivore, it also unearths and eats various small animals. The patches of churned soil which mark its feeding sites are found both in heavily wooded country and along the margins of grassland. In the Santa Cruz mountains, feral pigs are especially numerous in tanbark oak groves in the fall when acorns ripen. Feral pigs are difficult to exterminate or otherwise control. (Local predators are too few to limit their numbers.)

The original stock of the European wild pig (locally called Russian boar) was brought from the Ural Mountains to North Carolina in 1912. In 1925, some of its descendants were sent to California and released on the San Francisquito Ranch, between the Carmel Valley and Los Padres National Forest (Pine and Gerdes, 1973, p. 126). The European wild pig interbreeds with feral domestic pigs, which are found in considerable numbers in the Sierra de Salinas and in the Gabilans. Being nocturnal, in contrast to the domesticated pig, the European wild pig is occasionally seen feeding early in the morning and late in the evening. Acorns, grass roots, and bulbs are its favorite foods (Dasmann, 1965, p. 35), but farther south, in the Salinas Valley, it also does considerable damage to ground crops. Areas in which coast live oak is dominant are the animal's favorite habitat, though they are found in lesser numbers in blue oaks as well (Pine and Gerdes, 1973, p. 129). The spread of the European wild pig has been mainly south from the site at which it was first released, into Los Padres National Forest. But it is said to occur in the Mount Toro area too. Ranchers claim that the animal comes close to isolated ranch houses there in the evenings, although it is possibly being confused with feral domesticated pigs or, more likely, with hybrids of the two. (What appear to be hybrids are now found northward in the Santa Cruz Mountains.) In 1968, there were estimated to be 2600 European wild pigs in Monterey County, with a population density within their range of 0.8 pigs per square kilometer (2.1 per square mile) (Pine and Gerdes, 1973, p. 126). Because of continued interbreeding with feral domesticated pigs, an accurate account is probably now impossible.

Native varieties of muskrat are found only along the eastern borders of California. Some of these spread westward as alterations in drainage systems were made for purposes of irrigation. A more valuable variety introduced from the eastern United States for commercial fur production had become common in the Pit River watershed by 1933; it had reached the lower Sacramento Valley and the San Joaquin River by 1943 (Seymore, 1954, p. 377). The muskrat is now present in the Monterey Bay area and has spread southward in the Salinas Valley. There, the muskrat, which feeds mainly on the roots and young shoots of the common cattail, is found in some of the larger irrigation ponds— for example, at Salachi Dam and southward off Old Stage Road and along the Salinas River itself. Local residents around Moss Landing and Castroville say the animal first appeared near there in the early 1960s. Since then, it has also been observed in Harkins Slough, in the San Lorenzo River, and within the city limits of Santa Cruz itself, in Nearys Lagoon—surprisingly, because the lagoon is surrounded by urban development. In 1970-1971, 206 muskrats were reported to the California Fish and Game Department as having been trapped commercially in Santa Cruz County.

In 1945, five golden beavers trapped in Yuba County were transported to the Salinas Valley and released near Chualar (Hemsley, 1946, p. 98). Since that time the beaver has multiplied and spread along the river wherever food is available. Its principal foods here are cottonwood and willow; the beaver seems to prefer cottonwood although the willow is much more plentiful. A survey made in the early 1970s by the Fish and Game Department south of Chualar found evidence of the presence of beavers wherever there were sizable stands of willow or cottonwood. In that stretch the beaver population was estimated at around 12 per km (20 per mile). Downstream beaver were found near the Salinas River bridge. Northward, one colony was eradicated from the virtually treeless Tembladero Slough, east of Castroville, where it had built a dam from a patch of willow growing near an irrigation ditch. Some have denied that the beaver's presence in the Salinas Valley is beneficial: There have been complaints of beavers plugging culverts and ditches and disrupting the operation of stream gauges. There has been an open season on beavers in the Salinas Valley, and their distribution along the river also was changed by the 1995 floods.

The gray fox, common in chaparral country, is a native—but the red fox is an introduced species (in all areas to the west of the Sierras).

Red foxes were brought to the southern Sacramento Valley from east of the Rockies for the production of fur in 1870s. During the following century numerous fox farms operated in California, and more stock was imported from various eastern sources. Some of the animals escaped, or were released for hunting, and the species spread over a good deal of the state.

A number of factors account for red fox's success: It is omnivorous, mainly nocturnal, and adapts readily to rural and suburban life. For instance, foxes often feed on the contents of garbage cans. They eat food put out for pets (and sometimes the pets themselves). In some places, residents give them further assistance: "In Orange County, foxes were fed by people at every site studied; some feeding was done on a daily basis" (Lewis et al, 1993, p. 21).

The red fox was absent from the Monterey Bay area until around 1985. Here, too, its introduction was probably deliberate—but the details are unclear. The animal found itself in ideal surroundings in this area, and its numbers swelled: Elevated populations of the fox's favorite prey species (such as meadow mice and pocket gophers) and reduced populations of native competitors (such as badgers, bobcats, and coyotes) probably contributed to the fox's success here.

Supplementing its well-rounded diet with native birds, especially ground-nesting birds, the fox has become a scourge to the clapper rail, least tern, snowy plover, and burrowing owl (Roberson and Tenney, 1993, pp. 164, 399, 413). In this regard, its effects are even worse than those of the house cat, because it ranges farther afield. The California Department of Fish and Game has undertaken a program to suppress the red fox population.

2. Birds

2.1. Original Bird Fauna

Few other areas in the United States have so rich an avifauna as coastal California. Over 300 bird species have been collected in the Monterey Bay area, some 90 of which are permanent residents, according to The Monterey Peninsula Audubon Society's *List of Birds of the Monterey Peninsula Region.*

Because of the scarcity of published data on animal numbers in the Monterey Bay area, quantitative statements made here are often on the crude order of "more than," "less than," or "approximately the same as." Numerical information is needed for reconstructing historical trends and developing a comprehensive ecological plan. For example, there is a close association of some bird species with a particular vegetation (carefully studied by Miller, 1951), and the population density of each species fluctuates within limits that can be determined by field census. A map that reconstructs the plant cover before the time of European settlement indicates as well, albeit roughly, the relative numbers of various bird species under natural conditions. Thus a series of sketch maps drawn up to show historical changes in plant cover will give, at the same time, some indication of the changing relative abundance of species.

2.2. Extinctions and Changes in Range, Numbers, and Habit

Although no animals are known for certain to have been exterminated here by prehistoric peoples, the subject has not been carefully studied archaeologically. A possible example has come to light: Many bones of an extinct diving duck, *Chendytes lawi*, known to have lived along the California coast in the Pleistocene period, have been found in middens to the north of Santa Cruz at Laguna Creek, in layers dating from approximately 5390 to 3780 years before the present.

The bird was flightless, was no doubt relatively easy to capture, and had large goose-sized legs which would have made it a preferred food item . . . . Overharvest by aboriginal man was probably the principal factor contributing to the extinction of this species. (Morejohn, 1976a, p. 210)

Accounts from the middle of the nineteenth century describe the California condor as present throughout the Monterey Bay area and northward in the Santa Cruz Mountains. Now the nearest condor territory is in the coastal mountains to the south, where the species faces extinction. In 1961, only some 40 to 60 birds survived in the wild (Peterson, 1961, p. 62). By 1985, this number had dropped to 7 (*Science*, Aug. 30, 1985, p. 844), and by 1994 to 4. There were, however, 85 in zoos; though 10 of these were scheduled for release into the wild, prospects for survival there are poor (*The New Scientist*, July 9, 1994, p. 13).

Spanish observation of the condor gave rise to the name of the Pajaro River. In 1769, Father Crespi described the interior of an Indian village on the banks of the Pajaro River:

Hanging on one of these poles we found half the body of a black bird, with the two wings fastened together; spread out these measured thirteen cuartas [nearly 3 m] from tip to tip; and because of this bird, this place . . . is known among the soldiers no otherwise than as the *Rio del Pajaro*, Bird River. (Stanger and Brown, 1969, p. 76)

A black bird with such a wingspread could hardly have been other than the California condor.

In the Monterey Bay area the condor was commensal with the turkey vulture. Both fed heavily on dead whales. Condors were still plentiful in 1861, when it was recorded in Monterey that hundreds of whale "carcasses have there decayed, fattening clouds of buzzards and vultures [condors]" (Brewer, 1949, p. 105). A local ornithologist, writing in 1888, remarked that the condor "was common a few years ago, when it could be seen feeding with the common turkey vulture. The last I saw were two in September, 1885. A few still breed in the wilder mountains north of Santa Cruz" (Anderson, 1891, p. 56).

As early as 1890 a perceptive observer, well aware of the ecological importance of changing land use, commented on reasons for this decline:

The causes of this are not hard to perceive. Besides poison used to kill wild animals on which the vultures then feed, two others may be given. One is the much less abundance of cattle, sheep, etc. kept in these parts of the State, where grazing is giving way to agriculture and fruit-raising. The other is the foolish habit of men and boys who take every opportunity of shooting these birds. (Cooper, 1890, p. 248)

As late as 1904, condors were "seen several times in the mountains on the north side of the Pajaro Valley" (Hunter, 1904, p. 24).

As the vulture and the condor were commensal, and the former is resident on the coast mainly in the summer, the immediate forces that acted to decimate the condor population, whatever they may have been, were perhaps most effective during the winter months. It may be noteworthy in this connection that although the humpback season in Monterey began in July, the main whaling season fell between January and mid-April, during which time the gray passes along this coast. Between mid-April and July, there was no whaling (*Santa Cruz News*, March 23, 1860)—hence a much-reduced food supply for the condor.

The condor may even have become more numerous in the days of cattlemen and shore whalers than it had been in Indian times. Cattle dead in the open fields and whale carcasses on the beaches probably provided more abundant food than dead deer, elk, and antelope in the more heavily wooded country of Costanoan times. Having been drawn away from its old, dispersed food sources and habituated to a more localized supply, the bird may have found readjustment difficult. In any case, the critical decrease in condor numbers occurred as American farming replaced Spanish ranching. The decrease coincides, too, with the near-extermination of the gray whale, and the collapse of the shore-whaling industry.

Another account, written at Monterey in 1871 during the peak period of shore whaling, noted the influence of the industry on bird numbers and distribution:

The whale fishery *attracted several species usually seen only far off shore*, of which the enormous Petrel, or "Gong" (*Ossifraga gigantea*), could often be seen swimming lazily near the try-works to pick up scraps of blubber, sometimes accompanied by the dusky young of the *Short-tailed Albatross* (*Diomedea brachyura*). The Pacific Fulmars (*F. pacificus*), called by the whalers "Tager" or "Haglet," were common off shore, feeding also on whale meat, but oftener observed chasing the Gulls to make them disgorge. (J. G. Cooper, 1871, pp. 757-758)

The short-tailed albatross is now near extinction as a result of its destruction in the feather industry, carried on in other parts of its range. By the beginning of the twentieth century, Californians began to miss it off their coast. According to Peterson (1961, p. 337), the last sighting of the bird off the California coast was in 1946.

The bald eagle is rarely seen in the area: "Two were seen in March, 1885" (McGregor and Fiske, 1892, p. 139). Golden eagle are occasionally seen and may be increasing in number.

The effects of commercial hunting before the enactment of game laws are illustrated in the following note from a historical diary written by a resident of Salinas, December 6, 1877:

> Never in the history of this section has wild game of all kinds been so plentiful. Over a ton of geese, ducks, quail, and pigeons [apparently band-tailed pigeons] have been shipped to the San Francisco market in the last few days. Ducks are a drug on the market, bringing but 10 cents apiece. Two Mexican boys brought in 20 from Santa Rita and were unable to dispose of them at any price. Quail sold for 75 cents per dozen. Mike Tynan of the Diamond Hotel killed 126 ducks on the ponds east of Salinas in six shots. (*Overton Manuscript*, 1877, p. 11)

Plainly these were times of limited conservational concern and only superficial interest in the local natural history. Newspapers rarely commented upon wildlife of the area except in hunting stories. Either there were no city ordinances controlling the use of firearms or they gave way readily before a boyish enthusiasm for target practice:

> Joe Watson saw a hawk [an osprey?] perched upon the cross surmounting the Catholic Church steeple Wednesday, and, getting out his rifle, brought down the bird at the third shot, together with the fish, a sucker, it held in its beak. (*Castroville Argus*, Oct. 19, 1878)

The clapper rail is found exclusively in tidal saltwater marshes, where it is associated with the pickleweed. The number had been much reduced by hunting for the market in 1913, at which time protective laws were enacted. In the Monterey Bay area, by 1972 there were only about ten pair left, all around Elkhorn Slough. Any that may have survived into the 1980s, were probably killed by the red fox (Roberson and Tenney, 1993, p. 413).

The least tern nested on beaches in the Monterey Bay area in the first half of the twentieth century; for example, near the mouth of the Salinas River and around Elkhorn Slough (Beck, 1907, p. 58). By 1944, increasing human use of beaches suitable for its nesting sites was recognized as a threat to the bird's survival (Grinnell and Miller, 1944, p. 175). Until 1954, a colony nested near the mouth of the Pajaro River (Wilbur, 1974, p. 2)—now the site of a large housing development—but no nesting terns have been observed in the Monterey Bay area since within a few years of that time.

According to an American pioneer's account of the Pajaro Valley in 1852, "In the fall there were great quantities of wild geese" (Kitchen, 1952, unpaginated). There is no way of knowing which geese these were; in autumn, snow, black brant, and other geese are occasionally found in Elkhorn and Bennett's sloughs, but nowadays geese are rarely seen in the Pajaro Valley itself.

The fortunes of the burrowing owl are tied to those of the California ground squirrel, the birds being almost "restricted to treeless fields and pastures inhabited by ground squirrels" (Grinnell and Wythe, 1927, p. 86). The owl nests only in subterranean sites provided by the larger burrowing mammals native to the area, especially the burrows of the ground squirrel. Like the range of the ground squirrel, that of the owl expanded with the great historical extension of grassland. In the nineteenth century it was reported as a common resident (McGregor and Fiske, 1892, p. 139). The author remembers it as being plentiful around Aromas in the 1930s, as was the ground squirrel. By 1947, around Santa Cruz, it was described as "now rare due to the poisoning of ground squirrels" (Streator, 1947, p. 19). Actually, owls and squirrels were killed together when carbon bisulphide gas was pumped into burrows (Sherwood, 1925, p. 78). The owl has so decreased in numbers that even dedicated bird-watchers have long found it noteworthy. For example, in July 1972 members of the Monterey Peninsula Audubon Society, after a successful field excursion, reported, "A bonus came in the form of a family of burrowing owls close to Highway 1, immediately north of Marina" (*The Sanderling*, 1972, vol. 29, no. 1). There are probably fewer than two-dozen breeding pair left in the entire Monterey Bay area (Roberson and Tenney, 1993, p. 164; *The Albatross,* Mar/Apr 1995, p. 10).

The white-tailed kite, which has been rare in the area since the 1920s, lost much of its habitat when the area's freshwater marshes were drained. The bird's decline was probably hastened by target hunters who took advantage of the fact that it is less fearful of people than most other raptors. In 1927, it was estimated that there were no more than 50 pair in all California (Hoffmann, 1927, p. 64). By 1940, the bird was still so rare in the Monterey Bay area that discovery of four nesting pair near Watsonville prompted a publication (Hawbecker, 1940b). The kite population is recovering slowly.

In 1892, the horned lark was much more abundant in Santa Cruz County than it is at present: "In the fall the young and old collect *in immense flocks*. When they are feeding, *I have killed as many as thirty at one shot*" (Harrison, 1892, p. 140). No such congregations of horned larks are seen hereabouts today. The birds are seen occasionally on dunes and in other treeless areas. But often the entire flocks number no more than 30. In the five years 1990-1994 inclusive, the Christmas count of birds found 13 horned larks in Santa Cruz County (*The Albatross*, Mar/Apr 1995, p. 11). The horned lark favors a plant cover of short grasses, and the bird is still numerous in the foothills of the Gabilans where cattle keep the grass closely cropped (Roberson and Tenney, 1993, p. 224).

One might wonder, reading the above account, why anyone shot such small birds: Small birds were long a special item in European cookery. Blackbirds were not the only ones baked "four and twenty" in pastries. Birds of many species were shot, netted, or trapped— including the horned lark, which is native to Europe as well as America. In central California, horned larks were the favorites; and, following European custom, they were taken in large numbers for sale in the markets of San Francisco:

Six of them ranged side by side with a skewer running through them . . . one to ten dozen small birds upon the counters of game and poultry stalls . . . the scant morsel of flesh on either side of the keel of the breast bone may be served as an *entrée* in the better class San Francisco restaurants . . . . Generally speaking it is a horned lark . . . .The hunting is almost exclusively done by Frenchmen. (Bryant, *Zoe*, 1891, p. 142)

Actually, by that time habitat for the horned lark had been extended by deforestation and early agricultural developments here; certainly the bird flourished in those years. The horned lark is still abundant in other parts of its range, hunting of it having long since stopped.

Many of the birds that have extended their range and become more numerous, and many of those that have adapted easily to human presence, are birds of the "grassland formation" (see Miller, 1951). The areal extent of forest species has been correspondingly reduced: Nowadays the only place in the northern part of the area in which the Steller's jay comes to the shoreline is in the pine forest between Año Nuevo and Waddell Creek. On the other hand, changes have occurred within the forest, too: Steller's jays congregate near tourist campsites; at Mount Madonna County Park, the jays obviously depend on campers for a good part of their food. Rarely do such changes in number occur without effects elsewhere in the ecological system. For example, in the Big Basin area,

their presence in abnormal numbers around camping areas appeared to be definitely correlated with a reduction in the numbers of small passerine birds in such places, especially during the nesting season. On more than one occasion jays were seen hunting for the nests and young of smaller birds. (Orr, 1942, p. 321)

Some of the "grassland" bird species that have increased their numbers and are now found mainly in the rural and urban bioassociations probably existed in transitional vegetation between the woody and herbaceous plant cover of the area before human settlement began. The western mourning dove and the western meadowlark, for example, have benefitted greatly from the extension of grassland associated with the cattle industry. The western meadowlark strongly prefers tall grass as its nesting site. The dove is now the most abundant single upland game bird in California. In hill country, the dove favors for food the seeds of the turkey mullein, a native weed that has, itself, spread extensively with grazing on the drier rangelands. Doves have also taken up residence in the towns, where they nest in trees and rest on telephone wires—singly or in pairs in summer, sometimes in groups in winter. Curiously, in Santa Cruz in 1888 the dove was described as an "abundant summer resident, arriving about April 1" (McGregor and Fiske, 1892, p. 139). Similar statements appear in several other early accounts. Mourning doves now winter within Santa Cruz city limits. Is the bird adapting to new habitats? The removal of certain seasonal restrictions with urbanization has been noted elsewhere and appears to be a trend. To the south of the Monterey Bay area the robin and the band-tailed pigeon, formerly only winter residents in the city of Santa Barbara, have, in the last decades, been observed to remain there throughout the year, nesting in downtown parks. Similarly, a variety of the dark-eyed junco (Thurber's) that was a visitor in Santa Barbara only in winter before 1936 has gradually become a year-round resident (E.Z.R. and J.W.H., 1961, p. 3).

In the Monterey Bay area, as elsewhere in the United States, the American robin became one of the most numerous birds following American settlement: "there appears a semi-domestication, connected with lawns for feeding and scarcity of enemies" (Beecher, 1942, p. 62). Further evidence of the robin's increased involvement in artificial habitats is the fact that one of the earthworms that forms an important part of its diet is in fact an introduced species.

The American kestrel, the tamest of the local hawks, perches on telephone wires over empty town lots, feeding on mice and grasshoppers, and is said even to nest occasionally in birdhouses.

Although not so tolerant of human presence as the mourning dove, the meadowlark comes to the outskirts of towns. Around airports its song, certainly one of the most familiar natural sounds of rural California, mingles with the roar of aircraft motors. On the other hand, it appears to avoid cultivated fields (Orr, 1942, p. 332).

The house finch (California linnet) has also benefitted greatly from human alterations of the natural plant cover. The following habitat description shows well its association with the cultural landscape: "weedy stretches of open hills and fields, trees bordering watercourses or roadsides, orchards, barnyards, parks, gardens, and isolated weed-covered city lots. Perches familiarly about houses and on telegraph and telephone wires" (Grinnell and Miller, 1944, p. 109). The house finch, which subsists to a large extent on the seeds of exotic weeds, garden plants, and orchard fruits, is one of the three or four most abundant land birds in the area.

The California towhee is one of the more common birds in city backyards and flower gardens, and certainly one of the tamest native birds in the area; one can approach the bird to within a few meters. Hummingbirds, too, are probably more numerous than formerly, nourished as they are by the many introduced flowering plants that bloom almost throughout the year in city gardens—fuchsias, for instance. In pre-European times, nectar from the bush monkey flower, a long-blooming native plant, was probably one of their principal foods.

The clearing and reclearing of forest and woodland tracts in historical times has greatly elongated the lines of ecotone vegetation and probably extended the habitat of a number of species. The California thrasher, for example, can commonly be heard rustling the dry leaves in bushes bordering open fields and seen flying in and out of the margins of thickets.

The valley quail, which also prefers ecotone vegetation and brush and thickets along the margins of open fields, is probably at least as common now as it was before European settlement began.

The American coot is probably more common now than formerly. A hunting season is posted on it and a limit of 20 set, but few are taken. Local hunters, unlike those in several European countries, disregard the bird or take it only as a last resort; here the flesh is not considered tasty. As a result the mudhen is commonplace. The birds are a nuisance on golf courses, where they foul the fairways. Flocks of several hundreds can be seen in February, feeding along the highway near the old salt ponds north of Moss Landing. They are numerous, too, in freshwater irrigation ponds, where pondweed is one of their favorite foods.

Barbed wire fences and telephone lines have established an artificial network within which the movements of some birds are, to some extent, channeled. Some species appear to make their territorial claims within this artificial network. The sparrow hawk, or American kestrel, commonly scans the ground for prey from telephone and power lines even in towns. The shrike, also known as the butcherbird, ordinarily perches on telephone wires and fence posts along country roads; it often impales its prey on the barbed wire. For similar reasons fruit-eating birds influence plant distribution; for instance, poison oak and California blackberry are now more plentiful than ever and have a more linear distribution pattern than previously, congregating along fences and property boundaries.

Brewer's blackbird, which probably originally occupied alluvial meadows, tule patches, etc., has spread to open fields, orchards, and pastures, and particularly into the suburban environment, where it is one of the most common birds on lawns, in parks, and on golf courses. It is, by the way, one of the few land birds that ventures into the salty

Gulls following disk harrow and feeding on earthworms, north of Moss Landing. (Photo B. Gordon)

tidal environment. It can be seen on the beaches along West Cliff Drive in Santa Cruz and on Point Pinos, at low tide, walking among the tide pools. It picks up lunch scraps on the pier leading to the concrete ship at Seacliff Beach State Park, a hundred yards from land. In this respect it differs from its relatives: Neither the redwing nor the tricolor blackbird commonly appears among the tide pools, though both join the Brewer's to feed at garbage dumps.

The areal extent of oak woodland and riparian forest is particularly important to bird life in this area. Because they covered the lower, more fertile lands toward the coast, these plant associations lost relatively large parts of their areas to agriculture (larger proportions than did chaparral and redwood forest). The fact that the avifauna in oak woodland and riparian forest is particularly rich is probably explained by the general diversity of plant forms in these associations and the comparatively abundant and varied food materials they supply. For example, oak woodland appears to have a relatively large winged-insect population compared with neighboring coniferous forest or chaparral with an associated abundance of insectivorous bird species such as flycatchers and warblers (Orr, 1942, p. 280). Also, the proximity of water in riparian forest no doubt partly accounts for the large insect populations there. True, the richness of oak-woodland bird life is not solely a matter of that plant cover's having a large and distinctive avifauna of its own: Because of its transitional character several bird species typical of neighboring plant associations (particularly of chaparral and redwood-Douglas fir forest) are almost equally abundant in oak woodland (Orr, 1942, p. 280).

At least one native bird, the northern mockingbird, has extended its range into the Monterey Bay area in historic times in association with changes attending human occupancy, spreading northward and westward from the San Joaquin Valley. Residential areas have become a principal habitat. The mockingbird appears to have reached the Monterey Bay area from the south. In Santa Barbara, the first sighting of a mockingbird nest was reported in 1882. It was sighted and listed as a rare bird in the vicinity of Watsonville in 1904 (Hunter, 1904,

p. 24). Mockingbirds were not present, or very rare, in Santa Cruz in 1891: "Our local ornithologists say they have not seen this bird about Santa Cruz . . . . Dr. Cooper saw it at Monterey" (Anderson, 1891, p. 65). Around 1920 it appeared in Santa Cruz as a winter visitant, but did not begin to nest there until about 1930 (Arnold, 1935, p. 197). In 1947, the bird was listed as "very common in Santa Cruz . . . . It is extending its range in the coastal district . . . . I do not think it will ever inhabit the higher mountains back from the coast. They first appeared here about twenty-five years ago" (Streator, 1947, p. 27). In Santa Cruz, mockingbirds are commonly seen perched on the crosspieces of telephone poles (mourning doves prefer the wires).

The spread of the mockingbird has been attributed to the planting of trees and shrubs. "The planting of ornamental shrubbery, such as pyracantha, cotoneaster, toyon, and other berry producers has helped the mockingbird to establish residence in the vicinities of Santa Cruz . . . " and elsewhere (Arnold, 1935, p. 198). Thus, townspeople hear a new summer bird song, and sometimes at a surprising hour: No other bird in the area, and few elsewhere, are known to break into full song at midnight.

The brown-headed cowbird, another native American species, has experienced marked changes in range and number since the introduction of cattle from Europe. Although cowbirds were virtually unknown west of the Sierras a century ago, nowadays flocks numbering in the thousands are not uncommon in the Sacramento Valley. There the birds " . . . invade riparian forest habitat, where they burden other species with the task of incubating their eggs and raising their young" (Gaines, 1980, p. 64). Though pastures are among the cowbird's principal forage grounds, it roosts and nests in trees. Cowbirds may be less numerous in the lower Salinas Valley than in the first quarter of the twentieth century, because there are fewer home dairies, barnyards, and feedlots—and because there is less riparian forest. Nevertheless, the bird is increasing its range in the southern Monterey Bay area, where it is said to threaten the survival of several native species (Roberson and Tenney, 1993, p. 374).

The killdeer has extended its range from shores and stream bars into ploughed fields, where it feeds on insects, and sometimes makes its nests.

Of native bird species, the gull is one of the least timid of human presence. Gulls loiter around piers accepting whatever turns up, be it only crusts of bread from tourists. They steal bait from under the fisherman's nose. Their food includes both vegetable and animal matter—living or carrion. They are more truly amphibious than most other shore birds. They follow tractors across the fields eating earthworms turned up by the plough, and thousands can be seen flocking around inland city garbage dumps, e.g., Watsonville, feeding on all sorts of waste. (At dumps the flocks, largest in winter, are made up of about 90% California gulls, the remainder being mainly immature western gulls.) They also feed on floating sewage in the tanks at the sewage-processing plant near Salinas; and there, gulls and Brewer's blackbirds perch calmly together on the giant sprinkler frame, as it rotates over the trickling filter, occasionally dropping off to snatch slugs and fly-larvae from the rocks in the filter tank below. Few beaches are too polluted for the gull; insecticides are a threat to some birds, but the gull seems to go unscathed. Even changes in habit have been brought about, such as learning to respond to the sound of a caterpillar motor's starting up, and to follow the machine across the fields— behavior certainly unknown to their ancestors. Its activity as mouse predator in artichoke fields is but another example of the gull's remarkable adaptability.

While the gull's tolerance of human presence gives the bird a competitive advantage over other species, it also leads to an increased dependency: When W.W. II began, fishing operations in the bay were sharply curtailed and many gulls which had fed on fish scraps were left starving. Gull populations are now held at disproportionately high levels as a result of the bird's access to a copious and growing food supply in city garbage dumps.

The barn owl has changed its nesting habits and adapted remarkably to the presence of humans. In addition to natural nesting places in

Barn swallow nest, *left*, and **cliff swallow nests**, *right*, on buildings. (Photos B. Gordon)

holes in the banks of ravines and tree trunks, the owl has taken to using the interior of barns and old buildings for nesting sites. As the barn is no longer the essential and common building it was in the early part of the twentieth century, the owl is either less abundant now or less conspicuous. More than other owls, the barn owl finds its food in the cultural landscape, in fields, gardens, and orchards.

The barn swallow, or fork-tailed swallow, and the northern cliff swallow, both summer residents of the Monterey Bay area, have adjusted similarly to human presence. Both have benefitted from growth of the human population which has led to a great increase in the number of suitable nesting sites: During the early American period of settlement the northern cliff swallow, which nests naturally on beach cliffs and sometimes on tree trunks, took to nesting on the walls of buildings as well. Similarly, the barn swallow, which used caves and ravines, now also nests under the eaves of buildings. While the barn swallow builds open nests of mud, one or two together and usually

Left, **Sapsucker holes**, in a walnut tree. Many native animals here have taken to alien plants for food. The yellow-bellied sapsucker, a winter visitor to the Monterey Bay area, favors trees with a smooth, light-colored bark—especially the English walnut. Sapsucker holes are usually arranged in horizontal rings. There are no holes below in the rough bark of the black walnut. Sapsuckers also drill in introduced acacias, as well as in apple and other fruit trees. The birds seem to avoid eucalypts, though many of these have light, smooth bark, too. Sapsuckers sometimes drill sycamores and live oaks; these are among the native trees on which the birds depended heavily in aboriginal times. (Photo B. Gordon).

Right, **Holes drilled** in Monterey pine by the California woodpecker for storing acorns. Such holes are drilled in both native and alien trees—even in palms. Woodpeckers attack squirrels and jays trying to remove acorns from the holes. In the spring (when this picture was taken) many holes are empty, the birds having eaten acorns stored here in the fall. The large quantities of acorns carried about by the woodpecker suggest that the bird is important in disseminating oaks. (Photo R. Buchsbaum) inside buildings, the northern cliff swallow sticks pellets of mud together to form its narrow-mouthed nests, usually in colonies on the outsides of buildings. Both species have also been favored by the extension of irrigation in the area, because of both the increased availability of mud for nest building and the increased supply of insects for food.

The black phoebe also often makes its mud nests on abandoned houses and on the understructures of bridges. A characteristic perch for the bird is on water troughs in barnyards.

After the Europeans introduced the horse, various native birds took to using its hair in making their nests. With the advent of tractors and automobiles, such nests became hard to find. Similarly, in the days when the area was a major poultry producer, nests of the violet-green swallow were ". . .composed entirely of chicken feathers" (C.L. Anderson, 1891, p. 58).

Cedar waxwings visit this area in winter. Nowadays the birds are found mainly in urban sites; they commonly congregate on telephone wires and in the city gardens, where they feed especially on the berries of pepper tree, cotoneaster, and pyracantha. (All of these are introduced plants.) Judging from the cedar waxwing's habits and preferences today, the attractions of the Monterey Bay area must have been very different in prehistoric times.

Where floodlights play on beaches, sanderlings run back and forth at the edge of the swash as if it were daytime.

The names of such native birds as the barn swallow, the cowbird, the barn owl, and the house finch themselves suggest changes in habit which have been made since European settlement began.

2.3. Introduced Species

Certainly the best-known introduced birds are the house sparrow (English sparrow) and the pigeon (rock dove).

The trend toward domestication and increased freedom from seasonal restrictions induced by association with humans (mentioned above in the case of the robin, junco, and other synanthropic native birds) is well illustrated in these two species.

The house sparrow, native to southwest Asia, began its adjustment to human activities in antiquity: It was present around houses in the Levant some 11,000 years ago—when people first gathered in villages. The sparrow became a follower of human settlement, and eventually spread to the villages and towns of Europe. The bird has long since ceased to exist in a truly wild state, and is unable to survive in undisturbed plant communities. (For example, it soon became extinct on several small north European islands when human residents left, all domesticated animals were removed, and a regrowth of native plants took over.) More than a dozen separate importations of the sparrow into the eastern United States are recorded between 1850 and 1881—at least one for the purpose of controlling an insect pest (though the bird is mainly a seed eater). In California, the sparrow first appeared in San Francisco, around 1871. Although it was probably first brought purposely, the bird also entered the state spontaneously a number of times—for instance, along railroad lines, accompanying grain and stock cars. The Southern Pacific Railroad was extended into the Monterey Bay area in 1872, and the sparrow may have entered shortly thereafter. In any case, it was common in the towns of Santa Cruz County by 1888 (McGregor and Fiske, 1892, p. 141). Thus, the sparrow flourished in California towns in horse-and-buggy days, at which time its food is described as having consisted largely of undigested oat seeds in the horse droppings then plentiful in the streets.

By the end of the nineteenth century, the sparrow was so numerous that it was considered a nuisance. In 1916, the California Fish and Game commission initiated a campaign against it (*Calif. Fish and Game,* 1916 (2), p. 141): Government circulars, noting that the sparrow had been eaten in the Old World for centuries, praised the bird's palatability and recommended it for human consumption in America (Dearborn, 1912, p. 24).

Although still abundant in the Monterey Bay area, the sparrow has become decidedly less so since automobiles and parking lots have

Pigeon guillemots and **pigeons** (rock doves) in Santa Cruz, off West Cliff drive. Four bird species nest in holes on the cliff: two are natives — the guillemot (*down arrow,* inset) and northern cliff swallow; and two are aliens—the pigeon (*up arrows,* inset) and starling. (Photo B. Gordon).

replaced horse-drawn vehicles and stables. The bird has never been able to establish itself in any local natural plant association: Nowadays, house sparrows are even rare around isolated dwellings.

Turning from the house sparrow to the pigeon: This bird shows even more the effects of close association with humans. A native of the Mediterranean area, where populations still exist in a more or less wild state, the pigeon spread northward in Europe during the Neolithic—following the expansion of agriculture. As a result of artificial selection by people, and life in humanized environments, the pigeon has lost physiological traits common to most wild birds: The breeding cycle of wild pigeons is seasonal and photoperiodic, but in both the feral and domestic pigeon breeding may continue throughout the year; "eggs may be laid in any month with squabs reaching independence at any time" (Murton et al., 1972, p. 221).

In medieval Europe pigeons were a major source of fresh meat. Dovecotes were a characteristic architectural feature—as they still are in parts of the Mediterranean area. Many varieties of pigeon were bred. Squabs were once an important food on many an American farm, and some are still produced there commercially. Thus, the pigeon has a long record of service to humankind. (Only in 1994 did the Swiss military give up its use of homing pigeons.) However, in urban centers where pigeons are now both useless and an expensive nuisance, people are more than willing to break these old associations. As it turns out, with the pigeon (and with the sparrow) this is not easily done.

A few pigeons may still be raised for food in the Monterey Bay area, but most are feral. Although some flocks feed in cultivated fields, they are much more numerous in cities and towns—where they subsist mainly on weed seeds and scraps, and on the grain scattered about by those people who still appreciate the birds.

Though they compete with native seed-eaters in urban and rural areas, house sparrows and pigeons are not among the serious threats to native species.

Because of their old ties to inland farms, one hardly associates pigeons with the marine environment. Thus, it is noteworthy that the birds nest in the sea cliffs of Santa Cruz—in holes only about 20 feet (6 m) above water, barely out of reach of the spray. Perhaps this should not be so surprising since coastal cliffs around the Mediterranean Sea are said to be the bird's ancestral habitat. The pigeon's selection of this nesting site has given rise to a new interspecific relationship. A native marine bird, the pigeon guillemot, also nests in these holes, and was no doubt doing so long before the pigeon arrived. The nests of the two are intermixed, and the birds compete for space: Occasionally, a guillemot can be seen forcing pigeons off the cliff.

Between 20 and 30 adult guillemots are usually present, and counts made over the last couple of decades indicate no great change in the size of this colony. Although guillemots nest elsewhere in these cliffs—for example, at Lighthouse Point and at the end of Getchell St.—this colony is the largest in Santa Cruz. The guillemots arrive in March or early April. For example, in 1983, they were present on March 22; in 1993, on March 8. They depart around the end of August. During at least the last half of the twentieth century, guillemots have occasionally nested on timbers under the wharves at Santa Cruz and Monterey harbors (Streator, 1947, p. 17).

Although this species of guillemot is called the pigeon guillemot, it bears slight resemblance to the pigeon. In fact, the two birds are so utterly different that one can only wonder that they have the same nesting place. The guillemot is heavy bodied compared to the pigeon. When the pigeon takes flight it climbs immediately and strongly from its perch. The guillemot dives off the face of the cliff and flies some distance before it can stop losing altitude. In landing, the guillemot approaches the cliff at slightly below the level of its perch; beating its wings rapidly, it literally flies onto the cliff, slowing itself by rising at the last minute to perch level. The pigeon, on the other hand, approaches the cliff from aloft, braking and lowering itself in a series of swoops; then spreading its wings widely, it falls onto its perch. Guillemots come and go singly or in pairs; the pigeons are usually in flocks. Guillemots rarely fly higher than the top of the cliff, much less inland from its edge, though they are remarkably tolerant of human presence on the cliff edge while nesting. They leave the cliff early in the morning and fly along the coast to feed on benthic marine life—especially sculpins (Follett and Ainley, 1976, p. 28), often returning only after dark. They rarely venture more than a few hundred meters offshore (Stallcup, p. 1976, p. 132). The pigeons forage inland, parts of the flock coming back frequently for short periods during the day, and all return well before sunset. The guillemot is here only during the summer; the pigeons stay on—although on really stormy days they spend their time elsewhere.

The ring-necked pheasant is a native of Eurasia. The State of California liberated some of these birds at Monterey in 1889. However, the pheasant was probably not well established in the Monterey Bay area until around 1916, by which time state game farms had supplied the birds in large numbers. It is surprising to see such a large game bird close to human habitations, but, in fact, pheasants favor settled areas, especially irrigated and other well-watered sites. In the 1970s they could be seen within the city limits of Santa Cruz e.g., near Natural Bridges State Park and Neary Lagoon. The ring-necked pheasant does not thrive in any natural plant communities of the area. Judging from the example of abandoned orchard land in Larkin Valley, changes in cover produced by plant succession eliminate the bird within a couple of decades. Now rarely bred and released hereabouts, the pheasant has almost disappeared in the Monterey Bay area.

Another exotic species is the European starling. One hundred starlings are said to have been released in New York in 1890 by a group of Shakespeare enthusiasts who wished to honor the poet by introducing into this country the birds named in his writings. In 1940 (p. 148), Peterson remarked that the starling "has at this date reached the base of the Rockies and Utah. To be looked for on the Pacific Coast." In 1961 (p. 241), he gave the starling's range as "from Vancouver I. to southern California." At a time between these two dates a few had been seen in the Point Reyes area (Sibley, 1952, p. 32), and their first appearance in the Monterey Bay area was probably in Carmel Valley in 1953 (Roberson and Tenney, 1993, p. 304). They were probably here some years before most people recognized them. The owner of a ranch by the Salinas River Road, a few miles southwest of Spreckels, states that starlings appeared on his place for the first time in 1968, and within a year the birds were already a serious pest, taking figs from the trees in his yard. The author saw a flock near the Moss Landing cemetery in November 1969. Starlings nest in sycamore trees along the creek at the entrance to Toro Regional Park and are said to compete with acorn woodpeckers for nesting sites in the park. They are occasionally seen in areas remote from settlement in the Sierra de Salinas.

Few birds rival the starling in adaptability. On August 9, 1970, a flock of Brewer's blackbirds was observed feeding on insects in a lawn near West Cliff Drive in Santa Cruz. Flying and feeding with them, apparently completely at ease as a member of the flock, was a single starling. Throughout 1972, starlings and blackbirds often fed together on the same lawn and perched in nearby Monterey pines. Again, on August 30, 1973, half a dozen starlings intermixed with about a dozen blackbirds fed together. (At this time of year the differences between the two birds are particularly marked; in fall the starling's plumage turns lighter and becomes speckled.)

In the Monterey Peninsula Audubon Society's bird count of December 1973, more starlings were seen than any other bird (*The Sanderling*, vol. 29, no. 6). In 1994, starlings were still among the three most common birds in the Monterey Bay area.

The cattle egret, a native of Africa, having spread to South America, appeared in Texas in 1955. Around 1970, the first cattle egrets were seen in the Monterey Bay area. They have been observed around Elkhorn Slough, and were reported on the Monterey Peninsula in December 1970 (*The Sanderling*, vol. 26, no. 6).

Wild turkeys were first introduced into California in 1908. Since that time more birds have been imported from the southwestern United States and Mexico, where the species is native. Wild turkeys are established in southern parts of the Monterey Bay area, and subject to an open hunting season.

Some humanized landscapes have relatively diverse bird populations (Pitelka, 1942), particularly areas of suburban park and garden where elements of the native flora are incorporated. It may be noted at this point that overly tidy parks and gardens, carefully trimmed and sprayed, have but limited appeal for wildlife; reduction in birdlife often "parallels significantly the establishment of *formality*—the removal of elements of naturalness" (Grinnell, 1943, p. 185). Birds even seek out what may to us seem unkempt surroundings. Because of inborn preferences, particular species favor specific parts of a single tree, including parts that are present only at certain stages of the tree's natural growth. For example, different bird species may either feed on leaf buds, take larvae off young foliage, take food from flowers, hunt insects in furrowed bark, nest in trunk cavities, eat grubs in decaying branches, perch on snags, or feed on the seeds of weedy undergrowth. The planting and arranging of parks for maximum variety of animal life may one day add a dimension to urban horticulture and give a new meaning to the term "zoological garden."

The destructive effects of human presence are much emphasized at present, and for the most part appropriately. But under suitable conditions, diversification and enrichment may accompany settlement. Such conditions have been observed elsewhere in rural California. A study of bird life in the San Joaquin Valley in 1922 described the very destructive effects of marsh drainage on avifauna there. But at the same time the study concluded that not only had the number of species increased in parts of that area following irrigation and other agricultural development, but the actual number of birds per unit area had greatly increased (Grinnell, 1943, p. 124). Although this statement was written before the development of modern insecticides and herbicides, it may still be valid. With suitable management of vegetation in agricultural and suburban parts of the Monterey Bay area much can be done to increase the diversity of bird life there.

On the other hand, the general observation has been made that artificial grassland and tree plantations are "conspicuous for a fauna impoverished in species though rich in individuals" (Hesse, 1937, p. 544). This statement seems applicable to most of the grassland of the Monterey Bay area (which has large numbers of individuals of relatively few species; e.g., mourning doves, meadowlarks, and

California ground squirrels). In at least one kind of artificial forest, namely, eucalyptus groves, not only the number of species but the number of individuals is small.

Quantitative data on the responses of local animals to human activities are scarce. This is unfortunate, because such ethological information is needed for preserving native species in areas subjected to increasingly intensive settlement.

Early explorers frequently remarked on the tameness of animals in areas never settled by people. In his *Voyage of the Beagle*, Darwin noted that most terrestrial bird species on the Galapagos Islands (prehistorically uninhabited) could be approached and killed with a stick; and that the earliest visitors to the Islands had birds alight on their hats. That wild animals become increasingly tame as they experience frequent non-alarming contacts with humans can be readily seen in almost any park or game refuge. On the other hand, the great differences in tameness from species to species cannot be explained by learned behavior alone. Darwin, for instance, concluded that "in regard to the wildness of birds toward man, there is no way of accounting for it, except as an inherited habit"; that wildness "is not acquired by individual birds in a short time, even when much persecuted; but that in the course of successive generations it becomes hereditary."

The whole subject of timidity or tameness in animals is complex. It is not necessarily a special psychological tolerance of humanity alone that draws a species into areas of dense human population, but rather some other factor, say ready acceptance of new foods (e.g., the seeds of alien weeds attract house finches to settled areas). Timidity in some species varies seasonally, or according to the age of the individual animal, or according to the scene of the animal's activity at the time it is approached, and so on. [For example, the harbor seal, one of the wariest of pinnipeds while on land, behaves differently in the sea: There, surfers say, it nears and even brushes against their boards. Off Lighthouse Point in Santa Cruz, surfers sometimes paddle to within touching distance of sea otters.] Even whether our various native birds are alarmed primarily by sight or sound seems to be poorly known.

What might be called a "timidity table" can be drawn up, based on field observations. In similar tables prepared for bird censusing purposes, species are classified according to relative conspicuousness, the scale being based on the average distance at which they first come to the census taker's notice (Kendreigh, 1944). For instance, the brown towhee is first noticed at an average distance of 21 feet (6.3 m), the song sparrow at 66 feet (20 m), the robin at 328 feet (100 m). Plainly the table is also to some extent a measurement of bird wariness (i.e., the towhee is first noticed at an average of 6 m only because it permits approach to within such distances). An actual timidity table, on the other hand, would list average distances at which the various birds become alarmed and take flight. Below are a few examples comparing birds [and mammals] that are related or share similar habitats:

[On land, harbor seals remain close to the water's edge and dive in before they can be approached closely. Elephant seals, on the other hand, are sometimes almost indifferent to human intruders; at Año Nuevo, one can walk among them as they drowse on the beach. The tameness of the California sea lion is between the two. The sea lion soon learns to take advantage of patterned human behavior. For example, on the breakwater at Monterey it can be approached to within unusually short distances. A fence there prohibits human traffic beyond a certain point; and sea lions haul out and rest on breakwater rocks only a few yards beyond, unperturbed by tourists standing nearby. According to some, the Steller's sea lion is almost as wary as the harbor seal.]

The downy woodpecker appears to be the tamest local woodpecker species. The author's average approach to sanderlings feeding on the beach is to within 43 feet (13 m). When they have just begun feeding, the sanderlings seem reluctant to stop, and one can come closer. On the other hand, snowy plovers, which are much rarer birds here, being seen only on a few beaches in the area (e.g., near the mouth of the Pajaro River and north of Natural Bridges State Park), are easier to approach; one can walk to within 33 feet (10 m) of them. On the cobble beach at Point Año Nuevo in late September three black brants were feeding on tufts of fresh Ulva and what appeared to be surf grass. We approached to within 10 feet (3 m), the geese continuing to feed calmly; thus, wariness in black brants varies according to where they are (no hunting is allowed in Año Nuevo State Reserve). The northern phalarope is uncommonly fearless: "I have got within four feet [1.2 m] of one before it would fly" (McGregor and Fiske, 1892, p. 138). While the rufous-sided towhee tends to move out of an area as development occurs, the brown towhee remains. The varied thrush is warier than its relative, the robin. Bonaparte's gull stays farther from people than western and California gulls. Both the purple finch and the house finch are tolerant of people, but the purple finch is less so. Although the band-tailed pigeon sometimes visits bird feeders in outlying residential areas, it is not a town dweller. The mourning dove, on the other hand, often nests in town and is a regular visitor at feeders (where, incidentally, its treatment of other birds is aggressive). Both redwing and Brewer's blackbirds thrive in well-settled areas, but redwings keep to a greater distance from humans. When starlings and Brewer's blackbirds flock together, the starling takes flight sooner; starlings generally fly when approached to within 50 feet (15 m), whereas one can walk to within 6 feet (2 m) or less of blackbirds. Cormorants are among the most timid of sea birds while nesting; on the Farallons they "flee their nests if a human shows himself within 164-328 feet (50-100 m)" (Ainley and Lewis, 1974, p. 436). The birds are less disturbed, however, when their nests are separated from people by water: In the spring of 1995, a colony of Brandt's cormorants built nests and raised their young on an offshore stack at Natural Bridges State Park—having ousted a pair of western gulls that have nested there for years. The stack is less than 100 feet (30 m) from a path and road, and from numerous human observers. In parks and in areas scheduled for residential development such quantitative information, systematically arranged and made more accurate, will have predictive values useful in spacing buildings, paths, and so on for minimum ecological disruption.

3. Fish

3.1. Native Fishes: Changes in Number

The relative numbers of the various fish species present in Monterey Bay have changed greatly as a result of commercial fishing. These ratios periodically change even under natural conditions, as does the total fish biomass in the bay. Such facts will continue to frustrate plans for the rational management of marine animal populations until a model of the dynamic natural ecosystem is postulated, based on thorough study of all records.

The giant schools of fish near shore described in old accounts are no longer present. These reports of fish numbers would seem exaggerated if they were not in general agreement:

Herrings and sardines are frequently so abundant in this bay, that boatmen find it difficult to make their way through the shoals. (*Santa Cruz Sentinel*, Sept. 12, 1868)

California sardine, *Clupea sagax* . . . . The bay near the beach is darkened for long distances, at certain seasons, with this little fish. It is excellent food and, owing to its great abundance, *must sometime prove valuable*. (C. L. Anderson, 1891, p. 33)

Another surf smelt, *Hypomesus olidus* . . . . Found at all seasons, but in August go in great schools near shore. (Harrison, 1892, p. 116)

Still other accounts testify to the large populations of fish in the bay, and at the same time record a curious and apparently natural feature of local fish behavior which is as yet unexplained—namely, the tendency of several species toward mass self-destruction, by swimming ashore. The accounts refer to "sardines," but that term was often applied to small fish indiscriminately. The following note was written April 10, 1775, at Carmel:

> Today there is a great shoal of small sardines on the beach, and they said that *they were so abundant that they made the ground black at the edge of the water*. The commander went there in the afternoon with the fathers to walk and see this wonder. (Bolton, 1933, p. 420)

In 1841, an English visitor at Monterey reported occasions "when a *westerly gale has driven millions of sardines on the strand.*" (Simpson, 1930, p. 105)

The following accounts are from the American period:

> The number of fish in Monterey Bay is almost incredible . . . . In 1863, an immense shoal of herrings, *from some unknown cause was stranded* . . . along the beach, on the Santa Cruz side of the bay. *They extended for nearly three miles, and were spread to the depth of from six inches to nearly two feet over the entire beach.* (Cronise, 1868, p. 131)

> Horse mackerel or Scad, *Trachurus picturatus* . . . . Sometimes our beaches are strewn with these fish, *driven ashore by other fish pursuing them.* (C. L. Anderson, 1891, p. 114)

Neither pursuit by predators nor gale winds can explain all such events. The "herring" referred to in the quoted passages above may actually have been anchovy.

Several fish found in this area in the nineteenth century are now absent or rare—for example, the mullet, long-jawed mudsucker (Anderson, 1891, pp. 29 and 32), and grunion. Nowadays latitudinal changes in fish distribution along this coast are often attributed to temperature changes associated with El Niño fluctuations. While these fluctuations may account for the disappearance of the mullet, the present lack of mudsuckers can more likely be ascribed to the destruction of lagoon habitat.

The grunion, now common only southward from Morro Bay, is renowned for its remarkable breeding cycle. Grunion come to the beach at night, but only for an hour or two immediately after high tide following each full or new moon and, wriggling into the sand just above the water line, deposit their eggs. Some two weeks later the next spring tides uncover their eggs, at which time they hatch.

The only verified spawning of the fish within the Monterey Bay in the twentieth century comes from the vicinity of New Brighton beach (Spratt, 1980, p. 134). The following account, apparently written in the late 1850s, describes a fishing scene on the same stretch of beach:

"A correspondent of the *Santa Cruz Sentinel* writes that paper of *some extraordinary fishing at Aptos Landing, some eight or ten miles from the town of Santa Cruz .... We reached the fishing about twilight .... It was low tide,* the sea here forms a continuous, almost level beach, five or six miles long, and an average width of 160 yards at low tide, with a hard, smooth bottom, and not a pebble or a seaweed visible the whole distance. The ever-changeable bluff, some 100 feet in height, all the estuaries filled in with driftwood, accumulating for years. Now imagine some 100 people *arriving between twilight and dark,* the fine carriages, the omnibuses, two-horse teams, six-horse teams, ox teams, carts and California go-carts, all filled with *persons who have the highest expectation* of making a big haul. The piles of dry drift-wood, set ablaze for the distance of five miles, the *moon shining* his brightest rays on the silver-sand and phosphorescent water. Men, women, and children taking their positions at equal distances, *awaiting the coming of the fish, which occurs when the tide is on the point of coming in .... The incoming tide,* being stronger than the fish is used to, it deposits him through the breakers, often casting great numbers of them high and dry, but most generally depositing them *just through the breakers, into from three to six inches of water,* which causes them to *flounder and squirm* to regain their element; then the real sport commences, men and boys roll up their trowsers, ladies tie their dresses around their waists, and also pitch in ...; when the fish flounders he is both seen and *heard,* as he makes a great commotion ... five of us caught *over five hundred weight*" (*California Fisheries,* Set W, v. 33, Bancroft Library, University of California, Berkeley).

The writer of the account took the fish for stranded horse mackerel —grounded, he theorized, while pursuing anchovies through the breakers. But the details point to the grunion: The fact the event was planned for, the full moon, the rising tide, as well as the reference to noises made by the fish. (The name grunion comes from the Spanish for "grunter," referring to the faint sounds the fish makes while spawning.)

A reading of old accounts of the Monterey Peninsula strongly suggests that grunion once spawned in large numbers on Carmel Beach. Spanish accounts describe circumstances hard to associate with any other fish than the grunion; for example, translating from an account written at Monterey on July 19, 1774:

> The Indians come down to the edge of the beach, chase the fish and throw them ashore. The fresh fish are rich in oil. I have heard so often of these sardines that I would sometime like to go over to Carmel myself to catch some and salt them down on my own account. (Rivera y Moncada, 1774, p. 167)

Judging from the above accounts, the local grunion population may have been depleted by overfishing.

The best-known example of change in numbers among native marine fishes in the area is the sardine. As the local naturalist quoted above predicted, the fish did indeed "prove valuable." Commercial sardine fishing began in the bay around 1905. In 1920, sardine canning was described as a giant industry with a "growth unparalleled within the countries bordering the Pacific" (it has in fact been closely paralleled, since, both in its growth and decline by the Peruvian anchovy industry). In 1947, the sardine disappeared from the bay in commercial quantities rather abruptly, markedly changing the economy of Monterey and Moss Landing. Whether this drastic reduction in numbers was the result of overfishing, natural environmental changes, or (perhaps more likely) a combination of the two is still debated. In any case, the population of the northern anchovy, a species with similar ecological requirements, soon expanded dramatically. This change may be linked, in turn, to a subsequent decline in the populations of the double-crested cormorant, puffin, and Steller's sea lion (Ainley and Lewis, 1974, pp. 442-443).

Certain changes in habit have been observed in another marine fish, the onespot fringehead, which has moved from deeper water into the vicinity of wharves, taking shelter in submerged junk—glass containers and the like (David Lindquist, personal communication).

There is an old theory that the Sacramento and San Joaquin valleys were drained by an Ice Age river system which emptied, via the Santa Clara Valley, into Monterey Bay (Beard, 1941). The theory was first proposed at the beginning of the twentieth century by an ichthyologist seeking to explain the close relationships between the freshwater fish of the Monterey Bay area and those in the Sacramento and San Joaquin rivers (Gilbert, cited in Branner, 1907, p. 1). (The common names of several fish native to the Monterey Bay area—the Sacramento perch, Sacramento blackfish, etc.—express this relationship.)

As a result of the Holocene rise of sea level many small streams that once joined on the now-submerged coastal plain, today flow separately into Monterey Bay (see Branner, 1907, p. 9). Confined to a number of small drainage systems, native freshwater fish of the area have been especially vulnerable, and their numbers and distributions have changed greatly—both from human-caused hydrographic changes and because of the introduction of numerous exotic species. One native fish, the Sacramento sucker, has withstood such changes better than most; it is still common in parts of Pajaro River. Nevertheless, though a hardy species and rarely taken by anglers, even the sucker gives way before such introduced species as the carp and goldfish (Moyle, 1976a, p. 216).

3.2. Introduced Species

Of the 67 freshwater fish species listed for California, 32 are introduced (Lachner et al., 1970, p. 21), including some of the most abundant.

The common shad, probably the first fish to be introduced by man into California, was brought from the Hudson River in 1871. Shad were first planted in the Sacramento River near Tehama, and are now found along the coast from Alaska to San Diego. They were well established in the Salinas River: "After the original introduction, shad appeared at various points along the coast . . . . The only stable populations in California [outside the area that drains into the San Francisco Bay], however, have been those in the Salinas and Russian

Rivers" (Skinner, 1962, p. 86). Actually, there have been no shad in the Salinas for a long time now.

At a much later date, 1953, the threadfin shad was introduced into California from Tennessee as a food for gamefish species. Like the native sucker, it serves as food for trout. Threadfin shad have been planted in Pinto Lake and College Lake, where they are at times very numerous.

The carp was brought to California from Holstein, Germany, in 1872, only a short time after the shad. It is a hardy fish and thrives even in the warm and stagnant pools left in drying stream courses during the rainless summers. There is no doubt that it is the least popular fish ever brought to California. Great sums are spent on its eradication. This is strange because in the Old World carp has been considered to be a great delicacy for centuries, and as such was carried from the Far East into Europe at an early date. Complaints against the carp are many: For instance, that it muddies the water, eats the eggs of other fish, and digs up aquatic plant life. Some defense of the carp appears in early literature:

. . . while they probably have been the principal cause of the destruction of the California perch by eating the eggs and digging up the nests, at the same time they furnish the chief food of the black and striped bass [both introduced], two varieties of fish whose value more than offsets the damage by the carp. (Shebley, 1917, p. 4)

But the judgment against the carp seems now to be generally accepted.

The smallmouth bass was among the first fish introduced into California, having been brought here in 1874. The largemouth bass was introduced shortly afterward (Brown, 1939, p. 310). Both are widespread in the Monterey Bay area. The bluegill, introduced in 1908 as stock for largemouth bass, is now considered a threat to native frogs. It feeds, for example, on the tadpoles of the red-legged frog.

The striped bass, an anadromous fish, was introduced into the Sacramento River system from New Jersey in 1879, and spread very rapidly. It now ranges from the Russian River to Monterey. "Less than a year after being placed in Suisun Bay a specimen was taken in Monterey . . . . Small populations became established on the Salinas [River] as well as Elkhorn Slough" (Skinner, 1962, p. 71). It formerly spawned in the Salinas River (Skinner, 1962, p. 79). The striped bass appears to have established itself securely on this coast. Until 1935, it was even fished commercially. It has become one of the most important species to sport fishermen. There is a reproducing population in San Antonio Reservoir on the upper Salinas (Moyle, 1976, p. 285).

The eastern brook trout (speckled trout) was introduced into California in 1872, the brown trout was brought from Germany in 1895, and the lake trout was introduced in 1889. That they are valuable introductions has rarely been questioned. (The rainbow trout and the cutthroat trout are native to California.)

There are no native catfish on the Pacific slopes north of Mexico, but several species were introduced in the late nineteenth century. Catfish were imported into California in the early 1870s and planted around Salinas in 1876; the white catfish and the brown bullhead were introduced into California in 1874.

Panfish and crappies were first introduced into southern California in 1891 and made their way northward to the San Francisco Bay area through later transplantations. The green sunfish was also introduced in 1891.

Several introduced species are widely planted in ponds. For example, the author saw several boys fishing from an earthen dam between Prunedale and Natividad. One youngster, who had caught a few bluegills and a crappie, said that bass are also caught in the pond, and an occasional catfish; these appear to be the species favored for pond culture by the Department of Fish and Game.

A general despoilation of native fish habitats has taken place in the Salinas River. The position of the river's mouth has been changed, the flow has been reduced by damming and irrigation, and the channel is used heavily for sewage outlets.

In an archaeological excavation at Soledad, 41% of the fish bones collected belonged to the steelhead, "which ascended the Salinas River from the sea to spawn" (Follett, 1972, p. 11). Apparently the steelhead went even farther upstream. In 1776, Father Pedro Font, speaking of the many "good salmon" (i.e., steelhead) that ascend the streams, stated that "even at the mission of San Antonio some of the fish which ascend the Monterey [i.e., Salinas] river have been caught" (Bolton, 1933, p. 302). Few steelhead enter the river these days. Farther upstream, the introduced threadfin shad is common. Below Chualar fishing prospects are very limited. A local landowner on the banks of the Salinas near Gonzales told the author that carp and an occasional smallmouth black bass (both introduced species) and suckers were all that he could catch. The two anadromous introduced species, the shad and the striped bass, were driven out by alterations made in the course of the lower Salinas.

Regarding ecological change in the lakes east of Watsonville, the following note from the nineteenth century is of interest:

> The three largest of these are called College Lake, Laguna Grande [now Kelly Lake], and White Lake [Pinto Lake?]; they are from two hundred to five hundred acres [80 to 200 hectares] in extent, and, at their greatest depths measure sixty feet [18 m]. Being fed by subterranean mountain streams they do not vary in depth with the seasons. *They are prolific in native fish* of excellent quality, and also have been stocked by the Board of Fish Commissioners *with eastern white fish, perch, and landlocked salmon.* (*Overland Monthly*, vol. 10, no. 56, August 1887, p. 7)

The "native fish" mentioned in the quoted passage are unfortunately not identified, but even at that time three introduced species were present; the native species are now gone. In 1961, the city of Watsonville, advised by the Department of Fish and Game, treated Pinto Lake with an unspecified "anoxydizing agent" to eliminate the carp. Since then the lake has been restocked with black bass, crappies, threadfin shad, redear sunfish (first brought to California in 1948), and brown bullhead (catfish). The threadfin shad now reproduces in especially large quantities in the lake.

When carp were introduced here is uncertain. Kelly Lake, which is privately owned, has a fish population of several species too, but is still infested with carp. Although College Lake is now used by a local rod and gun club for hunting, and drained for agricultural use in the summer, with suitable damming it has a real potential for a more general recreational use. The lakes must, incidentally, have shoaled considerably since 1887—Pinto Lake is now only 23 feet (7 m) deep.

The goldfish was introduced into the United States from eastern Asia around the beginning of the twentieth century. It is now established in the Pajaro River, no doubt released from aquaria. The orange and yellow stock does not survive under natural conditions. Free-living specimens are usually olive color, resembling their relative, the carp. Goldfish are also carplike in their preference for warm ponds and sluggish waters.

The mosquito fish (top minnow) has been one of the few successful "biological controls" of mosquito populations. Having been distributed widely throughout the world for that purpose, it is now said to have the greatest range of any freshwater fish. The fish was brought to California from the southeastern United States in 1922, and is now abundant in the streams and irrigation ponds of the Monterey Bay area. A live-bearer, it is easy to reproduce. Distributed by the Mosquito Abatement program of the California Department of Public Health, the fish has been generally welcomed as a promising alternative to pesticides. Nevertheless, there have been complaints about its ecological effects in many parts of the world (Myers, 1965), and misgivings have been voiced about its continued use in the Monterey Bay area: The fish not only destroys mosquito larvae but many other organisms as well—for example, fairy shrimp populations in vernal ponds. Mosquito fish also feed heavily on the native red-legged frog whose population has been steadily decreasing. A few years previous to the introduction of mosquito fish, a well-known ichthyologist had recommended a native fish, "the stickleback (*Gasterosteus*), as a mosquito destroyer in California, particularly in coastal regions" (Hubbs, 1919, p. 21). The time has come to reconsider the propagation of the stickleback, or of other native species, for that purpose.

Although most freshwaters of the Monterey Bay area now swarm with fish from elsewhere, "Even today, undisturbed habitats tend to be dominated by native fishes, while disturbed habitats tend to be dominated by introduced species" (Moyle, 1976b, p. 108).

4. Amphibians and Reptiles

The Santa Cruz long-toed salamander is threatened with extinction, because ponds in which it lives are being filled for construction purposes. The species is known from only a few localities—from Valencia Lagoon, near Aptos; from an area about one kilometer northwest of Ellicott Railroad Station, also in Santa Cruz County; and from a few spots near Elkhorn Slough. It has been placed on the list of endangered species published by the Department of the Interior.

One native that definitely has become rarer here during the last decades is the coast horned lizard. "Horned toads" were once so common that rural children often collected these beautiful little animals for amusement and fed them ants. Several might be carried off to school in a cigar box to be traded back and forth according to size, shape, and markings. But it is hard to believe that this practice alone much reduced their population, since most were released eventually, unharmed. In towns, horned lizards and pond turtles were sometimes also sold for pets at fairs and carnivals.

The bullfrog, native east of the Rocky Mountains, was introduced into California for food.

The spread of the bullfrog in California has been dramatic. The earliest presumed occurrence dates back to about 1905. In a little over 30 years it had become common over most of the Sacramento and San Joaquin valleys, the lowland waters of southern California, in many valleys of the Coast Range, and in scattered localities elsewhere .... The animals are sufficiently abundant to supply the local demand for frog legs ... the state has set a limit. (R. C. Stebbins, 1951, p. 345)

It is said that the bullfrog has had a destructive effect on some native species—for example, that it eats the red-legged frog, an increasingly rare animal.

No exotic reptiles have been established here, either accidentally or purposely.

5. Mollusks and Some Other Aquatic Invertebrates

Within a few decades after east-coast Americans arrived in California, the abalone had become their favorite native food mollusk—a taste they acquired from Chinese Americans, who had started the abalone-meat industry.

Only the red abalone was taken commercially. Huge quantities have been collected in the Monterey Bay area. Over 1,360,000 kg (3,000,000 pounds) per year were harvested from 1929 through 1931. Thus, the population of red abalone has been influenced more by people than have other abalone populations. In the 1930s great heaps of discarded shells could be seen along the road as one left Monterey for Castroville. (Abalone was one of the principal items processed on Cannery Row, made famous by John Steinbeck.) After the Chinese take of abalone in shallow water was restricted by law, Japanese Americans, who were experienced divers, moved into the industry: "Between 1916 and 1929, almost the entire [California] abalone catch, over 2 million pounds per year, was taken by Japanese crews and landed at Monterey" (Cox, 1962, p. 84). When the Japanese were moved inland by the government in 1942, the abalone industry virtually disappeared. It revived here weakly after World War II. The industry's main centers were located mainly to the south of the Monterey Bay area where, for a time, black abalone were harvested in rapidly increasing quantities. All commercial collection of abalone is now forbidden in the Monterey Bay area. On the other hand, the recent development of inexpensive wetsuits has had its effect on the abalone population: The noncommercial take of red abalone has increased. (Black abalone are now protected by a permanently closed season.)

Mussels have never been much used as a food by Californians of north European ancestry. The fact that they are rendered poisonous by blooms of a protozoan, *Gonyaulax catenella*, during midsummer and early fall has given them a bad reputation. Mussels are among the most common mollusks on rocky shorelines and are probably even more abundant now than in the eighteenth century, their Indian collectors having disappeared. Fishermen commonly strip them from the rocks for bait—using either the mussels themselves or, more often, the mussel worms that live among them.

The native Olympia oyster was once more plentiful in Elkhorn Slough than it is at present. As noted previously, on one Indian midden site near the slough, shells of the native oyster are almost the only ones to be seen. In 1926, several oystermen worked the beds there, greatly depleting them. In 1931, a diked bed for growing native (and eastern) oysters was laid out on the mud flats in Parsons Slough, a branch of Elkhorn Slough. These experimental plantings of the native oyster were apparently successful, but except for a small harvest in 1935, no commercial venture developed. The oyster is found on pilings in Elkhorn Slough and Monterey Harbor. It is said to be "especially partial to iron as a place of attachment" (MacGinitie, 1935, p. 720). Its partiality for iron is, of course, a postindustrial adaptation.

Pismo clams were reportedly taken at Santa Cruz Beach in 1861 (Smith and Gordon, 1948, p. 162); they are not found there now. They are still taken between Aptos Creek and the mouth of the Pajaro River; Watsonville Beach has long been a favorite site for their collection. Old residents tell of times before the beginning of the twentieth century when farmers took horse teams and ploughed the beach at low tide to obtain Pismo clams for hog food.

5.1. Introduced Saltwater Mollusks

Several exotic oysters have been planted in California. Even where growing conditions are good, these alien species rarely reproduce themselves, and none seems to have established itself; spat has to be imported periodically.

Probably the first to be introduced was the eastern oyster, from the Atlantic coast of the United States. It arrived at San Francisco in

Clumps of bay mussels on pilings at Sandholdt Bridge, Moss Landing—an example of human influence on local animal distribution: The colonies thrive here in an area of soft, silty bottom only because of the presence of the bridge and old pilings. The mussel grows best where it has a solid surface to fasten on. In Elkhorn Slough, a large colony grows in an old oyster bed on the shells of dead Japanese oysters. In many countries, such heaps of mussels, free for the taking, would be a great attraction to passersby. (Photo B. Gordon)

1869 or 1870, on the newly completed transcontinental railroad.

Elkhorn Slough has been used for oyster experimentation for some time. The date of the first plantings of the eastern oyster there is uncertain. A planting made in 1923 gradually disappeared. In 1929, Mexican oysters from the vicinity of Acapulco were tried, but this venture, too, was abandoned. In 1929, the Japanese (Pacific) oyster was tried and was so successful that a much larger planting was made the following year. Eastern oyster spat was again planted in 1932 and 1936—the last planting there until after World War II (*Pacific Fisherman*, Feb. 1936, p. 42). In 1946, a small amount of Japanese oyster spat was planted, but no commercial enterprise developed. Both eastern and Japanese oysters were growing in the slough in 1948 (Smith and Gordon, 1948, pp. 169-170), and some very large Japanese oysters until 1970.

Although the oysters themselves were unable to reproduce here, several plant and animal species accidentally introduced with them did establish themselves. For example, the oyster drill, an Atlantic species of snail, was introduced with the eastern oyster and has spread, attacking other mollusks. The oyster drill had already been introduced in 1898, in the same way, into San Francisco Bay, where it is still abundant. Although the drill was reported to be "fairly common" in Elkhorn Slough in 1948 (Smith and Gordon, 1948, p. 189), there are few if any there now.

The soft-shell clam, native to the southern Atlantic coast of the United States, is now one of the most important food mollusks in California; it is even collected commercially. The clam is believed to have been accidentally introduced into San Francisco Bay with the first importations of the eastern oyster around 1870. However, it was purposely planted in the Monterey Bay area (Hanna, 1939, p. 306) at a later date. In 1948, it was described as common in the mud at Elkhorn Slough (Smith and Gordon, 1948, p. 176).

The Japanese cockle, introduced around 1930, is now found from Elkhorn Slough northward and appears to be replacing the native rock clam, or rock cockle (Hedgpeth, 1962, p. 116). It is believed to have been introduced with the Japanese oyster.

A small Japanese mussel, *Musculus senhousia*, has been collected in Elkhorn Slough (Ricketts and Calvin, 1968, p. 379). And the Japanese horn snail is common behind the dunes north of Jetty Road. For example, in April 1974, one could see patches of sandy bottom at the shallow margins of the slough there with more than 200 shells per square meter. This introduced species is even more abundant on mud flats in the upper parts of the slough. Still other species introduced with the oyster industry are probably to be found (Carlton, 1975).

Two cosmopolitan species, the bay mussel and the shipworm, neither apparently native on this coast, are found in the Monterey Bay area. But their dates and modes of introduction are disputed. According to most authorities teredo, a scourge in Europe since classical times, was unknown in California at the beginning of the twentieth century (Ricketts and Calvin, 1968, p. 370). It is "practically certain that *Teredo navalis* has been imported to San Francisco Bay within recent years, probably between 1910 and 1912" (Kofoid et al., 1927, p. 194). Although it is often called the European shipworm, its actual origin is rather uncertain. The teredo either appeared in the San Francisco Bay region between 1910 and 1914 or, if it was already there, suddenly became abundant at that time. It especially infested pilings at Mare Island, where, by 1917, its effects became catastrophic: Many pilings of ferry slips collapsed as a result of teredo infestations. The shipworm is estimated to have done about 25 million dollars' worth of damage in San Francisco Bay between 1917 and 1921. Our role in its dissemination is obvious; wherever pilings and wharves are built, they create a special habitat for the animal.

The pier at Port Watsonville, located at what is now called Palm Beach, is said to have been destroyed by shipworms: "Teredo worms had caused extensive damage to the pilings" (Locke-Paddon, 1964). Early in November 1904, heavy seas broke up the wharf. However, this damage could well have been done by a native species: "The native species, *Bankia setacea*, was noted as a serious pest as early as 1870" in California (Hanna, p. 309). It is claimed that the materials released by Kaiser's effluent in Moss Landing Harbor suppress shipworms and that they do little damage in that vicinity. Both species may be present in pilings around Monterey Bay, but *Teredo navalis* has not recently been identified hereabouts. (The gribble—an isopod, not a mollusk—also does much damage to wooden pilings: Two of the several species found along the central California coast may have been introduced from the Atlantic in the nineteenth century [Carlton, 1975, p. 18].)

The bay mussel has an uncommonly wide distribution, being found around the world in north temperate regions. According to most authorities it was introduced here by people: "The common bay mussel is not a native species, but is thought to have reached our coast from Europe by way of sailing vessels several hundred years ago" (Skinner, 1962, p. 106).

Because it is exceptional, the case of the bay mussel is especially interesting: An introduced species, the mussel appears to have completely replaced its native relative the surf mussel in a large part of the latter's range. During the first half of the twentieth century, the surf mussel is said to have disappeared, almost unnoticed, along the whole coast to the south of San Francisco Bay—possibly as a result of competition from the invader (J. B. Geller, as cited in *Science*, January 20, 1995, p. 331).

As with cultural landscapes, much altered seascapes provide alien species with favorable environmental conditions: While deep oceanic waters and open coasts are inhospitable to alien organisms, marine harbors (heavily trafficked and far from a natural state), appear to welcome them. Arriving ships, carrying exotics from port to port on hulls and in ballast-water, ensure a constant supply of potential immigrants. Nevertheless, naturalization is by no means assured. After all, maritime commerce has been carried on since antiquity, and in California for several centuries. On the other hand, since "ships have used water as ballast regularly [only] since the 1880s," the number of transfers is increasing (Carlton and Geller, 1993, p. 79).

On the other hand, the bay mussel has often been identified in prehistoric shell middens—a contradiction, unless bay-mussel shells confined to midden surfaces have been mixed during archaeological excavation with those of the native surf mussel, taken from lower levels.

Curiously, there has been no attempt made to grow the bay mussel commercially for food in California; in fact, in the Monterey Bay area few are even gathered. In Europe the bay mussel is an important aquacultural species, rivaling the oyster in places.

5.2. Introduced Land and Freshwater Mollusks: Snails and Slugs

The brown garden snail (*Helix aspersa*) was brought to the vicinity of San Jose around 1856 by a French family and planted for use as food on a few acres of vineyard on Guadalupe Creek (Stearns, 1882, pp. 129-130). It was also introduced into southern California. From these sites it has spread to become one of the worst garden pests in coastal districts of the state. As an example of its abundance, in one evening over a thousand were collected from the lawn around a house in Santa Cruz, and the supply was by no means exhausted. On the other hand, the snail has not yet spread to yards around buildings in remoter areas (such as Mount Madonna County Park and Pinnacles National Monument). It spreads most readily in towns and in tract housing, where yards adjoin. As yet, curiously, no native birds seem to have learned to prey on the snail—although the starling (which is also from Europe) does so frequently—thrashing the snail's shells to bits against hard surfaces to free the flesh. Starlings, now numerous, have greatly reduced snail populations along West Cliff Drive in Santa Cruz.

A similar, and somewhat larger, lighter-colored, introduced species, *Otala lactea*, arrived in California around 1940, and is now found in the Monterey Bay area. At least some colonies of this snail were established in the state intentionally as a food source. It is reported to have a better flavor than the more common brown garden snail (Hanna, 1966, pp. 12-14).

A small foreign snail, *Cochlicella ventrosa*, infests several blocks in Santa Cruz (Hanna, 1966, p. 26); it has been found, for example, on David Way near West Cliff Drive.

Several species of slug have also been introduced accidentally from Europe and are now destructive garden pests (Hanna, 1966, pp. 29-35).

5.3. Introduced Crustaceans and Other Aquatic Animals

There are no native crayfishes in this part of California (Riegel, 1959, p. 48). But in 1912, large batches of a northwestern species,

Pacifastacus leniusculus, obtained from the Columbia River, were shipped to the California Fish and Game hatchery at Brookdale: Later, many were released into the nearby San Lorenzo River. The species is now also established near Swanton and in the Pajaro and Carmel rivers; it is probably in many other streams as well. An eastern crayfish, *Procambarus clarkii*, probably brought to California from Louisiana, is also present in the Monterey Bay area. It appears to be better adapted to warm sloughs than is the northwestern species; for example, it is found in Tembladero Slough, near Castroville. It is said to survive the seasonal drying up of streams here by burrowing to water level. How this eastern crayfish reached California is uncertain, but it seems to have arrived sometime between 1939 and 1941 (Riegel, 1959, pp. 34, 46, 48). It was collected in the southern part of the state as early as 1925 (Bonnot, 1930, p. 212).

The Japanese anemone, a small, salmon-colored, occasionally green-tinted, species appeared suddenly in Elkhorn Slough after the Japanese oyster was introduced. (It has since journeyed even farther eastward, having turned up on the Texas coast in 1947.)

The naked hydroid *Syncoryne mirabilis* is found in the Monterey Bay area:

> Agassiz found this form in San Francisco Bay in 1865. There is at least a *distinct possibility that it is a relic of the days of wooden ships*, for the same species occurs on the East Coast, and it seems unlikely that its natural distribution would account for its occurrence on this coast also. (Ricketts and Calvin, 1968, p. 332)

5.4. Early Pollution and Depletion of Shoreline Life by Collectors

Pollution by sewage had already significantly damaged the mollusk habitat in the nineteenth century. Unfortunately, these effects on the littoral zone are likely to be obvious to specialists only. An extract from a letter to the editor of the periodical *Nautilus* in 1892, by a well-known naturalist, describes conditions at Monterey:

Monterey as a collecting ground [for mollusks] is already seriously injured, and will probably be nearly ruined before long, on account of the Hotel Del Monte, the new town of Pacific Grove, and the increased population of old Monterey, all of the sewage of which is turned into the bay in front of the town. Beaches which would formerly afford several hundred species are now nearly bare, or offensive with stinking black mud. (Dall, 1892-1893, p. 48)

A similar report was made in 1893:

Monterey is no longer the famous collecting ground it used to be. The increasing population at and around Pacific Grove is driving away all the land shells. The deadly sewage flowing from the various towns into Monterey Bay is killing the marine shells. (Wood, 1892-1893, p. 70)

Spoken at that time, these words of warning stimulated little popular interest. On the other hand, some marine mollusks actually thrive in this environment; the black turban population around the Pacific Grove sewer outfall is the largest I have seen.

Overzealous collectors have become a prime factor in molluskan ecology in the bay area.

No longer is it possible to collect two hundred species as Dall did in 1866 [at Monterey]. Even at extremely low tide the rocky shores are less productive, as many of the movable rocks have been overturned in the ever-increasing search for specimens of marine life. (Smith and Gordon, 1948, p. 153)

Fortunately collection in the area has recently been curtailed, for example since the creation of California state beaches and parks; nevertheless, the shoreline has been severely depleted. Probably collection for amusement and specimens is now a more important factor in this depletion than is collection for food.

6. Insects and Mites

Even among native insects one can see adjustments to changes made by human inhabitants in the area.

One of our best-known native insects is the monarch butterfly. Monarchs pass the winter at many places along the coast, but they congregate in swarms at Pacific Grove (where they are protected by city ordinance). Nowadays the swarms can be seen not only in the native cypress tree, but on the introduced eucalyptus as well, as in the groves at Moss Landing and at Natural Bridges State Park. This may, however, be but one small part of a marked transformation in the butterfly's habitat and behavior resulting from human activities: According to one investigator, "the monarch's seasonal mass migration is a recent phenomenon, an artifact of colonial and modern land-use patterns and concomitant vegetation changes in temperate North America" (Shapiro, p. 1984, citing R. I. Vane-Wright).

Another well-known native is the sulphur butterfly, also known as the alfalfa butterfly. When the alfalfa plant, a native of Eurasia, was introduced into California between 1850 and 1860, the larvae of the sulphur butterfly found it an especially attractive food. As alfalfa cultivation spread in the state, the sulphur butterfly became a major pest of the crop.

The plume moth, a principal pest in artichoke fields, is also a native; its other main host here is the bull thistle, which is, like the artichoke, from Europe. But such instances of native insects that have taken immediately to alien plants as food are not common. Natives are a minority among the rural-urban insect pests—and, on the other hand, few alien insects have entered the natural plant associations, except in disturbed sites.

Since oak moths sometimes denude oaks both in suburban areas and on sites which are at present but slightly disturbed, it seems likely that recurrent moth infestations are a natural phenomenon here. Burgeoning oak-moth populations are believed to be brought under eventual control mainly by a viral disease. Ordinarily this disease afflicts only a small percentage of the moths, but when the insects appear in exceptionally large numbers, they are more susceptible to infection by reason of overcrowding, and the virus spreads through the population as an epidemic (Baker, 1965, p. 10). Large predators such as birds play little part in moth control (Harville, 1955, p. 115). In the

Berkeley hills, severe moth infestations are said to occur about once every seven years (Baker, 1965, p. 10).

As an agent of natural biological disturbance, the oak moth may play an important role in maintaining habitat diversity within live-oak woodlands. Although some oaks are almost completely defoliated and temporarily unsightly, they are rarely killed. By defoliating the oaks, the moths in effect render these evergreen trees "occasionally deciduous," thus removing shade and allowing lower-growing heliophile species (bush monkey flower, manzanita, poison oak, and perhaps also such rare species as Monterey manzanita) to establish themselves.

Coast live oaks defoliated by oak moths, south of Aptos. Here oak moths feed only on live-oak leaves. Although elsewhere in the Monterey Bay area the moths are sometimes present on deciduous oaks, populations there are comparatively small because when leaves of the deciduous trees drop in winter, the moth larvae lose their food supply and die (Essig, 1958, p. 689). As shown in the photograph, oak moths occasionally sweep through whole tracts of coast live oak. (Photo B. Gordon)

Ticks of the genus *Ixodes* are the primary vectors of the spirochete that causes Lyme disease—in California, the western black-legged tick, *I. pacificus.*

In the eastern United States, mice and deer are primary hosts for ticks carrying the disease. In California, the black-tailed deer is a common carrier, but the host reservoir for the disease, demonstrated or suspected, also includes mice, dogs, rabbits, raccoons, etc. The geographic origin of Lyme disease is uncertain. An ailment with similar symptoms was described, off and on, in Europe as early as the nineteenth century. Thence, the spirochete may have spread to New England—where it was first identified after an outbreak of the disease in Lyme Connecticut, in 1975—and from there westward throughout most of the United States. In California, the first case was reported in 1978, and at present the disease is a major public health problem.

Food requirements as well as habitat requirements of many animals are quite specific. For example, there are 144 insect species closely associated with one native plant, the coyote brush (Tilden, 1951, p. 175); the list includes a number of insects that feed on nothing else. Thus, the coyote brush supports a distinctive fauna, and at the same time attracts the larger wildlife that preys on these insect associates: Another species of evergreen shrub, though of similar form, planted in its place will have by no means the same biotic effects. The remarkable dependence of our native butterflies on particular plant families (or even on particular species) has been summarized (Tilden, 1965, pp. 60-70). Many insects are so closely dependent on certain kinds of food plants that the association is actually a valuable aid in identification. Cumulatively, such data again point up the practicability of spacing plant cover and microhabitat for purposes of controlling animal distribution. They show the need, in fact, for a systematic regional program of greenery dispersal, both for maintaining wildlife and for controlling pests. This would not be simply greenery as such, but greenery arranged according to chemical variety, as evidenced, for example, by its palatability to certain animal species.

Of introduced insects, the body louse, which has been associated with humans from their beginnings, and the flea were probably brought across the Bering Straits by the earliest immigrants. In any case, these pests were known to the Costanoan Indians when the Spanish arrived.

The common housefly, one of the oldest and most prevalent of synanthropes, may also have reached the Americas at an early date. The lesser housefly, on the other hand, is definitely a European species, having probably come to California in the ships of the first Spanish settlers (Essig, 1931, p. 318).

Two species of cockroach were introduced first by the Spanish, then repeatedly by Americans. The most widespread exotic is the oriental roach (black roach), an insect that has spread with maritime commerce almost throughout the world. In the Monterey Bay area it is common in basements and sewers. The light-colored German cockroach is an even more serious pest in this area, particularly in kitchens, bakeries, and restaurants. Another exotic roach, the American cockroach (also known as Mexican cockroach) is thought to have reached the southeastern United States in slave ships; the Australian cockroach arrived later. Despite their names, all of these roaches are of African origin.

The bedbug infested early sailing ships and probably arrived with the first Europeans; it is never far from human habitations.

The grape phylloxera is native to eastern North America. There, the insect lives on the roots of native grapes, which are undamaged by its presence. In 1852 the phylloxera was somehow introduced in California, and attacked the roots of the European grapes which have been grown here since the days of the Spanish Missions. Within a short time the phylloxera had destroyed a thriving wine industry. Toward the middle of the twentieth century the industry was reestablished in California, and a few decades later in the Monterey Bay area itself—both in the Santa Cruz Mountains and, especially, along the east side of the Salinas Valley between Chualar and Soledad. By the mid 1980s, however, phylloxera had reappeared and growers were forced to begin replacing their vines with resistant stock.

(European grape varieties grafted on the roots of native American grapes are undamaged by phylloxera.)

The honeybee, often presented as a symbol of nature itself is, in fact but another introduced domesticated animal. Although some claim that the honeybee was brought to California by the Spanish, or even by the Russian settlers at Fort Ross, it seems fairly certain that the first hive of bees to reach California was brought to San Jose by Americans in 1853, by way of the Isthmus of Panama (Essig, 1931, pp. 265, 273). Swarms were sold in Soquel in 1859. In parts of eastern North America the honeybee is said to have become known to Indians before they ever saw a white man, swarms of the insects having moved westward well ahead of European settlement. But it is unlikely that the first bees to reach California swarmed overland.

Many domesticated plants—apples, cherries, pears, and so on—depend on pollination by the honeybee to set fruit. Driving through the apple orchards near Aromas in winter one will see buckets and cans hanging in the leafless trees. These serve as "drinking fountains" for bees. As the red delicious, an increasingly popular apple variety here, is especially difficult to pollinate, bees, the principal pollinators, are needed in large numbers. In spring, when the trees are in blossom, drinking water is poured into the cans so that the bees needn't journey back and forth between the orchard and the Pajaro River, some distance away.

The ecological importance of the honeybee in California has grown steadily since its arrival: Foraging for nectar and pollen, the bee visits and pollinates a great variety of plants, both introduced and wild. Over those large areas in which agriculture and urban development have destroyed their habitats, native insect pollinators have been replaced by the honeybee. Studies of wild plant communities in the Southwest show that where honeybees range into the wild, they often out-compete and crowd out native pollinators (carpenter bees, bumble bees and others)—that, in fact, honeybees "preempt the most productive habitats and flower species" (Schaffer, et al., 1983, pp. 564-565).

True, some native insects are also able to pollinate both native and introduced plants: Native leafcutter bees pollinate domesticated members of the sunflower family, and native bumble bees pollinate alfalfa and clover. Then too, there are native plants that honeybees are unable to pollinate; for instance, bumble bees pollinate certain long-tubed native flowers "that honeybees and other short-tongued bees cannot" (Powell and Hogue, 1979, p. 353); besides, the flowers of some native plants (including the buckeye) are toxic to the honeybee. Despite all this, the honeybee—because of its cosmopolitan foraging activities and the wide range of environments in which it flourishes— pollinates a greater number of plants than any native insect. Whether the honeybee has disruptive effects on the structure of native insect communities in the Monterey Bay area seems not to have been investigated, and the extent to which the area's native plants are now dependent on honeybees for pollination also appears to be unknown. Elsewhere, because of its role in cross-pollination, the honeybee is recognized as an important factor in the evolutionary process.

Although orchards still consider honeybees essential for successful pollination, and invite beekeepers to place hives near their trees, the commercial propagation of several native fruit-tree pollinators has recently shown signs of success.

Two of the more serious orchard pests introduced into this area in the early 1870s were the coddling moth and San Jose scale. By 1906, the coddling moth, a native of Europe, had become one of the most injurious insects to apples in the Pajaro Valley (*Watsonville Register-Pajaronian*, May 10, 1906). San Jose scale, a native of Asia, was imported into the Santa Clara Valley, probably on Chinese flowering peach trees, around 1870. It entered the Monterey Bay area not long afterward.

In 1874, there occurred an event in Santa Clara Valley that was to have a profound effect on the future of the Pajaro Valley. Red (San Jose) scale attacked the apple trees, wiping out nearly every orchard. This created a void which stimulated the planting of apple trees in the Pajaro Valley, which had not been infested . . . . Oddly, prunes which had been grown in the Pajaro Valley were torn out for apples, while in Santa Clara, dismayed growers tore out their apple trees and planted prunes . . . . The Pajaro Valley did not entirely escape the terrible red scale . . . . A lime-sulfur combination, which proved effective against scale, made a timely appearance. (*Watsonville Register-Pajaronian*, June 6, 1968)

The European white cabbage butterfly, now probably the world's most widely distributed butterfly, arrived in California by way of Canada in the 1880s. It is one of the few butterflies harmful to the human economy. The butterflies feed not only on cabbage but on cauliflower and sprouts, and on some native crucifers as well.

The Argentine ant is the most important ant pest of farm and household. This native of the American tropics is thought to have been brought by ship from Brazil to New Orleans in 1891. The species was first collected in California in 1905, and was found near Campbell in the Santa Clara Valley in 1908. It probably appeared in the Monterey Bay area around that time, too. The workers of this species are almost black, are odorless, and do not bite or sting effectively. In towns their nesting places are often found in manholes and basements, where they are kept warm by steam pipes (Cook, 1953, pp. 234-235). The Argentine ant has replaced native ants in many areas. The ant spreads and tends the native Monterey pine scale for the honeydew the scale produces. This native scale causes serious injuries to Monterey pine seedlings. The ants tend mealybugs, too, and protect them from enemies (Swain, 1952, p. 61).

A number of insects have been introduced with domesticated animals. The hen louse, a parasite on domestic poultry, is well known to local poultry growers, as is the red poultry mite. The latter, now found throughout much of the world, infests poultry and their roosts, and occasionally people, as well.

The horse botfly, which somewhat resembles the honeybee, lays its eggs on the hair of horses' forelegs. "The species is European and has been distributed with horses throughout the world" (Essig, 1958, p. 575). Though sometimes found in horse-watering troughs, and mistakenly thought by some rural people to be animated horse hairs, the hairworm, *Gordius*, has a life history unrelated to horses.

Other insects have come to the area on accidentally introduced animals, and some parasites and diseases were transferred to native species:

Neither the so-called domestic rats, Norwegian, Alexandrian, black, nor the house mouse, nor their 3 common fleas—the Oriental rat flea (*Xenopsylla cheopis*), the European rat flea (*Nosopsyllus fasciatus*), nor the mouse flea (*Leptopsylla segnis*) are native of this country. All seem to have been introduced through shipping channels. (Hubbard, 1947)

These fleas are the principal vectors of bubonic plague, an Old World disease, and of murine or endemic typhus. The fleas are now found on native animals in California, to a limited extent.

Several European insects which are bird parasites are believed to have entered North America with either the house sparrow or starling—and at least one has spread to native birds (Brown and Wilson, p. 156-157).

The citrus mealybug, (another source of honeydew for the Argentine ant) was introduced on citrus trees from the Mediterranean area; it also attacks other fruit trees. Its infestations were a problem in the Carmel Valley in the 1930s when pear orchards were extensive there. It, or a similar mealybug, is also found on poison hemlock around Elkhorn Slough (Essig, 1931, pp. 131-133).

The pear slug, a native of Europe, is found on cherry and pear trees here and in the Santa Clara Valley (Essig, 1931, pp. 257-259). (Despite the name "slug" it is actually an insect larva.) Unlike neighboring areas, the Monterey bay area has been spared major infestations by the Mediterranean fruit fly.

The clothes moth, introduced from Europe at an early date, is a destructive household pest.

The European earwig was discovered in Berkeley in 1923, and reached the Monterey Bay area shortly thereafter. Another European species, the green apple aphis, has spread around the world in midlatitudes, wherever its hosts have been introduced. In addition to the apple, its host plants include cotoneaster, pyracantha, and loquat.

The corn earworm, a moth larva that is a major pest on maize and tomato plants, is an introduced species here, although native to the Americas.

The above list of introduced insect species is quite incomplete. No other group of introduced animals is so large or, in terms of disruptive effects on human occupancy and problems of control, so important. On the fertile flatlands of the lower Salinas and Pajaro valleys the natural mosaic of native plant associations inhabited by native insects, each with its special dietary needs and subject to natural controls, has been erased. The infinitely more uniform plant cover that has replaced it (consisting of row upon row, mile after mile, of lettuce, orchard trees, brussels sprouts, etc.) stands as an open invitation to itinerant insect species, long adapted to just such fare. Here, the subject matter of natural history is reduced to little more than the study of a few crops and their pests.

Arguments for diversity are by no means based on aesthetic appeal alone. Considerable evidence has accumulated showing that areas of great diversity in plant cover are more stable in terms of fluctuating animal numbers than are areas of "clean culture" (i.e., large tracts devoted exclusively to crop plants). Such diverse settings provide habitats for all varieties of predator and parasite and therefore limit the growth of pest-insect populations (Pimentel, 1961). The artichoke plume moth, for example, has become extremely difficult to control under present agricultural usage.

In 1869, the cottony cushion scale was discovered in California on specimens of *Acacia latifolia*, which had been introduced from Australia. Within 20 years, the scale threatened to destroy the state's citrus industry. It was in response to this threat that "the first successful introduction of a beneficial insect into any country to prey on an injurious one" was made (Essig, 1958, p. 415). The vedalia, the most famous ladybird beetle in California, was introduced from Australia to southern California in 1888 and 1889 and quickly brought the cottony cushion scale under control. An Australian fly, *Cryptochaetum iceryae*, an internal parasite of cottony cushion scale, was introduced into California citrus groves in 1888. In northern California it became a more efficient enemy of cottony cushion scale than was the vedalia, keeping the scale under almost perfect control (Essig, 1958, p. 616). All three insects are now rare in the Monterey Bay area.

Biological control of California insect pests has been studied for over a century. The mosquito fish (noted earlier) and the vedalia are well-known and successful examples. Because its consequences cannot be foreseen completely, the introduction of an alien species is a potentially hazardous procedure—but probably less so than is control based on the use of toxic substances. Certainly research on biological controls is one of the more promising practical aspects of the study of human influences on the environment.

A helpful alien, in terms of soil quality, is the large European earthworm introduced into the eastern U.S. with soil brought with European plants and animals, or used as ballast in ships returning from Europe. On land the worm was widely dispersed with the cattle industry, its eggs having been spread especially on the hooves of horses. Other smaller earthworm species are now being cultivated and sold as garden and agricultural aids. Two species of land planarians also have been introduced in California (Storer, 1933, p. 780).

As the foregoing pages indicate, about a dozen exotic birds and mammals reproduce in the area, untended. More numerous are the alien mollusks and fish, and most numerous of all, the species of foreign insects: a veritable menagerie. Whereas the introduced fish were brought purposely, many of the other animals, including most of the insects, arrived by accident. Of animal species that arrived by chance and thrive here without care, few are now considered beneficial.

Considering the facts that the Monterey Bay area's written history is short, and that it is rich in endemic species, unrecorded extinctions may well have taken place. But balancing the list of introduced plants and animals against known extinctions, the total human effect on the area has been biotic "enrichment," at least in terms of the number of species present. On the other hand, simply increasing the total species number is not necessarily desirable; more agricultural pests could easily be imported. Plainly, it would have been better not to introduce many of the alien animals listed above. *Chance, rather than planning, has characterized the area's historical development.* But condemning the introduction of all aliens in the name of conservation seems unreasonable. Surely the honeybee, striped bass, and ringnecked pheasant are no offense to nature lovers. Granted, even these may have disrupted some native animal communities. (Greater care must be taken in allowing exotic species into the area.) But to reject these three—while tolerating such major sources of ecological disturbance as cattle, pigs, and housecats—is to "strain at a gnat and swallow a camel." (Nor, for that matter, has the dog been a boon to wildlife.) Such condemnation of alien species is inconsistent because the human species is itself a recent intruder in this whole western hemisphere. And in California proper, not only is our species an alien, but virtually all of the food-producing species upon which we depend are alien as well: No plant or animal important to our subsistence was domesticated here. Without introduced species, the state would rely entirely on imported food or its population would shrink drastically—perhaps stabilizing, after learning to forage in the Costanoan manner, at roughly a hundredth its present size. True, alien species cannot be thought of as permanent contributions to the area's biota, because most could not long survive the departure of people. (In fact, many could not withstand drastic changes in land use.) Yet properly selected and restricted, their threat to native species can be minimized.

If the least tern, burrowing owl, and clapper rail in the Monterey Bay area are wiped out by the red fox, what lesson is to be learned? To place the blame solely on an introduced animal would be misleading, and a great over-simplification: Doing so is to disregard those critical earlier events which made the birds' extermination possible. Doing so also fosters the view that introduced animals and plants invade pristine environments and annihilate natives—and that the conservation of native species is largely a matter of eradicating aliens. The three birds mentioned above were on the verge of local extinction well before the red fox appeared on the scene. They were in that condition as a result of a long series of disruptive human activities: Destruction of nesting sites by residential developments, habitat reduction by agriculture, poisoning programs, hunting, the decimation of native predators, etc. Introduction of the fox was but a last step.

Plant succession determines a sequence of faunal changes. Information on succession in the area is still so incomplete that the fate of introduced animals in the absence of human activities is largely conjectural. But, as with plant species, the trend is definitely toward the exclusion of aliens. If the human population were entirely removed, most of the domesticated animals would soon disappear. Cattle might linger for several of their generations, maintaining patches of grassland. Feral pigs have adapted well to oak woodland—and, like the cattle, might persist until the populations of native predators built up. Disease would eventually eliminate honeybees living in untended hives, and probably feral swarms as well. Untended aliens closely associated with habitations, such as cockroaches and the housefly, would soon follow. Populations of English sparrow, house mouse, and garden snail would decrease sharply as farms and gardens became overgrown. (Around Larkin Valley, garden snails were a pest while orchards there were still in production—eating apple tree leaves and the blossom ends of the fruit—but by the time tall shrubby regrowth was established in the abandoned orchards, the snails had entirely disappeared.)

Introduced aquatic and amphibious species would fare better: In fresh waters, the carp, mosquito fish, and eastern crayfish might survive, as might the bullfrog. As for the estuaries, the soft-shell clam, Japanese horn snail, and others are well established in Elkhorn Slough. In watery environments, the general rule that aliens are replaced by natives during the successional process may be subject to more exceptions than on land: The human influence being incessant, there is little opportunity to test the outcome of natural succession.

Nevertheless, it is unlikely that more than a small minority of introduced animals could become a permanent part of the area's fauna in an environment long without people.

5

Cultural Origins
and Local Ecological Conditions

IN COASTAL CALIFORNIA, as in many other areas, specific
cultural influences on the biotic environment appear among the
general effects of human presence. The ecological consequences
of human action have varied in character and intensity, with the
settlement of the area by different ethnic groups.

1. Culture, Cuisine, and Ecology

One can readily see relationships between culture, cuisine, and
ecology in the Monterey Bay area. The Indians were comparatively
omnivorous, whereas their successors, coming from different climates
and cultures, were ignorant of many native food sources. The
Costanoans ate ground squirrels, acorns, and buckeyes; none of these
is eaten by Californians today. Costanoans also ate quantities of the
California mussel; not so the Americans. The Spanish-Mexicans in
the Monterey Bay area were largely beef eaters and made little use of
shoreline resources generally.

The coastal Indians collected and dried quantities of marine algae.
In the nineteenth century the Chinese, too, set up camps along the
coast for drying and sacking seaweed, their favorite being a small

ruffled red alga, *Porphyra perforata*. Anglo-Americans almost never collect these plants for food.

The garden snail was introduced into California by a Frenchman as a food source, but it is not used as such in California today. In addition to its strictly culinary merits, the snail was long important in Catholic Europe because it could be eaten on Friday. The mollusk is still a favorite food in France where there are heavy fines for snail-gathering before the beginning of the summer season. In the United States, "strange to say, epicures who like snails for food seem to prefer them from imported cans from Europe rather than picking them from western gardens" (Hanna, 1966, p. 11). For almost a quarter of a century after its introduction at Guadalupe Creek near San Jose the snail remained localized in that vicinity; its "increase *was quite likely the measure of consumption as food by the parties owning the locality.*" It was noted, too, that local French families seemed "very unwilling to give any information, which may be because Americans are prejudiced against snails as an article of food" (Stearns, 1882, pp. 129-130). Similarly, the Asiatic pond snail which was introduced into California for food by Oriental Americans, is eaten only by their descendants.

Italian and Portuguese seafood appetites contrast strongly with those of Anglo-American Californians. Thus, their assessment of food resources in the littoral zone is quite different. For instance, the Italians consider the goose barnacle and black turban snails to be choice food, and the eel delectable. From their homeland the Italians brought the custom of eel fishing with pokepoles—a method growing increasingly popular among other California fishermen. If sea urchins were a popular food in California, as in Italy or Japan, they probably would not be the nuisance that they are in the southern part of the state. In Italy one sees beaches littered with their split tests, and in Japan they have had to be protected by law (Kato, 1972, pp. 23-29). Near Año Nuevo the author also came upon a little pile of split urchin tests, with a squeezed half lemon lying nearby—possibly left over from lunch by an immigrant fisherman. Only the gonads are eaten.

The carp, having traveled as a choice food fish from the Far East to Europe, received a less than enthusiastic welcome in North America. Only first-generation immigrants continue the carp-eating tradition. In California, it is, in fact, considered the worst pest among fishes. And it is overly abundant simply because it is seldom eaten—for cultural reasons.

2. A Littoral Ecological Chain

When central California was still virtually terra incognita, the coastal ecology of the Monterey Bay area was already responding to cultural attitudes and economic developments in very distant places. One cultural trait of particular importance involved the use of animal pelts. Mandarin Chinese had long used fine furs for decorative clothing. This trait spread to Europe, and in the seventeenth century a great demand for fur coats developed there among sophisticated women. The furs were prized far beyond any practical value they may have had in the making of warm clothing, and the fur of the sea otter was coveted above all others. (This continues to be true today—despite a groundswell of support for animal rights and the rejection of fur as the ultimate fashion statement, the pelt of the sea otter still is said to be more valuable than that of any other furbearer.)

Furbearing animals, particularly the sea otter, were hunted even in such then-remote and inaccessible areas as California. The resulting changes in their numbers caused the populations of several other animals in the California littoral to fluctuate as well. Three centuries ago, as now, offshore kelp beds were the favorite habitat of the sea otter—once one of the most common mammals in the littoral zone. Abalones and sea urchins also inhabit the kelp beds, feeding on these plants. The sea otter feeds, in turn, on the abalone and sea urchins. By the end of the nineteenth century, fur hunters had virtually exterminated the southern sea otter, causing abalone and sea urchin populations to increase. Around this time American immigrants in

California developed a taste for abalone, following the example of local Chinese settlers. The large-scale harvesting of the red abalone, which began in the early part of the twentieth century, benefitted the abalone's competitor, the sea urchin.

Human Effects on Littoral Populations

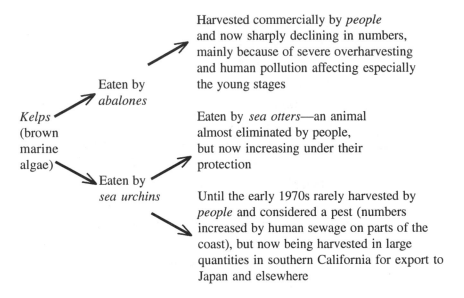

Kelps (brown marine algae)

Eaten by abalones → Harvested commercially by *people* and now sharply declining in numbers, mainly because of severe overharvesting and human pollution affecting especially the young stages

Eaten by *sea otters*—an animal almost eliminated by people, but now increasing under their protection

Eaten by sea urchins → Until the early 1970s rarely harvested by *people* and considered a pest (numbers increased by human sewage on parts of the coast), but now being harvested in large quantities in southern California for export to Japan and elsewhere

A study (Ebert, 1968) of the food habits of the sea otter in the Monterey Bay area shows that the animal locally exerts a potent influence on benthic biocommunities, in spite of its present reduced numbers. The red abalone, the red sea urchin, the giant kelp, and the bull kelp are noticeably affected. By foraging on the urchins and abalones, which are herbivores, the otter also encourages maximum growth in the kelp beds. (The otter feeds principally on the red sea urchin in the benthic zone, the purple sea urchin being mainly intertidal.)

Although the otter's diet consists mainly of sea urchins, abalones, mussels, snails and, in some places, crabs, the proportions of these animals in the diet vary considerably. This variation reflects the relative availability of the food animals as much as it does the otter's own preferences. Pismo clam populations are frequently decimated by otters.

A tentative reconstruction of biogeographical changes in the littoral zone (based partly on Ebert, 1968) is as follows: Before the arrival of Europeans, when sea otters were plentiful, red abalone and red sea urchins were not abundant in the offshore zone. Abalones were then numerous only in the intertidal zone, where otters could not easily reach them; the huge quantities whose shells are to be found in the Indian middens along the coast were mainly obtained there. Between Indian fishermen and sea otters, the red abalone population was kept relatively small. Thus, when sea otters were almost exterminated, red abalone and red sea urchins became more common throughout the offshore kelp beds in the deeper water. There the red abalone became the basis of the commercial abalone-fishing industry. Nowadays, where sea otters reappear, they quickly limit the red sea-urchin population and compete with the commercial fishermen for the red abalone, activities which favor the growth of kelp, which then supports other invertebrates.

3. Lawns

Lawns are another example of cultural peculiarity. Lawnmaking in California is a persistent north European cultural trait; nothing of the sort existed in Indian times. Nor were lawns planted for each individual house by the Spanish-Mexicans. They are scarcely functional, other than for public display. Nowadays, as a matter of custom, thousands of them, prim and rectangular, and likely bounded on either side by trimmed privet hedges, are planted in the dooryards of every town. In fact, dooryard and park lawns, with their associated exotic ornamental trees and shrubs, are the dominant biotic features of urban areas. As a new animal habitat, lawns have had a marked effect on the range and abundance of certain species; for example, the garden snail (introduced) and Brewer's black bird and the pocket gopher (natives). Golfing, another north European cultural trait (which arrived here at a much later date), and lawns together produce a major form of land use in the area. Something over 60 hectares (250 acres) is required for a first-class eighteen-hole golf course. Thus, if we add to dooryard lawns those of the large golf courses, especially around the Monterey Peninsula, it is clear that the total acreage of this type of plant cover is considerable, as is the water demand for its maintenance.

Although long established elsewhere in what is now Latin America, the rectangular street grids (and fenced yards) that demarcate today's urban bioassociations are, like lawns, a north European—that is, Anglo-American—contribution here. Note the following description of Monterey in 1836, before Anglo-American settlement:

> The houses—about a hundred in number—were dotted about here and there, *irregularly*. There are in this place, and in every other town which I saw in California, *no streets*, or fences . . . so that *the houses are placed at random* . . . . (Dana, 1911, p. 73)

6

Physiographic and Hydrographic

Changes and Their Effects

TOPOGRAPHIC CHANGES are made in the Monterey Bay area on an almost daily basis. The general effect is to subdue relief: Cut-and-fill levelling is a prime engineering activity. It has smoothed the terrain for highway construction throughout the hill lands; for agricultural use up and down the Salinas Valley; and for residential development in and around every city and town. Those changes that have had the greatest effect on plant and animal life are discussed here.

1. Irrigated Lands and Earthen Reservoirs

Beyond the floodplains of the Salinas and Pajaro rivers, especially in the rougher land in the northern part of the Monterey Bay area, the surface is dotted with small earthen reservoirs—for example, in the area between Natividad, Aromas, and Castroville, and the mouth of the Pajaro River, and on northward along the coast between Santa Cruz and Año Nuevo.

These reservoirs are on the higher ground, neighboring flat tracts of land suitable for artichokes, strawberries, or brussels sprouts. Water from the reservoirs is used both for ditch irrigation and for overhead sprinklers. Reservoirs of this type were made by farmers here in the early twentieth century by heaping dirt with "Fresno scrapers," devices shaped something like a huge dustpan and drawn by a team of horses. Most of the reservoirs postdate World War II, however, and were made with powered machinery. A few have been made by impounding small streams, but the water in most is pumped from nearby wells.

Within a surprisingly short time after the reservoirs are filled they are inhabited. Willow herb, cattail, and duckweed arrive within a year. Insects that are strongly dependent on water-mosquitoes, midges, and dragonflies appear, and within a short time so do others that actually live in or on the water itself, including water boatmen, back swimmers, water striders, and water beetles. Frogs and garter snakes are soon present. Coots arrive, perhaps even before plant growth develops. Mallards, too, feed and rest in the ponds. In the evenings swallows can often be seen swooping over the water, feeding on insects. Brewer's and redwing blackbirds are common. Such quantities of an aquatic snail can be seen in the ponds that the species can fairly be said to have experienced a "population explosion." When the ponds are drained, their bottoms are so densely covered with the shells of these snails that, in places, one can hardly press a finger into the mud without touching a shell. The snail appears to be *Lymnaea nuttalliana*. Whether this species is native here or a European introduction is uncertain.

Because most of the reservoirs are periodically dried and the vegetation destroyed, plant succession usually does not proceed for more than a few years. Thus there is usually no tree growth, although in ponds left undisturbed for four or five years, willows are likely to be established.

Exotic field weeds—mustard, mallows, amaranths, and the like—commonly appear in a fringe around the reservoirs, but they are well

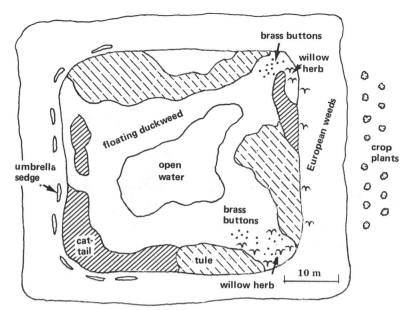

Sketch of an irrigation pond and associated vegetation. The more strictly aquatic plants include tule, cattail, umbrella sedge, duckweed, willow herb, and brass buttons. Although such irrigation ponds extend the freshwater marsh flora beyond its natural limits, the actual number of plant species spread in this way is not large. Because of periodic draining, few ponds contain more than a dozen native plant species—while over 50 native herbs, growing in surviving remnants of natural marsh, can be collected within 10 km of the pond shown above. Common freshwater marsh species that are absent from the ponds include bur reed and silver weed.

away from the water's edge. In the reservoirs themselves, most of the aquatic plants and animals are native species (exceptions are mosquito fish, and muskrats).

The manner in which several of the species are disseminated to the ponds is something of a puzzle. Presumably such plants as the cattail are wind disseminated, but it seems unlikely that this is true for umbrella sedges and tules, the ponds being well separated in large tracts of cultivated land. Thus bird dissemination must be a very important factor. How else could the snail have arrived? Possibly its eggs are carried in on the feathers and feet of coots and ducks. The western pond turtle must travel overland over surprisingly long distances. Mosquito fish, present in some ponds, are planted by mosquito-abatement personnel.

Irrigation ponds near Salinas Road north of Moss Landing.

Left, tules (in the background) and cattails grow together around the ponds, the tules extending into somewhat deeper water; but the two form mutually exclusive clusters. The plant flowering in the foreground is mustard, one of the alien species that approach the pond from the surrounding fields.

Right, tules. Blackbirds seem to prefer them as perches, perhaps finding their stems easier to grasp than the flat leaves of the cattail. (Photos B. Gordon)

Below, two mollusks, *Lymnaea*, a large population of which is found in the ponds, and ram's horn, which is occasionally present. (Photo R. Buchsbaum)

There are some 300 such reservoirs, mainly in the northern half of the Monterey Bay area but also scattered generously along the eastern side of the lower Salinas Valley. Their effect on the biota of the area as a whole must be considerable. They preserve part of a marsh flora that, as noted earlier, once existed in natural freshwater lakes, now drained (especially between Salinas and Castroville), and have extended patches of such habitat over a far wider area. In most respects they must be beneficial, at least in terms of increases made in habitat and species diversity; because of them, various water-loving animals have been more widely distributed; the ponds have established resting places for birds (the subject of their importance to migrating waterfowl would bear study); they provide feeding grounds for various birds of prey; and so on.

The growth of aquatic plants can be controlled by adjusting water levels in the ponds and shaping their vertical cross sections. The ponds can also be made more attractive to wildlife by planting shrubs and trees back from waterline.

While under natural conditions winter and spring are the times of greatest herbaceous plant growth (because of concentration of the rainfall in those seasons), in irrigated areas the season of strongest growth not only is changed to summer and fall but is accelerated, as well, by the higher temperatures occurring then. This growth is mostly in crop plants. Weeds, such as mustard, that otherwise flower mainly in January and February, bloom in August, too, along irrigation ditches. Many insects thrive throughout the summer in the Salinas and Pajaro valleys on the artificial supply of water from sprinklers, increasing the need for spraying operations from aircraft.

As lawns and parks of the area remain evergreen only because of the artificial water supply in summer, plainly the whole urban bioassociation is largely dependent on the practice of irrigation.

The effect of irrigation on the distribution and number of insects can hardly be overstated. A large part of the mosquito abatement program deals with mosquitoes associated with irrigation waters.

2. Saltwater Intrusion

Diverting streams to supply water for irrigation is an old Spanish-Moorish custom which was continued in the Monterey Bay area. The missionaries grew irrigated crops to help feed the Indians who had been concentrated around the missions, especially at Mission Soledad and Mission San Antonio. However, irrigation was virtually given up in the area when the missions were secularized in 1833.

A few decades later, irrigation agriculture was renewed by the Americans. Between 1874 and 1890, irrigation water in the Salinas Valley was obtained mainly from wells, with pumps operated by windmills. Toward the end of the century a canal was built along the side of the valley, carrying water from upstream tributaries. In 1904, several thousand hectares of sugar beets were being irrigated with water supplied by wood-fueled steam pumps, which burned mainly willow and cottonwood growing along the river. Very large amounts of wood were needed; for example, on one 200-hectare (500-acre) tract it was noted that "the consumption of fuel is at the rate of one-half cord per acre irrigated" (Hamlin, 1904, pp. 80-81). Mineral fuels were being sought at the time because riparian forests had been cleared and the local supply of wood was inadequate.

Intensive exploitation of groundwater began between 1910 and 1920, with the spread of commercial vegetable growing in the Salinas Valley and the introduction of gasoline fuel, electrical power, and deep-well pumps. By 1963, about 95% of the water used in the Salinas Valley came from beneath the surface and, of this, 95% was used for irrigation (Manning, 1963, pp. 107, 109).

Two main aquifers carry water seaward beneath the floor of the Salinas Valley: One is approximately 180 feet (55 m) below the surface; the other is at a depth of about 400 feet (122 m). The lower ends of these aquifers are exposed and discharge along the sides of the submarine canyon offshore from Moss Landing. Seawater intrusion into the 180-foot (55-m) aquifer, a result of heavy pumping of well water, became evident in the early 1940s. By 1945, seawater had advanced 1.5 miles (2.5 km) inland and polluted some 2428 hectares (6000 acres) (Todd, 1953, p. 752). Since that time intrusion has been detected progressively farther inland.

In 1954 the 55-m aquifer was polluted by seawater for a distance of about 4 km inland from the coast, and water levels in the wells were below sea level for about 8 miles [13 km] inland. At that time the 122-m aquifer had been polluted by seawater for a distance of more than 3 km from the coast. (Manning, 1963, p. 108)

To appreciate fully the changes made in subsurface hydrography, compare the circumstances noted above in the 55-m aquifer with those in the following early description:

In 1880, a well was drilled at Castroville to a depth of 178 feet [54 m] *producing a volume of fresh water, which at high tide flowed in large quantity over the casing and at low tide ceased flowing.* This well is near the mouth of the Salinas River, and the surface of the ground is 20 feet [6 m] above the river. (Hamlin, 1904, p. 32)

The rate of saltwater intrusion varies; in one year, 1944-1945, saltwater moved 600 feet (183 m) farther inland. The intrusion has been observed to vary seasonally and to be correlated with the pumping of irrigation water on truck crops in the lower part of the valley (Todd, 1953, p. 752). Indications of seawater intrusion were also noted in 1967 in the Springfield area, to the north of the lower Elkhorn Slough, and subsequently in the lower Pajaro Valley where it has become a serious problem (Pajaro Valley Water Management Agency).

The State Department of Public health recommends drinking water with chloride concentrations of less than 250 mg/l (PVWMA). Salt water intrusion threatens wells which supply drinking water for the city of Salinas. A few agricultural plants are sensitive to prolonged irrigation with water having a chloride concentration as low as 100 mg/l; at values over 350 mg/l, production of some of the more valuable crops is sharply reduced (PVWMA). Artichokes are comparatively tolerant of salt, but between Mulligan Hill and Castroville, even this crop plant has been damaged by salty irrigation water. Artichoke

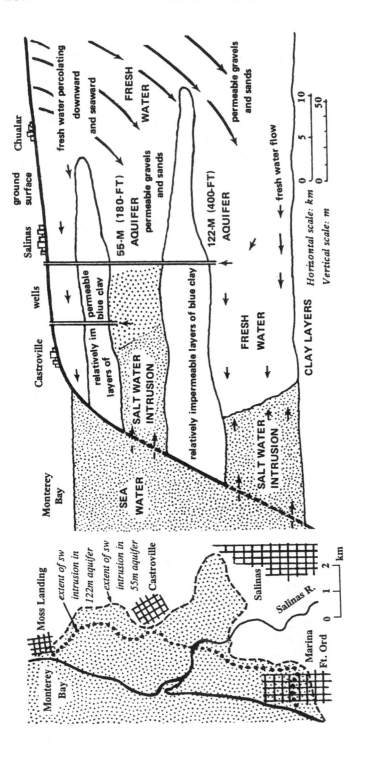

Section through Monterey Bay and adjacent area under Castroville and Salinas, showing saltwater intrusion into freshwater aquifers

Saltwater intrusion in Salinas Valley, 1992 (concentrated intrusion only: 500 mg/l or more) (Bunte; Hurst; Manning; Todd)

growers near Castroville have given up pumping from the 180-foot (55-m) aquifer, and are relying instead on the 400-foot (122-m) aquifer—or on an even deeper one at about 896 feet (273 m) (Hurst, 1993, p. 6). Although Monterey cypress will tolerate relatively saline ground water, many other native trees will not.

In the Pajaro Valley water is pumped mainly from two layers in the Aromas red sands: One layer ranges in depth from 90-200 feet (30-60 m); the other, between 200 and 600 feet (60-180 m). By 1992, salt water with a chloride concentration of 500 mg/l had intruded inland as much as 1.3 miles (2.1 km), and caused the abandonment of many wells (PVWMA, Fig. 4). The most severely intruded areas are on the north side of the Pajaro River. Increased pumping during drought years has accelerated the rate of encroachment.

Because yearly and seasonal differences in streamflow cause uncertain supply, only small amounts of diverted stream water are used for irrigation in the Salinas Valley.

3. Deflection of the Salinas River and Elkhorn Slough and Tidal Control of Moro Cojo Slough

In the early part of the twentieth century the Salinas River flowed northward in the lower part of its course, paralleling the shoreline and separated from the bay for about 6 miles (10 km) by only a narrow stretch of sand dunes. The mouth of the river was then located about 1 mile (1.6 km) north of Moss Landing. Between 1908 and 1910, the river began to empty into the bay at a location about 5.5 miles (8.8 km) southward, near Mulligan Hill (G. C. Jones, 1933, p. 2). Thus, the old mouth was to the north of the submarine canyon, and the present mouth is well to its south.

A question arises as to which is the more stable position of the river mouth. An official surveyor pointed out that "the proper location of the mouth of the Salinas is a very difficult problem" (Hermann, 1879, p. 20). The subject has long been a matter of controversy, and for very practical reasons: Here, as elsewhere, the hydrographic net-

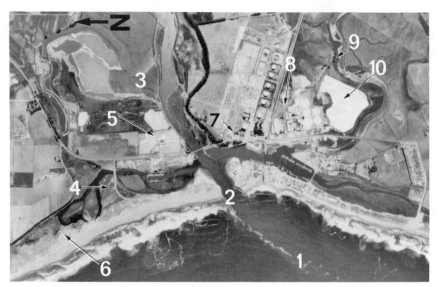

The submarine canyon (1) that approaches the shoreline near the entrance to Moss Landing Harbor (2) is a controlling feature in the circulation of the waters of Monterey Bay. The nearby salt marsh of Elkhorn Slough (3) is one of the richest and most distinctive wildlife habitats in California. Jetty Road (4) is a favorite spot for birdwatchers. Note the former salt-production ponds (5) and the location of the old Salinas River mouth (6). The photograph shows industrial growth that has already taken place at this critical spot—for example, the P.G. and E. power plant (7) and Kaiser Aluminum and Chemical's refractories plant (8). Note the extensive tailing heap (9) of the Kaiser plant on Moro Cojo Slough (10). Over the years, various proposals have been made for the development of a deepwater port here. The overall environmental effects of such a project would have been destructive. For example, a certain amount of oil would certainly have been spilled, with harmful consequences to fish-breeding and bird-feeding areas, and to sea otters in and around Elkhorn Slough—as well as to beach use, pleasure boating, etc., in the vicinity. Fortunately, this danger has been avoided by the establishment of the Monterey Bay National Sanctuary. (Photo USGS, 1966)

work is a basic reference in determining property boundaries. The complicated drainage characteristic of low coastal lands such as these presents special problems to the surveyor. Furthermore, the Salinas River and the sloughs tributary to it have been controlling agents in the physiographic and biogeographic development of the area. Thus, interpretation of the local natural history depends on accurate reconstruction of hydrographic change.

Geological evidence indicates that the mouth has been at its present position over long periods of time. The underground flow of the Salinas River is through aquifers reaching the bay on the south slopes of the submarine canyon, directly offshore from its present mouth. One principal aquifer, at a depth of about 180 feet (55 m), is "apparently a stream channel deposit laid down by an ancestral Salinas River and is probably upper Pleistocene to Recent in age" (Manning, 1963, p. 108). Another feature indicates long duration of this outlet: "The position of the apex and shape of the fan [a broad, thin, deltaic wedge of river sediment, offshore from the river mouth, shown on U.S. Coast and Geodetic Survey charts 5402 and 5403] show that the location of the present mouth of the Salinas River has been maintained for the duration of the deposition of the fan" (Yancey, 1968, p. 9).

On the other hand, the river's mouth was located well to the north of its present position, and even somewhat to the north of the submarine canyon, throughout most of the historical period, until 1908-1910. Natural wave refraction patterns in the bay produce increasingly high beach berms southward from Moss Landing and favor a location of the river mouth upcoast, near the head of the submarine canyon (Bascom, 1954, p. 603). Counteracting this trend are the great variations in winter rainfall here and occasional flooding, which explain abrupt changes in the river channel with flood waters sometimes breaking through the dunes. A report written before the river changed its outlet describes a gradual movement of the river mouth northward, stating that drift sand

has been crowding the mouth of the river northward until it is now in comparatively close proximity to that of the Pajaro. It is conceivable that this same movement may continue until a union of the two streams takes place, and moreover one should not entirely overlook the possibility that such a union may have occurred before. (Snyder, 1913, p. 54)

In fact, a geologist who visited the area in 1854 had already made a detailed mapping of physiographic evidence that the two rivers had but recently reached the bay in a single mouth (Johnson, 1855, p. 22).

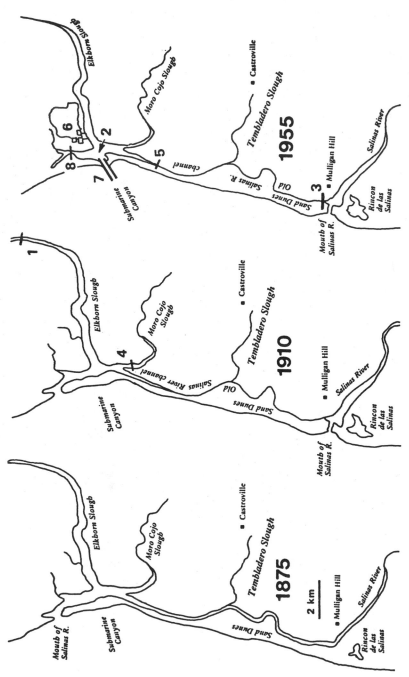

Principal hydrographic changes made in the Salinas River Mouth-Elkhorn Slough area, comparing conditions in 1875, 1910, and 1955. 1. Floodgates near Hudson's Landing. 2. Moss Landing Harbor. 3. Earthen dike across old Salinas River channel. 4. Tide gate on old Salinas River channel. 5. Tide gate on Moro Cojo Slough. 6. Salt ponds. 7. Jetties at Moss Landing Harbor. 8. Tide gate at Jetty Road.

Thus, the fish and other aquatic life of the rivers have been alternately joined and separated over the years.

In the nineteenth century, during winter floods, the river sometimes broke or was directed through the dunes to the south near the "Big Bend of the Salinas" that is, near Mulligan Hill:

> all old Residents to whom I during the survey applied for information agree to the fact that at high water during and after the winter rains, the river here breaks the Sandbar and empties into the ocean. That *sometimes the Settlers along the river Bottoms help this breaking through process with shovel, plough, and spade, so as to avert the danger of inundation . . . that in dry or half dry seasons no such breaking through occurs, and that not one of them ever knew of the opening being kept open by the River for an entire summer season.* (Hermann, 1879. p. 21)

It seems that during the recent geologic past the river mouth has shifted back and forth between the two positions, and that when the mouth was in the more northerly position, or midway between the two, its sediments disappeared into the submarine canyon.

Although it has been claimed (Fisher, 1945, pp. 15-16) that the displacement of the river's mouth southward to its present site was caused by the April 18, 1906, earthquake, there is little evidence of a connection between the two events. There are indications that the shift actually occurred some time later: An ichthyologist's detailed account of the streams tributary to Monterey Bay based on field observations in the summer of 1909 described the Salinas as emptying into the bay to the north of Moss Landing:

> The mouths of the Pajaro and Salinas are in close proximity, less than 3 miles [5 km] of land separating them . . . (Snyder, 1913, pp. 50-51)

In 1910, the river flowed through the Rincon de las Salinas before making a 1300-m northward adjustment and emptying in its present position by Mulligan Hill (Westdahl, 1910, p. 2; G.C. Jones, 1933, p. 2). No reference to the event has been found in local newspapers, but it appears that the Salinas changed its outlet from north of Moss

Present mouth, an artificial outlet, of the Salinas River at flood stage, from above an offshore point south of Moss Landing, March, 1995. Each year, when the river reaches a critically high level, county flood-control personnel make a ditch across the berm or sand dam separating the river channel from the bay, starting a flow in that direction. In rainy years floodwaters impounded behind the berm may rise to between 3 and 4.5 m above sea level and escape into the bay at high velocity when the cut is made. A dike preventing northward flow of the river in its old bed is located on the north bank of the present mouth. During summers, when stream flow dwindles, ocean wave action rebuilds the berm. One of the many consequences of these engineering activities is that the Salinas River deposits its heavy load of sediment in this area, south of the submarine canyon, rather than to the north of the canyon, as it did formerly. (Photo U.S. Army Corps of Engineers)

Landing to south of Mulligan Hill in the winter of 1909 or the spring of 1910. As in the old days, the local residents probably directed the flooding river to the sea by excavating a channel for it through the sand as they still do, with county assistance, almost every winter, following the summer buildup of berm and dune sand at the river's mouth. A great expansion of agricultural land was underway at the time, and deflecting the river through the dunes made its bed northward available for crops and helped protect the site of Moss Landing from flood.

The river still shows a strong tendency to flow northward into its pre-1909 bed:

The mouth of the river is opened in the winter either by the river itself or *by artificial means.* Sometimes during this process the water is high enough that some of the water escapes into Elkhorn Slough by way of the old channel. (Beard, 1941, p. 8)

This overflow of the Salinas into its old bed and into Elkhorn Slough has occurred a number of times. Within the nine-year period 1926-1935, it spilled over in 1929, 1930, 1931, and 1934 (MacGinitie, 1935, p. 635), and this despite the earthen dike placed between Mulligan Hill and the beach to block such northward flow.

In the nineteenth century, the Salinas sometimes flooded violently in winters: "Its usual width, at the entrance to the bay, is about four hundred and fifty feet (137 m). In 1862, during the wet season, it exceeded a mile (1610 m)" (Cronise, 1868, p. 83). That means that a large part of the dunes between Moss Landing and Zmudowski Beach were swept away. In the upper part of the valley the Salinas Dam was built in 1941, the Nacimiento in 1957, and the San Antonio in 1966. By reducing flooding, these dams have helped confine the river to its present outlet and made the present site of Moss Landing habitable.

Before 1909, the dunes separating the lower course of the Salinas River from the bay were breached not only by the river but by ocean waves: "A natural dam has been formed across the Salinas River near Moss Landing by cutting of the surf through the sand hills separating the river from the ocean" (*Salinas City Index*, March 7, 1878). Duflot de Mofras' early-nineteenth century map of Monterey Bay shows a peculiar, delta-like protrusion of shoreline in the same vicinity, possibly made by a breakthrough of the river in the opposite direction. The protrusion has since disappeared.

The vulnerability of the dunes immediately south of Moss Landing has been much reduced since 1910. With the Salinas River emptying to the south of the submarine canyon, the beach there has been supplied with additional sand and broadened.

According to contemporary accounts, in 1859 the mouth of the Salinas River was some 137 m (150 yards) wide, and at low tide in late summer the water depth on the bar at the river mouth was about

4 feet (1.2 m). Inside the entrance a small bay, deep enough for oceangoing sloops and schooners, covered the area where the Salinas River and Elkhorn Slough joined. Commercial agriculture began in the Pajaro Valley in the middle of the nineteenth century. Within a few years produce was shipped to San Francisco, ships were loaded by surfboats off the mouth of the Pajaro River, and development of port facilities in the lower Salinas and Elkhorn Slough was being considered. The following note was written in Santa Cruz in the fall of 1859:

We again call the attention of the residents of Pajaro to the project of rendering navigable the mouth of the Salinas . . . . By inquiry, on our recent visit, we ascertained, beyond a doubt, that *there is four feet of water on the bar at low tide, the depth of water is sufficient for the entrance of vessels* without deepening the channel at all. *The harbor inside the bar is perfectly calm, and of ample dimensions, and the slough will admit the passage of boats to a point within two miles of Watsonville.* (*The Santa Cruz News*, September 28, 1859)

Another report on the subject was written at Watsonville on March 16, 1860:

The passage of a sloop across the bar at the mouth of the Salinas river, on Saturday last, and its arrival *in the little bay* inside, created a great excitement in our town . . . this being the first time a vessel has ever entered the channel . . . . Captain Williams says . . . there is no doubt of the perfect safety of the channel for the entrance of *schooners* . . . . Warehouses will be built on the margins of the river, at its junction with the slough or, *perhaps on the slough itself much nearer town*, and soon the glory of the surf-boats will have departed . . . . About sixty of us went aboard the sloop and sailed down to the entrance and back to the bay again. The captain offered to take us out to sea and return, saying he had sailed out and in with ease. (*The Santa Cruz News*, April 20, 1860)

In the 1870s, the port for Watsonville was located at the head of Elkhorn Slough. In the winter of 1876, an ocean-going steamer was plying its waters:

The stern-wheel steamer, *Vaquero*, has arrived from San Francisco, and is making regular trips up and down Elk Horn Slough, taking grain out of the

Watsonville warehouse and freighting it to Moss Landing. (*The Salinas City Index*, Dec. 21, 1876)

This ship is further identified elsewhere: "The stern-wheel steamer *Vaquero* drawing about three feet [1 m] of water and of one hundred tons [90 metric tons] register" (Elliott and Moss, 1881, p. 114).

Some old pilings at a spot called Hudson's Landing still stand at the head of the slough, but today it is impossible to reach them except in small boats and at high tide.

Near Werner Lake, a pass of low ground separates the drainage of the Pajaro Valley from that of Elkhorn Slough. During floods of the nineteenth century, the Pajaro River frequently "overflowed and passed through some of its water via Werner Lake into Elkhorn Slough" (Reid, 1963, p. 17). Most of this overflow stopped when a railroad was built through the pass. At that time, fill material was carried in—and the ground level in the pass, raised. According to one account, over the years the railroad company has dumped "several thousand" carloads of gravel and other fill between Werner Lake and a place called "Bulkhead" (now part of Kirby Park) in order to stabilize the constantly sinking roadbed. Despite all this, the Pajaro River rose so high during the floods of March, 1995 that its freshwater again overflowed into Elkhorn Slough.

Very large amounts of fill were dumped into the upper part of Elkhorn Slough, both by the railroad company and as a part of public works projects. In 1908, plans were drawn up for construction of floodgates to reduce tidal flow in the upper part of the slough so that land there could be used agriculturally

. . . the concrete bridge and flood gate across Elkhorn Slough near the Hudson place . . . *including a fill of some 1500 feet* [457 m] *across the marsh*. There are to be six culverts with a flood gate in each. The bridge will rest on a pile foundation. *The farmers of that section have agreed to stand the expense of putting in the flood gates as a means of reclaiming their lands.* (*The Salinas City Index*, Dec. 10, 1908)

The wreckage of the bridge, which was actually made of wood, can still be seen east of Elkhorn Road. Above the floodgates there are still many acres of pickleweed marsh which were never successfully used agriculturally, except for limited cattle grazing.

In short, Elkhorn Slough has been subjected to many recent human-made changes, the greatest of which, ecologically speaking, took place when the connection between the slough and the Salinas River was severed in 1909. Although the slough is now a saltwater estuary, there is no question that its character has changed remarkably since that time. Before, when the slough was an arm of the lower Salinas, its water must have been seasonally almost fresh. In winter the slough was probably often a lake of the river's impounded floodwaters. The author of the most thorough early study of the slough's ecology, G.E. MacGinitie, clearly had this in mind when he made the following statement:

> The connection between the Salinas River and the Slough is disestablished. To all intents and purposes, therefore, Elkhorn Slough *at the present time* may be considered strictly a saltwater estuary. (MacGinitie, 1935, p. 635)

Hence, many of the ecological conditions described by MacGinitie in his excellent monograph were clearly brought into existence by human action: Namely, the diking of the channel of the Salinas near Mulligan Hill, preventing the river from flowing northward into the lower part of Elkhorn Slough.

The curious absence of cord grass, a characteristic species of California's coastal salt marshes, from Elkhorn Slough may be explained by the slough's history of repeated freshwater incursions.

The above comments on seasonally fresh water in the slough are confined to the historical period—that is, to conditions that have existed since European settlement began. There may well have been earlier periods when Elkhorn Slough was, as now, strictly speaking a marine estuary, with its waters saline throughout the year (for example, in the geologic past when the Salinas River emptied naturally into the bay near Mulligan Hill).

The previously mentioned oyster industry that developed in the slough in the 1920s and 1930s would have been impossible before the deflection of the Salinas River. In 1931, as noted above, flood-waters of the Salinas reentered the slough briefly. And in 1932, it was reported that as a result "of last winter's storms . . . the native oysters were nearly all killed off . . . by seepage of freshwater into the Elkhorn Slough where the beds are located" (*Pacific Fisherman*, Oct. 1932, p. 70).

The slough was changed, too, by the many dikes built to exclude tidal overflow and extend private use of land. Dikes were also built to prevent salt water from spilling over into wells along the north edge of the slough, and still others in establishing the salt industry, the oyster industry, and so on.

Before 1909, Elkhorn Slough (formerly known as Estero Grande and Roadhouse Slough) joined the Salinas River and emptied into the bay north of Moss Landing. Between 1909 and 1946, the slough continued to drain into the bay through the old mouth of the Salinas. In 1946, a private firm under contract with the U.S. Army Corps of Engineers cut through the dune barrier: Thus, Elkhorn Slough now empties into the bay almost directly at the head of the submarine canyon at Moss Landing. Jetties were built to protect the new entrance to the slough. The old mouth, about 1 mile (1.6 km) north of Moss Landing, began to fill with sand immediately. Dunes, now partly stabilized with Holland dune grass and native dune vegetation, have built up almost to the level of the older dunes on either side and have hidden the old mouth of the river and the old opening of the slough.

Accounts often differ as to whether Elkhorn Slough as a whole is being shoaled or scoured. This is because shoaling may predominate in one part of the slough and, at the same time, scouring in another. Since no large streams drain into the slough, it shoals very slowly under natural conditions. There can be little doubt that shoaling is the tendency in the upper slough during periods of intensive agricultural use. For example, in 1910, it was noted that "the principal changes (in Elkhorn Slough since the last years of the nineteenth century) seem to be a diminution in width and depth of the main

View over upper Elkhorn Slough, from Hudson Landing Road. The pilings of old Port Watsonville rise from the slough on the left. The dark lines of raised earth are levees (now broken), which were placed between 1949 and 1951 approximately at mean high water line to confine the higher tidal waters to the slough channel. In the background on the right is Nature Conservancy land on which coast live oak and other native plants are reclaiming an abandoned farm. The clusters of taller trees are mostly eucalyptus. The low growth extending outward from the water's edge is pickleweed. (Photo B. Gordon)

slough and its laterals, and a reduction of the marshy area in its vicinity" (Westdahl, 1910, p. 2), that is, sedimentary fans produced by gully erosion covered parts of the marsh. Since 1946, however, scouring seems to have been the rule especially in the lower part of the slough (and this despite the movement of littoral drift and wind-blown sand into the harbor entrance itself). Since the cut was made through the dunes, the slough is more directly subject to tidal fluctuations. In the late 1960s, a plume of suspended silt was often spread at ebb tide over several acres of the bay outside the harbor mouth. Little of this sediment was carried back into the harbor. One result of this scouring has been a deepening and widening of the channel in the lower part of the slough. In places the banks there have been protected with riprap. Nowadays soil erosion, associated with strawberry culture in the upper watershed, again supplies the headwater area with quantities of sediment.

In 1935, it was observed that "above the highway bridge there are no mudflats" (MacGinitie, 1935, p. 637). But since that time erosion above the highway bridge has removed patches of pickleweed and lowered the surface to form intertidal mudflats, now covered with *Enteromorpha* and *Gracilaria*. This mudflat area is being extended by undercutting at the edges of the channel. Undercutting and slumping can be seen along the edges of the lower part of the slough, exposing banks honeycombed with mud crab burrows. Other mudflats have recently been eroded in pickleweed areas at the upper end of the slough, where high water has broken through dikes running approximately along mean high water line. (In this connection, it is noteworthy that pickleweed is an example of a plant whose zonal limits actually have been used in survey; lacking point-by-point determinations of elevation, surveyors have sometimes used the sloughward boundary of pickleweed to delineate mean-high-water line, this being the limits of the original public domain.)

Furthermore, local residents say that because of the 1946 cut through the dunes, and an associated increase in tidal range, pickleweed grows farther inland, having replaced willows in spots along the north side of the slough; that the many small stream courses that meander over the surface of the salt marsh have all been deepened; and that at high tide salt water flows farther up the arroyos in the low hills north of the slough, spoiling the grazing and necessitating increased diking.

There has been a marked redistribution of plant life near the old mouth of Elkhorn Slough. *Enteromorpha intestinalis*, for example, which formerly grew there, has now filled in the mud flats behind the harbor entrance, while pickleweed grows behind the dunes in the slough mouth.

Behind the dunes at Salinas River State Park, the flatland is covered with native vegetation—but it consists, surprisingly, of marsh plants such as salt grass, pickleweed, spear saltbush, and coastal gumplant. This land having been the bed of the Salinas River, one would expect a freshwater vegetation; however, since 1909, this whole stretch has been under increased tidal influence. At high tide salt water moves southward up the channel from Moss Landing Harbor. Thus, although these salt-marsh species are natives, they do not make up the original plant cover here. Indeed, in the nineteenth century a Salinas River port was located here (as shown on J. H. Garber's "Map of Moss, Salinas, and Watsonville Landings"). At the beginning of the twentieth century, patches of tule, a few cottonwoods, and other freshwater plants still grew on the east banks of Moss Landing Harbor, across Highway 1 from the Pacific Gas and Electric power plant.

In 1932, a tide gate was constructed in Moro Cojo Slough.

> Moro Cojo Slough has been equipped with some form of tide gate structure since the early years of the Twentieth Century . . . . For various reasons . . . these gates were more or less ineffective in preventing saltwater action and some tidal fluctuation until 1932, when gates were installed at State Highway No. 1 crossing near Moss Landing. (*U.S. Senate Document No. 50 Monterey Bay [Moss Landing] California 79th Congress, 1st session, May 24, 1945*, 1946, p. 22)

Actually, the first tide gates were installed between 1886 and 1890, when a dam (now called Sandholdt Dam) was built to carry the county road across the slough. Construction of tidal gates on Moro Cojo changed the hydrographic character of the whole slough system in the area (Elkhorn, Bennett, Moro Cojo, etc.), probably reducing by at least 1/5 the total tidal prism.

When Moro Cojo and Elkhorn sloughs were connected by the lower course of the Salinas River, and subject at least seasonally to tidal influence, their mollusk faunas were similar. But since 1932, little seawater has been able to enter Moro Cojo Slough. The chemical content of water in the slough has fluctuated greatly. In 1973, the water was brackish (with salt content dropping to around 4 parts per 1000 in the rainy season, low compared to seawater, which has about 34 parts per 1000). But since that time salty drainage water pumped from nearby fields into the slough has increased the salinity greatly (Hansen, 1976).

The only living native mollusk common in the slough today is a small snail, *Tryonia imitator* (see Kellogg, 1980). The decaying shells of white sand clam cover the bottom in the shallow water of the lower slough near Highway 1. A few hundred meters eastward, a heap of soil dug from a ditch near the slough was found to contain dead mollusks, including many bent-nosed clams, Washington clams, jackknife clams, Pacific littleneck clams, and bay mussels. Installation of the tide gates plainly exterminated virtually the entire molluskan fauna of the Moro Cojo. All of these mollusks now live in Elkhorn Slough. In 1975 a large drainage ditch was excavated and a levee constructed along the south side of the slough, extending from its Castroville tributary upslough to within 656 feet (200 m) of the railroad crossing. Masses of shell were excavated in making the levee, showing that a rich marine benthic community, including over a dozen species of mollusks, once extended 1.86 miles (3 km) inland from the mouth of the slough. Above the railroad crossing a narrowing strip of salt-marsh vegetation (e.g., pickleweed and salt grass) extends almost to Castroville Boulevard. Beyond Castroville Boulevard the headwaters of the slough are freshwater marshland.

If tidal restraints were to be removed, the slough would again become a breeding ground for fish and other marine organisms; the benthic mollusk community (a significant economic resource) would recolonize the lower slough; maricultural activities might prove to be tolerable from a conservational standpoint; and so on. For those interested in restoring California's despoiled estuaries, Moro Cojo Slough is one of the most promising sites in the state.

4. El Estero: An Urbanized Estuary

Coastal lowlands are among the most attractive sites for agriculture, industry, and urban expansion—but all of these activities depend heavily on freshwater. Since saltwater is of little use, estuaries and saltwater marshes have usually been seen as obstacles to economic development. Many small estuaries along California's coast have been simply filled in, and their sites used for other purposes—despite their importance as distinctive wildlife habitats.

The first half of the twentieth century was a time of ambitious engineering plans for dealing with the estuary problem. The Reber Plan is a grandiose example. This project called for turning most of San Francisco Bay into a great freshwater lake: Broad dams were to be built across the bay, so located as to impound the waters of the Sacramento and San Joaquin rivers. The plan came close to adoption. Other extreme solutions to the estuary problem have been proposed: At one time it was even suggested that the mudflats and saltwater marshes of Elkhorn Slough be dredged and pumped away, so that a deepwater port for oceangoing vessels could take their place.

No place better illustrates the problem of making an estuary conform to a traditional urban setting than El Estero, in Monterey.

Under natural conditions, El Estero was seasonally either a marine estuary (as its Spanish name indicates) or a brackish-water lake. Wind generated ocean waves, especially high winter waves, built a berm— a nearly horizontal ridge or dam of beach sand—across the mouth of the estuary, separating it from the ocean. This ridge impounded the water of the several small streams that drain into the estuary during the winter season, forming a lake. Sometimes water in the lake rose enough to overtop and cut through the ridge, and the entire lake drained quickly into Monterey Bay. For some time thereafter, especially at times of high tide, ocean water entered the estuary freely. Under this natural flushing action little sediment accumulated in the estuary channel. During the summer season, when inland streams supplied little or no water, evaporation lowered the lake's surface. This constant change in the lake's depth and outline made it difficult to use its shores for the construction of buildings or for other urban purposes.

In the winter of 1847, according to an account written by the city's former mayor, the lagoon:

... began to threaten with inundation the buildings upon its margin .... As it lay several feet above the level of the sea, with only an intervening ridge of sand, it occurred to me that it would be a good scheme to cut a channel between the two .... The work was easily accomplished; but my channel of two feet soon widened to 40, and the whole lake came rushing down in a tremendous torrent ... and left on its sandy bottom only a few floundering fish .... (Colton, 1859, pp. 137-138)

Since that time, El Estero has been subjected to numerous and drastic changes: The estuary has been dammed, dredged, drained, and reshaped. It has been polluted, purified, and even perfumed. Native plants have been repeatedly cleared from its shores, and its waters stocked and restocked with fish imported from far outside the Monterey Bay area.

The following brief calendar of changes that El Estero has undergone (divided here into three periods) is based mainly on accounts in the *Monterey Peninsula Herald* (MPH) and the reports of Monterey's Parks and Recreation Director (P&RD). It reads like a planner's nightmare:

Conversion of the estuary (El Estero) into a saltwater lake (Lake El Estero): El Estero was dammed in 1872 when tracks for the Southern Pacific Railroad were built along with sand ridge separating it from the bay. Outlets were installed to prevent the lake's waters from rising and spilling over during winter floods. After this damming, El Estero was no longer flushed by tidal action or by lake water escaping into the bay. As a result, the lake was shoaled in winter by sediment in incoming streams. During the dry summer months, the lake's surface was lowered by evaporation, and its water was stagnant. Ocean water was pumped in to maintain a constant water level.

Repeated dredging was required to maintain water depth (the lake was used for recreational boating), and the dredge spoil was used to reshape the shores. Each dredging produced an unpleasant odor which permeated the surrounding neighborhood.

Conversion of Lake El Estero from a saltwater lake into a freshwater lake: In 1945, El Estero was referred to as "the city-owned saltwater lake that has never in the memory of man lived up to its potentialities" (MPH 9/5/45). Plans for its change were considered. (Henceforth, such plans were customarily described as being for purposes of "rejuvenation," "renovation," or "restoration.") After an investigation to "determine whether freshwater or saltwater would be maintained in the lake," El Estero was converted into a freshwater lake—because saltwater killed lawns, garden flowers, and planted trees, etc. No more ocean water was to be pumped in (MPH, 9/5/45). Throughout these deliberations over the fate of El Estero, two divergent philosophies (both still very much alive) were expressed: "Prominent in the debate was the suggestion that the lake be filled . . . and the entire area opened for commercial development" (MPH, 3/5/48, p. 13). Opposing this suggestion, a spokesperson for those with a conservational outlook, held that "We are throwing away our heritage if we toy with El Estero" (MPH, 3/17/48). (In any case, the property is protected by deed restrictions which limit its use to parks and roads.)

The entire lake was pumped dry, and the shoreline cleared of vegetation. A lawn was planted from Fremont Street to Franklin Street (MPH, 3/5/48).

From time to time, an assortment of introduced freshwater animals had been planted in the lake, most of them by the Fish and Game Department. These included crayfish, carp, catfish, goldfish, smallmouth bass, bluegill, green sunfish, mosquito fish, and a species of trout. Only one, the Sacramento perch, was native to the area. Carp were especially numerous.

Bridges were built over El Estero, connecting Monterey and Oak Grove (MPH, 4/27/57). The lake was enlarged: Two existing ponds, Washerwoman's Pond and Lagunita Mirada, were improved and two new ponds created (MPH 12/8/83).

Parts of the lake were used as a trash dump (MPH 8/3/50), and shoaling continued to be a problem ". . . what water was left—and it was barely knee-deep in places—was filthy." Green algae (freshwater species of *Cladophora*), which had been less abundant when water in the lake was mainly salty, now formed tangled mats blanketing much of the lake's surface. The algae were controlled by applications of bluestone (copper sulfate).

The shallower water was overgrown with tule—a native plant common in California's freshwater lakes and ponds. A contract was awarded for machinery to tear out and remove the tules: "Fish and Game reviewed and approved the removal project, saying it will cause no long-term harm to the wild-fowl population in the lake." At two locations the tules were to "be left undisturbed to provide wildfowl nesting sites" (MPH, 1/12/81).

Over the years, large numbers of pigeons, seagulls, and domesticated ducks had taken up residence in and around the lake. Feeding these birds having become something of a tradition, a place was set aside as "the major public feeding area for birds" (MPH, 10/2/81).

The "Rehabilitation of El Estero": Again in 1983, it was decided that conditions in Lake El Estero were in urgent need of improvement, and a major new plan was called for. The lake was said to contain "so little oxygen that it will not support fish and plant life" (MPH, 12/30/83). "The water of El Estero has become fouled by the extensive spread of algae, fed by an abundance of nitrogen and phosphorus [compounds] in the droppings of water birds which live there and feast off human handouts" (MPH, 12/13/83).

The considerations led to a policy reversal on public bird feeding. The plan called for "a ban on the feeding of birds to keep their population down" (MPH, 7/7/84). It was hoped that this ban would gradually improve water quality enough, "so that recreational fishing can be resumed" (MPH, 12/8/83), and that "fish like bass, perch, and bluegill can be stocked" (MPH, 12/13/83).

Lake El Estero was completely drained in July, 1984 (MPH 7/20/84)—though again "some citizens . . . suggested filling in the lake altogether" (MPH, 6/28/84). When the lake was actually drained, the amount of aquatic life left floundering on the exposed lake bed came as a great surprise: "There are thousands of fish . . . many more than the City of Monterey estimated" (MPH, 7/13/84).

Foul odors had been expected: ". . . in anticipation of odors that might arise from the exposed lake bottom, the city has purchased deodorants . . . the deodorant has an orange fragrance" (MPH, 6/6/84). A thick layer of black sludge was hauled away, increasing the depth of the lake to an average of 6 feet. The banks of the lake were landscaped and planted with grass.

Algal growth was controlled with yet another application of bluestone. The plan also called for "alum stripping . . . a process that involves adding chemicals to the lake to inactivate nitrogen and phosphorous in the water" (MPH, 12/8/83).

Within a year there had been a significant improvement in water quality, but a new problem was announced—namely, a colonization of the lake by widgeon grass which "clogs our pumps and makes them inoperable" (P&RD, 10/11/85). Earlier plans had called for leaching salt from the mud exposed when the lake was drained but—since widgeon grass grows best in brackish and highly alkaline water—such flushing was apparently incomplete. This colonization by widgeon grass was nothing more than natural plant succession in a changed aquatic environment (as was the case with the tules and green algae which had preceded it).

The response to all this planning and engineering was something less than enthusiastic: The outcome was characterized as the "El Estero Mess": "Nobody was prepared for one shocking consequence of clean water—an infestation of scumlike weeds that have turned the refilled lake into an eyesore and an embarrassment" (MPH, 9/3/85).

An attempt was made to control the "weeds" by spraying them with an herbicide, Aqua Thol-K (MPH, 10/18/85), but the herbicide killed all plant growth, indiscriminately (P&RD, 10/11/85).

Widgeon grass is an annual species, and it was feared that it would pose a recurrent problem. However, an aeration system was installed in the lake (P&RD, 7/31/85), and gradual changes in water chemistry appear to have eliminated the plant.

In 1985, plans for El Estero's future were again modified with a laudable innovation: A resolve "to protect the lake from the introduction of foreign species" (P&RD, 4/10/85). Four fish, once found naturally in the Monterey Bay area, were to be established in the lake: the Sacramento hitch, Sacramento blackfish, Tule perch, and Sacramento perch. Within a few months stocking with these species had begun (MPH, 8/27/85). With this first step, it was naively concluded that "We have come a long way in returning the natural beauty of Lake El Estero" (P&RD, 4/10/85).

This promising beginning seems to have come to little. Despite the resolve to exclude alien species, the fish planted in the lake during the next decade were selected mainly for their value to the recreational fishing industry: By 1994, bluegill and catfish were again being caught, and there had been a major stocking of rainbow trout by the Department of Fish and Game (MPH, 6/5/94).

Although the rainbow (the most abundant and widespread of California trouts) is a great favorite with sport fishermen, stocking with this species (in one or another of its hatchery-altered varieties) is a questionable contribution toward returning El Estero to nature: Although the prehistoric fauna of El Estero is unknown, it is unlikely that it included trout. The fish present before European settlement would mainly have been those more tolerant of brackish water. In 1891 a mullet was recorded as living ". . . in the ocean and muddy lagoons" of Monterey Bay—and a goby, the longjaw mudsucker, as burrowing ". . . in the muddy bottom of the lagoons" (Anderson, 1891, pp. 29 and 32).

El Estero is but the largest of many similar physiographic features scattered along this coast. All have been altered to some degree: At the northern end of Monterey Bay, Schwan Lake, Corcoran Lagoon, and Woods Lagoon were once, like El Estero, seasonal estuaries. Schwan Lake (now part of Twin Lakes State Park) has been dammed and made a freshwater lake: Now its seaward banks are covered with such freshwater plants as tules and willows. Ocean water still enters Corcoran Lagoon (through a culvert), and its seaward edges are still covered by salt grass, patches of pickleweed, and other native salt-marsh vegetation.

Woods Lagoon, having been dredged to make the Santa Cruz Small Craft Harbor, was completely opened to sea water and marine fish in 1963. Since then, big schools of northern anchovy have occasionally entered the lagoon and died in large numbers—fouling the air for miles around and posing a sanitation problem. For example, in 1974 "some 80-100 tons of anchovies were removed by hand, and an additional 40 tons by local fishermen"; in 1984, an estimated 150 tons of dead fish were removed—from an single school (*Santa Cruz Sentinel,* Aug. 25, 1974 and July 22, 1984). Subsequently, installation of pumps to aerate the harbor's water appears to have decreased this die-off.

Elkhorn Slough is unique among estuaries in the area because of its location at the head of the Monterey Bay submarine canyon. The effect of the submarine canyon on the refraction of ocean waves is to reduce wave height and wave energy near the canyon head. Consequently, the wave-built berm is lower in that vicinity than along the coast to the south or north. As this low ridge of sand has little damming effect, the ebb flow from Elkhorn Slough is (unlike ebb flow from the other estuaries) able to clear an entrance to the sea throughout the year.

5. Altered Littoral Drift and the Monterey Bay Sand Budget

Beaches, already a major economic resource of the Monterey Bay area, will become increasingly valuable in the future. Below are some general remarks on the natural conditions of sand supply and the effects of human-made physiographic alterations.

Littoral drift is the net movement of sand parallel to the shoreline during any given period. Because the prevailing winds along the California coast are from the northwest, most ocean waves arrive from a northwesterly direction. Accordingly, the predominant movement of sand is southward, or downcoast.

Over a long period of time Monterey Bay has acted as a great trap for sand moved southward along the coast by littoral drift. This is because of the configuration of the southern half of the bay, with the Monterey Peninsula jutting sharply northward. Losses of sand out of the bay around Point Pinos appear to be negligible.

The Monterey Bay submarine canyon is a major depository for sand moving into the bay. It catches not only sand moving downcoast, but upcoast as well: Westerly and southwesterly waves approaching the shore in winter produce an upcoast movement in the southern half of the bay, and much of this sand, too, is lost into the submarine canyon (Wong, 1970, p. 37).

Although sand moves into the Monterey Bay from the north, local streams supply most of the sand kept in motion by wave action along the bay's shoreline. The largest streams entering the bay are the Salinas, Pajaro, and San Lorenzo rivers. All deposit quantities of sediment in the surf zone, part of which accumulates in beaches. The Salinas River is the largest of the three, its flow averaging three times that of the Pajaro; the San Lorenzo is the smallest. Next to streams, erosion of coastal cliffs yields the principal supply of sediment (Wong, 1970, p. 39).

Probably the greatest single human-made change in natural littoral sand movement began after 1909, when the Salinas River was prevented from returning to its old effluent, north of Moss Landing. Before 1909, the sediment carried by the Salinas was deposited in the northern half of the bay; since that time it has been deposited in the southern half. Although littoral drift can move some sand past the head of the Monterey submarine canyon (Yancey, 1968, p. 23), it is likely that the canyon now divides the bay into two rather distinct sand provinces. Thus, the supply of sand to the northern part of the bay has been reduced and the supply to the southern part increased.

Between Moss Landing and the present mouth of the Salinas there is a slight seaward bow in the shoreline, marking the above-mentioned offshore fan-shaped lens (see U.S.C. and G. Charts 5402 and 5403). There is no corresponding bow to the north of Moss Landing, around the pre-1909 mouth of the Salinas—very likely because much of the material deposited upcoast from the submarine canyon was soon transported southward by littoral drift into the canyon itself. On the other hand, emptying south of the canyon as it now does, the river appears to be feeding sediment to the lens. In a study of the shoreline made through comparison of historical maps, the U.S. Army Corps of Engineers concluded:

> From the . . . Monterey Submarine Canyon south to the vicinity of the mouth of the Salinas River, the offshore area shoaled . . . . The most extensive seaward advance of the shoreline during the period of record occurred at the mouth of the Salinas River. (*House Document No. 179*, 1958, pp. 61 and 68)

Nevertheless, along a half-mile stretch of dune just north of the river mouth there was considerable wave erosion during the storms of early 1995, and heavy driftwood was carried to the upper edge of the berm.

The building of the jetties at the Elkhorn Slough-Moss Landing Harbor entrance has probably had the effect of deflecting sand more strongly into the head of the submarine canyon. A study made of the effects of the jetties' construction on littoral drift over an eight-month period in 1946-1947 predicted that a sandbar would develop between the jetties (Bascom, 1947, pp. 1-3), similar to the one that seasonally blocks the entrance to Santa Cruz Small Craft Harbor. However, at Moss Landing it appears that a larger portion of the drift sand than anticipated falls into one feeder branch of the submarine canyon which extends shoreward toward a point between the jetties. Some of the dredging to keep the harbor entrance clear is necessary, not to remove sand deposited by littoral drift, but rather to remove sand which has been blown from beach and dunes adjoining the jetties and settled in inland parts of the entrance.

In the late nineteenth and early twentieth centuries, agricultural activities such as clearing, grazing, and ploughing increased erosion throughout the area, with a corresponding increase in stream loads. But this was soon counterbalanced by the damming of streams. The reduction of beach-sand supply as a result of damming is likely to become increasingly critical for the Monterey Bay area, since streams are the largest source of sand. For example, the building of dams on the upper Salinas River has reduced its sediment load, and other dams are planned.

Cliff erosion has been severe in the northern part of the bay—for instance, between Capitola and Santa Cruz and westward along West Cliff Drive. There riprap has been dumped along the bases of the cliffs, reducing the rate of erosion, but at the same time reducing the amount of sand supplied to the beaches.

At both Santa Cruz Small Craft Harbor and Moss Landing, dredge spoil taken from between the jetties has been distributed elsewhere. The spoil from Santa Cruz Small Craft Harbor has been pumped onto the beach immediately southward. At Moss Landing benthic invertebrates are in the process of recolonizing dredge spoil transported from between the jetties and distributed offshore in the vicinity of Moss Landing pier (J. S. Oliver and P. N. Slattery, 1973).

The effects of the old iron-sand workings near Aptos at Rob Roy were probably small, at least in terms of volume of sand displaced, but the evidence has been obscured by real estate development. Other real estate projects, such as Rio del Mar, have disturbed sand and influenced its movement along the shore. At Pajaro Dunes, particularly, large amounts of sand were scooped from the mouth of the Pajaro River and piled up as foundation for a housing development.

Road-surfacing and building materials are being quarried on the Pajaro River, near Aromas. Tailings dumped into the river have thoroughly changed its sediment-transport regimen.

5.1. Santa Cruz Small Craft Harbor and the Depletion of Capitola Beach

Following a feasibility study made by the U.S. Army Corps of Engineers, the Santa Cruz Small Craft Harbor was completed in 1963. Although the preliminary study did not indicate strong littoral drift, it was hoped that the jetty protecting the west side of the harbor entrance would trap enough downcoast drift to extend the beach west of the entrance, causing the waves to break well away from the cliffs, which were subject there to wave erosion. The desired effect was attained: A fine broad beach, at times as much as 600 feet (180 m) in width, developed west of the harbor; ice plant now grows down the face of the cliffs. However, in the fall of 1964, the year after the harbor was completed, Capitola, about 3.5 miles (5.6 km) to the east, began losing its beach. Such a loss is normal during the winter, but the beach did not return the following summer. Waves began to undercut the foundations of buildings behind the beach, and a storm sewer was exposed by removal of beach sand. Riprap was placed along the cliff at the west end of the beach to protect it from wave erosion. Between Santa Cruz Small Craft Harbor and Capitola, part of the beach at 26th Avenue also disappeared, and cliffs in the intermediate stretch had to be protected from increased erosion with riprap.

Capitola is one of the state's oldest seaside resort towns, economically heavily dependent on the attractions of its beach for vacationers.

In the early part of the twentieth century there was no shortage of sand supply. Probably because of increased erosion attending the intensive agriculture and lumbering practiced at the time, the amount

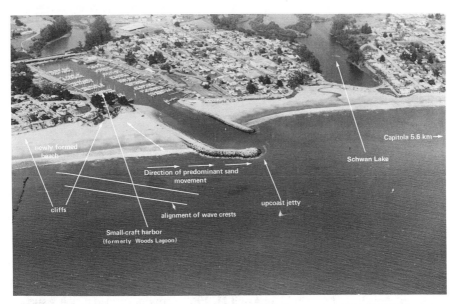

Ebbtide shoreline at Santa Cruz Small Craft Harbor on April 11, 1968, showing the cliffs along East Cliff Drive protected from wave erosion by a broad, newly formed beach. (Photo B. Gordon and D. Hawley)

of sediment deposited in the bay by Soquel Creek was much greater than it is at present:

> *The Soquel Creek landed so much sand at its mouth* this year that the water at the end of the Capitola wharf is so shallow *that a landing on* [sic] *boats is impossible* at present, but it is probable that the sand will wash out. *Two years ago so much sand and soil came down the stream that at low tide it was possible to walk on the beach to the end of the wharf. (The Santa Cruz Surf,* February 4, 1909)

Capitola residents claim that nowadays the principal source of sand supply to their beach is littoral drift, and that the amount of sand carried to the shore by Capitola Creek, or eroded from seacliffs in the vicinity, is small by comparison. They claim that their beach losses in 1964 were a consequence of the erection of the jetties at Santa Cruz Small Craft Harbor, and blame the U.S. Army Corps of Engineers for deciding mistakenly that there was too little littoral movement of sand at the Santa Cruz Small Craft Harbor to justify a sand bypass across the entrance. (A sand bypass is a continuous

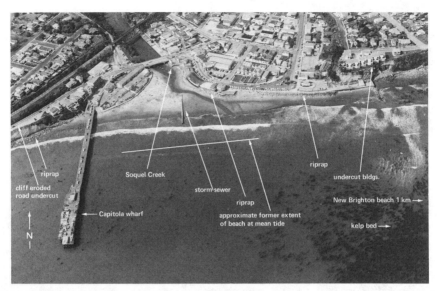

Ebbtide shoreline at Capitola on April 11, 1968, showing eroded beach, exposed storm sewer, and riprap placed to prevent waves from undercutting cliffs, roadway, and buildings. (Photo B. Gordon and D. Hawley)

Capitola groin in April 1971 (completed in July 1970). Capitola beach is replenished by littoral drift trapped on the upcoast side of the groin. (Photo U.S. Army Corps of Engineers)

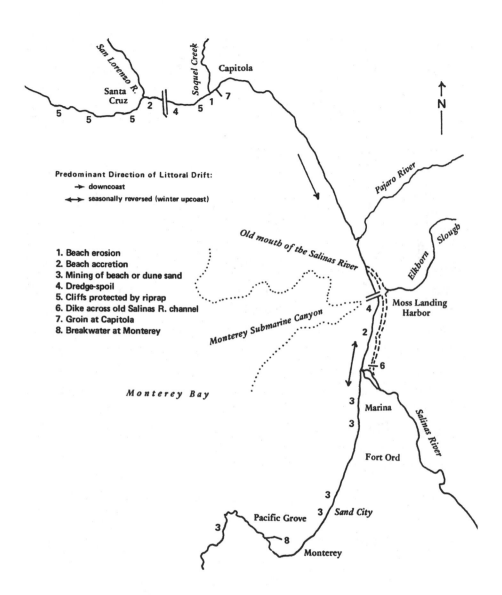

**Sketch Map Showing Artificial Changes in
Sand Supply and Deposition**

dredging operation which would supply sand continuously to the downcoast side of the harbor entrance, where it could be carried on down the coast by littoral drift.)

In 1966, the city of Capitola even trucked in sand to replenish its beach, at considerable expense; but the sand was quickly swept away. As a solution to the problem Capitola has built a groin of its own to trap littoral drift. (*House Document No. 179*, 1958, records earlier shoreline changes in this vicinity.)

Fears that these engineering feats might have repercussions farther downcoast were soon realized. Cliff erosion between Capitola and New Brighton became intense. This was especially noticeable in December 1976 (and welcomed by fossil hunters, because in the process masses of marine mammal bones, shells, etc., were exhumed there and fell into the surf. After having been conveniently washed by the waves, the specimens could be picked over at low tide). Erosion of the sandy cliffs along this stretch continues. A bit farther south at Seacliff State Beach, the winter storm waves of 1979-1980 required the building of a mile-long protective barrier of riprap. Yet more severe storms in 1983 led to the construction of the present seawall, completed in 1985.

5.2. Sand Mining

Within the bay sand mining is concentrated in two stretches of shoreline in the southeast, one near Marina and the other near Sand City. A third area is along the western shore of the Monterey Peninsula (Hart, 1966, pp. 84-92).

From the dunes at Lapis Siding (near Marina), sand is pumped in suspension to a processing plant, in a year-round operation. During the winter, when the grains are largest, hence more desirable commercially, sand is collected from the surf zone. Large water-filled pits mark the source of the mined dune and beach sand.

Around Sand City dune landscape has been greatly altered by sand-mining operations. Aside from the open pits and an area of

Sand-mining operation near Marina (Photo J. Christenson and D. Hawley)

shifting dune, disturbance is on a small scale around Marina. On the other hand, on the Monterey Peninsula, several hundred acres of beautiful white dunes and a large part of their associated biota have been eliminated. And there the dune and beach sand resources can be considered "essentially non-renewable, sand replenishment by wave and wind action being much less than the excavation rate" (Hart, 1966, p. 91).

Within the bay, the coarsest dune sand appears to be in the vicinity of Fort Ord, grain size diminishing to both the north and the south. Were its extent not restricted by Fort Ord, sand mining would probably be practiced along the whole stretch of shoreline from Marina to Sand City.

According to local sand-mine operators, questioned in 1970, the shoreline near Sand City had moved landward in recent years, and the average sand-grain size had been reduced. One estimated that the shoreline had moved back 175 feet (53 m) between 1950 and 1970.

Some attribute these changes to effects of the building of Santa Cruz Small Craft Harbor. This seems rather unlikely, because the harbor is separated from this part of the bay by the submarine canyon. The following report was written in 1966: "The Beach Erosion Board, U.S. Army Corps of Engineers, *considers shore erosion in the Fort Ord vicinity to be severe* and currently is studying the situation to determine the causes of erosion" (Jack Stirton, cited in Hart. 1966, p. 86). This erosion of the shoreline apparently took place despite the increased supply of sand which had been provided by the Salinas River after 1909 (when the Salinas began to empty to the south of the submarine canyon) and before the large dams were constructed upriver. Sand mining at Lapis began around 1906. Probably, sand-mining operations themselves account for some landward movement of the shoreline. The mining of sand from higher parts of the dunes may have little effect on beach equilibrium, but the effects of dredging the surf zone, even taking relatively small amounts of sand, could be considerable. The stripping of the coarser sand from the surf zone probably influences sand-grain size on neighboring beaches, too. Sand excavated from the surf near Marina (at Prattco) was exported to the San Francisco Bay area to help maintain three beaches of the East Bay Regional Park (Goldman, 1967, p. 3). (For more recent information on sand mining in the dune and surf zones see *Big Sur Land Trust,* 1992, pp. 18-21.)

Like freshwater, sand has become an important commodity in the local economy—and is increasingly in short supply. Like water, sand is shifted from place to place as needed: Thanks to the tourist industry, n square meters of beach sand equals, so to speak, one hamburger stand—and xn square meters, a hotel. Obviously, a sand budget is needed for the embayment as a whole.

5.3. Littoral Drift, Artificial Reefs, and Planning in the Offshore Zone

That sand accumulations form a special habitat is well known.

When artificial changes cause the erosion or accretion of beaches, this characteristic sand fauna is redistributed, too.

Artificial changes in littoral drift may redistribute offshore kelp beds, as well. Kelp grows only where rocks are exposed for its holdfasts; if these rocky surfaces are buried in sand, the kelp beds soon disappear, and their large associated fauna disappears also.

The effects of artificial reefs on the ecology of sandy areas offshore have been studied along the coast of southern California (Carlisle et al., 1964); the results may be significant for planning in the Monterey Bay area.

These studies were concerned primarily with the improvement of sport fishing in the coastal waters. Sites for artificial reefs were selected in flat sandy areas where fishing for kelp bass, sand bass, and sheepshead (sport-fish species that favor rocky areas and kelp beds) is generally poor. There are broad expanses of such bottom in Monterey Bay—for example, offshore from the Salinas River mouth and Fort Ord. In southern California, the reefs were placed at depths of not more than 50 to 60 feet (15 to 18 m), since kelp does not flourish at greater depths, yet deep enough that they posed no hazard for navigation. Naturally seeded giant-kelp beds became established within a few months after the reefs were placed, and marine life, including fish populations in the vicinity of the reefs, built up rapidly. There can be no doubt that kelp beds provide a new habitat, rich in more than fish species: "A separate sublittoral faunal group [in Monterey Bay] is *the giant kelp assemblage which includes about one hundred and forty five mollusks and one brachiopod*" (Smith and Gordon, 1948, p. 154).

Although reefs built of old cars quickly attracted fish and produced kelp in the southern California study area, the car bodies disintegrated into low mounds of rubble within three or four years, at which time kelp and fish life again diminished. Furthermore, although no chemical studies were made, chemical alterations of the seawater, which very likely accompanies disintegration of the cars, may well have harmful effects as yet undescribed. It appears that artificial reefs will not make suitable graveyards for the unwanted bodies of our old cars.

Quarry rock turned out to be the best (though most expensive) material for the construction of durable reefs. Properly located, such artificial reefs might be of considerable value for dissipating wave action and reducing erosion, as well as for maintaining a varied littoral flora and fauna.

6. Moss Landing Salt Ponds

Until around 1973, salt was manufactured on the Elkhorn Slough at Moss Landing by the Monterey Bay Salt Company. The special physical conditions necessary for commercial production of salt from ponds, namely, a tidal flat that is protected from the surf and underlain by a relatively impermeable layer and that is not subject to flooding by fresh water, are not common along the coast. Two of these three conditions are now to be found in Elkhorn Slough, but before the 1909 displacement of the Salinas River mouth the slough was frequently flooded with fresh water, precluding a successful salt industry. Although some salt was manufactured on Elkhorn Slough during the 1890s, commercial salt production did not begin until 1916, well after displacement of the river mouth.

The Monterey Bay Salt Company used about 3 hectares of its property for rectangular crystallizing ponds, ranging in size between 0.2 and 0.4 hectares (0.5 and 1 acre). "Seawater pumped from Elkhorn Slough circulates through the concentrating pond system and returns as pickle saturated with sodium chloride in the vicinity of the crystallizing ponds . . . ." (Ver Planck, 1968, pp. 68, 71). The whole cycle required several years for completion.

During periods of salt production, the various colors in the ponds depicted an ecological succession: As the salinity of the ponds increased, they were inhabited by different species of blue-green algae, the metabolic products of which colored the water (Carpelan, 1957).

The colors were most intense, and their range greatest, in the fall. When harvested, the salt crystals were washed to remove a red covering produced by dinoflagellates concentrated in the ponds. Most of the mollusks of adjacent tidal flats were absent, probably because the pond waters were too saline for these animals.

On the other hand, the ponds swarmed with brine shrimp, not common in the neighboring slough. Phalaropes fed heavily on these shrimp, and the ponds were important to other estuarine birds as well.

Since around 1973, salt making in these evaporation ponds has stopped, at least temporarily. Their use shifted for a time to the commercial production of brine shrimp, an industry similarly dependent on an artificial increase in the salinity of sea water. In 1984 much of the salt-pond property was acquired by the California Department of Fish and Game. The former salt ponds are now unused and, dikes having broken, some are flooded with slough water. The variety of bird life has diminished accordingly.

Salt has long been manufactured in this general area. Indeed, *salinas* is the Spanish word for salt ponds. However, the original salt-manufacturing sites, which gave the Salinas River its name, were located somewhat farther south. In Spanish times salt was brought from

. . . the Salinas lagoons, or salt ponds, situated between the ocean sand dunes and the Monterey River ["Monterey" is one of several names applied to the Salinas River in the days before salt manufacturing began here] . . . . The commander of the guard [at Monterey Presidio] would bring Indians from Soledad and Carmelo and gathering all the salt from *the three lagoons* into one pile, covered it with sticks and branches, to which they set fire, so as to melt over the surface and form a crust over the mass, which would protect it from the dampness . . . (Bancroft, 1888, p. 486)

Cattle need quantities of salt, and much of the salt prepared in these ponds was used in salt licks on the great cattle ranches of the time.

The "three lagoons" mentioned as being used as *salinas* were probably at Rincon de las Salinas, where an old Spanish cadastral sketch (*Diseño* No. 16) specifically labels four. There were also natural salt ponds in the vicinity. At Marina, too, there are several low, very saline ponds just behind the dunes. Unfortunately, these Marina ponds were destroyed or much altered by residential development before being thoroughly studied. From the water in one pond, two Dutch biologists described a new species of saltwater flagellate, *Dunaliella peircei* (E. Nicolai and L. Baas Becking, 1936, p. 319).

7

Custodial Planning for the Monterey Bay Area: Biota and Land Use

THE ECOLOGICAL EFFECTS of industry are now felt on a global scale, and virtually all species are affected. Indeed, such sustained selective influences of human cultures on biota and ecology as those described here and elsewhere affect the course of evolution, introducing into that process an element of human choice (B.L. Gordon, 1957, p. 91). If the world's human population continues to grow, people will have to take responsibility for the condition of many species, both those with decreasing and those with increasing numbers—a responsibility that will entail more than mere "game laws" and "wilderness areas." In fact, conservational responsibility may ultimately require a global inventory and the apportionment of biomass and range, species by species.

1. Anthropogenic Evolution

The evolutionary effects of human activities are generally subtle, and proceed almost unnoticed. Several activities that cause evolutionary change in plant and animal life—including the breaking down of ecological barriers, artificial selection, and the creation of synanthropic populations—are discussed below. (As previously noted, synanthropic species are those that are tolerant of, or favored by, the selective effects of human activities.)

The natural environmental barriers which separate habitats often disappear during land use operations. The resulting redistribution of species has its evolutionary effects—for example, as a result of introgressive hybridization: When two species interbreed, the hybrids "may back cross to one or both parents, and so modify the adjoining populations of the parental species through introgression . . . " (Anderson and Stebbins, 1954, p. 378). For example, in the Santa Cruz Mountains the Douglas iris, generally a coastal species, is an aggressive colonist on such disturbed sites as roadsides, pastures, and burned-over areas. There it comes frequently into contact with other irises. When Douglas iris hybridizes with the slender-tubed iris, for example, introgression occurs (Lenz, 1959, pp. 287, 300, 304). Thus, a person trying to identify irises in some areas (say, between Eagle Rock and Boulder Creek) may be faced with a confusing array of flower shapes and colors.

On the Monterey Peninsula, along clearings made for firebreaks, a pair of ceanothus species (blue blossom and cropleaf) sometimes hybridize so freely as to produce "every conceivable intergradation" between the two (Stebbins, 1950, p. 205-206). The same pair produced similar hybrid swarms in parts of Fort Ord which were accidentally burned in 1967 (Griffin, 1976, p. 27). Whether introgression occurred in these cases in uncertain.

Human land use changes and the resulting breakdown of ecological barriers may also explain the occurrence of some hybrid forms of *Quercus* and *Arctostaphylos* that exist in this part of California.

Hybridization also occurs when native animal species are shifted about. For example, rainbow trout from the Shasta area were the first to be selected for hatchery culture:

Widespread planting of derivatives of this form over California (and over the world) combined with *hatchery selection pressures and hybridization with other forms* has largely eliminated whatever distinctive traits they might once have had. (Moyle, 1976a, p. 127)

Planted rainbow trout have hybridized "extensively with Lahontan cutthroat trout, golden trout, and redband trout" (Moyle, 1976b, p. 101). As noted before, the introduced English (Persian) walnut hybridizes with the native black walnut.

The northern ("red-shafted") flicker of the western United States and the eastern ("yellow-shafted") flicker now interbreed in the Great Plains. In parts of that generally treeless area, human settlements—with their trees planted for shade, windbreaks, etc.—created new habitats in which the two birds came together. In the introgression which followed, gene flow has been predominantly from east to west (B.W. Anderson, 1970, p. 343)—and hybrids are now found in California, including the Monterey Bay area (Roberson and Tenney, 1993, p. 202).

Natural selection is the cornerstone of modern evolutionary theory: "No other concept in evolutionary biology is as important" (Mayr, 1988, p. 93): *Artificial* selection has received less attention.

Following the Pleistocene development of human culture, an entirely new selective influence appeared. Largely the product of human volition, artificial selection now permeates the evolutionary process, supplementing the operation of natural selection.

In his work on domesticated plants and animals, Darwin writes at length on the subject. That he was well aware of the distinction that must be made between the human (i.e., the cultural) and the natural can be seen in such passages as the following: "With domestic productions, natural selection comes to a certain extent into action, independently of, and even in opposition to, the will of man" (Darwin, II 177-178). He repeatedly distinguishes between the natural and the artificial as selective processes.

In discussing the appearance of new breeds of domestic pigeon, Darwin refers to two types of artificial selection—"methodical" and "unconscious" selection. In methodical (deliberate) selection, "the breeder has a distinct object in view"—while in unconscious selection "the breeder selects his birds unconsciously, unintentionally, and without method" (Darwin, 1987, I, p. 224).

However, Darwin's interest in artificial selection focused on the part it played in the evolution of domesticated species: Geographically the selective efforts of human action go far beyond the breeder's pens and gardens.

The following case is an example of unconscious artificial selection:

> The evolution of insecticide-resistant races of insects within a few years indicates the speed with which simple adaptive changes may take place under constantly applied selection, being in fact *a negative type of artificial selection.* (Allee et al., 1965, p. 654)

Such purposeful actions, with their unintentional effects on evolution, underlie the synanthropic trend. (Human disturbance of the environment is mainly deliberate and purposeful—whether undertaken with the intent of influencing evolution or not.)

The same unconscious artificial selection is illustrated in the use of herbicides. It is not generally appreciated how widely herbicides are used in the Monterey Bay area: Their use is unrestricted by law except on plants to be marketed, and they are available in any garden-supply store. Herbicides (Roundup™ is a common brand) are even used by conservationists in restoration projects. As to the evolutionary effects, spraying any one plant works to the advantage of its neighbors—and, as in insects, a number of weeds are evolving a resistance to pesticides. Like insecticides and herbicides, anti-coagulants for the extermination of small mammals are readily available in stores—as well as from the local agricultural commissioner.

The evolutionary influence of new chemical products is now widespread: Within the twentieth century hundreds of chemical compounds, many of which do not exist in nature, have been synthesized and manufactured in quantity; more are added every year. Because different organisms have distinctive, genetically-determined, tolerance levels, when released into the open environment such compounds have a highly selective effect. These chemical artifacts have penetrated the natural world far beyond the human settlement; a well-known example is the DDT found in ospreys, pelicans, and even in antarctic penguins. Thus, it will be increasingly difficult in the future to divide the earth's surface sharply into two spatial realms—the wild versus the humanized.

Exotic species make up a large part of the Monterey Bay area's plant and animal life. Most of these come from Eurasia where they have been exposed to artificial selective action for millennia. Agriculture, with all its selective effects, had its beginnings more than 10,000 years earlier in the eastern Mediterranean area than in the Monterey Bay area.

Under what Darwin calls "the will of man" methodical artificial selection has produced our crop plants and domesticated animals— and unconscious selection, hundreds of other synanthropic species such as insect pests and weeds. Most weeds have evolved "from wild colonizers, through selection towards adaptation to continuous habitat disturbances"—or "as derivatives of hybridization between wild and domesticated species" (De Wet and Harlan, 1975, p. 100). Plants have been selected for the annual habit, by yearly ploughing (practiced in southern Europe more than 5000 years ago); for withstanding intensive grazing, by exposure to domestic herds (see p. 143); for reduced photoperiodicity, by being transported to various latitudes; and so on. Because of its relatively sparse population, and the simple technology of its inhabitants, the synanthropic process had not gone so far in pre-European California. Nevertheless, under the newly-added pressure of agricultural practices, a small number of native California plants, including several fiddlenecks, have evolved rapidly and produced weedy varieties (see p. 78). According to one geneticist, "none of these weeds could be more than 200 years old" (Stebbins, 1965, p. 174).

Evolution operates at the species level (Mayr, 1988, p. 475)— and with each extinct species, one line of evolutionary development terminates. Thus, the human extirpation of any species has the effect of restricting subsequent evolutionary possibilities. In places like the

Monterey Bay area, where few animals are known to have been completely exterminated, less drastic reductions of populations may be even more important from the evolutionary standpoint than outright extinction: A "major component of the decline in bio-diversity is the loss of genetically distinct populations . . . extirpation of populations is the dominant element of the extinction crisis in temperate regions today" (Ehrlich, 1991, p. 175). These losses are irreversible: Severely inbred, small remnants of a species saved from extinction are unlikely to have the same genetic resources as the original population. The elephant seal is a case in point (Bonnell and Selander, 1974, p. 90).

It is generally agreed that artificial selection tends to reduce the fitness of plants and animals for survival under natural conditions. (As discussed above, synanthropic species are usually excluded during natural plant succession.) Consequently—some contend—synanthropic organisms, being dependent on the continued ecological dominance of the human species, represent in the long term an evolutionary dead end. On the other hand, completely natural conditions are fast disappearing: The cultural landscape continues to expand—even into remote tropical forests (B.L. Gordon, 1982). Furthermore, the evolutionary changes already made have lasting effects even if the human species were to disappear now.

Synanthropic behavior is a preliminary to domestication: When synanthropic species are further selected for usefulness they are said to be domesticated. A number of plants, the so-called "cultivars," are incapable of survival without direct human tending. Maize is an example: The plant has been so altered that it hardly resembles the grasses found in nature—and if its seeds were not planted, the species would soon become extinct. The creation of transgenic organisms, and their release into the environment, continues the humanizing trend (R.A. Gordon et al., 1991, pp. 190, 198). This human desire to improve on nature is apparently irrepressible, and goes beyond meeting perceived biological needs: Witness, the topiary gardens of earlier centuries and the marine parks of today; the many flowers bred solely for their beauty; the various grotesque new breeds of animals; and so

Yellow-flowered evening primrose (*Oenothera glazioviana*), an example of the evolutionary effects of transporting plants from place to place: Several weedy evening primroses from eastern North America were accidentally exported to Europe in the seventeenth century. Two of them came together in the same geographical area and crossed, producing the hybrid species shown above (Obersdorfer, 1990, p. 688, Jepson, 1993, p. 803); it is about 1 m tall. Imported to the United States as a decorative plant, the hybrid escaped from cultivation on disturbed ground; for instance, it grows as a garden weed in Santa Cruz and Pacific Grove. (Photo B. Gordon)

on. That the long-term trend is toward further embellishment (and—transcending the strictly organic—toward outright forgery) can be seen in the increasing use of artificial bouquets in restaurants, plastic corsages on clothing, plastic turf ("Astroturf") on playing fields, and non-flammable Christmas trees. The plastic shrubs now common in shopping malls, office buildings, and hospitals are advertised as indistinguishable from, or even improvements on, nature (no irrigation required, few bugs, no hay fever). These artifacts are now made with such skill that the simulation is, in fact, hard to detect. One prediction has it that "Future gardens will have artificial plants that can be

programmed to change colors, or even species, with the seasons"
(Vick, 1989, p. 29).

Despite all this, the resurgent forces of nature are very much in
evidence and, though there is no prospect of completely resurrecting
pre-human nature in the Monterey Bay area, natural plant succession
eliminates most evidence of past human presence. Notwithstanding
the genetic changes discussed above, most native plants and animals
remain in their familiar forms, and much that is natural can be restored.

2. Depleted Areas and Their Replenishment

Doubtless the establishment of "wilderness areas" has been a great
step forward in the conservation movement. For example, Los Padres
National Forest, just to the south of the Monterey Bay area, was
converted into the Ventana Wilderness Area in 1969. But future
wilderness areas should include more than broad expanses of
coniferous forest in rough, high country, ecologically neither the most
complex of plant associations nor in the most danger of extermination.
Public parks tend to be located in such vegetation. Toro Regional
Park and Royal Oaks County Park are notable exceptions.

A mosaic of native plant communities scattered throughout the
area will be useful as a reference base in decision making. The
wilderness-area idea should be extended to include many small tracts
of various natural plant formations—riparian forest, oak woodland,
coniferous forest, chaparral, freshwater marsh, and so on. Remnants
of these original formations should be located and extended in a
patchwork of whichever patterns best fit the terrain. Such tracts,
scattered over their natural areas of growth throughout the cultural
landscape, would serve as seedbeds for redirecting ecological change
and as habitats for native animal species. They would, in a sense, be
living historical records and invaluable as controls in studying
changing land use. The ribbons of ecotone vegetation at their edges
would be greatly elongated by such a distribution of plant cover; and
since the ecotone is the site of greatest successional potential, rapid

changes in plant cover would be facilitated as later needs arose. Studies elsewhere have shown that the population density of most nesting birds "varies as a direct function of the *amount of edge per unit area*" (Beecher, 1942, p. 39), and increases with the diversity of the plant cover. General observations suggest that the same relationship holds in the Monterey Bay area and that it applies as well to various animals other than birds. Within the overall mosaic of plant cover, the animal species present will change sequentially as successional progresses.

Considering the Monterey Bay area as a whole, the comprehensive management of vegetation has an unrealized potential for regulating terrestrial animal numbers, plant cover being the basic "biological control." Although the greatest present need is for what might be called "wilderness renewal districts" and for replanting programs, there will continue to be a need for selective clearing as well—and for the use, under appropriate weather conditions, of low-intensity fires. Where woody cover is heavy enough to supply valuable fuels, mechanical methods of clearing may be used, followed on some sites—depending on the kind of succession desired—by the controlled burning of slash.

As mentioned earlier, maximum diversity in plant cover will be favored by maintaining existing areas of natural vegetation, by allowing natural successional trends to proceed unchecked on a variety of available sites, by partially replanting tracts from which natural associations have long been cleared, and by keeping all possible phases of plant succession in existence simultaneously through selectively disturbing localized portions of climax vegetation. These conditions are prerequisites for a varied and balanced fauna. An early replanting project to support wildlife was undertaken on a site in the Monterey Bay area: The planting was done between 1932 and 1937 as a cooperative effort by a local landowner, the U.S. Soil Conservation Service, and the California Department of Fish and Game (Hawbecker, 1940, p. 272).

Some nineteen species of trees and shrubs were planted on a 50-hectare (120-acre) farm in the San Andreas District, west of

Watsonville, from which the natural plant cover had long since been cleared. Within two years of the first plantings a marked increase in number of bird and mammal species was reported. Despite this promising beginning, the long-term accomplishment was slight. The reasons for the project's failure are instructive. The plants were not well chosen. Some were introduced from distant parts of California or from elsewhere in the United States—for example the lemonade berry (*Rhus integrifolia*), the laurel-sumac (*Rhus laurina*), and the Arizona cypress. Others, though native within the Monterey Bay area, are not a part of the potential natural vegetation of the San Andreas District, and failed to reproduce themselves on the site. (Although the terms "alien" or "introduced" are usually applied to plants from outside the state, for purposes of restoring the Monterey Bay area's natural plant cover these terms should be interpreted in a narrower sense and include all Californian species whose ranges have been extended by human action—admittedly, a difficult task since distributions have been so thoroughly reshuffled). Furthermore, the project's emphasis was strongly on game animals—on increasing the number of quail, establishing pheasants, etc.—rather than on restoring wildlife as a whole. But these shortcomings are technical details that could have been gradually revised. The critical flaw in the whole venture was the absence of sustained responsibility. Within a few years, ownership of the land changed hands. And despite a firm statement of intent to "continue study" and "evaluate results" (Hawbecker, 1940, p. 277), the project was soon forgotten. The project site has since been used for an army camp, as a private school grounds, for truck crops, and for residences. The plantings have all died off, except for a grove of Monterey pines and a few senescent knobcone pines. Plainly, successful management of living resources will have to be based on longer views into the future. The life spans of some native plants cover centuries; planning within a commensurate time scale is essential if the biotic potential of the area is to be realized.

Since 1975, several admirable replanting and restoration programs have been undertaken with much public support and involvement.

2.1. Dune Restoration

Exotic species commonly establish themselves on terrain disturbed by human activities, but in the coastal dune environment (as on river floodplains and in estuaries) the disturbance may also be natural. Thus, introduced plants are doubly likely to gain a firm foothold in the dunes.

In a dune restoration program in the southern Monterey Bay area—at Asilomar, Marina, and several other state beaches, and at Moss Landing Marine Laboratories—many native species have been planted: beach-bur, coast buckwheat, Menzies' wallflower, coastal sagewort, etc. Some that had become rare are now plentiful. A major effort has also been made to limit the spread of introduced plants that have spread aggressively and taken territory from native plants—the Hottentot fig, for example.

Generally, there is little doubt as to which plants are native, and which introduced—but in the dune environment this is sometimes not the case. In restoration programs devoted to replanting and managing native plants, the question becomes critical, as in the case of the sea fig—a plant found in both Chile and California, and which has been claimed as a native in both areas.

Although the sea fig is problematical because of its discontinuous distribution, the native status of several other common dune plants could well be questioned on similar grounds: The beach morning glory, beach strawberry, and sandmat also grow untended in both California and Chile (and elsewhere). Because all are found in other parts of the world, and because it is unknown how long they have grown in California, a question arises from the standpoint of dune restoration: Should all be classified as aliens?

The problem of the sea fig is complicated by the presence in California dunes of the closely related, and plainly undesirable, Hottentot fig—with which the sea fig occasionally hybridizes. (If introgression occurs, the gene flow is probably toward the Hottentot fig populations.) The problem is further complicated by use of the term "ice plants" which is applied to both the sea fig and the Hottentot fig, as well as to a number of other species in the genera *Carpobrotus* and *Mesembryanthemum*. In 1925, the Hottentot fig appears to have been confined to an area near Los Angeles (Jepson, 1925, p. 343). Since then, it has been widely planted in coastal California to check soil erosion on roadcuts and sea cliffs, and to stabilize dunes: In 1978, the California Transportation Department maintained some 6000 acres of "ice plants" (*Santa Cruz Sentinel,* August 10, 1978). From such plantations, the Hottentot fig has invaded many disturbed dune surfaces—and, in places, it appears to have replaced the sea fig.

The question of which ice plants are native to California, and which introduced, is still unsettled. Because of its abundance and wide distribution along this coast—and a concern that like the Hottentot fig it may exclude other plants—the case of the sea fig is especially important.

Studies of California's dune vegetation have long treated the sea fig as a native and characteristic species (Purer, 1936; Cooper, 1936; Williams and Potter, 1972). Standard floras have either treated the plant as a native—or at least failed to identify it as introduced (Jepson, 1925; Abrams, 1944; Thomas, 1961; Munz, 1968).

The following chronology shows that the sea fig and some of its relatives have been in California for a long time: The first reference to these plants in California was written by the botanist Archibald Menzies. In listing the species growing in the vicinity of San Diego in 1793, Menzies noted, "I saw also *Mesembryanthemum edulis.*" (This is one of the old botanical names for the Hottentot fig—but the taxonomy of these plants had not been well worked out at the time and, according to an outstanding authority on the botanical exploration of California, what Menzies saw was actually the sea fig [Eastwood, 1924, p. 334]).

Between 1834 and 1836, Thomas Nuttall found two species of "*Mesembryanthemum*" in California: "One [presumably the sea fig] Mr. Nuttall suspects to be native" (Torrey and Gray, 1838-1840, p. 556). The sea fig was again collected in the years 1848-1849, and

"Ice plants": Sea fig (*above*); Hottentot fig (*below*) with one fruit cut open. The two plants are quite similar, except that the Hottentot fig has yellow flowers (turning pink as they dry) while the flowers of the sea fig are a light rose-purple, and somewhat smaller. Both have succulent leaves, triangular in cross-section—those of the sea fig being the shorter and having a bluish-green tint. In both species the contents of the fruits have a fig-like consistency.

Sea rocket. A European species, the sea rocket was first reported from Stinson Beach north of the Golden Gate and from the coast of San Mateo County in 1935 (Rose, 1936, p. 224). Since then, it has almost entirely replaced a closely related plant (*Cakile edentula*) which had been introduced from the eastern United States about half a century earlier (Barbour and Rodman, 1970). The sea rocket has become an important part of the dune community; there, it is an aggressive colonist on devegetated foredunes—and reardunes, though to a lesser extent. It is even found growing on thin layers of blown sand accumulated in macadam parking lots. Though an alien species, the sea rocket is welcomed (and sometimes planted) in restoration programs. In any case, its extermination would be difficult, if not impossible: The plant is an annual and its seeds, carried along the coast by littoral drift, are constantly supplied to beaches by ocean waves.

identified by John Torrey in 1857 (Abrams, 1944, p. 199).

In a study of plant collections made in California between 1860 and 1865, the sea fig's distribution was described as follows: "On the sea shore and in saline soils *from San Diego to Punta del Reyes. Also in Chile and abundant in Australia and Tasmania ...*" (Brewer and Watson, 1880, p. 251). Assuming the plant did not arrive in California until historical times, the Spanish come to mind as those who might have brought it; perhaps the seeds were accidentally mixed in ship ballast at their old settlements in Chile. On the other hand, the Spanish mission in San Diego was not founded until 1769, and from San Diego to Point Reyes is some 600 miles: To cover that distance between 1769 and 1860, the plant would have had to spread northward at the unlikely rate of more than 6 miles per year—somehow passing over many stretches without dunes. Even if the Spanish dropped sea fig seeds off at several coastal points, the time interval seems scarcely sufficient for the plant to have covered the distances involved. By 1870 the sea fig had been collected in the vicinity of San Francisco (Bolander, 1970, p. 24), and in 1881 at Santa Cruz (by Marcus Jones, whose herbarium sheet is at the Rancho Santa Ana Botanic Garden). (In trying to determine the date of a species' arrival here, it must be kept in mind that the *absence* of a plant in a botanist's collection does not prove that it was not growing in the area at the time; and, similarly, with the absence of the plant's pollen from a palynologist's soil core.) Some have suggested that the seeds of the sea fig and beach strawberry were carried to California on the feet or feathers of migrant birds well before the arrival of Europeans.

The sea fig often grows intermixed with such natives as the silky beach pea and yellow sand verbena in what appears to be a stable dune plant cover. In one of the earliest discussions of dune-plant

Dunes footpaths, leading from cars to beach. This photograph, taken in 1969 before dune restoration began, illustrates the problem of providing public access to beaches and, at the same time, maintaining dune vegetation. Residential use of the dunes eliminates even more natural plant cover. (Photo B. Gordon and D. Hawley)

restoration in the Monterey Bay area, the sea fig is described as a native and carefully distinguished from the invasive Hottentot fig: "Since it [the sea fig] is a natural part of the native plant community, it can be used freely with other plants and wildflowers without danger of crowding them out" (Cowan, 1975, p. 7). Present in California for at least two centuries—the sea fig has, so far as is known, been responsible for the extinction of no fellow dune plant. In recent years, however, some have classified the sea fig as an import—and, as part of a major effort to protect and restore native dune vegetation, it is one of the "ice plants" being eradicated (*The Big Sur Land Trust,* 1992, p. 22).

Where the sea fig has been designated an alien species and its complete eradication attempted, there is some disagreement as to the best method of extermination. One opinion holds that all "ice plants" including the sea fig and the Hottentot fig should be dug up, and that chemical methods should be avoided "because spraying with herbicides also could affect non-targeted native species" (*The Big Sur Land Trust,* 1992, p. 22).

Another opinion is that digging up the plants is not the best way to proceed—that herbicides are the answer. Herbicides have been used locally in alien plant eradication at least since 1976 (*Fremontia,* July 1976, p. 14).

Yet, even in digging up sea fig, it is impossible to avoid destroying some intermixed native pioneers such as the coastal sagewort and beach-bur. Furthermore, thin soil profiles are broken up, and blowouts initiated. Considering the fact that the sea fig forms extensive dune plant cover from southern Oregon to Baja California (Cooper, 1936, p. 153), attempting its total destruction is both impracticable and unadvisable.

Without guiding principles or an overall plan, conservational efforts remain uncoordinated—and to some extent at cross purposes. For example, during the first half of the 1990s, while ice plant was being dug up or sprayed with herbicides in the southern parts of the Monterey Bay area, the Hottentot fig was being *planted* in the north at Natural Bridges State Park—and by the City of Santa Cruz, along West Cliff Drive.

When a more complete knowledge of successional variations in dune-plant cover is available, it may be possible to restore damaged plant cover through replanting alone without recourse to the selective destruction of unwanted species.

2.2. Other Restoration Programs

Several other parts of the Monterey Bay area are in need of replanting operations, and of protected tracts in which successional trends may proceed without interruption.

The coastal area along the present route of Highway 1, northward from Santa Cruz past Davenport and Año Nuevo, has been deservedly much acclaimed for its beauty. As the human population is small, it is sometimes even pointed to, mistakenly, as a remnant of untrammeled California nature. But, as noted earlier, natural plant associations have long since been largely eliminated there. Foreign annuals grow along the road and dominate neighboring pastures. The area could be made even more attractive than it is at present, and much more varied, by reviving tracts of the natural vegetation.

Another promising area for revegetation is the surface of the Aromas Red Sands, lying between Moro Cojo Slough and the Pajaro Valley and including much of the Prunedale and Hall districts. Although this land has long been used agriculturally, especially during the depression of the 1930s, its soils are not very fertile. Since the 1970s, with the aid of mineral fertilizers, strawberry culture has become economically successful in the area: This land use is preceded by a complete clearance of natural vegetation and often followed, on the steeper slopes, by severe erosion. Nevertheless, small patches of oak woodland survived and, where agricultural use lessened, many new live oak stands have appeared. In fact, live oaks are more numerous now than at any other time in the twentieth century.

Erosion scar in Aromas Red Sands resulting from clearing and overgrazing in the upper drainage of Elkhorn Slough off Garin Road. The sands are actually more tan than red (Allen, 1946). The original cover was coast live oak; note the several oaks still growing on the knoll in the distance. All material eroded here was deposited immediately below in Werner Lake, a small body of water partially visible in the left foreground, where the considerable shoaling produced by this scar alone could be calculated. The lake is now Nature Conservancy property. That the Aromas Red Sands are susceptible to erosion can also be seen hereabouts where strawberries are grown on the steeper slopes.

On erosion scars such as the one shown above, as well as on roadcuts and shifting dunes, any plant cover (even though it includes alien plants which may be undesirable elsewhere) is better than none because, with the eroding surfaces stabilized, soil-forming processes can begin.   (Photo B. Gordon)

Live-oak woodland makes an attractive setting for homesites: Surfaces in the Aromas Red Sands area are mainly sloping, and the soils are well drained. If low-density residential settlement (accompanied by restoration of native plant cover) takes place on surfaces now used for growing strawberries, there will be a sharp increase in wildlife. Certainly it is more reasonable to build homes here than on the productive alluvium of the Pajaro and Salinas valleys.

Some of the best prospects for restoration are at Fort Ord, where more rare plants and plant associations survive than anywhere else in the Aromas Red Sands area. (One can only conclude that half a century of urban development and strawberry culture can do more damage to nature than the traffic of marching thousands, the gouging and churning of soil by tanks, and other preparations of war.)

A few patches of freshwater marsh still survive because draining them has been impractical—for instance, parts of Gallighan, Harkins, and Struve sloughs near Watsonville, and several of the old lake beds between Castroville and Salinas, where the banks of numerous drainage ditches extend this type of habitat. Rebuilding patches of marsh vegetation on such sites will be of great importance to wildlife.

Most of these prospective restoration sites are now incorporated in the plans of the Watershed Ecology Outreach Program (W.E.O.P.), a project that has come into existence since 1990; its headquarters are at California State University Monterey Bay. The program includes an educational agenda for public school teachers and their students, and much valuable restoration has already been accomplished—for instance, on Natividad Creek near Salinas, on Moro Cojo Slough, and at Fort Ord (in cooperation with the Bureau of Land Management). Native species are being propagated, and planted in the areas where they once naturally grew.

A third area, the lower Salinas Valley, is particularly in need of a renewal program. Drainage, field leveling, and other operations for the purposes of commercial agriculture have largely eliminated the native plant cover—for example, the floodplain marshes, oak woodland, and parts of the riparian forest.

Ponds in peat-mining pits on Scott Creek near Highway 1 (*above*) and on Gallighan Slough west of Watsonville (*opposite*). Peat was being mined at the Scott Creek site around 1948 (Rudd, 1948, fig. 6). The photograph illustrates how plant distribution around such ponds is controlled by the shape of the excavation. At the pond on Scott Creek, note the broad, light-colored zone marked by cattails (the leaves of which are dry in this, the winter, season), indicating that the slopes of the pit are gentle: cattails grow only in water less than about 50 cm deep. At Gallighan Slough peat has been mined off and by a local food company for use in mushroom-growing beds. Alien fish have been planted in the ponds—catfish, carp, and bluegills. Because of their steep slopes, cattail is unlikely to grow extensively around the edges of these pits.

Peat has also been mined in the marsh at Camp Evers (Thomas, 1961, p. 32), and there are sizable deposits elsewhere in the Monterey Bay area, particularly under Elkhorn Slough—as well as in the drained lake beds of the lower Salinas Valley, where farmers dragging "subsoilers" across the fields to loosen the underlying peat have sometimes brought up chunks of wood, e.g. of the bay tree.

Geologically speaking, small lakes and ponds are short-lived features—since they soon fill with sediment: several small lakes southwest of Corralitos have filled with sand and disappeared completely within the period of human memory (Reid, 1963, p. 16). Some of the peat beds underlying marshlands along this coast are only a few thousand years old: peat on Año Nuevo Point has been dated at 2800 years B.P. (Lajoie, 1972, p. 36).

Because of their temporary nature, it may be desirable to deliberately create such small bodies of open water for purposes of maintaining dependent species—to excavate, for example, some lake beds now filled with sediment. If we were dealing here with a country untouched by human hands, one might have misgivings about the ecological justification for such a plan—on the grounds that it interferes with a natural progression. But the countless human changes already made and the need for restoration should be kept in mind—remembering, for example, that lumbering and agriculture in the hill country shown above have greatly accelerated sedimentation rates. (Photos B. Gordon)

Although it is economically impractical to use large parcels of prime agricultural land for the growth of native plants, many tracts scattered throughout the rural area are available. These include the following lands, which are publicly owned, or in which the public has a stake.

Within the network of state and county roads there are many small patches of roadside median, and roadcut well suited for replanting efforts.

The banks of the lower courses of the Pajaro river are privately owned but have long been maintained by the local counties and the U.S. Army Corps of Engineers; the artificial levees along the Pajaro were built with public funds. Because of clearing operations and tillage, riparian forest in the lower Salinas and Pajaro valleys is now confined to narrow strips along the river banks, where the principal tree growth is made up of sandbar willow, arroyo willow, Fremont cottonwood, box elder, sycamore, and blue elderberry. Roads along the level tops of the artificial levees are ideal for bicycling and well suited for use by conducted excusions of schoolchildren. Stretches of this riparian land can be made into valuable educational parks. In 1995, restoration of riparian tree growth along the Pajaro River suffered a setback as a result of unnecessarily drastic clearing, done in the name of flood control.

Golf courses cover a large area. Portions of the courses can easily be developed to function also as parks and arboretums. Where possible, native vegetation should be used in landscaping unused grounds. This is not to say that alien ornamentals should be excluded, but surviving native plants should be preserved and, wherever practicable, more planted.

Cemetery owners can probably be interested in developing burial grounds with the preservation of plant and bird life in mind. Several cemeteries in the area are already favorite sites for bird-watchers. To many, this use will seem appropriate for purely sentimental reasons. Devoting productive land to cemeteries and golf courses will be increasingly criticized in the future unless such multiple uses are found.

Railroad rights-of-way are almost unused for planting nowadays. At one time the Southern Pacific Railway Company had a program that included seeding the tracksides with poppies and lupines. But interest in such beautification has waned for the time being. Today roadside vegetation is often killed with sprays.

Tailing heaps and old mine pits do not cover a large part of the area, but such barren and constantly growing surfaces are a real challenge for reclamation by plants. Some of the most conspicuous are those of Kaiser Refractories at Natividad and Moss Landing. The quarrying scars made by the Davenport Cement Company in the Santa Cruz Mountains are more extensive, but are better hidden, being generally surrounded by well-wooded slopes. Parts of the sand-mining properties in coastal dunes along the southern part of the bay are also in need of revegetation.

With increased popular interest, various tracts of privately owned land might become available for planning an improved plant cover.

In hilly country near the coast, gullies and erosion scars have sometimes been planted to coyote brush in their drier, upper courses and to willows in their lower, wetter parts. (In the 1930s the WPA made such use of these plants.) Woody vegetation should be encouraged on such sites. Generally all slopes too steep to withstand grazing should be kept well wooded.

Because of the cover and food they provide, fencerows, hedges, and windbreaks are potentially important in the regulation of animal numbers, particularly in areas where the original vegetation has been cleared. In parts of the eastern United States, the importance of contour hedges to agriculture and wildlife management is well recognized. The multiflora rose and Osage orange have been widely planted as hedge. In Britain, where they have been maintained for centuries, hedges have developed a distinctive and stable animal community. Hedges and fencerows might well be a beneficial addition in the Monterey Bay area, replacing, where practical, barbwire fences.

Hedges and fencerows made up of small trees and shrubs are especially attractive to wildlife, because cover is most effective where it is close to the ground (Pedrides, 1942, p. 279). Windbreaks of tall trees will support more animal life if an understory can be added, preferably made up of native shrubs. The following are good prospects for hedge and fencerow plants, because their fruits are eaten by both mammals and birds: The islay prune, besides being an uncommonly attractive plant, will grow on a variety of terrains—as a shrub on thinner soils, and as a small tree on more fertile sites. The toyon, usually seen as a shrub may, like the islay prine, grow to tree size, thriving on both dry ridges and stream banks. The blue elderberry has a wide distribution. Although especially common along streams and roadsides, it is also found on hilltops—for example, on Fremont Peak—where its seeds were no doubt carried by birds. The coffee berry and red berry are two attractive, closely related, and easily planted shrubs; red berry is better suited to drier parts of the area. Creek dogwood will prove especially valuable on moister soils. Because their fruits are eaten and their seeds disseminated by birds, poison oak and California blackberry will appear spontaneously in many hedge sites.

2.3. A Biogeographic Model

Population ratios among native species in the Monterey Bay area have become markedly disproportionate: Whatever the equilibrium that existed under natural conditions, it has been disrupted.

Development of the present imbalance is illustrated in one well-known consequence of exterminating predators—namely, an overpopulation of rodents, making the use of poisons necessary.

Except those by the Department of Fish and Game and the Audubon Society, few censuses are made in the Monterey Bay area; for example, no counts comparable in accuracy to those available for birds exist for most land mammals. The need for such information becomes ever more obvious.

Population control programs have generally been undertaken mainly for purposes of protecting crops, livestock, and game animals; for example, local agricultural commissioners once supplied strychnine-laced bird bait to viticulturalists for the control of such native species as robins, finches, orioles, scrub jays, house finches, and towhees (Bourdeau, 1972, pp. 50-51); the practice lasted until the late 1980s.

Efforts to control populations of native animals (as well as introduced pests) continue on an increasing scale. The fact that many native species are overly abundant can be seen in the number of advertisements in local telephone directories: More than a dozen pest-control businesses are listed in Santa Cruz alone. These provide poisons, anticoagulants, gassing equipment, etc. One for example, offers "Humane removal of squirrels, raccoons, skunks, bats, birds, fox, moles, gophers, and snakes"—most of which are natives.

Outside towns, ground squirrels and voles are still at the top of the list, but in urban parts of the Monterey Bay area other native mammals, the raccoon for example, are more troublesome. In suburbia's lawns and flower gardens, poisoning pocket gophers is the major pest-control activity. Getting rid of moles is even more problematical and expensive—though there are fewer of them. (Being a carnivore, the mole doesn't take vegetable bait.)

These pest control efforts are guided toward no overall ecological goal, and little exists in the way of a comprehensive regional program.

The following statement of principle was made by one of California's great naturalists:

"I believe that it is unwise to attempt the absolute extermination of any native vertebrate species whatsoever. At the same time it *is* perfectly proper to reduce or destroy any species in a given neighborhood where sound investigation shows it to be positively hurtful to the majority of interests. For example, coyotes, many rodents, jays, crows, magpies, house wrens, the screech owl and certain hawks may be best put under the ban locally" (Grinnell, 1943, p. 165).

Grinnell recommended local destruction of Cooper's and sharp-shinned hawks (Grinnell, 1943, p. 69; written in 1915).

The statement may be acceptable to many conservationists—except for the examples given. Thus, in the Monterey Bay area, screech owls—though common in oak woodlands and suburbs—appear to have no major negative effect on the populations of other birds; nor does the house wren. Similarly, sharp-shinned and Cooper's hawks are now too rare to be considered threats to other species—indeed the populations of both have themselves sunk to precariously low levels (Roberson and Tenney, 1993, pp. 93, 275).

Despite its importance for practical ecological planning, no theoretical statement has been published describing an optimum balance in numbers for species resident in the Monterey Bay area. Nor do such statements appear for comparable areas. Although there is an important literature on "wildlife management," only the most general statements are available on what constitutes balanced animal populations. Except for models so abstract that they have little value for planning purposes, writings on the subject appear to be confined to determining suitable populations of game animals. There has been much argument over the meaning of the term "balance of nature" (Ehrlich and Birch, 1967, p. 106). Much of this disagreement stems from the misunderstandings over the time intervals under consideration. Granted that all environments and populations are subject to constant change in the long term, and even to drastic short-term fluctuations. Nevertheless, most studies evidence a natural balance in the sense of "the persistence of ecological systems as a result of their tendency to compensate for perturbations" (Slobodkin et al., 1967, p. 119). Examples of such persistence and compensation, acting at least over the time spans involved in the history and plannable future of the Monterey Bay area, may be found in the natural plant associations.

In fact, for most of the area a pre-human, or at least a pre-European, biogeography and natural balance can be described in approximate quantitative terms. But to do so is too considerable a task to complete here, and only brief review is made of concept and method: In nature all animal species tend to maintain population densities that are in "a more or less consistent numerical relation to each other," because of interactions among the animals themselves or interactions between them and their physical environment (Doutt and DeBach, 1964, p. 119). Furthermore, and the fact is of particular importance in planning, when these numerical ratios or equipoise densities are disturbed, there is a natural tendency for corrective return to equilibrium position (Huffacker, 1964, p. 76). Thus, the set of all such numerical ratios that pertained in the Monterey Bay area when human occupancy began constituted the natural balance: (1) Animal populations in surviving patches of the natural plant associations, and in other but-slightly disturbed habitats, can be censused to determine areal carrying capacities and numerical ratios between the species present. (2) The original extent of all natural habitats in the area can be estimated (e.g., by successional studies and a mapping of the potential natural vegetation) and the numerical values obtained by census expanded accordingly. (3) Quantitative historical and archaeological data such as those assembled here can also be applied in postulating prehuman conditions.

With such a model in mind, land use and other human activities can be regulated to give all native animals species "such protection as will enable them to maintain their proper numerical strength in proportion" to each other (Henderson, 1927, p. 48). Without such a concept, the determination of animal populations probably will be left to chance, or else be based on legal restrictions that grow either from the economic interests of the moment or simply from polls of public sentiment. The present confusion over appropriate populations for the sea lion, mountain lion, deer, sea otter, etc., is a case in point. (The proper balance between sea lion and fish populations along this coast has been debated in the press for well over a hundred years).

In applying ecological principles to the management of plant and animal populations, the natural plant formations can serve as variable parameters for assessing the consequences of change, and adjusting wildlife populations over time—for example, in the Elkhorn Slough area, the changed bird populations attending the reduction of salt marsh and the expansion of mudflats since 1946 (Ramer et al., 1991).

In rural and urban surroundings human custom is the controlling factor. Within broad environmental limits, cultural practices (land use, food habits, pest-control methods, quarantine procedures, game laws, etc.) will determine which species are present and control their fluctuations in number: Population explosions and rapid invasions are commonplace. Species content and numerical ratios in these surroundings will increasingly be a response to optional human actions, planned or unplanned. Here, too, animal populations tend to stabilize at levels dependent on current environmental conditions. But one can speak of no natural balance, the balances attained being culturally induced; each change in land use, for example, initiating a new process of adjustment.

Ideally residents and gardeners will know both the successional trends and potential natural vegetation of the properties they care for. Using this information, landscape architects can gradually shape residential surroundings that are distinctly Californian, outlined by the forms of native trees and shrubs that authentically express the area's varied natural growth potentials: coast live oak, sycamore, bay, digger pine, black oak, madrone, tanbark oak, and so on, each with its own distinctive configuration and growing in its appropriate environment.

Gradually, the collage of exotic plants now favored in residential areas will give way to a growth ecologically more functional and permanent, and based on persistent natural interrelationships—a growth adapted to local climate and soils and supporting a predominantly native animal life. Native plants reproduce themselves untended and can often be maintained at less expense than aliens (for example, without costly summer irrigation). Thus, horticulturalists will use the total growth potential of the area to economic advantage by allowing the forces of nature to operate for them—practicing wherever possible an accommodating action within the natural plant cover, rather than destructive action against it.

By regulating successional development on their property and, in places, reconstructing the climax vegetation natural to the area, residents will at the same time encourage reestablishment of the original fauna. To name only a few examples, the acorn woodpecker will reappear with the regrowth of oak woodland, the yellow warbler with strips of riparian forest, wren tits with chaparral, the pygmy nuthatch in closed-cone pine forest, and winter wrens in dense redwood groves. The replanting of oak woodland and riparian forest will be especially important to bird life in the Monterey Bay area, because these are the plant associations that are richest in numbers of bird species (Miller, 1951, p. 554) and at the same time those that have suffered most from clearing operations.

CONCLUDING REMARKS

IN THE settlement of the Monterey Bay area, peoples of contrasting cultures with varying levels of technology have modified the natural setting and affected the biota differently. Imprints of early changes are still discernible in the countryside. These imprints, and the historical records, have been inspected here for evidence of interrelationships between human occupancy and nature, culture, and landscape.

The author's reason for describing such differences in custom and subsistence is not solely to judge their relative benefits to environmental quality, but also to emphasize that styles of land use, food habits, economic goals, esthetic preferences, and the like (each with its potential ecological effects) differ according to tradition among peoples who have used the California coastlands. Such traits are optional cultural expressions. They stem from personal choices, made at various times and places, which have been established in folk custom by consensus. In short, although one hears much about irresistible socio-economic forces, there is no good reason to suppose that the area's future character is prescribed by a specific "natural and inevitable economic development" for example, by a development under which all resources, including the biota, must be expendable.

Land-use options abound in the Monterey Bay area. Some lead to biotic enrichment and diversification. In the long run, these probably will prove to be the soundest economically. As knowledge of past relationships between people and nature improves, retrospect will become increasingly useful in planning.

Common and Scientific Names for Animals

Mollusks

* Atlantic gem clam	*Gemma gemma*
* Asiatic pond snail	*Vivipara sp.*
Banana slug	*Ariolimax columbianus*
Basket cockle	*Clinocardium nuttallii*
* Bay mussel	*Mytilus galloprovincialis (M. edulis)*
Bent-nosed clam	*Macoma nasuta*
Black abalone	*Haliotis cracherodii*
Black turban	*Tegula funebralis*
Blue top shell	*Calliostoma ligatum*
* Brown garden snail	*Helix aspersa*
* Eastern oyster	*Crassostrea virginica*
Gaper (Horseneck) clam	*Tresus nuttallii*
Gumboot chiton	*Cryptochiton stelleri*
Jackknife clam	*Solen sicarius*
* Japanese horn snail	*Batillaria attramentaria*
* Japanese littleneck clam	*Tapes japonica*
* Japanese (Pacific) oyster	*Crassostrea gigas*
Littleneck clam (Rock cockle)	*Protothaca staminea*
Mossy chiton	*Mopalia muscosa*
Olivella	*Olivella biplicata*
Olympia (California) oyster	*Ostrea lurida*
Pismo clam	*Tivela stultorum*
Purple-hinged scallop	*Hinnites giganteus*
Red abalone	*Haliotis rufescens*
Red turban	*Astraea gibberosa*
Sea hare	*Aplysia californica*
Shield limpet	*Lottia pelta*
* Shipworm (Teredo)	*Teredo navalis*
Slipper shell	*Crepidula adunca*
* Soft-shell (Mud) clam	*Mya arenaria*
Surf (California) mussel	*Mytilus trossulus (M. californianus)*
Washington clam	*Saxidomus nuttalli*
White sand clam	*Macoma secta*

* Introduced species

Insects and Mites

* American cockroach	*Periplaneta americana*
* Argentine ant	*Iridomyrmex humilis*
Artichoke plume moth	*Platyptilia carduidactyla*
* Asiatic (Black) cockroach	*Blatta orientalis*
* Australian cockroach	*Periplaneta australasiae*
* Bedbug	*Cimex lectularius*
Black stink beetle	*Eleodes*
* Body louse	*Pediculus humanus*
Buckeye butterfly	*Junonia coenia*
Bumble bees	*Bombus* spp.
* Cabbage butterfly	*Pieris rapae*
California sister butterfly	*Adelpha bredowi*
Carpenter bees	*Xylocopa* spp.
* Clothes moth	*Tineola biselliella*
* Coddling moth	*Cydia pomonella*
* Common housefly	*Musca domestica*
* Corn earworm	*Heliothis zea*
* Cottony cushion scale	*Icerya purchasi*
Drywood termite	*Incisitermes minor*
* European earwig	*Forficula auricularia*
* German (Common) cockroach	*Blattella germanica*
Globose dune beetle	*Coelus globosus*
* Grape phylloxera	*Phylloxera vitifolia*
* Green apple aphis	*Aphis pomi*
Ground squirrel flea	*Diamanus montanus*
* Hen louse	*Menacanthus stramineus*
* Honeybee	*Apis mellifera*
* Horse botfly	*Gasterophilus intestinalis*
* House cricket	*Acheta domestica*
* House mosquito	*Culex pipiens*
* Human flea	*Pulex irritans*
Kelp flies	*Coelopa* spp. and *Fucellia* spp.
* Ladybird (Vedalia)	*Rodolia cardinalis*
Leafcutter bees	*Megachile* spp.
* Lesser housefly	*Fannia canicularis*
* Mediterranean flour moth	*Anagasta kuehniella*
* Mediterranean fruit fly	*Ceratitis capitata*
Monarch butterfly	*Danaus plexippus*
Oak moth	*Phryganidia californica*
* Mediterranean fruit fly	*Ceratitis capitata*

Moro Blue butterfly	*Plebejus icarioides moroensis*
* Pear slug	*Caliroa cerasi*
* San Jose scale	*Quadraspidiotus perniciosus*
Smith's blue butterfly	*Euhilotes enoptes smithi*
Spittle bugs	*Aphrophora* spp.
Subterranean termite	*Reticulitermes hesperus*
* Vinegar (Fruit) fly	*Drosophila* spp.
Xerces blue butterfly	*Glaucopsyche xerces*
Sulphur (Alfalfa) butterfly	*Colias eurytheme*
White-faced hornet	*Vespula maculata*

Other Invertebrates

Beach hoppers	*Orchestoidea* spp.
* Eastern crayfish	*Procambarus clarkii*
* European earthworm	*Lumbricus terrestris*
Fairy shrimp	*Linderiella occidentalis*
Goose barnacle	*Pollicipes polymerus*
* Gribble	*Limnoria lignorum*
* Japanese anemone	*Diadumene leucolena*
Krill	*Euphausia* spp.
Mud crab	*Hemigrapsus oregonensis*
Mussel worm	*Nereis* sp.
* Northwestern crayfish	*Pacifastacus leniusculus??*
Purple sea urchin	*Strongylocentrotus purpuratus*
Red sea urchin	*Strongylocentrotus franciscanus*
Sand dollar	*Dendraster excentricus*
Striped shore crab	*Pachygrapsus crassipes*

Fish

* Bluegill	*Lepomis macrochirus*
* Brown bullhead	*Ictalurus nebulosus*
* Brown trout	*Salmo trutta*
* Carp	*Cyprinus carpio*
Coho (Silver) salmon	*Oncorhynchus kisutch*
* Common shad	*Alosa sapidissima*
* Eastern brook (Speckled) trout	*Salvelinus fontinalis*
* Goldfish	*Carassius auratus*
Great white shark	*Carcharodon carcharias*
* Green sunfish	*Lepomis cyanellus*
Grunion	*Leuresthes tenuis*
* Largemouth bass	*Micropterus salmoides*

	Longjaw mudsucker	*Gillichthys mirabilis*
	Sacramento (Western) sucker	*Catostomus occidentalis mniotiltus*
*	Mosquito fish	*Gambusia affinis*
	Mullet (Striped mullet)	*Mugil cephalus*
	Northern anchovy	*Engraulis mordax*
	Onespot fringehead	*Neoclinus uninotatus*
	Pacific herring	*Clupea harengeus*
	Rainbow trout	*Salmo gairdneri*
*	Redear sunfish	*Lepomis microlophus*
	Sacramento blackfish	*Orthodon microlepidotus*
	Sacramento hitch	*Lavinia exilicauda*
	Sacramento perch	*Archoplites interruptus*
	Sardine	*Sardinops caeruleus*
*	Smallmouth bass	*Micropterus dolomieui*
	Steelhead	*Salmo gairdneri gairdneri*
	Stickleback	*Gasterosteus aculeatus*
*	Striped bass	*Roccus saxatilis*
*	Threadfin shad	*Dorosoma petenense*
	Tule perch	*Hysterocarpus traski*
*	White catfish	*Ictalurus catus*

Amphibians and Reptiles

	Alligator lizard	*Gerrhonotus* sp.
	Black legless lizard	*Anniella pulchra nigra*
*	Bullfrog	*Rana catesbeiana*
	Coast horned lizard	*Phrynosoma coronatum*
	Red-legged frog	*Rana aurora*
	Santa Cruz long-toed salamander	*Ambystoma macrodactylum croceum*
	Slender salamander	*Batrachoseps attenuatus*
	Tree frog	*Hyla regilla*
	Western fence lizard	*Sceloporus graciosus*
	Western pond turtle	*Clemmys marmorata*

Birds

Acorn woodpecker	*Melanerpes formicivorus*
American coot (Mudhen)	*Fulica americana*
American kestrel	*Falco sparverius*
American robin	*Turdus migratorius*
Ash-throated flycatcher	*Myiarchus cinerascens*
Bald eagle	*Haliaeetus leucocephalus*
Band-tailed pigeon	*Columba fasciata*

	Barn owl	*Tyto alba*
	Barn (Fork-tailed) swallow	*Hirundo rustica*
	Bewick's wren	*Thryomanes bewickii*
	Black-headed grosbeak	*Pheucticus melanocephalus*
	Black phoebe	*Sayornis nigricans*
	Bonaparte's gull	*Larus philadelphia*
	Brandt's cormorant	*Phalacrocorax penicillatus*
	Brewer's blackbird	*Euphagus cyanocephalus*
	Brown pelican	*Pelicanus occidentalis*
	Brown-headed cowbird	*Molothrus ater*
	Burrowing owl	*Athene cunicularia*
	Bushtit	*Psaltriparus minimus*
	California condor	*Gymnogyps californianus*
	California gull	*Larus californicus*
	California quail	*Lophortyx californicus*
	California thrasher	*Toxostoma redivivum*
	California (Brown) towhee	*Pipilo crissalis*
*	Cattle egret	*Bubulcus ibis*
	Cedar waxwing	*Bombycilla cedrorum*
	Chestnut-backed chickadee	*Parus rufescens*
	Clapper rail	*Rallus longirostris*
	Cliff swallow	*Petrochelidon pyrrhonota*
	Common murre	*Uria aalge*
	Cormorants	*Phalacrocorax* spp.
	Dark-eyed junco	*Junco hyemalis*
	Downy woodpecker	*Picoides pubescens*
	Golden eagle	*Aquila chrysaetos*
	Horned lark	*Eremophila alpestris*
	House finch (Linnet)	*Carpodacus mexicanus*
*	House (English) sparrow	*Passer domesticus*
	Hutton's vireo	*Vireo huttoni*
	Killdeer	*Charadrius vociferus*
	Lark sparrow	*Chondestes grammacus*
	Least tern	*Sterna antillarum*
	Lesser goldfinch	*Carduelis psaltria*
	Loggerhead shrike	*Lanius ludovicianus*
	Mountain quail	*Oreortyx pictus*
	Mourning dove	*Zenaida macroura*
	Northern flicker	*Colaptes auratus cafer*
	Northern mockingbird	*Mimus polyglottos*
	Northern phalarope	*Lobipes lobatus*
*	Pigeon (Rock dove)	*Columba livia*

Plain titmouse	*Parus inornatus*
Purple finch	*Carpodacus purpureus*
Pygmy nuthatch	*Sitta pygmaea*
Red-winged blackbird	*Agelaius phoeniceus*
* Ring-necked (Chinese) pheasant	*Phasianus colchicus*
Ruddy duck	*Oxyura jamaicensis*
Rufous-sided towhee	*Pipilo erythrophthalmus*
Sanderling	*Crocethia alba*
Scrub jay	*Aphelocoma coerulescens*
Shrike (Butcherbird)	*Lanius ludovicianus*
Snowy plover	*Charadrius alexandrinus*
Song sparrow	*Melospiza melodia*
Sooty shearwater	*Puffinus griseus*
* Starling	*Sturnus vulgaris*
Steller's jay	*Cyanocitta stelleri*
Turkey vulture (Buzzard)	*Cathartes aura*
Valley quail	*Lophortyx californicus*
Violet-green swallow	*Tachycineta thalassina*
Western meadowlark	*Sturnella neglecta*
Western screech owl	*Otus asio*
White-tailed kite	*Elanus leucurus*
Willet	*Catoptrophorus semipalmatus*
Winter wren	*Troglodytes troglodytes*
Wood duck	*Aix sponsa*
Wrentit	*Chamaea fasciata*
Yellow-billed magpie	*Pica nuttalli*
Yellow warbler	*Dendroica petechia*

Mammals

Badger	*Taxidea taxus*
Black bear	*Euarctos americanus*
* Black rat	*Rattus rattus*
Black-tailed deer	*Odocoileus hemionus*
Blacktail jackrabbit	*Lepus californicus*
Bobcat (Wildcat)	*Lynx rufus*
Brush rabbit	*Sylvilagus bachmani*
California gray whale	*Eschrichtius gibbosus*
California ground squirrel	*Citellus beecheyi*
California sea lion	*Zalophus californianus*
Chipmunk (Merriam chipmunk)	*Eutamias merriami*
Cottontail rabbit	*Sylvilagus auduboni*

	Coyote	*Canis latrans*
	Deer mouse	*Peromyscus maniculatus*
	Dusky-looted wood rat	*Neotoma fuscipes*
*	Eastern fox squirrel	*Sciurus niger*
*	Eastern gray squirrel	*Sciurus carolinensis*
	Elephant seal	*Mirounga angustirostris*
*	European wild pig	*Sus scrofa*
*	Golden beaver	*Castor canadensis*
	Gray fox	*Urocyon cinereoargenteus*
	Guadalupe fur seal	*Arctocephalus townsendi*
	Harbor seal	*Phoca vitulina*
*	House mouse	*Mus musculus*
	Humpback whale	*Megaptera novaeangliae*
	Long-tailed weasel	*Mustela frenata*
	Meadow mouse (Vole)	*Microtus californicus*
	Mountain lion (Cougar)	*Felis concolor*
*	Muskrat	*Ondatra zibethica*
	Northern elephant seal	*Mirounga angustirostris*
	Northern (Pribilof) fur seal	*Calorhinus ursinus*
*	Norway rat	*Rattus norvegicus*
	Pocket gopher	*Thomomys bottae*
	Porcupine	*Erethizon dorsatum*
	Raccoon	*Procyon lotor*
*	Red fox	*Vulpes fulva*
*	Rocky Mountain elk	*Cervus canadensis nelsoni*
	Sea otter	*Enhydra lutris*
	Steller's sea lion	*Eumetopias jubata*
	Tule elk	*Cervus canadensis nannodes*
	Western gray squirrel	*Sciurus griseus*
	Western harvest mouse	*Reithrodontomys megalotis*
*	Wild pig	*Sus scrofa*

Common and Scientific Names for Plants

Alder	*Alnus rubra*
* Amaranth	*Amaranthus retroflexus*
Arroyo willow	*Salix lasiolepis*
Beach-bur	*Ambrosia chamissonis*
Beach morning glory	*Calystegia soldanella*
Beach primrose	*Camissonia cheiranthifolia*
Beach saltbush	*Atriplex leucophylla*
Beach strawberry	*Fragaria chiloensis*
* Bermuda grass	*Cynodon dactylon*
Big-leaved maple	*Acer macrophyllum*
* Bindweed (Field morning glory)	*Convolvulus arvensis*
Bishop pine	*Pinus muricata*
Black cottonwood (Alamo)	*Populus balsamifera*
Black oak	*Quercus kelloggii*
Blue beach lupine	*Lupinus chamissonis*
Blue blossom	*Ceanothus thyrsiflorus*
Blue elderberry	*Sambucus mexicana*
Blue-eyed grass	*Sisyrinchium bellum*
* Blue gum	*Eucalyptus globulus*
Blue oak	*Quercus douglasii*
Bonny Doon manzanita	*Arctostaphylos silvicola*
Bluff lettuce	*Dudleya farinosa*
Box elder	*Acer negundo*
Bracken	*Pteridium aquilinum*
Branching beach aster	*Lessingia filaginifolia*
* Brass buttons	*Cotula coronopifolia*
Bristlecone (Santa Lucia) Fir	*Abies bracteata*
Buck brush	*Ceanothus cuneatus* var. *cuneatus*
Buckeye	*Aesculus californica*
Bullwhip kelp (Sea-Otter cabbage)	*Nereocystis leutkeana*
* Bull thistle	*Cirsium vulgare*
* Bur-clover	*Medicago polymorpha*
Bur-reed	*Sparganium eurycarpum*
Bush monkey flower	*Mimulus aurantiacus*
Button (Black) sage	*Salvia mellifera*
California blackberry	*Rubus ursinus*
California croton	*Croton californicus*
California laurel (Bay)	*Umbellularia californica*
California poppy	*Eschscholzia californica*
California sagebrush	*Artemisia californica*

	California scrub oak	*Quercus dumosa*
	California tule	*Scirpus californicus*
*	Cape oxalis (Bermuda buttercup)	*Oxalis pes-caprae*
	Cat-tails	*Typha* spp.
	Chamise	*Adenostoma fasciculatum*
	Chaparral pea	*Pickeringia montana*
	Chia	*Salvia columbariae*
	Chinquapin	*Chrysolepis chrysophylla*
	Coast buckwheat	*Eriogonum latifolium*
	Coast cryptantha	*Cryptantha leiocarpa*
	Coast liveoak (Encina)	*Quercus agrifolia*
	Coast redwood	*Sequoia sempervirens*
	Coast wallflower	*Erysimum ammophilum*
	Coast whitethorn	*Ceanothus incanus*
	Coastal sagewort	*Artemesia pycnocephala*
	Coffee berry	*Rhamnus californica*
*	Common groundsel	*Senecio vulgaris*
*	Common plantain	*Plantago major*
	Cord grass	*Spartina foliosa*
	Coulter pine	*Pinus coulteri*
	Coyote brush (Greasewood)	*Baccharis pilularis*
	Creek dogwood	*Cornus sericea*
	Cropleaf ceanothus	*Ceanothus dentatus*
*	Crystalline iceplant	*Mesembryanthemum crystallinum*
*	Curly dock	*Rumex crispus*
*	Dandelion	*Taraxacum officinale*
	Deerweed	*Lotus scoparius*
	Digger (Gray) pine	*Pinus sabiniana*
	Douglas fir	*Pseudotsuga menziesii*
	Douglas iris	*Iris douglasiana*
	Duckweed	*Lemna* sp.
	Dune bluegrass	*Poa douglasii*
	Dune knotweed	*Polygonum paronychia*
*	Dwarf nettle	*Urtica urens*
	Eastwood's ericameria	*Ericameria fasciculata*
	Eel grass	*Zostera marina*
	Fiddleneck	*Amsinckia* spp.
*	Field mustard	*Brassica rapa*
	Feather boa kelp	*Egregia* sp.
	Flowering currant	*Ribes sanguineum*
*	Forget-me-not	*Myosotis latifolia*
*	Foxtail	*Hordeum murinum*

Fremont cottonwood	*Populus fremontii*
* French broom	*Genista monspessulana*
* German ivy	*Senecio mikanioides*
Giant kelp	*Macrocystis pyrifera*
Golden eardrops	*Dicentra chrysantha*
Gowen cypress	*Cupressus goveniana*
Hairy honeysuckle	*Lonicera hispidula*
Hartweg's spineflower	*Chorizanthe pungens*
Hazelnut	*Corylus cornuta*
* Himalayan blackberry	*Rubus discolor*
Hooker's manzanita	*Arctostaphylos hookeri* ssp. *hookeri*
* Hoarhound	*Marrubium vulgare*
* Hottentot fig	*Carpobrotus edulis* (*Mesembryan-themum edule*)
Hutchinson's larkspur	*Delphinium hutchinsoniae*
Ice plants	*Mesembryanthemum* spp. and *Carpobrotus* spp.
Indian hemp	*Apocynum cannabinum*
Interior live oak	*Quercus wislizenii*
Islay prune	*Prunus ilicifolia*
* Jimson weed	*Datura stramonium*
Knobcone pine	*Pinus attenuata*
Lace lichen	*Ramalina menziesii*
* Lawn daisy	*Bellis perennis*
Lizard tail (Golden yarrow)	*Eriophyllum staechadifolium*
* Long-beaked filaree	*Erodium botrys*
Lotus	*Lotus* spp.
Madrone	*Arbutus menziesii*
Man-root (Wild cucumber)	*Marah fabaceus*
Manzanitas	*Arctostaphylos* spp.
* Marram grass (European beach grass)	*Ammophila arenaria*
Marsh baccharis	*Baccharis douglasii*
Marsh pennywort	*Hydrocotyle ranunculoides*
Maul oak (Gold cup)	*Quercus chrysolepis*
Menzies' wallflower	*Erysimum menziesii*
* Milk thistle	*Silybum marianum*
Milkweed	*Asclepias* spp.
Miner's lettuce	*Claytonia perfoliata*
Mock heather	*Ericameria ericoides*
Monterey ceanothus	*Ceanothus cuneatus* var. *rigidus*
Monterey cypress	*Cupressus macrocarpa*
Monterey gilia	*Eriastrum virgatum*

	Monterey manzanita	*Arctostaphylos montereyensis*
	Monterey pine	*Pinus radiata*
*	Mustard	*Brassica* spp.
*	Myoporum	*Myoporum laetum*
	Needlegrasses	*Nassella (Stipa)* spp.
	Nodding needlegrass	*Nassella (Stipa) cernua*
*	New Zealand spinach	*Tetragonia tetragonioides*
	Pajaro manzanita	*Arctostaphylos pajaroensis*
*	Pampas grass	*Cortaderia jubata*
*	Pepper tree	*Schinus molle*
*	Periwinkle	*Vinca major*
	Phantom orchid	*Cephalanthera austiniae*
	Pickleweed	*Salicornia virginica*
	Pink sand verbena	*Abronia umbellata*
	Plantains	*Plantago* spp.
*	Poison hemlock	*Conium maculatum*
	Poison oak	*Toxicodendron diversilobum*
	Ponderosa pine	*Pinus ponderosa*
	Purple needlegrass	*Nassella (Stipa) pulchra*
*	Quaking grass	*Briza maxima*
	Red berry	*Rhamnus crocea*
*	Red-stem filaree	*Erodium cicutarium*
*	Red fesque	*Festuca rubra*
	Redwood sorrel	*Oxalis oregana*
	Ribbon kelp	*Egregia menziesii*
*	Ripgut grass	*Bromus diandrus*
*	Rye grasses	*Lolium* spp.
	Rockweed	*Fucus* spp.
	Saltgrass	*Distichlis spicata*
	Sand gilia	*Gilia tenuiflora* var. *arenaria*
	Saltrush	*Juncus lesueurii*
	Sandmat	*Cardionema ramosissimum*
	Sandmat manzanita	*Arctostaphylos pumila*
	Sandbar willow	*Salix hindsiana*
	Santa Cruz cypress	*Cupressus abramsiana*
	Santa Cruz manzanita	*Arctostaphylos andersonii*
	Santa Cruz tarplant	*Holocarpha macradenia*
	Santa Cruz wallflower	*Erysimum teretifolium*
	Saw grass (Sedge)	*Carex barbarae?*
	Schreiber's manzanita	*Arctostaphylos glutinosa*
*	Scotch broom	*Cytisus scoparius*

Sea fig	*Carpobrotus chilensis (Mesembryan-themum chilense, M. aequilaterale, M. dimidiatum)*
Sea lyme (Dune rye grass)	*Leymus mollis*
Sea pink (Thrift)	*Armeria maritima*
Sea palm	*Postelsia palmaeformis*
* Sea rocket	*Cakile maritima*
Seaside amsinckia	*Amsinckia spectabilis*
Seaside daisy	*Erigeron glaucus*
Seaside paintbrush	*Castilleja latifolia*
Sea thrift (Sea pink)	*Armeria maritima*
* Sheep sorrel	*Rumex acetosella*
Silky beach pea	*Lathyrus littoralis*
Silver weed	*Potentilla anserina* ssp. *pacifica*
Slender hairgrass	*Deschampsia elongata*
* Slender-leaved iceplant	*Mesembryanthemum nodiflorum*
Slender-tubed iris	*Iris macrosiphon*
Soap plant	*Chlorogallum pomeridianum*
Squaw bush	*Rhus trilobata*
Squaw grass	*Xerophyllum tenax*
Stream orchid	*Epipactis gigantea*
Surf-grass	*Phyllospadix* spp.
* Sweet fennel	*Foeniculum vulgare*
Sword fern	*Polystichum munitum*
Sycamore (Plane tree)	*Platanus racemosa*
Tanbark oak	*Lithocarpus densiflorus*
Telegraph weed	*Heterotheca grandiflora*
Tidestrom's lupine	*Lupinus tidestromii*
Toyon (Christmas berry)	*Heteromeles arbutifolia*
Tree lupine	*Lupinus arboreus*
* Tree tobacco	*Nicotiana glauca*
Tules (Bulrushes)	*Scirpus* spp.
Turkey mullein	*Eremocarpus setigerus*
Turpentine weed	*Trichostema lanceolatum*
Umbrella sedges	*Cyperus* spp.
* Valerian	*Centranthus ruber*
Valley oak	*Quercus lobata*
Wax myrtle	*Myrica californica*
Whip-strap kelp	*Pterygophora californica*
* White goosefoot	*Chenopodium album*
Widgeon (Ditch) grass	*Ruppia maritima*
Wild licorice	*Glycyrrhiza lepidota*

* Wild oat   *Avena fatua*
  Wild buckwheat   *Eriogonum* spp.
* Wild radish   *Raphanus sativus*
  Wild rose   *Rosa californica*
  Willows   *Salix* spp.
  Willow herb   *Epilobium ciliatum*
  Woody chain bladder   *Cystoseira osmundacea*
  Yellow pincushion   *Chaenactis glabriuscula*
  Yellow sand verbena   *Abronia latifolia*
  Yerba buena   *Satureja douglasii*

BIBLIOGRAPHY

Abbott, I. A., and G. J. Hollenberg. 1976. *Marine Algae of California.* Stanford: Stanford University Press.

Abrams, L. 1944. *Illustrated Flora of the Pacific States*, vol. 2. Stanford, CA: Stanford University Press.

Addicott, W.O. 1966. *Late Pleistocene Marine Paleoecology and Zoogeography in Central California.* Contributions to Paleontology. Geological Survey Professional Paper 523-C, Washington D.C.

Ainley, D. G., and T. J. Lewis. 1974. The History of the Farallon Island Marine Bird Populations, 1854-1972. *Condor,* 76: 432-446.

Allen, G. M. 1942. *Extinct and Vanishing Mammals of the Western Hemisphere.* Cambridge, MA: American Committee for International Wildlife Protection.

Allen, R. H. 1935. The Spanish Land Grant System as an Influence in the Agricultural Development of California. In *Agricultural History,* vol. 9.

Allee, W.C., A.E. Emerson, O Park and T. Park. 1965. *Principles of Animal Ecology.* Philadelphia and London: W.B. Saunders Company.

Anderson, B. W. 1971. Man's Influence on Hybridization in Two Avian Species in South Dakota, *Condor,* 73:342-347.

Anderson, C. L. 1891. *The Natural History of Santa Cruz County.* Oakland: Pacific Press.

Anderson, Edgar. 1956. Man as a Maker of New Plants and New Plant Communities. In *Man's Role in Changing the Face of the Earth,* ed. W. L. Thomas, Jr. Chicago: University of Chicago Press.

Anderson, E. and G. L. Stebbins. 1954. Hybridization as an Evolutionary Stimulus. *Evolution,* 8: 378.

Andrews, H. L. 1945. The Kelp Beds of the Monterey Region. *Ecology,* 26 (1): 24-37.

Antisell, T. 1854-1855. *Geological Report of Exploration from San Francisco to Los Angeles West of the Coast Range,* vol. 7. U.S. Government Printing Office, Washington, D.C.

Arnold, J. R. 1935. The Changing Distribution of the Western Mockingbird in California. *Condor,* 37: 193-199.

Assessor of Monterey County. 1865. Annual Report for 1865. Sacramento, CA: *California State Agricultural Society, Transactions.*

Audubon Society. 1974. *American Birds.* Vol. 28, no. 2. New York: National Audubon Society.

Avey, R. R. 1970. "Mound Microrelief: A Case Study of the Santa Cruz Area, California." Unpublished M.A. Thesis, San Francisco State University.

Azevedo, J. J., Jr. 1965. The Ecology of Insects Associated with Some Introduced and Native Plants. M.A. dissertation, California State University, San Francisco.

Baker, H. G. 1965. A Timely Note on the California Oak Moth. *The Four Seasons* 1 (3): 9-10.

—— —— 1974. The Evolution of Weeds. *Annual Review of Ecology and Systematics.*

Baldwin, T. A. 1963. Landforms of the Salinas Valley. In *Guidebook to the Salinas Valley and the San Andreas Fault, No. 1.* American Association of Petroleum Geologists.

Bancroft, H. H. 1888. California Pastoral San Francisco: The History Company.

Barbour, M.G. 1970. The Flora of of Bodega Head, California. *Madroño,* 20: 289-312.

Barbour, M.G. and J.E. Rodman. 1970. Saga of the west coast sea-rockets: *Cakile edentula and C. maritima. Rhodora,* 72: 370-386.

Barbour, M.G. and J. Major (eds.). 1977. *Terrestrial Vegetation of California.* New York: Wiley.

Barnes, T.S., H.S Bryant and T. J. Hoover. 1925. Map of Middens on Año Nuevo Point (Available at San Mateo County Museum).

Barrett, E. M. 1963. The California Oyster Industry. *California Dept. Fish and Game, Fish Bull.* No. 123, Sacramento.

Bascom, W. N. 1947. Investigation at Moss Landing, California: June 6, 1946, to March 31, 1947. In *University of California Dept. of Engineering Fluid Mechanics Laboratory Memorandum HE-1 16-243,* Berkeley.

—— —— ——1954. The Control of Stream Outlets by Wave Refraction. *Journal of Geology,* 62: 600-605.

—— —— ——1964. *Waves and Beaches. The Dynamics of the Ocean Surface* New York: Anchor Books.

Baumhoff, M. A. 1963. Ecological Determinants of Aboriginal California Populations. In *University of California Publications in Amer. Arch. and Ethnol.* vol. 49.

Beal, F. E. 1907 and 1910. Birds of California in Relation to the Fruit Industry. In *U.S. Biological Survey Bulletin,* vol. 30, 34.

Beard, C. N. 1941. *Drainage Development in the Vicinity of Monterey Bay, California.* Ph.D. dissertation, University of Illinois, Urbana.

—— —— ——1948. Land Forms and Land Use East of Monterey Bay. *Economic Geography* 24: 286-295.

Beardsley, R. K. 1946. The Monterey Custom House Flag Pole: Archaeological Findings. *California Historical Society Quarterly,* 25(3): 204-281, San Francisco.

Beck, R. H. 1907. Monterey Bay Notes. *Condor,* 9: 58.

Becker, R.H. 1964. *Diseños of California.* San Francisco: The Book Club of California

Beecher, W. J. 1942. Nesting Birds and the Vegetation Substrate. Chicago Ornithological Society.

Beechey, F. W. 1831. *Narrative of a Voyage to the Pacific and Beering's Strait.* Vol. 2. London: Henry Colburn & Richard Bentley.

Beetle, A. A. 1947. Distribution of the Native Grasses of California. *Hilgardia,* 17: 309-357.

Bentham, G. 1844. *Botany of the Voyage of Her Majesty's Ship Sulfer... During the years 1836-1842.* London: Smith Elder & Co.

Berry, W. D., and E. Berry. 1959. *Mammals of the San Francisco Bay Region.* Berkeley: University of California Press.

Big Sur Land Trust. 1992 *The Monterey Bay State Seashore. A Study for the Preservation of the Monterey Bay Dunes (October).*

Biswell, H. H. 1969. Prescribed Burning for Wildlife in California Brushiand. *Thirty-fourth North American Wildlife Conference,* 338-446.

Blake, W. P. 1856. Report of the Physical Geography and Geology of the Coast of California from Bodega Bay to San Diego. In *Report of the United States Coast Survey,* 1855, Appendix 65: 376-398, Washington, D.C.

Bluestone, V. B. 1970. *Distribution of Selected Coastal Beach and Dune Plants along Monterey Bay, California.* M.A. dissertation, San Francisco State University, San Francisco.

— — 1981. Sand Dune Vegetation at Salinas River State Beach. *Madroño,* 28(2):49-60.

Bolander, H.N. 1870. *A Catalogue of the Plants Growing in the Vicinity of San Francisco.* New York: A. Roman & Co.

Bolin, R. L. and D. P. Abbott. 1963. Studies on the marine climate and phytoplankton of the central coastal area of California, 1954-1960. *California Cooperative Oceanic Fisheries Invesigations Reports,* 9: 23-45.

Bolton, H. E. 1927. *Fray Juan Crespi, Missionary Explorer on the Pacific Coast, 1769-1774.* Berkeley: University of California Press.

— — 1930. *Anza's California Expeditions. Vols.* 11 and IV. Berkeley: University of California Press.

— — 1933. Diary of an Expedition to Monterey by Way of the Colorado River, 1775-1776 (by Fray Pedro Font). In *Font's Complete Diary, A Chronicle of the Founding of San Francisco.* Berkeley: University of California Press.

— — trans. 1926. *Historical Memoirs of New California. Fray Francisco Palou.* Vol. 3. Berkeley: University of California Press.

Bonnell, M. L., and R. K. Selander. 1974. Elephant Seals: Genetic Variation and Near Extinction. *Science,* 184: 908-909.

Bonnot, P. 1926. Report on the Seals and Sea Lions of California. *California Dept. Fish and Game, Fish Bull.* No. 14, Sacramento.

— — 1928. The Sea Lions, Seals, and Sea Otter of the California Coast. *California Fish and Game* 37(4): 371-389.

Boudreau, G. W. 1972. Factors Related to Bird Depredations in Vineyards. *American Journal of Enology and Viticulture,* 23 (2): 50-53.

Bradley, W. C. 1956. Carbon-14 Date for a Marine Terrance at Santa Cruz, California. *Geol. Soc. Amer. Bull.,* 67: 675-677,

— — — 1957. Origin of Marine-Terrace Deposits in the Santa Cruz Area, California. *Geol. Soc. Amer. Bull.* 68: 421-444.

— — — 1958. Submarine Abrasion and Wave-cut Platforms. *Geol. Soc. Amer. Bull.* 69: 967-974.

Branner, J.C. 1907. A Drainage Peculiarity of the Santa Clara Valley Affecting Fresh-Water Faunas. *Journal of Geology,* 15: 1-10.

Brant, D. H. 1962. Measures of the Movements and Population Densities of Small Rodents. *University of California Publications in Zoology,* 62(2).

BRCF, *Biennial Report of Fish Commissioners.* Calif. Dept. of Fish and Game, (1870-1871, Sacramento).

Brewer, W. H. 1949. *Up and Down California in 1860-1864.* Berkeley: University of California Press. (Ed. F. P. Farquhar.)

Brewer, W. H., A. Gray, and S. Watson. 1876. Geological Survey of California. *Botany. Vol.* 1. [Explorations, 1861-1864]. Cambridge, Mass.

Brewer, W. H. and S. Watson. 1880. Polypetalae. In *Geological Survey of California* 2nd edition, Vol. I (J.D. Whitney, Ed.) Cambridge, MA: John Wilson and Son.

Broadhurst, J. 1910. The Eucalyptus in California. *Torreya,* 10(4): 84-90.

Brown, A.K. and F.M. Stanger 1969. Discovery of the Redwoods *Forest History,* 13 (3): 6-11.

Brown, M. V. 1939. A Brief History and Identification of the Three Species of Black Bass Now Occurring in California. *California Fish and Game,* 25(4): 310-312.

Brown, N. E. 1928. *Mesembryanthemum* and allied genera. *Journal of Botany,* 66: 322-327.

Brown, N. S. 1975. A Comparison of the Ectoparasites of the House Sparrow *(Passer domesticus)* from North America and Europe. *American Midlands Naturalist,* 94: 154-159.

Browning, B.M et al. 1972. *The Natural Resources of Elkhorn Slough.* Department of Fish and Game, Coastal Wetland Series no. 4.

Bunte, L. S., Jr., et al. 1967. Basic Data and Operation Report for Water Year October 1, 1966, to September 30, 1967. *Monterey County Flood Control and Water Conservation District, Hydrology Section.*

Burcham, L. T. 1957. *California Range Land.* Sacramento: State of California, Division of Forestry, Sacramento.

Butterfield, H. M. 1935. The Introduction of Eucalyptus into California. *Madroño,* 3: 149-153.

Cannon, W. A. 1913. A Note on Chaparral-Forest Relations at Carmel, California. *Plant World,* 16: 36-38.

Carlisle, J. G., C. H. Turner, and E. E. Ebert. 1964. Artificial Habitat in the Marine Environment. Sacramento: *Department of Fish and Game, Fish Bulletin* No. 124.

Carlton, J. T. 1975. Introduced Intertidal Invertebrates. In *Light's Manual: Intertidal Invertebrates of the Central California Coast.* pp. 17-25. Edited by R. I. Smith and J. T. Carlton. Berkeley: University of California Press.

Carlton, J.T. and J. B. Geller. 1993. Ecological Roulette: The Global Transport of Nonindigenous Marine Organisms. *Science,* 261:78-82.

Carpelan, L. H. 1957. Hydrobiology of the Alviso Salt Ponds. *Ecology,* 38(3).

Carpenter, E.J.,andS. W.Cosby. 1929. Soil Survey of the Salinas Area, California. *U.S. Dept. Agric., Bur. Chem. and Soils,* No. 11, Washington, D.C.

Chittenden, N. 1884. *Health Seekers, Tourists, and Sportsmen's Guide.* San Francisco: C. A. Murdock & Co.

Clar, C. R. 1957. *Forest Use in Spanish-Mexican California.* Sacramento: Division of Forestry, Department of Natural Resources.

——— 1959. *California Government and Forestry.* State of California, Division of Forestry, Sacramento.

Clements, F. E. 1935. Experimental Ecology in the Public Service. *Ecology,* 16: 342-363.

Colton, Walter. 1859. *Three Years in California.* New York: S. A.Rollo & Co.

Cook, S. F. 1943. The Conflict between the California Indian and the White Civilization. Pt. 1: The Indian versus the Spanish Missions. *Ibero-Americana,* No. 21, Berkeley.

———1946. A Reconsideration of Shellmounds with Respect to Population and Nutrition. *American Antiquity,* 12: 50-53.

Cook, T. W. 1953. *The Ants of California.* Palo Alto: Pacific Books.

Cooper, J. G. 1871. Monterey in the Dry Season. *American Naturalist,* 4: 756-758.

Cooper, W. S. 1936. The Strand Flora of the Pacific Coast of North America: A Geographic Study. In *Essays in Geobotany in Honor of William Albert Setchell.* (Ed. T.H.Goodspeed)

———1967. Coastal Dunes of California. *Geological Society of America.* Memoir 104, Boulder.

Costansó, M. 1910. The Narrative of the Portola Expedition, 1769-1770. *Publications of the Academy of Pacific Coast History* 1(4).

Costas Lippman, M. 1977. More on Weedy "Pampas Grass" in California. *Fremontia,* 4: 25-27.

Cowan, B. 1975. Protecting and Restoring Native Dune Plants. *Fremontia,* 3: 3-7.

Cowan, R.G. 1956. *Ranchos of California: A List of Spanish Concessions, 1775-1822, and Mexican Grants.* Fresno: Academy Library Guild.

Cronise, T. F. 1868. *The Natural Wealth of California.* San Francisco: H. H. Bancroft & Co.

Crowell, J. C. 1952. Submarine Canyons Bordering Central and Southern California. *Journal of Geology,* 60: 58-83.

CSD, *Mean Number of Thunderstorm Days in the United States.* Climatological

Services Division, U.S. Weather Bureau, Technical Paper No. 19 (Washington D.C., 1952).

Cullerton, J. 1950. *Indians and Pioneers of Old Monterey.* Fresno: Academy of California Church History.

Dale, R. F. 1966. Climate of California. In *Climates of the States: California.* Rev. ed.: 1-8. Washington, DC: U.S. Government Printing Office.

Dall, W. 1892-1893. An Extract from a Letter to the Editor of Nautilus on Collecting at Monterey. *The Nautilus,* 6(4). Philadelphia.

Dana, R. H. 1911. *Two Years before the Mast.* Boston: Houghton Mifflin Co.

Darwin, Charles. 1897. *The Variation of Animals and Plants Under Domestication.* New York: D. Appleton and Company.

Dasmann, W. P. 1965. *Big Game of California.* State of California, The Resources Agency, Sacramento.

Davis, J. and A. Baldridge 1980. *The Bird Year. A Book for Birders with Special Reference to the Monterey Bay Area.* Pacific Grove, CA: The Boxwood Press.

Davis, J. H. 1957. Dune Formation and Stabilization by Vegetation and Plantings. *Beach Erosion Board Technical Memorandum,* No. 101.

Dawson, W. L. 1923. *The Birds of California.* San Diego: South Moulton Co.

Dearborn, N. 1912 *The English Sparrow as a Pest.* Farmer's Bulletin 493, U.S. Department of Agriculture, Washinton

De Vogelaere, A. P., J. E. Holte and ABA Consultants. 1993. *Elkhorn Slough Bibliography.* Watsonville, CA: Elkhorn Slough National Estuarine Research Reserve.

DeWet, J.M. and J. P. Harlan. 1975. Weeds and Domesticates: Evolution in The Man-made Habitat. *Economic Botany,* 29: 99-107.

Dietz, S.A., W. Hildebrandt and T. Jones 1988. *Archaeological Investigations at Elkhorn Slough: CA-MNT-229 A Middle Period Site on the Central California Coast.* Papers in Northern California Anthropology Northern California Anthropological Group, Berkeley, California.

Dodge, R. E. 1914. *Records of the Past.* Vol. 13, Records of the Past Exploration Society, Washington, D.C

Dougherty, A. 1965. *Marine Mammals of California.* State of California, The Resources Agency, Sacramento.

Douglas, J. 1929. A Voyage from the Columbia to California in 1840. *California Historical Society Quarterly,* 8: 97-115.

Doutt, R. L., and P. De Bach. 1964. Some Biological Control Concepts and Questions. In *Biological Control of Insect Pests and Weeds,* edited by P. De Bach. Reinhold Publishing Corporation.

Duflot de Mofras, E. 1937. *Duflot de Mofras' Travels on the Pacific Coast.* Edited and translated by M. E. Wilbur. 2 vols. Santa Ana: The Fine Arts Press.

Eastwood, Alice. 1924. Archibald Menzies' Journal of the Vancouver Expedition. *California Historical Society Quarterly,* 2(4):265-340.

E. Z. R., and J. W. H. 1961. Birds, Suburbs, and Civilization. In *Museum Talk,* 36(i): 1-5. Santa Barbara Museum of Natural History.

Ebert, E. E. 1968. A Food Habits Study of the Southern Sea Otter, *Enhydra lutris nereis. California Fish and Game,* 54(l): 33-42.

Egenhoff, E. L. 1952. *Fabricas.* Sacramento: Division of Mines, State of California.

Ehrlich, Paul. 1991. Population diversity and the Future of Ecosystems. *Science,* 254: 175.

Ehrlich, P. R., and L. C. Birch. 1967. "Balance of Nature" and "Population Control." *The American Naturalist,* 101: 97-107.

Elliott and Moss (publishers). 1881. *History of Monterey County.* San Francisco.

Elton, C. S. 1958. *The Ecology of Invasions by Animals and Plants.* New York: John Wiley & Sons.

Emmel, T.C. and J. F. Emmel. 1973. *The Butterflies of Southern California.* Natural History Museum of Los Angeles County

Essig, E. 0. 1931. *A History of Entomology.* New York: The Macmillan Co.

— — — 1958. *Insects and Mites of Western North America.* New York: The Macmillan Co.

Evans, A. S. 1873. *A La California.* San Francisco: A. L. Bancroft & Company.

Everman, B. W. 1915. An Attempt to Save California Elk. *California Fish and Game,* 2: 85-96.

— — — 1916. The California Elk. *California Fish and Game,* 2: 70-77.

— — — 1923. The Conservation of the Marine Life of the Pacific. *Scientific Monthly,* 16: 521-538.

Fages, P. 1911. *Expedition to San Francisco Bay in 1770, Diary of Pedro Fages.* University of California Press, Berkeley. (Ed. H. E. Bolton.)

Fages, P. 1937. A *Historical, Political, and Natural Description of California by Pedro Fages, Soldier of Spain, Dutifully Madefor the Viceroy in the Year 1775.* University of California Press, Berkeley. (Translated by H. I. Priestley.)

Fisher, A. B. 1945. *The Salinas: Upside-Down River.* New York: Farrar & Rinehart.

Fisher, E. 1934. Early Fauna of the Monterey Region, California. *Journal of Mammology,* 15: 253.

— — — 1935. Shell Deposits of the Monterey Peninsula. *University of California Archaeological Survey* Manuscript No. 17, Berkeley.

Fitch, H. S. 1948. Ecology of the California Ground Squirrel on Grazing Lands. *American Midlands Naturalist,* 39: 513-596.

Follett, W. I. 1972. Fish Remains from Mission La Soledad Cemetery, Mtn.-233, Monterey County, California. *Monterey County Archaeological Society Quarterly 1(3).*

Follett, W.I. and D. G. Ainley. 1976. Fishes Collected by Pigeon Guillemots, *Cepphus columba* (Pallas), Nesting on Southeast Farallon Island, California. *California Fish and Game,* 62(1):28-31.

Forde, M. B. 1964. Variation in Natural Populations of *Pinus radiata* in California. *New Zealand Journal of Botany,* 2.

Foster, R. H. 1968. *The Persistence of Mexican Land Grant Boundaries in the Present-Day Landscape.* M.A. dissertation, Department of Geography, San Francisco State University, San Francisco.

Fremont, J. C. 1849. *Notes on Travel in California.* Dublin: J. McGlashan.

————— 1887. *Memoirs of My Life....* Chicago: Belforde, Clarke, & Co.

Frenkel, R. E. 1970. *Ruderal Vegetation along Some California Roadsides.* Berkeley: University of California Press.

Frey, H. W. 1971 *California's Living Marine Resources and Their Utilization.* Department of Fish and Game. The Resources Agency. State of California

Gaines, D. A. 1980. The Valley Riparian Forests of California: Their Importance to Bird Populations Riparian Forests in California. In *Riparian Forests in California. Their Ecology and Conservation.* A. Sands (Ed.) Agricultural Sciences Publications, University of California, Berkeley.

Galliher, E. W. 1932. Sediments of Monterey Bay, California. In *Mining in California.* State of California, Department of Natural Resources 28: 43-79.

Galstoff, P. S. 1932. Introduction of Japanese Oysters into the United States. *U. S. Bureau of Fishery, Fishery Circular* No. 12.

Garfield, N., T. A. Rago, K. J. Schnebele and C. A. Collins 1994. Evidence of a turbidity current in Monterey Submarine Canyon associated with the 1989 Loma Prieta earthquake. In *Continental Shelf Research*, 14(6):673-686.

Garnier, P. 1967. *A Medical Journey to California.* Translated by L. J. Oliva. Los Angeles: Zeitlein & ver Brugge.

Gill, R. 1979. Status and Distribution of the California Clapper Rail (*Rallus longirostris obsoletus*). *California Department of Fish and Game,* 64 (1):36-49.

Goddard, P. E. 1903. *Life and Culture of the Hupa.* Berkeley: The University Press.

Goldman, H. B. 1967. Salt, Sand and Shells. *Mineral Resources of San Francisco Bay.* California State Division of Mines and Geology.

Goode, G. B. 1884. California Gray Whale. In *Natural History of Useful Aquatic Animals. The Fisheries* and *Fishery Industries of the United States* (Section 1, Part 1): 31-32.

Gordon, B. L. 1957. Human Geography and Ecology in the Sinú Country of Colombia. *Ibero-Americana.* No. 39. Berkeley: University of California Press.

————— 1982. *A Panama Forest and Shore. Natural History and Amerindian Culture in Bocas del Toro.* Pacific Grove, CA: The Boxwood Press.

Gordon, R. A. 1991. Does Bioscience Threaten Ecological Integrity? In *Bioscience and Society*, D. J. Roy, B. E. Wynne and R.W. Old (Eds.). New York: John Wiley and Sons. pp. 185-200.

Graustein, J. E. 1967. *Thomas Nuttall, Naturalist, Explorations in America, 1808-1841.* Cambridge, Mass.: Harvard University Press.

Greene, H. A. 1929. Historical Note on the Monterey Cypress at Cypress Point. *Madroño,* 197-198.

Greene, H. G. 1970. Geology of Southern Monterey Bay and Its Relationship to the Groundwater Basin and Saltwater Intrusion. *U.S. Dept. of the Interior, Geol. Surv.* Open File Report.

Greengo, R. E. 1952. Shellfish Foods of the California Indians. *Kroeber Anthropological Society Papers,* No. 7, Fall.

Greenlee, J.M. and J.H. Langenheim. 1980. *The History of Wildfires in the Region of Monterey Bay.* California State Department of Parks and Recreation.

Greenlee, J.M. and A. Moldenke. 1981. *History of Wildland Fires in the Gabilan Mountains Region of Central California.* National Park Service.

Greenway, J. C. 1958. Extinct and Vanishing Birds of the World. *American Committee for International Wildlife Protection Special Publication No.* 13, New York.

Griffin, J. R. 1964. Isolated *Pinus ponderosa* Forests on Sandy Soils near Santa Cruz, California. *Ecology,* 45(2): 410-412.

— — — 1973. Valley Oaks: The End of an Era. *Fremontia,* 1:5-9.

— — —1976. Native Plant Reserves at Fort Ord. *Fremontia,* 4(2):25-28.

— — — 1978. Maritime Chaparral and Endemic Shrubs of the Monterey Bay Region, California. *Madroño,* 25: 65-80.

Griffin, J.R. and W. B. Critchfield. 1972. The Distribution of Forest Trees in California. *U.S. Dept. of Agric. Forest Service Research Papers* PSW 82-1972.

Grinnell, Joseph. 1943. *Joseph Grinnell's Philosophy of Nature; Selected Writings of a Western Naturalist.* Berkeley: University of California Press.

Grinnell, J., and A. H. Miller. 1944. *The Distribution of the Birds of California.* Cooper Ornithological Club, Berkeley.

Grinnell, J., and J. M. Linsdale. 1936. Vertebrate Animals of Point Lobos Reserve, 1934-1935. *Carnegie Institution of Washington 481.*

Grinnell, J., and M. W. Whythe. 1927. *Directory of the Bird-life of the San Francisco Bay Region.* Berkeley: The Club.

Grinnell, J., J. S. Dixon, and J. M. Linsdale. 1937. *Fur-Bearing Mammals of California.* Berkeley: University of California Press.

Gudde, E. G. 1960. *California Place Names: The Origin and Etymology of Current Geographical Names.* Berkeley: University of California Press.

Hamlin, H. 1904. Water Resources of the Salinas Valley, California. *Department of the Interior, U.S. Geological Survey* Series J. Water Storage 9, Water Supply and Irrigation Paper No. 89.

Hanna, G. D. 1939. Exotic Mollusca in California. *Bull. Dept. Agric. State of California,* 28: 298-321.

— — — 1966. Introduced Mollusks of Western North America. *Occasional Papers of the California Academy of Sciences* No. 48, San Francisco.

Hansen, J. 1976. *A Pilot Study- Moro Cojo Environmental Analysis.* Watsonville, CA: Soil Control Laboratory Technical Report No. 76-4.

Hare, L. G. 1916. Drainage Problems near Salinas. *The Salinas Daily Journal,* April 12 and 13, Bulletin. No. 15 (Partial Report).

Harrington, J. P. 1942. Culture Element Distribution, Central California Coast. *Anthropological Records,* 7 (1). Berkeley.

Harrison, E. S. 1889. Monterey County. *Harrison's Series of Pacific Coast Pamphlets* No. 3, Salinas.

— — — 1892. *History of Santa Cruz County.* San Francisco: Pacific Press Publishing Co.

Hart, E. N. 1966. Mines and Mineral Resources of Monterey County, California. *Division of Mines and Geology.* County Report 5, Sacramento.

Hartnack, H. 1939. *202 Common Household Pests of North America.* Chicago: Hartnack Publishing Co.

Hartweg, T. 1847. Journal of a Mission to California in Search of Plants. *Journal of the Horticultural Society.* London 2: 187-191.

Harville, J. P. 1955. Ecology and Population Dynamics of the California Oak Moth *Phryganidia californica* Packard. *Microentomology,* 20: 83-166.

Hawbecker, A. C. 1940a. Planting for California Wildlife. *California Fish & Game,* 271-277.

— — — 1940b. The Nesting of the White-tailed Kite in Southern Santa Cruz County, California. *Condor,* 42: 106-111.

Hedgpeth, J. W. 1962. *Introduction to Seashore Life of the San Francisco Bay Region.* Berkeley: University of California Press.

Heizer, R. E. 1940. The Introduction of Monterey Shells to the Indians of the Northwest Coast. *Pacific Northwest Quarterly October:* 399-402.

Heizer, R. E., and A. Treganza. 1944. California Indian Mines and Quarries. *California Journal of Mines and Geology* 40(3): 291-359.

Hemsley, A. L. 1946. A Progress Report on Beaver Movement in California. *California Fish and Game,* 32(2).

Henderson, J. 1927. *7he Practical Value of Birds.* New York: The Macmillan Company.

Hendry, G. W. 1939. The Adobe Brick as an Historical Source. *Agricultural History,* 110-127.

Hendry, G. W., and M. K. Bellue. 1925. Plant Content of Adobe Bricks. *California Historical Society Quarterl,y* 4: 361-373.

Hendry, G. W., and M. K. Bellue. 1936. An Approach to Southwestern Agricultural History through Adobe Brick Analysis. *University of New Mexico Bulletin* No. 296: 65-72.

Hermann, A. T. 1879. *Report, City Lands of Monterey, tracts 1, 2, 3 & 4.* San Jose, Nov. 15, 1879.

Herre, A.W.C. 1910. The Lichen Flora of the Santa Cruz Peninsula, California. *Proceedings of the Washington Academy of Sciences*, 12(2):27-269.

Hesse, R. 1937. *Ecological Animal Geography.* New York: John Wiley & Sons.

Hewatt, W. G. 1937. Ecological Studies on Selected Marine Intertidal Communities of Monterey Bay. *American Midland Naturalist,* 18: 161-206.

Hittel, J. S. 1882. *The Commerce and Industries of the Pacific Coast of North America.* San Francisco: A. L. Bancroft & Co.

Hoffmann, Ralph 1927. *Birds of the Pacific States.* Houghton and Mifflin Co., Boston.

Hood, L., ed. 1975. *Inventory of Natural History Areas, vol.* 1. Sonoma: California Natural Areas Coordinating Council.

Hooker, W. J., and G. A. W. Arnott. 1841. *The Botany of Captain Beechey's Voyage... in the Years 1825, 26, 27, and 28.* London: H. G. Bohm.

Hoover, M. B. 1966. *Historic Spots in California.* Stanford: Stanford University Press.

Hoover, R.F. 1957. Monterey Cypress as a "Naturalized" Species. *Leaflets of Western Botany*, 8(5):141-143.

House Document. 1948. Salinas River, California. United States Congress, 80th, 1st Session, House, 1948, Document 208. Washington, D.C.

House Document. 1958. Santa Cruz County, California, Beach Erosion Control Study. United States Congress, 85th, 1st Session, House, 1958, Document 179. Washington, D.C.

Howitt, B. F. 1972. *Forest Heritage: A Natural History of the Del Monte Forest.* Berkeley: California Native Plant Society.

Howitt, B. H., and J. H. Howell. 1964. The Vascular Plants of Monterey County, California. *Wasmann Journal of Biology,* 22.

Hubbard, C. A. 1947. *Fleas of Western North America.* Ames: The Iowa State College Press.

Hubbs, C. L. 1919. The Stickleback: A Fish Eminently Fitted by Nature as a Mosquito Destroyer. *California Fish and Game,* 5(1):21-24.

Hubbs, Clark. 1947. Mixture of marine and freshwater fishes in the lower Salinas River, California. *Copeia,* 1947(2):147-149.

Huffacker, C. B., and P. S. Messinger. 1964. The Concept and Significance of Natural Control. In *Biological Control of Insect Pests and Weeds,* edited by P. De Bach. Reinhold Publishing Corporation.

Hunter, J. S. 1904. Records from the Vicinity of Watsonville, California. *Condor,* 6: 24-25.

Hurst, W.F. 1993. Time is Running Out! *Water Resources Quarterly*, Monterey County Water Resources Agency, 4(2):1-8.

Hutton, W. R. 1961. Two Letters on Post-Conquest Monterey. *Monterey History and Art Association Quarterly, Noticias . . .* 5, June.

Ingles, L. G. 1945. Ecology and Life History of the California Gray Squirrel. *California Fish and Game,* 31:139-158.

——— 1965. *Mammals of California and Its Coastal Waters.* Stanford: Stanford University Press.

Ingram, W. M. 1959. Asiatic Clams as Potential Pests in California Water Supplies. *Journal of the American Water Works Association,* 51(3):363-370.

Jenkins, O. P. 1973. Pleistocene Lake San Benito. *California Geology,* July: 152-162.

Jensen, H. A. 1939. *Vegetation Types and Forest Conditions of the Santa Cruz Mountains Unit of California.* Berkeley: California Forest and Range Experiment Station.

———1947. A System for Classifying Vegetation in California. *California Fish and Game,* 33:199-266.

Jepson, W. L. 1910. The Silva of California. In *University of California Memoirs* 2, Berkeley. 1911. California Tanbark Oak. *U.S.D.A., Forest Service Bulletin* 75, Washington, D.C. 1923. *The Trees of California.* Associated Students Store, U.C., Berkeley.

——— 1925. *Manual of Flowering Plants of California.* Associated Students Store, U.C., Berkeley.

———1993. *The Jepson Manual: Higher Plants of California.* James C. Hickman (ed.) Berkeley: University of California Press.

Johnson, R. F. 1954. The Summer Food of Some Intertidal Fishes of Monterey County, California. *California Fish and Game,* 40:65-68.

Johnson, W.C. and C.S. Adkisson. 1986. Airlifting the Oaks. *Natural History,* 95(10):40-47.

Johnson, W. M. 1855. Extracts from a Report on the Features of the Country between Pajaro and Salinas Rivers, California. *Ann. Rept. U.S. Coast Survey, 1854* App. 22: 31-32, and *Map of the Coast of California from Pajaro River Southward,* Sheet No. T473-8, 1854.

Johnston, R. B. 1970. *Old Monterey County: A Pictorial History.* Salinas: Monterey Savings and Loan Association.

Jones, G. C. (Chief of Party). 1933. Monterey Bay: Salinas River to Moss Landing, Descriptive Report to Accompany Topographic Sheet No. B47788. Coast and Geodetic Survey, Washington, D.C.

Jones, R.E. 1967. A *Hydrodamalis* skull fragment from Monterey Bay, California. *Journal of Mammalogy,* 48:143-144.

Kato, S. 1972. Sea Urchins: A New Fishery Develops in California. *Marine Fisheries Review,* (Sept.-Oct.): 23-29.

Keen, A. M. 1896. West Coast Species of *Haliotis. The Nautilus,* 9(11):129-132.

Keen, F. P. 1938. *Insect Enemies of Western Forests.* Washington, DC: U.S. Dept. of Agriculture miscellaneous publication 273.

Keep, J. 1935. *West Coast Shells.* Stanford: Stanford University Press. (Revised by J. L. Baily, Jr.)

Kellogg, M.G. 1980. *Status of the California Brackishwater Snail,* Tryonia imitator, *in Central California.* California Dept. of Fish and Game, Inland Fisheries Endangered Species Program, Special Publication 80-3.

Kendreigh, S. C. 1944. Measurement of Bird Populations. *Ecological Monographs,* 14:67-106.

Kenyon, K. W. 1970. *The Sea Otter in the Eastern Pacific Ocean.* U.S. Bureau of Sport Fisheries and Wildlife.

Kitchen, J. R. 1952. J. R. Kitchen Recalls "How It Was in '52." *The Watsonville Register-Pajaronian* Centennial Edition, July 2.

Kofoid, C. A., and C. L. Hill. 1927. *Marine Borers and Their Relation to Marine Construction of the Pacific Coast.* San Francisco: San Francisco Bay Marine Piling Committee.

Koppel, 1. L. 1915. Opossums near San Jose Continue to Increase. *California Fish and Game,* 1:195.

Krebs, C. J. 1966. Demographic Changes in Fluctuating Populations *of Microtus californicus. Ecological Monographs,* 36:239-273.

Krebs, J. 1923. Natur-und Kulturlandschaft. *Z. Ges. f. Erdkunde zu Berlin,* Berlin.

La Peninsula. 1968. *Journal of the San Mateo County Historical Association,* 14(5).

La Pérouse, J. F. G. de. 1799. *A Voyage Round the World Performed in the Years 1785, 1786, 1787, and 1788 by the Boussole and Astrolabe.* London: G. G. & J. Robinson.

Lachner, E. A., C. R. Robins, and W. R. Courtenay. 1970. Exotic Fishes and Other Aquatic Organisms Introduced into California. *Smithsonian Contribution to Zoology,* No. 59.

Lajoie, K. R. 1972. Sediments on the Continental Shelf between Point Arena and Monterey Bay. *Guidebook for Friends of the Pleistocene.* U.S. Geological Survey Staff and J. C. Cummings, pp. 31-37.

Langenheim, J.H and J.W. Durham 1963. Quaternary Closed-cone Pine Flora From Travertine Near Little Sur, California. *Madroño,* 17(2):33-51.

Laycock, G. 1966. *The Alien Animals.* New York: Natural History Press.

Leechman, D. 1942. Abalone Shells from Monterey. *American Anthropologist,* 44:159-162.

Lenz, L. W. 1959. Hybridization and speciation in the Pacific Coast irises. *Aliso,* 4:237-309.

Leonard, Z. 1934. *Narrative of the Adventures of Zenas Leonard, Written by Himself* Chicago: The Lakeside Press. (Ed. M. M. Quaife.)

Lewis, J. C. , K. L. Sallee and R. T. Golightly. 1993. *Introduced Red Fox in California.* The Resources Agency, Department of Fish and Game, Wildlife Management Division. Game Bird and Mammal Section, Report 93-10

Lidicker, W. Z. 1966. Ecological Observations on a Feral House Mouse Population Declining to Extinction. *Ecological Monographs,* 36: 27-50.

Linsdale, J. M. 1931. Facts Concerning the Use of Thallium in California to Poison Rodents-Its Destructiveness to Game Birds and Other Valuable Wildlife. *The Condor,* 33: 92-106.

— — —1946. *The California Ground Squirrel.* Berkeley and Los Angeles: University of California Press.

Locke-Paddon, W. 1964. A Short History of the Beach at Pajaro and Vicinity. *The Watsonville Register-Pajaronian.*

Longhurst, W. M., A. S. Leopold, and K. F. Dasmann. 1952. A *Survey of California Deer Herds, Their Ranges and Management Problems.* Dept. of Fish and Game vol. 38, Sacramento.

MacGinitie, G. E. 1935. Ecological Aspects of a California Marine Estuary. *American Midland Naturalist,* 16(5): 629-725.

Manning, J. C. 1963. Resume of Groundwater Hydrology in Salinas Valley, California. In *Guidebook to the Salinas Valley and the San Andreas Fault.* Pacific Section of the Amer. Assoc. Petroleum Geologists and Soc. Econ. Paleontologists and Minerologists. Annual spring field trip, May, pp. 106-109.

Marsh, G. P. 1863. *The Earth as Modified by Human Action.* New York: Scribner, Armstrong & Co.

Mason, H. L. 1934. Pleistocene Flora of the Tomales Formation. Carnegie Institution of Washington Publication No. 415.

Mathes, W. M. (ed.). 1965. Carta Escrita al Presidente de la Audienca de Mexico por Sebastian Vizcaino: 28 de Diciembre, 1602. *Californiana: Documentos Para la Historia de la Demarcacion Comercial de California, 1583-1632.* Madrid.

Maule, S. M. 1959. *Xerophyllum tenax,* squawgrass, its Geographic Distribution and its Behavior on Mount Rainier Washington. *Madroño,* 15:39-48.

Mayr, Ernst. 1988. *Toward a New Philosophy of Biology: Observations of an Evolutionist.* Cambridge, MA: Harvard University Press.

McBride, J. R. and H. F. Heady. 1968. Invasion of Grassland by *Baccharis pilularis* DC. *Journal of Range Management,* 21: 106-108.

McBride, J.R. and E.C. Stone 1976. Plant Succession on the Sand Dunes of the Monterey Peninsula, California. *American Midland Naturalist,* 96:118-132.

McClean, D. 1958. *Upland Game of California.* The State of California, Department of Fish and Game, Sacramento.

McDonald, P. M. 1969. *Silvical Characteristics of California Black Oak.* Pacific Southwest Forest and Range Experiment Station, Research Paper PSW-53.

McGregor, R. C. 1901. A List of the Land Birds of Santa Cruz County. *Pacific Coast Avifauna* Issue No. 2, May 15, p. 22.

McGregor, R. C., and E. H. Fiske. 1892. Annotated List of the Land and Water Birds of Santa Cruz County. In E. S. Harrison's *History of Santa Cruz County.*

McHarg, I. L. 1969. *Design with Nature.* New York: Garden City.

McHugh, T. L. 1959. 125 Years of Lumbering in Santa Cruz County. *Frontier Gazette,* vols. 2, 3, 4.

McKelvey, S. D. 1955. *Botanical Exploration of the Trans-Mississippi West, 1790-1850.* Jamaica Plain, MA.: Arnold Arboretum.

McMillan, I. 1968. *Man and the California Condor.* New York: Dutton & Co.

McMillan, C. 1956. The edaphic restriction of *Cupressus* and *Pinus* in the Coast Ranges of central California. *Ecological Monographs,* 26: 177-212.

McWilliams, Carey. 1939. *Factories in the Field; the Story of Migratory Farm Labor in California.* Boston: Little, Brown.

Meighan, C. W. 1965. Pacific Coast Archaeology. In *The Quaternary of the United States.* Princeton. (Eds. H. E. Wright & D. G. Frey.)

Menzies, A. 1924. Menzies' California Journal. *California Historical Society Quarterly,* 2: 265-340.

Merriam, C. H. 1919. Is the Jaguar Entitled to a Place in the California Fauna? *Journal of Mammology,* 1: 38-40.

Miller, A. H. 1951. *An Analysis of the Distribution of the Birds of California.* Berkeley & Los Angeles: University of California Press.

Monterey Peninsula Audubon Society. 1972. *The Sanderling.* Bulletin of the Monterey Peninsula Audubon Society 29(i), Monterey.

Monterey County Planning Department and The California Coastal Conservancy (ABA Consultants). 1987. *Elkhorn Slough Wetlands Management Plan.* Capitola.

Morejohn, G. V. 1976a. An Analysis of Osseous Remains of Birds and Mammals from the Post Site (Mnt-88)," pp. 71-93. In *Big Sur Archaeology—A Guide* (Monterey, 1976) Angel Press.

—— —— 1976b. Evidence of the Survival to Recent Times of the Extinct Flightless Duck, *Chendytes lawi Miller. Collected Papers in Avian Paleontology Honoring the 90th Birthday of Alexander Westmore, Smithsonian Contributions to Paleobiology,* No. 27, edited by L. Olson-Storrs. Smithsonian Institution Press.

Mosquito Abatement in California. 1951. Bureau of Vector Control, State Department of Public Health, Bull. No. VC-1.

Mountjoy, J.H. 1979. Broom—A Threat to Native Plants. *Fremontia,* 6(4):11-15.

Moyle, P. B. 1976a. *Inland Fish of California.* University of California Press.

—— —— 1976b. Fish Introductions in California: History and Impact on Native Fishes. *Biological Conservation,* 9:101-118.

Munz, P. A. 1959. *A California Flora.* Berkeley and Los Angeles: University of California Press.

—— — —*Shore Wildflowers of California, Oregon and Washington.* Berkeley: University of California Press.

Murton, R., R. Thearle and J. Thompson. 1972. Ecological Studies of the feral pigeon, *Columba livia. Journal of Applied Ecology,* 9:835-974.

Myers, G. S. 1965. *Gambusia*, the Fish Destroyer. *Australian Zoologist,* 13(2):102.

Mylar, I. L. 1970. *Early Days at the Mission San Juan Bautista.* San Juan Bautista, CA: Valley Publishers.

Needham, P. R. 1940. Quantitative and Qualitative Observations on Fish Foods in Waddell Creek Lagoon. *American Fish Society, Transactions,* 69:178-186.

Newell, W., and T. C. Baker. 1913. The Argentine Ant. *U.S.D.A. Bureau of Entomology,* Bulletin 122:1-98.

Nicolai, E., and L. G. M. Baas Becking. 1935-1936. *Archiv für Protistenkunde.* Botanischen Institut der Reichsuniversität, Leiden (Holland), vol. 86, pp. 319-328.

Oberdorfer, E. 1990. *Pflanzensociologische Exkursionsflora* Eugen Ulmer GmbH & Co., Stuttgart

O'Connor, J. 1995. *Three Ways to Think about the Ecological History of the Monterey Bay Region.* Santa Cruz, CA: Guilford Publications Inc.

Oliver, J. S., and P. N. Slattery. 1973. *Dredging, Dredge Spoil Disposal and Benthic Invertebrates in Monterey Bay.* Operations Division, U.S. Army Corps of Engineers, San Francisco.

Orr, P. C. 1969. *Prehistory of Santa Rosa Island.* Santa Barbara: Santa Barbara Museum of Natural History.

Orr, R. T. 1942. A Study of the Birds of the Big Basin Region of California. *American Midland Naturalist,* 27(2): 273-337.

Orr, R. T., and T. C. Poulter. 1962. Año Nuevo Marine Biological Park. *Pacific Discovery,* 15(1): 13-19.

Orr, R. T., and T. C. Poulter. 1965. The Pinniped Population of Año Nuevo Island, California. *Proceedings of the California Academy of Sciences.* Fourth Series, Oct. 3, 32(13):377-404.

Overland Monthly and Out West Magazine. 1870. Vol. 4. 1887. Vol. 10.

Overton Manuscript. 1877. (A document handwritten by a resident of Salinas, donated by a member of the Overton family. Copy in the Salinas Public Library. Original in Salinas City Vault.)

Paine, R. T. 1966. Food Web Complexity and Species Diversity. *The American Naturalist,* 100:65-75.

Patch, D. and T. Jones 1984. Paleoenvironmental Change at Elkhorn Slough: Implications for Human Adaptive Strategies. *Journal of California and Great Basin Anthropology,* 6(1):19-43.

Peterson, R. S., and B. J. Le Boeuf. 1969. Population Study of Seals and Sea Lions. *Trans. 34th North American Wildlife and Natural Resource Conference.* Washington, D C: Wildlife Management Inst.

Peterson, R. T. 1949. *A Field Guide to Western Birds.* Cambridge, MA: The Riverside Press.

— —1961. *A Field Guide to Western Birds.* Cambridge, MA: The Riverside Press.

Petit-Thouars, Abel du. 1956. *Voyage of the Venus: Sojourn in California.* Translated by C. N. Rudkin. Los Angeles: Glen Dawson.

Petrides, G. A. 1942. Relation of Hedgerows in Winter to Wildlife in Central New York. *Journal of Wildlife Management,* 6: 261-280.

Pilling, A. R. 1955. Relationships of Prehistoric Culture among the Indians of Coastal Monterey County, California. *Kroeber Anthropological Society Papers,* No. 12, Spring.

Pimentel, D. 1961. Species Diversity and Insect Population Outbreaks. *Ann. Ent. Soc. Amer.,* 54:76-86.

Pine, D. S., and G. L. Gerdes. 1973. Wild Pigs in Monterey County, California. *California Fish and Game,* 59:126-137.

Pitelka, F. A. 1942. High Population of Breeding Birds within an Artificial Habitat. *Condor,* 44:172-174.

Powell, W. R., ed. 1974. *Inventory of Rare and Endangered Vascular Plants of California.* Berkeley: California Native Plant Society.

Purer, E. A. 1936. Studies of Certain Coastal Sand Dune Plants of Southern California. *Ecological Monographs,* 6:1-88.

PVWMA. 1993. Basin Management Plan (including the Executive Summary, May). Pajaro Valley Water Management Agency.

Radford, K. W., R. T. Orr, and C. L. Hubbs. 1965. Reestablishment of the Northern Elephant Seal *(Mirounga angustirostris)* off Central California. *Proceedings of California Academy of Sciences.* Fourth Series 32(22).

Ramer, B.A., G.W. Page and M.M. Yoklavich. 1991. Seasonal Abundance, Habitat Use, and Diet of Shorebirds in Elkhorn Slough, California, *Western Birds,* 22:157-174.

Rashkin, P. 1972. Monterey Peninsula Shell Mounds, Some General Remarks. *Monterey County Archaeological Society Quarterly,* 1(4).

Reid, R. M. 1963. Route of the Portola Expedition, 1769, from Blanco Crossing on the Salinas River to the San Lorenzo River at Santa Cruz. Mimeographed. Watsonville Public Library, Watsonville, Calif.

Repenning, C.A., R.S. Peterson and C.L. Hubbs. 1971. Contributions to the systematics of the southern fur seals, with particular reference to the Juan Fernandez and Guadalupe species. *Antarctic Research Series,* 18:1-34. American Geophysical Union.

Reynoldson, F. 1932. A Flora of the San Francisco Sand Dunes. M.A. thesis, University of California, Berkeley.

Rice, D.W. 1977. *A List of the Marine Mammals of the World.* NOAA Technical Report NMFS SSRF-711, U.S. Department of Commerce.

Ricketts, E. F., and J. Calvin. 1968. *Between Pacific Tides.* 4th ed. Palo Alto: Stanford University Press. (Revised by J. W. Hedgpeth.)

Riegel, J. A. 1959. The Systematics and Distribution of Crayfishes in California. *California Fish and Game,* 45:29-49.

Ritter, W. E. 1938. *The California Woodpecker and I.* Berkeley: University of California Press.

Rivera y Moncada, F. 1774. *Diario del Capitan Comandante Fernando de Rivera y Moncada. In Coleccion Chimalistac, 24,* 2 vols., J. Porrua Turanzas, Madrid, 1967. (Ed. by E. J. Burrus.)

Robbins, W. W. 1940. *Alien Plants Growing without Cultivation in California.* California Agricultural Experiment Station, Bulletin 637.

Robbins, W. W., M. K. Bellue, and W. S. Ball. 1951. *Weeds of California.* Sacramento: California State Department of Agriculture.

Roberson, D. and C. Tenney. (Eds.) 1993. *Atlas of the Breeding Birds of Monterey County, California.* Monterey, CA: Monterey Peninsula Audubon Society.

Robinson, A. 1947. *Life in California.* Oakland: Biobooks.

Roquefeuil, M. Camille. 1823. *A Voyage Round the World between the Years 1816-1819.* London: Sir Richard Phillips & Co.

Rose, L. S. 1936. An Unreported Species of *Cakile* in California. *Leaflets of Western Botany,* vol. 1.

Roy, D. F. 1957. *Sylvical Characteristics of Tanoak.* California Forest and Range Experiment Station Technical Paper No. 22. Berkeley.

— — —1966. *Sylvical Characteristics of Monterey Pine.* Berkeley: Pacific Southwest Forest and Range Experiment Station Research Paper PSW-3 1.

Rudd, R. L. 1948. The Mammals of Santa Cruz County, California. M.A. thesis, University of California, Berkeley.

Rudkin, C. N. 1954. *Camille de Roquefeuil in San Francisco, 1817-1818.* Los Angeles: Glen Dawson.

Santa Cruz Bird Club. *The Albatross* (bimonthly bulletin).

Sauer, C. O. 1952. *Agricultural Origins and Dispersals.* New York: The American Geographical Society.

Scammon, C. M. 1874. *The Marine Mammals of the Northwestern Coast of North America,- Described and Illustrated, Together with an Account of the American Whale-fishery.* San Francisco: J. H. Carmany and Company.

Schaffer, W.M. et al. 1983. Competition for Nectar between Introduced Honey Bees and Native North American Bees and Ants, *Ecology,* 64: 564-577.

Scheffer, V. B. 1972. The Weight of the Steller Sea Cow, *Journal of Mammology,* 53(4):912-914.

— — — 1984. A Case of Prairie Pimples. *Pacific Discovery,* April-June, pp.5-8

Schneider, C. L. 1949-1950. Natural Establishment of Eucalyptus in California. *Madroño,* 10:31-32.

Schwartz, D. L., H. T. Mullins and D.F. Belknap. 1986. Holocene Geologic History of a Transform Margin Estuary: Elkhorn Slough. *Central California Estuarine, Coastal and Shelf Science,* 22: 285-302.

Scofield, W. L. 1954. California Fishing Ports. *California Dept. Fish and Game, Fish Bull.* No. 96.

Senate Document. 1946. Monterey Bay (Moss Landing), California. United States Congress, 79th, Ist Session, Senate, 1946, Document 50, Washington, D.C.

Seymour, G. D. 1954. Recent Extension of the Range of Muskrats in California. *California Fish and Game,* 40(4): 375-384.

Shapiro, A. M. 1993. *Science* Vol. 260:1983-84, a review of *Biology and Conservation of the Monarch Butterfly* (Los Angeles, 1993). S.B. Malcolm and M.P. Zalucki (Eds.) Natural History Museum of Los Angeles County.

Shapovalov, L., W. A. Dell, and A. J. Cordone. 1959. A Revised Check List of the Freshwater and Anadromous Fishes of California. *California Fish and Game,* 45(3): 159-180.

Shebley, W. H. 1917. History of the Introduction of Food and Game Fishes Into the Waters of California. *California Fish and Game,* 3:3-12.

Shepard, F. P. 1948. Investigation of the Head of the Monterey Submarine Canyon. *Scripps Institution of Oceanography Submarine Geology Report 1,* La Jolla.

Sherwood, J. 1925. Extermination of Burrowing Owl, the Farmer's Friend. *Oologist,* 42: 78.

Shreve, F. 1927. The Vegetation of a Coastal Mountain Range. *Ecology,* 8(1): 27-44.

Sibley, C. G. 1952. *The Birds of the South San Francisco Bay Region.* Privately published by the author, San Francisco.

Silberstein, M. and E. Campbell. 1989. *Elkhorn Slough.* Monterey, CA: Monterey Bay Aquarium.

Simpkinson, F. S. 1969. *H. M. S. Sulphur at California, 1837 and 1839.* San Francisco: San Francisco Book Club. (Ed. by R. A. Pierce and J. H. Winslow.)

Simpson, G. 1930. *Narrative of a Voyage to California Ports in 1841-1842.* San Francisco: The private press of T. C. Russell.

Simpson, L. B. (ed. and translator). 1961. *Journal of Jose Longinos Martinez..... 1791-92.* San Francisco: John Howell Books.

Simpson, L. B. 1938. *California in 1792. The Expedition of Jose Martinez.* Publications, Marino, California: Huntington Library Publications.

Simpson, T. R. 1946. Salinas Basin Investigation. *California Division Water Resources Bull.* 52, 52a, 52b, Sacramento.

Skinner, J. E. 1962. An Historical Review of the Fish and Wildlife Resources of the San Francisco Area. *California Dept. Fish and Game, Water Projects Report No.* 1.

Skinner, M. W. and B.M. Pavlik (Eds.) 1994. *California Native Plant Society's Inventory of Rare and Endangered Vascular Plants of California* 5th ed. California Native Plant Society, Sacramento.

Slobodkin, L. B., F. E. Smith, and N. G. Hairston. 1967. Regulation in Terrestrial Ecosystems, and the Implied Balance of Nature. *The American Naturalist,* 101:109-124.

Smith, A. C. 1959. *Introduction to the Natural History of the San Francisco Bay Region.* Berkeley & Los Angeles: University of California Press.

Smith, A. G., and M. Gordon. 1948. The Marine Mollusks and Brachiopods of Monterey Bay, California, and Vicinity. *Proceedings of the California Academy of Sciences.* 4th Series 26(8).

Smith, G. M. 1944. *Algae of the Monterey Peninsula, California.* Palo Alto, CA: Stanford University Press.

Smith, R. T. 1949. Las Nueces y Bolbones. *Pacific Discovery,* 2: 9-17.

Snyder, J. O. 1913. Fishes of the Streams Tributary to Monterey Bay, California. *Bulletin of the U.S. Bureau of Fisheries* 32(776): 49-72, Washington, D.C.

Solarsano, A. Indian Story. *San Francisco Chronicle,* July 13, 1930.

Spratt, J. D. 1980. California Grunion, *Leuresthes tenuis*, Spawn in Monterey Bay, California. *California Fish and Game,* 67(2):134.

Stallcup, R. W. 1976. Pelagic Birds of Monterey Bay, California. *Western Birds,* 7:113-136.

Stanger, F. M. 1966. *A History of Point Año Nuevo in San Mateo County, California.* Prepared for the State Division of Beaches and Parks; 153 pp., maps and photographs (San Mateo Historical Museum No. 66-3).

Stanger, F. M., (ed.). 1968. La Peninsula. *Journal of the San Mateo Historical Association,* 14(5).

Stanger, F. M., and A. K. Brown. 1969. *Who Discovered the Golden Gate? The Explorer's Own Accounts.* San Mateo, CA: San Mateo County Historical Association.

Starke, G. W., and A. D. Howard. 1968. Polygenetic Origin of Monterey Submarine Canyon. *Geological Society of America, Bulletin,* 79:813-826.

Starks, E. C. 1922. A History of California Shore Whaling. *California Dept. Fish and Game, Fish Bull.* No. 6, Sacramento,

State Earthquake Investigation Commission. 1908. The California Earthquake of April 18, 1906. *Report of the State Earthquake Investigation Commission* 1(2), Washington, D.C. *State of California,* 28: 298-321.

Stearns, R. E. C. 1882. On *Helix aspersa* in California. *Annals of the New York Academy,* 2: 129-139.

Stebbins, G.L. 1950. *Variation and Evolution in Plants.* Columbia Univ. Press.

—— 1965. Colonizing Species of the Native California Flora. In *The Genetics of Colonizing Species,* edited by H. G. Baker and G. L. Stebbins. New York and London: Academic Press.

—— 1976. Ecological Islands and Vernal Pools. *Fremontia,* 4:12-18.

Stebbins, G. L., and J. Major. 1965. Endemism and Speciation in the California Flora. *Ecological Monographs,* 35:1-35.

Stebbins, R. C. 1951. *Amphibians of Western North America.* Berkeley & Los Angeles: University of California Press.

Stockwell, P., and F. 1. Righter. 1946. *Pinus:* the Fertile Species Hybrid between Knobcone and Monterey Pines. *Madroño,* 8:157-160.

Storer, T. I. 1933. Economic Effects of Introducing Alien Animals into California. In *Proceedings of the 5th Pacific Science Congress, Canada, 1933.* Toronto: Univ. of Toronto Press.

Storer, T. I., and L. P. Tevis. 1955. *California Grizzly.* Berkeley: University of California Press.

Streator, C. P. 1947. *Birds of Santa Cruz County, California.* Santa Cruz, CA: Santa Cruz Public Library.

Swain, R. 1952. *The Insect Guide.* Garden City, New York: Doubleday & Co.

Swan, J. 1874. Monterey in 1843—by a Pioneer. *Monterey Weekly Herald,* Aug. 1.

Sweeney, J. R. 1967. Ecology of Some "Fire type" Vegetation in Northern California. *Proceedings California Tall Timbers Fire Ecology Conference* Nov. 9-10.

Taylor, A. S. 1860-1863. The Indianology of California. *California Farmer and Journal of Useful Sciences,* 13-20. San Francisco.

The Record Union. 1901. October 12, 13. Sacramento.

Thomas, J. H. 1961. *Flora of the Santa Cruz Mountains of California.* Stanford: Stanford University Press.

Thompson, K. 1970. The Australian Fever Tree in California: Eucalypts and Malarial Prophylaxis. *Annals of the Association of American Geographers,* 60: 230-244.

Thompson, W. F. 1920. Gulls in the Monterey Bay. *California Fish and Game,* 6: 85-86.

Throckmorton, S. R. 1882. The Introduction of Striped Bass into California. *Bulletin U.S. Fish Commission for 1881* 1:61-62.

Tilden, J. W. 1951. The Insect Associates of *Baccharis pilularis* DeCandolle. *Microentomology,* 16:149-188

—— 1965. *Butterflies of the San Francisco Bay Region.* Berkeley: University of California Press.

Todd, D. K. 1953. Seawater Intrusion in Coastal Aquifers. *Transactions of the American Geophysical Union,* 34: 749-754.

Torchiana, H. A. V. 1933. *Story of the Mission Santa Cruz.* San Francisco: P. Elder & Co.

Torrey, John and Asa Gray. 1838-1840 *Flora of North America.* Vol. I, New York: Wiley and Putnam

Tüxen, R. 1956. Die heutige potentielle naturliche Vegetation als Gegenstand der Vegetationskartierung. *Angewandte Pflanzensoziologie.* 13: 5-42. Stolzenau/ Weser

U.S. Senate Document No. 50. 1946. *Monterey Bay (Moss Landing) California, 79th Congress, 1st Session, May 24, 1945.*

Vallejo, G. 1890. Ranch and Mission Days in Alta California. *Century Magazine,* 41(2).

Van Nostrand, J. 1968. *A Pictorial and Narrative History of Monterey, Adobe Capital of California, 1770-1847.* California Historical Society, San Francisco.

Vancouver, G. 1798. A *Voyage of Discovery to the North Pacific Ocean and Round the World.* Vol. 2. London: G. G. & J. Robinson.

————— 1954. *Vancouver in California, 1792-1794.* The Original Account, vol. 1, G. Dawson. Los Angeles. (Ed. and annotated by M. E. Wilbur.)

Vavilov, N. I. 1949-1950. Phytogeographic Basis of Plant Breeding. *Chronica Botanica*, Vol.13. (Trans. K. S. Chester).

Ver Planck, W. E. 1968. Salt in California. *California Division of Mines* Bulletin 175, San Francisco.

Vick, R. 1989. Artificial Nature: The Synthetic Landscape of the Future. *The Futurist,* 23:29-32.

von Bloeker, J. C. 1937. Four New Rodents from Monterey County, California. *Proceedings of the Biological Society of Washington,* 50:153-158.

——— 1938. The Mammals of Monterey County, California. M.A. thesis, University of California, Berkeley.

Wagner, H. R. 1937. *The Cartography of the Northwest Coast of America in the Year 1800.* Vol. 11. Berkeley: University of California Press.

Wales, J. H. 1962. Introduction of Pond Smelt from Japan into California. *California Fish and Game,* 48(2).

Wallick, P. K. 1969. An Historical Geography of the Salinas Valley. M.A. dissertation, San Francisco State University, San Francisco.

Walter, Heinrich. 1973. Vegetation of the Earth In Relation to Climate and the Eco-physiological Conditions. (Trans. J. Wieser). Heidelberg: Springer-Verlag.

Walton and Curtis (publishers). 1875. *The Handbook to Monterey and Vicinity.* Monterey.

Water Resources of California, Bulletin No. 1. 195 1. State Water Resources Board, Sacramento.

Webb, R. C. 1969. *Natural History of the Pinnacles National Monument, San Benito County, California.* Pinnacles Natural History Association.

Went, F. W., G. Juhren and M.C. Juhren 1952. Fire and Biotic Factors Affecting Vegetation. *Ecology,* 33:351-364.

W.E.O.P. Watershed Ecology Outreach Program. *Spring Report , March, 1995.* California State University—Monterey Bay.

Westdahl, F. (Chief of Party). 1910. From Pajaro River Southward, Supplementary Survey Descriptive Report to Accompany Topographic Sheet No. 473a. *Coast and Geodetic Survey.* Washington, D. C.

White, K. L. 1966a. Structure and Composition of Foothill Woodland in Central Coastal California. *Ecology,* 47: 229-237.

———1966b. Old-field Succession on Hastings Reservation, California. *Ecology,* 48.

— — —1967. Native Bunchgrass *(Stipa pulchra)* on Hastings Reservation, California. *Ecology, 48.*

Whitlatch, R. B. 1974. Studies on the Population Ecology of the Salt Marsh Gastropod *Batillaria zonalis. The Veliger,* 17: 47.

Whittaker, R. H. 1969. Evolution of Diversity in Plant Communities. *In Diversity and Stability in Ecological Systems.* Brookhaven Symposia in Biology, 22, U.S. Brookhaven National Laboratory, Upton, New York.

Wilbur, S.R. 1974. The Literature of the California Least Tern, Bureau of Sport Fisheries and Wildlife, Special Scientific Report—Wildlife No. 175, U.S. Department of the Interior.

Williams, E. L. 1892. Narrative of a Mission Indian. In *History of Santa Cruz County,* edited by E. S. Harrison. San Francisco: Pacific Press Publishing Co.

Williams, L. 1931. Further Notes on California Brown Pelicans at Point Lobos, California. *Condor,* 33: 66-69.

Williams, W.T. and J.R. Potter. 1972. The coastal strand community at Morro Bay State Park, California. *Bulletin of the Torrey Botanical Club,* 99(4):163-171.

Wilson, C. M. 1947. Port of Monterey and Vicinity. *Economic Geography* 23:199-219.

Wilson, M. E. 1907. Shore Topography near Davenport, Santa Cruz County. *California Physical Geography Club Bulletin,* 1:11-17.

Wilson, P. W., J. A. Hendrickson, and R. E. Kilmer. 1965. Feasibility Study for a Surge-Action Model of Monterey Bay, California. U.S. *Army Engineers Waterways Experiment Station Contract Report* 2-136, Vicksburg.

Wong, V. 1970. Moss Landing Harbor. California: A Case History. *Shore and Beach,* 26-39.

Wood, W. M. 1892-1893. On a Collecting Trip to Monterey Bay. *The Nautilus,* 7(6), Philadelphia.

WPA, *Special Collection on California Fires. A Works Progress Administration Project.* 69 vols. (3 vols. on Santa Cruz Co.). Forestry Library (Mulford Hall). University of California. Berkeley.

Xerces Society, in association with The Smithsonian Institution. 1990. *Butterfly Gardening.* San Francisco: Sierra Club Books.

Yancey, T. E. 1968. Recent Sediments of Monterey Bay, California. *Hydraulic Engineering Laboratory Technical Report* HEL-2-18. University of California, Berkeley.

Youngbluth, M. J. 1976. Vertical Distribution and Diel Migration of Euphausiids in the Central Region of the California Current. *Fisheries Bulletin,* Vol. 4, No. 4.

Zierer, C. 1956. *California and the Southwest.* New York: Wiley.

Index